I/O Design: Data Management in Operating Systems

I/O Design: Data Management in Operating Systems

Donald E. Freeman
IBM CORPORATION

Olney R. Perry

HAYDEN BOOK COMPANY, INC.
Rochelle Park, New Jersey

Library of Congress Cataloging in Publication Data

Freeman, Donald E
  I/O design.

  Includes index.
  1. Data base management. 2. Operating
systems (Computers). I. Perry, Olney R., joint
author. II. Title.
QA76.9.D3F73   001.6'44   76-54767
ISBN 0-8104-5789-X

Printed in the United States of America

4   5   6   7   8   9   PRINTING

79 80 81 82 83 84 85   YEAR

Text design and interior layout: Cobb/Dunlop Publisher Services Inc.

Preface

This is a book about computer input and output. Specifically, it is about that portion of an operating system called either the I/O system or data management. More specifically still, it is about the *design* of the I/O system. It is not about computers, though computers are an important supporting subject, and it is not about programming in the coding sense. When you have read this book, you should understand what I/O systems are, what they do, why they do it, how they are organized, and the techniques they employ. In some ways, the book is a rationalization. It does not crusade but, rather, it explains and evaluates. It is practical and pragmatic. It describes technology proven by general purpose use.

Measured by any standard, this book concerns an advanced topic. If programming is completely new to you, you are advised to start somewhere else. However, this book is independent and self-contained; so if you have a general knowledge of programming, why not try it? We have not assumed that you are versed in any particular programming language or that you are familiar with any particular computer system, but it will be helpful if you have some knowledge of *some* programming language and *some* computer systems.

This is not a book about IBM. However, quoting the immortal John von Neumann, "It is unavoidable that our account will be considerably biased by our own actual efforts in this field. . . ."[1] On the other hand, the authors have studied the documentation for the following systems, and this book includes what we believe is the best in them:

- Burroughs Corporation—Master Control Program
- Control Data Corporation—Scope and Master
- General Electric Company—GCOS III
- International Business Machines Corporation—Operating System/360 and Disk Operating System/360
- Honeywell, Incorporated—Series 200/Operating System
- National Cash Register Company—Operating System
- Radio Corporation of America—Time-Sharing Operating System and Input/Output Processing System
- Sperry Rand Corporation—Exec 2, Exec 8, and Real-Time System

You will find the text liberally sprinkled with examples from these systems. The preponderance of examples from one or another system does not

---

[1] *Collected Works of John von Neumann,* vol. 5, p. 1.

necessarily indicate its superiority. In many cases, examples were chosen on the basis that they illustrate a point most clearly without introducing terms at odds with the discussion.

At the end of each chapter, there is a set of exercises graded easy (e), moderate (m), and difficult (d). The easy exercises serve as a form of review; the answers are stated explicitly in the preceding text. Moderate exercises require that the information previously read be applied directly and properly. Difficult exercises require that you deal with the implications of the information previously read. If you are deeply interested in a particular topic, the difficult exercises will serve as an extension to the text, an extension the less avid reader can bypass without losing the train of thought.

Donald E. Freeman
Olney R. Perry

Contents

I/O Design: Data Management in Operating Systems

1 Introduction to Input/Output Systems

The I/O package was the seed pellet injected into the gathering cloud of ingenuity hovering over the computer industry. This was in 1958 or thereabouts. . . . Leo J. Cohen

An I/O (input/output) system is the programmed component of an operating system that stores and retrieves data. I/O systems are the spectacular achievement of a few dozens of people working in groups separated geographically and administratively. Surprisingly, the philosophies and techniques developed by these groups are quite similar, similar enough to constitute an emerging I/O system science. This book is devoted to that new and fascinating science, but before we plunge into that main study, courtesy requires that we give some attention to history. Beyond that, good judgment requires attention to the operating system environment within which an I/O system must perform.

Computer systems are a new phenomenon. The industry points with patronizing pride to Charles Babbage, whose machines and ideas in the nineteenth century were far ahead of his time.[1] But modern computer systems all use the stored program idea, and stored program machines date only from World War II. Many of the outstanding senior people in the computer industry today were already well into their professional careers when the first stored program computers were being built. I/O systems are much newer still, the most ancient of them dating from 1958 or thereabouts.

Before 1950, calculating machines were much less flexible than modern computers. Remington Rand, a parent of the present Sperry Rand Corporation, had a line of punched card handling products whose activities could be controlled somewhat by positioning mechanical levers. IBM had card machines whose actions could be altered by control panel wiring. An important forerunner of the modern computer was the Card Programmed Calculator (CPC), a system composed of several of IBM's card machines interconnected by electrical cables. As the name implies, the CPC was programmed by a deck of cards. Each complete pass of the cards might cause computation of one paycheck or one stage of a numerical approximation process. The instructions in the cards were interpreted by control panel wiring.

In the late 1940s John von Neumann authored several important papers describing a stored program computer, a computer where instructions would

---

[1] Neither high precision machining, electronics, nor an appreciative society assisted Professor Babbage in his magnificent efforts. The serious student of computer history will be fascinated by Charles' dogged persistence and by the unselfish support of his gifted admirer, the Countess of Lovelace, Lord Byron's daughter. The foreword, preface, and appendix of *Faster than Thought* by B. V. Bowden (1953) are recommended reading.

be stored in the "memory organ" along with other more conventional data. Von Neumann's papers were sometimes authored jointly with two associates, Burke and Goldstein. However, von Neumann was clearly the motivating force, and he is generally acclaimed the father of the stored program computer. Von Neumann's original papers can be found in the *Collected Works of John von Neumann,* volume 5, published after his untimely death.

HOW I/O SYSTEMS BEGAN

During the early 1950s, several stored program computers were introduced commercially. The names of those machines, including the Univac 1101, the IBM Type 650, the Electrodata 204, the Bendix G-15, and the ALWAC-III, may be unfamiliar to some readers. Commercial availability created an immediate demand for generally useful programs so that standard procedures need not be reprogrammed and retested.

The requirement for a generally available I/O program can be illustrated for the IBM defense calculator, later named the Type 701. For its day, the Type 701 was very fast, and like many of the early scientific computers, its I/O capabilities were quite rudimentary. Reading a punched card required execution of 24 COPY instructions, each resulting in the transfer of 36 binary digits of information to main storage. If the card contained decimal information, the newly stored information required sorting. For example, the 12 bits representing any holes punched in card column 1 would be found as the first bit transferred by each of the 1st, 3rd, 5th, . . . , 23rd COPY instructions. All of this had to be accomplished without the aid of index registers.

Beginning with these very first commercially available stored program computers, the manufacturers recognized that a few general utility programs would be required. Some of the first general utility programs furnished were the bootstrap loaders used to load a program and start its execution. Other programs gradually made available could duplicate a card deck, create a magnetic tape copy of a card deck, print a report from magnetic tape, read an input deck converting the data from decimal to binary, and so on. Such programs were either furnished in card deck form or printed in a computer operating manual to be punched by the user. Typically, a small stack of these utility programs sat near the card reader ready for use by one and all. When a card was lost or mutilated, or when decks became hopelessly intermixed, fresh copies were readily available from a filing cabinet close at hand.

One limitation of these early utility programs was that they were intended for independent use only, not for incorporation with the user's payroll or matrix inversion program. By the mid-1950s, general purpose I/O subroutines were available for most computers. These I/O subroutines were typically in the form of card decks that could be added to a user's program deck. The resulting deck, together with a bootstrap loader, was a complete and independent program ready for use whenever the computer was available.

Concurrent with the development of standard utilities and subroutines was the development of interpretive systems. An interpreter is a supervisory program that executes the instructions specified in another program; the latter is never executed directly. An early successful interpretive system was the "Speed Coding System" developed under the direction of John Backus, a famous name in computer science. The "Bell Interpretive System" developed by Bell Telephone Laboratories for the IBM Type 650 was very popular. Interpretive systems were popular for at least two important reasons:

1. They allow the users to specify their programs in a convenient language not closely related to the instruction set of the computer.
2. They retain a great deal of control over the users' programs, thereby simplifying problems such as user program testing.

The principal disadvantages were that interpreters preempted a significant portion of the very limited main storage space and that they tended to be slow. A good discussion can be found in Donald E. Knuth's book *The Art of Computer Programming,* volume 1.

The advent of a successful FORTRAN compiler in the late 1950s redirected operating systems by furnishing an even more convenient language for the user's program and by providing good execution speed for the compiled program without loss of space to the interpreter. One of the earliest noninterpretive systems was developed at the Rocketdyne Division of North American Aviation in California in about 1958. That system was called a "FORTRAN Compile and Go" system. It could accept a number of users' programs in the FORTRAN language, compile them, and execute them without operator intervention.

The Share Operating System (SOS) developed jointly by IBM and the organization of computer users called SHARE included I/O routines that were part of a monitor that remained in the computer. The term *input/output control system (IOCS)* was coined about that time and by the early 1960s IOCS was becoming a part of everyone's operating system, in theory if not in fact. At about that same time, the rapid development of a variety of I/O devices, the advent of independent channels, and the popularity of multiprogramming combined to compel the development of the current features of I/O systems.

OPERATING SYSTEMS, WHAT THEY DO AND WHY

An I/O system is a component of an operating system, typically the largest and most fascinating component. Just as a study of the human heart might begin with a survey of the entire circulatory system, our study of the I/O system begins with the entire operating system.

An operating system is a large and complex collection of computer instructions. A system might consist of from 50,000 to 500,000 instructions, and it may be so complex that no one person understands it completely. The largest operating systems are possibly the most complex products ever produced by humans, rivaling such developments as the Apollo missile systems.

Why We Need an Operating System

Nearly all general purpose use of medium and large computers is accomplished under operating system control. The major services furnished by an operating system will be described in just a moment. But first, it is useful to understand why an operating system is necessary. What needs justify a collection of programs so large and complex? When a user has a job for the computer, why doesn't he or she use the computer directly without an operating system? Several factors furnish the answers to these questions.

Most computer systems, as manufactured, presuppose operating systems. As it became clear that programs such as the IOCS mentioned earlier were inevitable, computer designers began to capitalize on their existence. Wherever programs could perform more flexibly or at less cost than electrical circuits, the operating system accepted a new responsibility. Yesterday's luxury has become today's necessity. All of the major manufacturers of computer systems furnish operating systems with their computers.

Operating systems improve operating efficiency in several ways:

• An operating system can overlap the setup time for one job with the execution of other jobs. The setup time required to ready the auxiliary storage units for a particular job often exceeds the execution time for the job. Without this overlap, the routine feat of running several hundred jobs a day on a single computer would be impossible.

• An operating system can arrange concurrent processing. For example, one job might require only one or two magnetic tape units, while another requires little use of direct access storage devices, and yet another requires very little main storage space. An operating system can arrange for several such jobs to be in process concurrently, thereby accomplishing more work in a given interval of time.

• An operating system can reduce the length of time that equipment is required by a job. For example, operating systems frequently use high-performance auxiliary storage devices as substitutes for card readers, printers, and other relatively slow devices. This substitution, accomplished without concern to the user, allows the user's program to perform its function more rapidly, thereby freeing the equipment devoted to that program sooner. At an unrelated time, the operating system will remove the information from its temporary storage and accomplish the printing or punching required by the user.

• An operating system can reduce the elapsed time from receipt of data to printing of results. Before the advent of operating systems, job processing usually included several peripheral operations before and after computer processing. The peripheral processes included activities such as collecting similar jobs onto a single magnetic tape and printing of final results from a computer output tape. Each peripheral operation involved clerical handling of data related to the service request. Not only were requests occasionally processed incorrectly, but also the peripheral machines were often backlogged for days at a time. By integrating the peripheral operations into the computing process, an operating system reduces the elapsed time for the combined operations.

Operating systems afford a useful combination of flexibility and standardization:

- The standardization of data formats imposed by operating systems provides greater interchangeability of data between computer systems and wider usefulness of programs.
- The standardization of procedures imposed by operating systems reduces operator errors.
- An operating system separates the user's program from the computer system in such a way that the latter can be expanded or contracted by addition or deletion of devices without modification to the user's program.
- An operating system separates the user's programs from the computer system in such a way that new, improved devices frequently can be substituted for older, less effective devices without modification to the user's programs.

An operating system can adapt a general purpose computer to any of several operating requirements. For example, an operating system can provide the responsiveness necessary for a communications based system, the reliability required for a missile guidance system, the efficiency of a conventional commercial data processor, or a combination of these attributes.

In summary, an operating system is used because it is profitable to use it, profitable because of the efficiency it produces, the combination of flexibility and standardization it imposes, and its ability to adapt a computer to special operating requirements such as responsiveness.

When one first encounters an operating system, one may feel uneasy because the system is not of real substance; it consists of computer instructions subject to change without notice. The physical devices that compose a computer system appear more solid and durable. Operating systems are, in fact, very real and, though they are frequently extended to make them more useful, their advertised functions are seldom altered or deleted. The reasons for the stability are primarily economic. A major operating system represents a direct investment of millions of dollars, even tens of millions. If one adds the investment in education of users and in development of users' programs that depend on the environment created by an operating system, the total investment for a single operating system may exceed a billion dollars. An investment of such proportions has such a stabilizing influence on an operating system that several major operating systems in use today have outlived the physical devices for which they were originally designed.

Major Activities of an Operating System

The general purpose operating systems of today bear great resemblance to one another. Most of them perform the following major functions:

Scheduling Jobs   An operating system accepts jobs and schedules the system resources to satisfy these jobs. Some systems simply schedule jobs in the order of their receipt, that is, first in, first out (FIFO). Others recognize a priority code furnished by the user as an expression of the urgency of the job. Job scheduling involves not only recognition of priorities, but also availability of necessary resources. The resources required for a particular job may not be immediately available because they are being used for another job, or because they are undergoing maintenance. A comprehensive operating system will defer running of jobs when possible within priority constraints to effect efficient use of resources.

Allocating Resources   The resources of a computing system include main storage space, I/O devices, and files of data. An operating system controls the use of all of these resources. For example, an operating system allocates a particular direct access storage device (DASD) to be used in processing a particular storage volume. Both the DASD and the files recorded on the storage volume are considered system resources.

Dispatching Programs   One very special resource that an operating system controls is central processing unit (CPU)[2] time. At the beginning of an interval of time to be used by a particular program, the operating system takes the necessary steps to start or restart CPU activity for that program. The process of preparing the system for executing a particular program and transferring control of the CPU to that program is called dispatching. The system dispatches programs in the same sense that a clerk might dispatch errand boys.

The list of operating system functions is not yet complete, but we should stop for a moment to reflect on the activities discussed so far: scheduling, allocating, and dispatching. The reader may feel that the distinction among these three requires hairsplitting because all three combined constitute the apparently artless reaction to a request for service. In a simple operating system, the three combined activities do constitute a modest process. For example, completion of one job might trigger the operating system to prepare for the next job by reading one or more cards from a particular card reader. The user's program might identify its I/O devices explicitly, thereby eliminating device allocation activity. And, if the user's program is simply to be started and allowed to run to completion, dispatching is trivial. But unlike a simple system, a comprehensive system may be inspecting a hundred or more service requests at any one time, analyzing priorities, allocating devices so that several programs can be executed simultaneously, and dispatching the programs for intervals of a few milliseconds at a time to achieve the best possible service. In such a system, each of the individual functions of scheduling, allocating, and dispatching is a major activity.

Resuming the list of operating system functions:

Communicating with the Operator   Philosophically, the computer-system operator should serve only one purpose: to be the hands for the computer, doing those things that require the mobility and dexterity of a human. This goal was suggested by Doctor Frederick Brooks in about 1968. Practically, operating systems have been unable to achieve the desired level of autonomy, so operators still serve as overall supervisors. In this role, they cancel improper service requests, reassign priorities, or even stop the system entirely when it appears that the operating

---

[2] The terms *CPU* and *arithmetic unit* are nearly synonymous. The term *CPU* is used extensively in this book, but *arithmetic unit* is used where appropriate.

system has lost control. Examples of communications from the system to the operator include requesting the operator to mount or demount storage volumes, notifying the operator of start and completion of each job, and apprising the operator of any unusual conditions, such as a high frequency of I/O device errors.

Recovering from Incidents   Computer systems, and particularly the I/O devices included within systems, are subject to a variety of unexpected (but not unanticipated) conditions. A comprehensive operating system must be prepared to deal with unexpected conditions at all times. Typical unexpected conditions include intermittent I/O device failure, permanent I/O device failure, operator error, improper action by a user's program, and intermittent main storage or CPU failure. The finesse with which an operating system deals with unexpected conditions is one very important measure of its value. A good system can diagnose many situations and recover with modest loss of work in process.

Recording of Statistics   The recording of operating statistics is unproductive and time-consuming, but it is essential for distributing costs to users and for analyzing system performance. In comprehensive systems, noteworthy events occur at such a rate that even simple counting of events in main storage tables with occasional copying of the tables to auxiliary storage may require as much as 1 or 2 percent of all available CPU time.

Storing and Retrieving Data   The I/O system, a major component of an operating system, is responsible for data storage and retrieval. Because the main body of this book dwells on I/O activity, no more will be said about it in this preliminary section.

Operating Modes

Four very important terms describe the general modes of operation of systems: (1) batch processing, (2) multiprogramming, (3) time sharing, and (4) multiprocessing. These terms will come up frequently during our discussion of I/O systems, so it is important to know what they mean.

Batch Processing.   The term *batch processing* refers to that very general working method in which a collection (batch) of related transactions is processed through the computer system as a group. For example, in a parts inventory application, the receipts and withdrawals from inventory might be accumulated manually and, at the end of each day, all transactions that had been accumulated might be submitted as a batch for processing. As illustrated in Fig. 1-1, a batch processing program typically accepts a batch of transactions and a master file as input creating printed reports and a new master file as results. This kind of processing is widely used in processing business data.

Batch processing has several important advantages:

1. Batch processing allows flexibility in scheduling of work, because the submitter usually is not expecting results while he or she waits. Typically, batches may require service within an hour, within one-half day, or overnight.

2. Batch processing allows significant efficiencies in the use of system resources. For example, a batch of transactions can be presorted into an efficient processing order, and the master files stored on removable storage volumes can be used heavily for processing those transactions and then removed from the system.
3. A batch is a convenient unit for accounting for costs and for rerunning of work when necessary.

The roots of batch processing are deep in data processing history. Punched card data processing was first used on a large scale during the 1890 United States Census. The data processing machines developed and manufactured from that time until World War II were batch processing machines. They required manual setup; they accumulated batch totals; they sorted batches of cards; and they performed simple extension and cross-footing. (These last two terms may be unfamiliar to some readers, but they were not strange to the industry in 1940. For the sake of history, extending is the process of multiplying unit price by quantity, and cross-footing is the process of summing the totals that exist at the feet of a set of columns.)

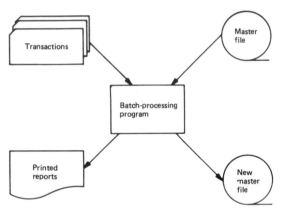

Fig. 1-1   Batch processing.

Much of the experimental work and much of the current literature about data processing concern individual transaction processing. But don't be confused by the difference between industry conversation and computer room practice. Most data processing accomplished by computers today is done in a batch processing mode. Using a simple operating system, operators can run batches one at a time. More comprehensive systems provide for batches to be multiprogrammed and/or multiprocessed as described below.

Multiprogramming.   Multiprogramming is the executing of two or more programs concurrently, using a computer system with a single CPU. The critical word in the definition is the word "concurrently": "executing two or more programs *concurrently,* using a computing system with a single CPU." The CPU of a system performs arithmetic and logical instructions, and it is capable of executing only one instruction at a time. In multiprogramming, the CPU is controlled to interleave the processing of several programs.

It is sometimes remarked that multiprogramming does not really accomplish concurrent processing, but, rather, gives the impression of concurrent processing. The remark is superficial; the system may, in fact, be performing I/O activities for many programs simultaneously and may even be performing more than one such operation for each of them.

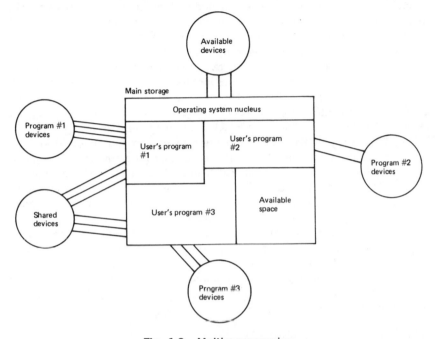

Fig. 1-2 Multiprogramming.

Figure 1-2 illustrates how computer facilities might be allocated to three programs for multiprogramming. In the figure, the main storage of the system is occupied by:

- The operating system nucleus which is that portion of the operating system that must be in main storage at all times to control moment-by-moment operations.
- The three programs that are to be executed concurrently.
- Available space (space not currently in use).

The devices in Fig. 1-2 have been allocated individually to the three users' programs except that some devices are shared by two or more programs and some devices are not in use.

The major justification for multiprogramming is efficiency. The opportunity for efficiency can be illustrated by two programs, A and B. Program A performs a great deal of computation using very little data, while program B performs minor computation affecting many records of a file. Program A might be selecting an optimum firing angle for a ballistic missile by repeatedly solving a set of simultaneous differential equations. Program B might be copying a file of parts inventory records. In many such cases, simultaneous execution of programs is quite efficient. Programs A and B might be executed simultaneously in a little more time than either program by itself. Contemporary multiprogrammed systems accomplish a less than optimum matching of simultaneous programs, yet they may achieve 35 percent or more improvement in total running time as compared to non-multiprogrammed systems.[3] (This improvement may be offset to some degree by the tendency for multiprogrammed systems to include more equipment than non-multiprogrammed systems. One has to pay something to reduce costs!)

Multiprogramming is a complex phenomenon. In 1955, Nathaniel Rochester described a trick called multiprogramming that was being used to increase computer productivity.[4] However, neither the required computer features nor the control-program design for generalized multiprogramming was understood until about 1960. The STRETCH computer, designed for the Los Alamos Laboratory of the Atomic Energy Commission and delivered in 1960, was probably the first computer designed for multiprogramming. The operating system for that computer included a limited form of multiprogramming. In 1962, Dr. Edgar F. Codd published the findings of his team concerning the practicality of multiprogramming.[5] He concluded correctly that multiprogramming was practical, and he predicted its widespread use. Today, a multiprogrammed operating system is available for every medium or large general purpose computer system. Some of the problems identified by these early researchers include efficient allocation of main storage, recoverability of damaged work, recreation of failure situations for testing purposes, and accountability adequate for customer billing. These four problems persist as today's major multiprogramming challenges.

Multiprocessing.   Multiprocessing is the use of a computer system containing more than one CPU to satisfy a collection of service requests. Figures 1-3 and 1-4 illustrate the two principal variations, symmetric and asymmetric multiprocessing. In symmetric multiprocessing, the CPUs are used symmetrically and interchangeably to perform any type of processing required. In the asymmetric case, the processing burden is divided by type of activity, and each CPU is assigned one type of activity. Figure 1-4 illustrates one CPU performing all I/O activity while another executes all user's programs.

Multiprocessing might be used for any of several reasons:

- To improve system reliability by addition of a redundant CPU (symmetric case). In a properly designed symmetric system, complete

---

[3] A paper by Tom Steel entitled "Multiprogramming—Promise, Performance, and Prospect," *Proceedings of AFIPS,* 1968 Fall Joint Computer Conference, cites average improvements of 30 to 70 percent.

[4] Nathaniel Rochester described multiprogramming using a magnetic tape unit controller available for the IBM Type 705. His paper is entitled "The Computer and Its Peripheral Equipment," published in the *Proceedings of the Eastern Joint Computer Conference,* 1955.

[5] Dr. Codd's comprehensive article, published in *Advances in Computers,* volume 3, 1962, is the last of several related reports beginning in 1959.

failure of a CPU simply reduces total system capacity without affecting the kinds of services rendered.

● To segregate system functions, thereby simplifying design and development of the system (asymmetric case).

● To increase the total CPU power in a system (both cases).

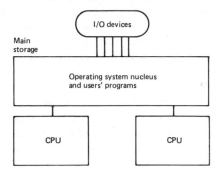

Fig. 1-3 Symmetric multiprocessing.

The asymmetric case has a load balancing problem; one CPU may be over-burdened, while another has no work to perform. The specialization of function, though, does actually simplify the design of the operating system, and simplification tends to improve both performance and reliability. The CDC SCOPE system is a good example of asymmetric multiprocessing. In SCOPE, one CPU executes all of the users' programs, and several "peripheral processing units" perform I/O activities.

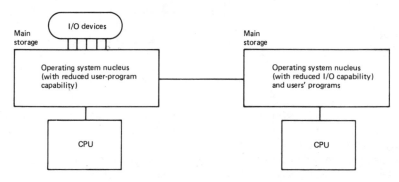

Fig. 1-4 Asymmetric multiprocessing.

Multiprocessing systems existed in the late 1950s. The earliest systems included two essentially separate computer systems with one in a "standby" rather than an active status. Such systems had significant switch-over problems in the event of failure because the failing system was required to detect its own failure and participate in an orderly transfer of work. Today more than half of the major operating systems include multiprocessing capability. Because redundancy can provide a system that is rarely out of service, organizations such as airlines, the military establishment, and the National Aeronautics and Space Administration are very interested in multiprocessing.

Time Sharing.   A time sharing mode of operation presupposes that each of a number of system users, usually from 10 to 100 or more, requires response within a few seconds to a series of simple service requests. Typically, time sharing users communicate with the computer system through keyboard terminals attached to the computer by telephone lines. Users may request services such as syntactic analysis of a programming statement, retrieval of a record from a file of data, execution of a mathematical procedure for finding a square root, or any of a variety of other services that individually make modest demands on system resources.

The primary objective in time sharing is to make the power of a centralized computing system available to several users simultaneously and to allow a cooperative relationship between user and system rather than the more conventional submit-a-request-and-wait-for-the-results relationship. Time sharing systems tend to accomplish less processing than other systems, but, in theory, their ready availability and their cooperative approach to problem solution improve the effectiveness of the users they serve.

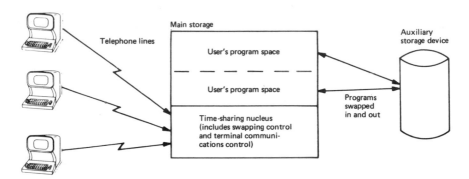

Fig. 1-5   A time sharing system.

In its simplest form, time sharing can be accomplished by a single program that performs a limited class of actions for several terminals. There are many such systems furnishing extended desk-calculator kinds of services. The more general time sharing systems use special operating system features such as a time slicing dispatcher and a swapping or paging mechanism. A time slicing dispatcher rotates use of the CPU to programs for fixed intervals of a few milliseconds each. A swapping or paging mechanism moves users' programs or pieces of users' programs called pages between main and auxiliary storage either on a preplanned or on a demand basis. Figure 1-5 illustrates a general time sharing system.

Time sharing was experimentally practiced in about 1961. A commercially usable system that offered several users time shared execution of FORTRAN-like requests was produced in 1964 by IBM under the direction of John Morrissey. In 1965, the General Electric Company produced a time sharing system providing the user a specially designed language called Basic. The latter was developed at Dartmouth College. General-purpose time sharing systems, where the user had less restricted use of computer facilities, were produced rapidly but with generally disappointing performance. By 1970, some of the initial luster of time sharing had dimmed, and the industry was beginning a careful, step-by-step development of time sharing technology.

Combinations of Operating Modes.   The operating modes described are by no means mutually exclusive. Rather, the computing industry is moving relentlessly toward systems that combine all four of the operating modes previously discussed. Some reasons for this tendency for coalescence are the following:

1. Modern society creates large volumes of data that must be widely available on a timely basis. Only a time sharing mode offers this capability.
2. The routine, systematic processing of these large volumes for massive modification of data, summary reporting, and reorganization must be as efficient as possible if the burgeoning volumes are to be processed at reasonable cost. A batch processing mode offers the efficiencies and controls necessary for such processes.
3. To allow batch processing without interruption to time sharing services, a multiprogrammed combination of time sharing and batch processing is appropriate.
4. And, finally, the modern society, its transportation, its defense, its financial systems, its education, and its recreation are becoming increasingly dependent on these large data systems with their efficient and timely services. The cost and inconvenience resulting from unavailability of these systems are increasing rapidly. A multiprocessing mode offering the availability that results from redundancy fills this need.

THE I/O SYSTEM: AN OPERATING SYSTEM COMPONENT

The programs that collectively constitute an operating system are of two major classes: (1) Programs that provide the environment and exercise the controls required to fulfill a user's processing request. These programs constitute the control program. Other terms sometimes used synonymously in the computer industry include executive, monitor, and supervisor. (2) Programs that are executed under control of the control program. These programs can be called users' programs, problem programs, application programs, or worker programs. The two classes are illustrated in Fig. 1-6 with some of their components identified. Our preoccupation throughout the book is with the control program; so we shall spend just a moment here with users' programs, thereby clearing our decks for the more comprehensive discussion.

As the name implies, the programs developed by the system user are classed as *users' programs,* but it is also true that some of the programs furnished with an operating system are classed as "users' programs." Included in this class are general-utility programs, such as programs that copy files, and the language processors that convert programs from source-language representation to a more concise nearly executable form. For any readers unfamiliar with the lore surrounding program development, Chap. 17 entitled "Program Libraries" includes a limited description of language processors and editors, as well as source, object, and executable forms of programs.

Strictly speaking, an operating system need contain only the few users' programs that are used in direct support of the control program. Such programs might include programs for analysis of operating statistics and for copying or reorganizing data that are to be used by the control program. In practice, other generally useful users' programs might be included in an operating system simply for ease of distribution.

AN OPERATING SYSTEM	
Control Program	User's Programs
Part 1. Scheduler	General Utility Programs
Part 2. Supervisor	Language Processors
Part 3. I/O System	Miscellaneous Programs

˙⎫
˙⎬ Parts of the
˙⎭ I/O System
	- Analyze operating
	  statistics
	- Reorganize control
	  program
	- Etc.

Fig. 1-6   Operating system components and subcomponents.

A control program includes at least three major components: (1) a scheduler that determines the gross order in which system resources will be applied to requests for service, (2) a supervisor that allocates main storage and dispatches programs, and (3) an I/O system that performs data handling services. This book is concerned with the I/O system directly and with the other parts of the control program indirectly. Because of the indirect concern, the scheduler and supervisor will be mentioned from time to time. Where necessary to avoid confusion, the scheduler and supervisor may be called the job scheduler and control program supervisor, respectively. The opportunity for confusion is excellent because the I/O system itself accomplishes many scheduling and supervising activities. You should understand that control programs have been developed by unrelated enterprises without access to any common set of rules. If you analyze the descriptive material for a control program, you may not find components that are called supervisor, scheduler, and I/O system. But if you dig deep enough, you will discover most of the functions described in this book.

I/O System Activities

Candidly, an I/O system is not a system but, rather, it is a subsystem, or a collection of subsystems. The I/O system is a collection of subsystems because (1) an I/O system is not self-sufficient. It requires assistance from other parts of the control program in the performance of its services. Examples of such assistance are allocation of main storage space for temporary storage of data and notification of the occurrence of an event. (2) The combined parts of an I/O system furnish an array of services that are all related to I/O but that are little related to each other. This latter point is illustrated in Fig. 1-7 which, though greatly simplified, serves to introduce the major parts of the I/O system. As that figure shows, the prominent I/O system activities concern I/O devices, the files of data that use those devices, and the data stored in the files (devices, files, and file contents). Figure 1-7 activities are considered prominent because they furnish explicit services to users. Less prominent, but nonetheless very important, are the philosophies, technologies, and programs added in Fig. 1-8. Each of the prominent I/O system activities with its related behind-the-scenes support is discussed briefly below.

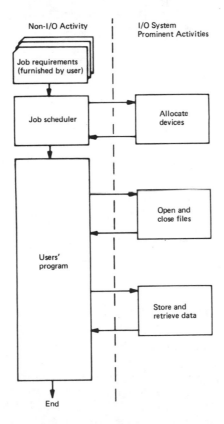

Fig. 1-7 I/O system activities.

Allocating Devices Job requirements are accepted and inspected by the job scheduler. Some requirements, such as the main storage space requirement, are not related to input and output. But most of the requirements concern the files of data that will be processed and, either explicitly or implicitly, the I/O devices required for those files. As a minimum, the device allocation programs of the I/O system must designate a workable combination of devices that will fill the requirements. More comprehensive device allocation programs accomplish matching of devices and files for the best system performance and the greatest convenience for the operator.

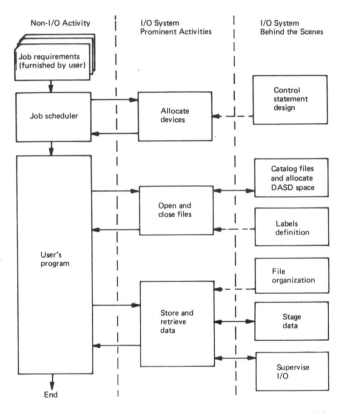

Fig. 1-8   I/O system activities, technologies, and philosophies.

Control Statements   Obviously, the users must communicate their requirements in a manner understandable by both themselves and the system. The terms and syntax to be used constitute a control language that is stipulated in the operating system manuals. Control statements describing I/O requirements are complex and detailed. The kinds of requirements and the techniques conventionally used for stating them constitute an important interface to the I/O system.

Opening and Closing Files   I/O systems identify collections of data as files in much the same way and for many of the same reasons as files are identified in manual systems. A single I/O system may be concerned with thousands of files, large and small, permanent and transient. Opening and closing files in a computer system are surprisingly complex activities. Actions included are determining what storage volumes are involved, requesting and verifying operator assistance, and protecting against unauthorized access.

File Cataloging   It includes construction maintenance and interrogation of records relating files with their physical locations.

Allocating DASD Space to Files   This includes maintaining an inventory of available space, identifying the space to be used for each specific need, and accepting the space that is returned when files are scratched (that is, deleted).

Labels   They are used to identify and describe storage volumes, files, and pieces of files. Label creation, interpretation, verification, and modification are important activities related to file opening and closing.

Storing and Retrieving Data   Moving blocks of data to and from I/O devices is the principal justification for an I/O system. A variety of programs often called *access methods* provide services matching the desires of the user's program and the requirements of any specific I/O device.

Organizing Files   Files are organized to allow efficient processing, and an organization appropriate for one file may be inappropriate for another. DASDs offer great flexibility for organizing files. File organization is an important factor affecting the access methods.

Data Staging   It is the process of moving data from one type of device to another in preparation for processing or subsequent to processing. The primary reason for staging is to improve system efficiency, but other advantages may also accrue.

I/O Supervision   This is an administrative activity that ensures efficiency, adjudicates conflicts, and protects files from unauthorized use. Centralized I/O supervision is essential in multiprogrammed systems.

I/O System Design

An I/O system consists of computer instructions, and those instructions are executed just as any other instructions are executed. In that sense, an I/O system is fundamentally related to all other computer programs. However, there are some characteristics that distinguish system programming in general and I/O system programming in particular from most other programming:

Instruction Mix   System programming involves very little arithmetic but, rather, is characterized by the setting and testing of indicators and extensive use of branching instructions. I/O system programming adds to those characteristics the heavy usage of data-moving instructions.

Performance Requirements   Many system activities must be as efficient as possible because they will be executed thousands or even millions of times in a single day on a single system. At the same time, system programs must be compact, because they will reside in main storage much if not all of the time.

Reenterability   Users' programs can be written with the assumption that they will be executed starting at the beginning and continuing as the branches in the program indicate. Most system programs must perform correctly under more stringent conditions in which a single program may be in use several times concurrently. For example, an I/O system program that is moving an array of information from main storage location A to location B might be interrupted at any instant, restarted to move information from C to D, and then resumed at the interruption point. The situation might be compared to a fictitious typist (analogous to a program), her typewriter (the computer), and several partially typed letters (jobs). Between any two keystrokes, not only might the typist be interrupted and her typewriter be taken from her, but she might find her very next keystroke on the same typewriter affecting an altogether different letter. And all of that without warning or even awareness that it has happened. It would take a special kind of typist, and it requires a special discipline in programs. (The techniques for achieving reenterability are well established, but they are outside the scope of this book.)

Program Testing   It is particularly important that system programs run correctly, for if they do not, users' programs have little chance of success. But the testing of control programs is much more difficult than testing of users' programs, because there is no convenient environment for testing control programs.

Three separate difficulties are immediately apparent. (1) Control program testing is very inefficient. The control program expects every user's program to be different, but there is no corresponding tool that allows efficient operation of a computer when a different control program is used every few seconds. (2) There is no control program that assists the control programs. The control program protects a user's program from accidental interactions, but who protects the control program? The control program can report circumstances attendant to a user's program failure, but who reports the circumstances when the control program fails? (3) Many of the conditions to be tested are difficult to create. For example, I/O system testing requires artificial creation of combinations of device failures. One cannot create a device failure at will.

Predictability of Use   There is no practical end to the variety of demands that are made on a control program. It is frequently impossible to determine what was happening at any particular instant in time, or to recreate that condition for analysis.

Device Support   The I/O system development department is customarily the first user of a newly developed I/O device. The combination of an untested program, an engineering model of the I/O device, and a delivery date that has been announced to the computer-using community at large is sobering.

These ideas are intended not to inspire awe but, rather, to indicate that differences in design requirements and in implementation problems are more than superficial. The differences are attested to by statistics for programmer productivity; a good programmer of commercial applications can easily produce two to ten times the number of machine instructions that an I/O system programmer can produce in the same period.

THE COMPUTER SYSTEM

The term *operating system* is used sometimes to include a certain collection of programs and sometimes to include those programs plus the machines they use and control. When the machines only are intended, the terms *computer, computer system,* and *computing system* are used.

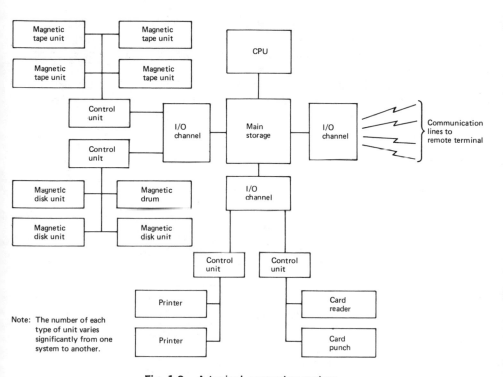

Fig. 1-9   A typical computer system.

Most of the information in this book is independent of the features of any particular computer system, but characteristics common to most computer systems are assumed. General purpose computer systems that are large enough to justify operating systems have many similarities:

1. They are manufactured from the same kinds of components, though at any one time, one manufacturer may achieve certain advantages over the others by some advance in the quality or cost of the components this manufacturer uses.
2. They are all of the stored program variety. That is, instructions are stored in the computer system in the same way that other data are

stored. Instructions are distinct from other data only in that, because of circumstances beyond their own control, they arrive at a station within the computer where they are interpreted as instructions.

3. They each include a CPU that executes instructions from consecutive main storage locations (except when branching) and that holds intermediate results in one or more registers. The CPU consists of a control section, which interprets instructions, and an arithmetic unit.

4. They each have a main storage that is used directly by the CPU.

5. They each include certain instructions that are intended for control program use only.

6. They each have channels that can accomplish I/O operations with limited CPU attention.

7. They include control units to attach I/O devices to channels and to control the activities peculiar to each type of device.

8. They each support a variety of I/O and auxiliary storage devices including printers, card readers, magnetic tapes, and direct access storage devices (magnetic disks and drums).

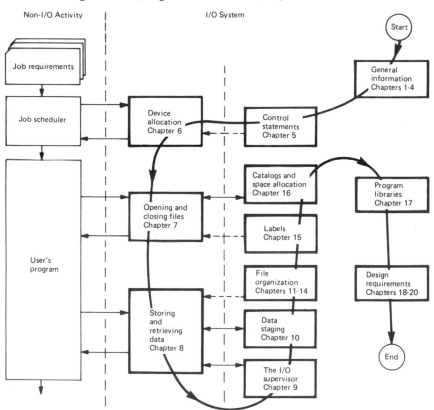

Fig. 1-10   Organization of this book.

Most of the systems in use today are illustrated by the generalized diagram in Fig. 1-9.

ORGANIZATION OF THE BOOK

Earlier, the activities of an I/O system were illustrated in Fig. 1-8. The activities illustrated form the main body of this book, Chaps. 5 through 16. Figure 1-10 completes the book by adding a few general chapters at each end.

SUMMARY

In the late 1940s, John von Neumann stimulated development of the stored program computer. The availability of stored program computers led inevitably to a demand for pretested programs. The need was particularly pressing in the I/O area. Bootstrap loaders were furnished with the first commercially available computers followed shortly by utility programs for copying card decks, printing reports, and so forth. I/O subroutines to be incorporated with the user's program were available in the mid-1950s. A strong side current of interpretive systems flourished for a time, but by 1958, the prototypes of current operating systems were in use. The I/O component, called IOCS, evolved to our current I/O systems.

Modern computers are designed with the assumption that an operating system will be used. An operating system improves the amount of work a system can process and reduces the elapsed time for the processing of any single job. Further, operating systems impose flexibility and standardization that are intangible but beneficial. And finally, an operating system can adapt a computer to any of several special operating requirements, such as quick response to service requests. Though operating systems have been in existence for only a short time, they are reasonably stable partly because of the very significant investment in their development and in programs that depend on them.

Some of the most important activities of operating systems include scheduling work, allocating resources, dispatching programs, communicating with the operator, recovering from incidents, recording statistics, and storing and retrieving data.

Most computer-based data processing is done in a batch mode, where groups of transactions are processed together. Batches can be processed one after another or, in multiprogramming, several batches can be processed concurrently. Though multiprogramming is complex and new, it is in wide use today. A computer system that includes more than one CPU is called a multiprocessing system. The processors in such a system can share work equally (the symmetric case), or each processor can be assigned specialized activities (the asymmetric case). In either event, the individual processors may use multiprogramming. When the primary use of a computing system is to respond quickly to a large number of demands for simple services, a time sharing mode of operating may be appropriate. In time sharing, each active request is given the use of resources on a rotational basis so that each user receives attention that appears to him or her to be continuous. Batch processing, multiprogramming, multiprocessing, and time sharing can exist simultaneously in a system.

An operating system includes two classes of programs: users' programs and the control program. Users' programs include utility programs, language processors, and those programs that the user develops. The control program includes a scheduler, a supervisor, and an I/O system. Some of the major activities of an I/O system are (1) allocating I/O devices according to the user's requirements as specified by control statements; (2) opening and closing files, maintaining and using a catalog of file locations, allocating DASD space, and creating and verifying labels; (3) storing and retrieving data, building and using several alternative organizations of data, staging data as required for greater efficiency, and supervising all input and output.

I/O system programming is significantly different from most computer application programming. The instructions used are primarily not arithmetic; performance and size are critically important; and most of the programs must be reenterable. I/O system testing is complicated because of lack of a convenient testing environment and the unpredictability of the conditions of use.

Throughout this book, a general purpose computer system is assumed. Fortunately, most general purpose computer systems are quite similar. They are manufactured from similar components; they execute stored programs; they include main storage used directly by a CPU; they include special instructions reserved for control program use; and they have channels, control units, and a variety of I/O devices.

Exercises

1. (e) The mechanical design of an I/O device frequently affects the order in which data are transmitted to or from a computer. Which of the following apparently describes the card reader used with the IBM type 701?

    a. Reads cards from one end, a column at a time.

    b. Reads cards from the bottom up, one row at a time.

2. (e) If a 500,000-instruction operating system were punched into a stack of cards, one instruction per card,

    a. how high would the stack be (assume 140 cards per inch)?

    b. how many tons would the cards weigh (assume 16 cards per ounce)?

    c. could the cards be read during an 8-hour shift of operators (assume 600 cards per minute)?

3. (e) Using Dr. Brook's philosophy, which of the following are appropriate activities for an operator?

    a. placing cards in a card reader

    b. stopping execution of a job that has exceeded its time limit

    c. separating the printed output of one job from another

    d. retrieving magnetic tape reels from a tape library room

    e. logging the start time of each user's job

4.(e) Which variety of multiprocessing has the best potential for overcoming computer component failure, symmetric or asymmetric? Why?

5.(e) In what operating mode and for what purpose is a paging or swapping mechanism used?

6.(e) Assume 100 engineers experience 10 percent improvement in efficiency by using a time shared computer exclusively dedicated to them. Is such use economically justified? Assume (1) an engineer's time is worth $20 per hour, (2) normal 8-hour days, 220 days per year, (3) a $5,000,000 computer with a 5-year life (no salvage value), (4) other factors (such as computer generating costs, depreciation allowance, cost of capital, etc.) are ignored.

7.(e) Does the control program supervisor have responsibility that would allow it to expedite a high-priority job? If so, what is the nature of that responsibility?

8.(e) Describe by example why a program that modifies its own instructions cannot be reenterable.

9.(m) Suggest at least four advantages of a stored program as compared with a program wired on a control panel.

10.(m) Frequently, the highest priority classifications for jobs are restricted to relatively small jobs. Suggest some justifications for that restriction.

11.(m) Magnetic tape is used extensively in batch processing. Suggest at least two reasons why magnetic tape is less used in time sharing.

12.(m) Why is each of the following a more difficult problem in a multi-programmed environment than in an environment where jobs are executed one at a time? Limit your answer to one sentence for each item.

a. recoverability of damaged work

b. control program testing

c. accounting for use of equipment

2 Input/Output Devices

Every input or output operation involves an I/O device. The purpose of this chapter is to familiarize the reader with the major classes of I/O devices. To understand their proper use, one should know how they work, what they can do, and any special problems arising from them. In most cases, devices of similar design are produced by several manufacturers. The classes of devices to be described are:

- data preparation devices such as keypunches
- end-use devices such as card readers, punches, printers, and keyboard terminals
- serial storage devices, notably magnetic tape units
- direct access storage devices such as magnetic disks and drums

The information presented for each class is necessary but not sufficient for the I/O system designer. If anyone would presume to control devices for another, he or she should touch those devices, operate them, and live with them for a time.

DATA PREPARATION EQUIPMENT

The next several pages are devoted to devices that are not attached to a computer. There are two important motives for describing these devices. One motive is related to history. During the first half of this century, earlier models of the same devices were the vanguard of automatic data processing. Most of today's senior data processing managers are well acquainted with these devices. What they expect from computers is conditioned by what they got from collators, sorters, and tabulators a few short years ago.

The second motive for discussing these unattached devices concerns accuracy of input data. A data processing system is vitally concerned with the accuracy of the data being processed. All too frequently, one sees a banner in the popular press, "Giant Brain Runs Amok." The folklore of data processing includes a cliche called the GI–GO principle, garbage in–garbage out, covering most such cases. There was a day when control program designers could cite the GI–GO principle to absolve themselves of responsibility for the failure of a system to produce useful results. That day is gone forever. A first step in sharing responsibility for accuracy of input data is an understanding of the equipment and processes used in data preparation.

24

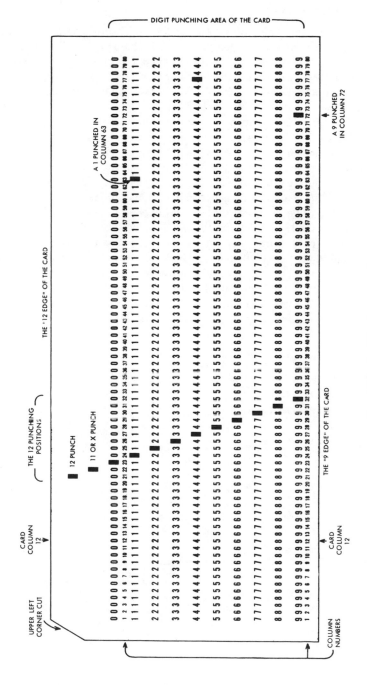

Fig. 2-1 An 80-column card.

25

Punched Card Equipment

Data outside computer systems typically consist of characters recorded by pencil or typewriter on paper documents. Characters and documents have a variety of styles and sizes, usually designed for human convenience. To prepare data for processing, the human-convenience form must be converted to a machine-processable form. The most popular medium for machine-processable input data is the punched card.

The 80-column punched card, sometimes called the Hollerith card or the IBM card, is used widely in the computing industry (see Fig. 2-1). Dr. Herman Hollerith was a pioneer in designing punched card equipment, and IBM was the first manufacturer of equipment for processing the 80-column card. Individual cards may differ in appearance due to differences in printing on a card, the existence of a perforated stub, rounded corners, or a diagonal corner cut on one or more corners. The overall dimensions of the card, 7⅜ in. by 3¼ in. by 0.007 in. thick, are widely accepted standards.

Other card forms are also in use. The Sperry Rand Corporation has equipment that uses a 90-column card. The 90-column card has 45 columns across the top half and 45 columns across the bottom half. A character is represented by some combination of the six possible holes in any column. IBM uses a relatively new and smaller card in some of its small systems. This card has 96 columns divided equally among 3 rows across the card.

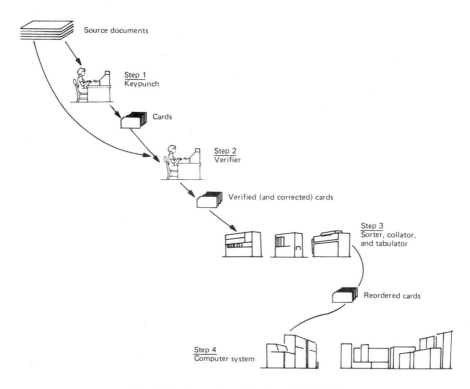

Fig. 2-2 Preparing data for processing.

Cards have at least two important advantages. The card is a unit record. It can be separated from adjacent cards for mailing or sorting. It is separately correctable and replaceable. (Card handling equipment is frequently called unit record equipment.) Card handling equipment is readily available. Most general purpose computers have card reading input devices. A wide variety of reliable equipment is available for punching, verifying, sorting, listing, and duplicating standard cards. Figure 2-2 illustrates the steps in preparing cards for computer processing:

Step 1 Source documents are visually interpreted by a keypunch operator who causes cards to be punched by depressing appropriate keys.

Step 2 The accuracy of keypunching is verified by an operator who visually interprets the source documents for the second time and depresses appropriate keys on a card verifier. The card verifier indicates whether the holes in the cards from the first operation correspond with the key depressions in this operation.

Step 3 The verified cards might be processed by electric accounting machines such as the sorter, collator, and tabulator to reorder the cards and to verify that totals of information contained in the cards match totals derived by desk calculators from the source documents.

Step 4 The reordered cards are presented to the computer system.

The Keypunch.   The most widely known piece of card handling equipment is the card punch, popularly known as the keypunch. More than a quarter million are in use.[1] The operator's keyboard resembles a typewriter keyboard with special keys that control card movement. When the operator depresses a key, the card positioned behind the punch station will be punched, and the card will advance toward the left by one column. The reading station can interpret information from the card that precedes the card being punched and, under operator control, that information can be duplicated into the card at the punch station.

Figure 2-3 shows the punched-hole code for common characters. The printing across the top of the card is accomplished by the keypunch as it punches the holes that represent that character. You will notice that the decimal digits are each represented by a single hole, while the characters of the alphabet require two holes each. A variety of special characters, not all of which are shown, require one, two, or three punches each.

The Verifier.   When small numbers of cards are punched, the accuracy of punching can be verified visually. For larger volumes, there is a machine verifier that resembles the card punch. As each already punched card is processed through the verifier, one or more error notches will be punched to indicate errors, or the verification notch will be punched to indicate successful machine verification. The two types of notches are illustrated in Fig. 2-4.

Cards that have been keypunched and verified contain few errors, particularly if the two operations are performed by different people. The mathematical

[1] The EDP Industry Report of October 19, 1971, puts the number at a quarter million—a number that is probably conservative.

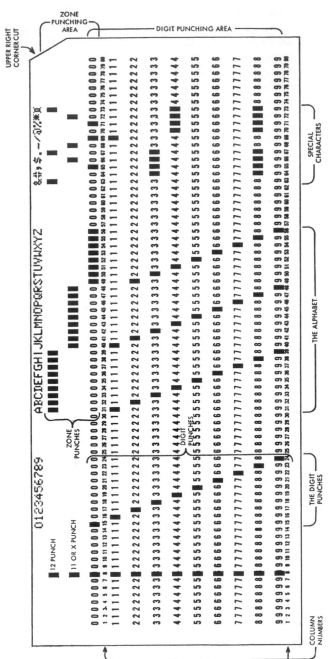

Fig. 2-3 Character codes.

28

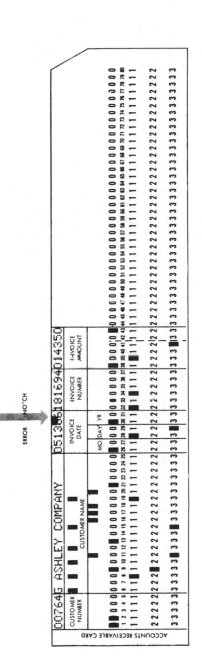

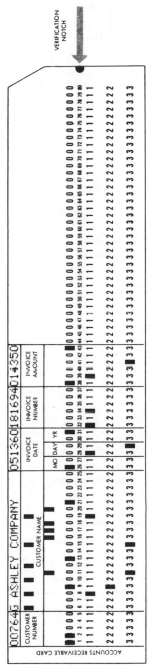

Fig. 2-4 Error and verification notches.

29

basis for this high accuracy is, of course, that if the probability of either a keypunching or verifying error for any particular character is 0.001, the probability of both a keypunching and a verifying error for that character is $(0.001)^2$ or 1 in a million. Unfortunately, that mathematical basis does not apply, and the experienced system designer knows that it does not apply. Some of the reasons for a higher error rate are:

1. The source document may be in error.
2. Hand-written characters on the source document may be misinterpreted. Both operators may make identical misinterpretations because they tend to view their goal as consistency rather than accuracy.
3. The process of correcting errors that were detected during verification may introduce other errors.

The Sorter.   The card sorter is used to rearrange a deck of cards so that the values punched in a particular field are in ascending order. As shown in Fig. 2-5, cards are moved from the hopper under the reading brush, where an electrical contact is made through any hole in the card. The operator collects the cards from the stackers and, if the sort is not yet complete, moves the sorter brush to another column and passes the cards through the machine again. A sorter feeds cards at speeds up to 2,000 cards per minute.

The sorter has control buttons that can inhibit sensing each of the individual hole positions 9, 8, 7, . . . , 1, 0, 11, 12. If a particular card column has alphabetic punching, the cards must be sorted twice on that column. On the first pass, punch positions 0, 11, and 12 will be inhibited, and on the second pass, 9 through 1 will be inhibited.

As an interesting mental exercise, try to visualize the steps necessary to sort a deck using the values in columns 1 and 2. First envision numeric values and then try it with alphanumeric. A skilled operator performs the necessary sequence of steps in an almost mechanical way—moving the brush, inhibiting hole sensing, and collecting cards from the stackers.

A sorter can be used to arrange cards in an order for efficient computer processing. The industry trend is away from this type of auxiliary processing of input data. Some reasons are that computers can sort quite efficiently; auxiliary processing may introduce errors; and auxiliary processing may cause delay while waiting for the operator or the auxiliary machine. On the other hand, a card sorter can perform a very inexpensive sort, particularly when the sort field is short.

The Tabulator.   An accounting machine is popularly called a tabulator or tab. Tabulators are used to edit and print the information from cards and to accumulate totals for printing on total lines. Most of the functions of the tabulator are controlled by a removable control panel.

The tabulator is a massive machine, and it is expensive as compared to other card handling machines. In the precomputer era, the tabulator was the center of the data processing facility. One may still hear the terms *tab room* and *tab room supervisor* occasionally.

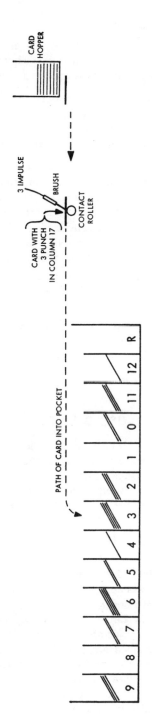

Fig. 2-5 Sorter operation.

Other Data Preparation Equipment

The use of punched cards is not without disadvantages. First of all, the cards are bulky to stock and store. Secondly, cards cost about one-tenth of a cent each, and they are not reusable. Third, card equipment tends to be noisy.

Keytape.   There is current interest in devices that record information from keyboards on magnetic tape. One such device records information on a magnetic tape in a small cartridge. Also available are systems of keyboards that can record information on a magnetic tape under control of a small special purpose computer.

Paper Tape.   Paper tape is widely used to record information transmitted over communications lines. Two alternative paper tape codes are shown in Fig. 2-6. In the eight-channel code, each character is complete in itself. The check position is used to make every character consist of an odd number of holes. The five-channel code is widely used in telegraphy. The "letters" and "figures" characters indicate that characters following should be interpreted as letters and figures, respectively.

Paper tape readers and punches are quiet, compact, and inexpensive. Some disadvantages are as follows:

1. Errors punched in paper tape are difficult to correct.
2. The tape is relatively fragile.
3. Paper tape handling equipment is not available in many computer installations.

END-USE DEVICES

Every I/O device can be designated as either an end-use device or a storage device. End-use devices are those that introduce data into a system or extract information from a system. End-use devices are sometimes called *source/sink devices,* a term borrowed from the science of thermodynamics. From a system viewpoint, data are generated by a source device, and it is absorbed at a sink.

Card Readers and Punches

In most computer installations, card readers are the principal devices for introducing new data into the system. A typical installation might include one or two card readers and one card punch.

Card readers and punches can be packaged separately, or a reader and punch can share a single package. Cards to be read are placed in an extended hopper. Blank cards to be punched are placed in a shorter hopper. As cards are read or punched, they are stacked in stackers ready for removal by the operator. Card readers and punches are available with a variety of speeds. A moderately high-performance unit such as the one shown reads 1,000 cards per minute and punches 300 cards per minute.

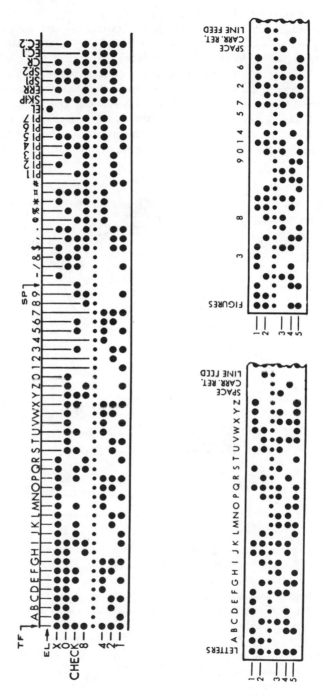

Fig. 2-6　Paper tape codes.

33

As shown in Fig. 2-7, card reading is accomplished by passing a card under reading brushes that establish electrical contact with the contact roll whenever a hole is encountered. Alternatively, some readers detect holes photoelectrically. Most high-performance card readers have 80 brushes at each reading station, one brush for each card column. Lower-performance card readers pass cards endwise beginning with column 1. This accomplishes two economies: the number of brushes is reduced to 12 at each station, and an entire character is sensed at one time and is ready for transmission. The second read brushes are used for automatic comparison by the device or for programmed comparison to ensure that the first reading was correct.

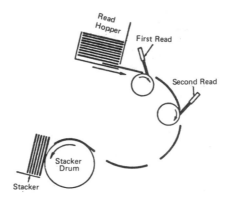

Fig. 2-7   Card reading.

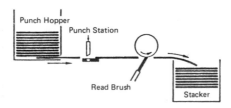

Fig. 2-8   Card punching.

The card punching illustrated in Fig. 2-8 is quite similar to card reading. The read brushes are used to verify that punching was accomplished accurately. Again, cards may be passed edgewise or endwise.

Some card units treat cards as if each column contains a character and each character has a particular hole combination as discussed earlier. For units of that type, reading a card results in transferring 80 bytes of information to main storage, properly converted to the internal character code of the computer. Other card units treat card information as if it were binary. When a card is read using such a unit, 960 binary digits are transferred to main storage, one digit for each of the 12 possible hole positions in each of the 80 card columns. If a unit treats all information as binary, an I/O system program may be used to convert the binary card image to the appropriate 80 bytes of information. The binary feature is useful because

1. It allows complete flexibility in interpretation of card codes. A nonstandard character representation in a deck of cards can be accommodated by changes in the conversion program.
2. Cards are sometimes used to store binary programs.
3. A card can contain more information when a binary form is used than when one column is used for each character.

Card handling devices include mechanical clutches. If programming is accomplished such that the clutches can remain engaged for significant periods, device performance will be excellent. If the device-controlling programs fail to do this by even a very small margin, device performance may be reduced by as much as 50 percent.

Printers

Printers are the principal devices used to record information that leaves a computer installation. A typical system might include from two to four or more printers. Most printers feed continuous forms up the front, and the printed results are stacked in back. Printing is accomplished a line at a time at speeds up to about 2,000 lines per minute.

Most printers use engraved type implemented in any of several mechanisms. Figure 2-9 shows a chain of engraved characters. The chain rotates continuously at high speed. As the appropriate character passes any particular print position, the corresponding hammer strikes the paper, forcing it against the ribbon and type. Other printers use a matrix of wires or an electrostatic process for recording.

A channel program causes a string of bytes of data to be sent to a printer. The bit combination in any byte to be printed is interpreted by the electrical circuitry of the printer, causing a hammer to be activated at some precise instant. The image that appears on the paper is completely dependent on the engraving on the type chain. For example, assume a particular byte of main storage contains a pattern of bits that constitute the letter A. As this byte is transmitted by a channel to a printer, it will still represent A. The mechanical motions of the printer will be timed to cause the proper printing hammer to "fire" at a predictable time in relation to the type chain, and something will be printed. Whether the printed result looks like an A or whether it looks like B, C, or any other character depends on the engraving at that point on the type chain.

Continuous forms are moved by sprocket wheels that engage perforations on both edges of the forms. A punched paper tape is used for printer-carriage control in many printers. The tape moves in synchronization with the printed forms, and the holes in the tape are sensed by electrical brushes. An example of the use of the carriage-control tape is as follows: If the information returned to the CPU after printing a line indicates that the brush number 12 on the paper tape has encountered a hole, the next channel program to be executed might include a command that causes the forms carriage to move forms continuously until brush number 1 encounters a hole. This set of actions can be used to provide high-speed skipping across the perforated fold of the continuous forms or for positioning printed lines properly on preprinted forms.

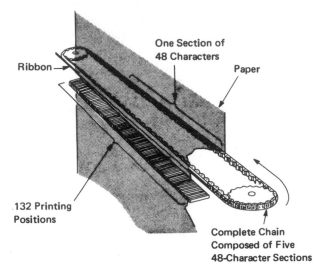

Fig. 2-9   An engraved-type chain.

Proper control of forms is a demanding responsibility. Printer performance can be adversely affected by inefficient spacing control. For example, a sequence of "print and space" commands might be executed more rapidly than "space and print" because the former commands allow transmission of a second print line during spacing. There is also the requirement of ensuring that the proper forms are being used for each special requirement. Paychecks must be on special forms, but a main storage dump should not use those same forms. When forms are torn or jammed, several illegible lines may be printed before the error is detected. The I/O system should include a recovery capability involving cooperative action by the operator to reprint several lines and continue. This capability is possible only when printing is a staged operation not involving the user's program.

Manned Terminals

A manned terminal is one that has virtually full-time attention of a terminal operator. From a computer system viewpoint, a manned terminal requires special support:

1. Terminal performance is limited by the operator. Keying rates vary widely from moment to moment. There may be unexplained delays for minutes at a time.

2. The terminal operator requires good response from the system. An unmanned terminal can be scheduled at the convenience of the system, not so with a manned terminal.
3. The terminal operator is capable of intelligent action. Messages verbally describing an action to be taken can be sent to the terminal.
4. The terminal operator must be kept informed. Cooperation between the system and the terminal operator is possible only if the operator understands what is happening. This is particularly true when the terminal is physically remote from the computer itself.

A great variety of terminal devices intended for communication between the terminal operator and the computer system exists. The typewriter keyboard and printer combination is widely used both because the typewriter is a familiar tool and because typewriter speeds of keying and printing are well matched to standard telephone-line capabilities. Graphic displays, using cathode-ray tubes, are similar in appearance to commercial television sets. They have the advantage of very rapid display and the ability to present charts and diagrams. The graphic display devices require communication lines much superior to standard telephone lines.

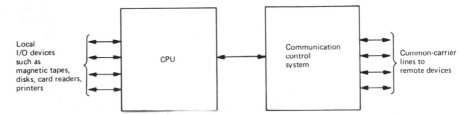

Fig. 2-10   A communication control system.

Another type is a low-cost terminal incorporating numeric keyboard and a manually operated card reader for entering data. An audio speaker is located behind the grill for receiving an audio response from the computer system. The audio response is furnished by a special device at the computer installation. Prerecorded messages are selected by the computer program for transmission to the terminal. A telephone handset completes the terminal.

Communicating with geographically dispersed devices using common-carrier facilities, giving prompt and intelligent attention to each requirement, is a challenge requiring special knowledge and special equipment. A department of I/O system programmers usually includes one or more specialists in the communications field. Usually, a computer system that deals with a large number of communications lines will include a "communications' front end" as illustrated in Fig. 2-10. The communication control system is a special purpose computer that furnishes the control codes required for automatic dialing, error correction, and terminal-device operation. Additionally, the communication control system sorts out the messages so that complete and accurate messages only are transferred to and from the main CPU. From the viewpoint of the I/O system in the CPU, the communication control system resembles a single high-performance, end-use device.

A few of the terms used in discussing the communication equipment are as follows:

Half Duplex Line   A half duplex line is capable of transmitting messages in one direction at a time. For example, when the terminal is sending information to the computer, the latter is powerless to interrupt or to communicate with the terminal in any way until that terminal voluntarily yields control of the line. A half duplex line may be adequate where long distances would make a full duplex line too expensive.

Full Duplex Line   A full duplex line is capable of two-way simultaneous transmission. Using full duplex, a receiving device can send an interrupting signal to a sender to request retransmission or to communicate urgent information.

Modem   The term *modem* (pronounced mō-dĕm) is an industry contraction for modulator/demodulator. A modem modulates signals that are being transmitted and demodulates signals being received. It is an adapter that converts signals conforming to one set of engineering conventions to another.

Leased Line Versus Dial-Up Line   A terminal might be connected to a computer using a leased line dedicated to that use. A leased line has the advantages of instant availability and constant and predictable quality. A dial-up line is less expensive, but establishing a connection at a desired time may be difficult, and the quality of the line is affected by the quality of the switching equipment used. Automatic dial-up equipment is available so that a computer can establish connection with a terminal without operator help at the computer end of a dial-up line.

Baud   The quality of a communication line is expressed in bauds. A 300-baud line is capable of carrying 300 binary digits of information per second. Information is transmitted in a serial-serial manner. That is, the binary digits of a byte are transmitted serially, and one byte is transmitted completely before the next byte is started.

The entire subject of data communications including common carrier equipment, communication conventions, terminal devices, and the system programming necessary to control all of these is sufficient subject matter for another book.

MAGNETIC TAPE

Most general purpose tape units process ½-in. plastic tape with magnetic coating on one side. A full-sized reel of tape is about 2,400 ft long. Information is recorded at densities up to 1,600 bytes per inch of tape at data rates up to 320,000 bytes per second.

Magnetic tape is typically used for processing where consecutive records are of interest and for long-term shelf storage of data. A general purpose system might include from 4 to 20 magnetic tape units.

General Description

A magnetic tape unit has two removable tape reels. Initially, the left-hand reel contains all of the tape. Tape feeds from the left-hand reel, down a vacuum column forming a loop, over the read/write head element, down another vacuum column and up to the right-hand reel. In operation, each reel is independently driven to furnish or take up tape in its vacuum column. The read/write head element has its own tape-moving capstan that moves tape between the two vacuum columns. This design allows the unit to accelerate tape from a standstill to full speed in as little as 2 ms while passing over about ¼ in. of tape.

Magnetic tape has several characteristics that distinguish it from most other media:

1. Tape length is variable. As tape wears out or is damaged, pieces are cut off and discarded. The using program has no way of knowing how much unrecorded tape remains available.
2. Tape surface is imperfect. Magnetic tape typically has small flaws or foreign particles that affect reading and writing. The system programs that process tape must assume that reading and recording problems will occur even when the tape and unit are in good operating condition.
3. Magnetic tape cannot support update in place. Due to variations in tape motion speed, recording densities vary by minor amounts. Therefore, whenever data are recorded on a tape, all data from that point to the physical end of the tape are assumed to be illegible. A file of data on magnetic tape can only be extended; it cannot be updated.
4. Recording formats are variable. There are no physical boundaries on magnetic tape other than the beginning and the end. Blocks of data can be of any reasonable length, and blocks can vary in length. No addressing is provided on tape; all processes are relative to the current position.

These characteristics apply to nearly all general purpose magnetic tape units. At least one computer of the 1950s, Burroughs Corporation's Datatron 205, used magnetic tape that had preaddressed fixed-length blocks. Any block could be read, written, or updated without affecting other blocks. More recently, the Atlas Computer at Manchester University is using preaddressed magnetic tape. For our purposes in this book, the variable format with no update-in-place capability will be assumed.

Magnetic Recording on Tape

Figure 2-11a shows a magnetic-tape read/write head. To record information, the electric current in the coils is changed causing a change in the magnetic field at the gap. The moving tape surface is in contact with the gap, and change in the magnetic field at the gap is recorded as a change in the magnetic condition of the tape surface. To read information, the magnetized tape is passed over the head. Changes in the magnetic field of the tape induce small but detectable currents in the read/write coils. Several read/write heads are packaged side by side so that several tracks can be recorded or sensed simultaneously. Typically, seven or nine tracks are used. Many tape units incorporate the two-gap head illustrated in Fig. 2-11b. By using such a head, a tape unit can sense the information just recorded and compare it with the original information, thereby ensuring that the recorded information is both legible and accurate.

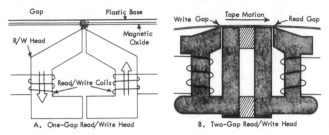

Fig. 2-11   Tape heads.

Information is recorded on magnetic tape as blocks of bytes separated by unrecorded gaps as shown in Fig. 2-12. When the tape unit receives the command to record data, it erases the gap as it accelerates the tape, and then it records the continuous block of bytes transmitted over the channel. When the transmission ends, the tape unit begins deceleration of the tape-erasing part of a gap as the tape comes to rest. Whenever a magnetic tape is at rest, the read/write head is positioned in a gap. Conversely, whenever tape is in motion, that motion will continue at least until a gap is created or encountered.

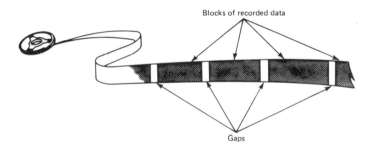

Fig. 2-12   Blocks and gaps.

One can readily perceive that block length has a significant effect on efficiency. For example, assume 1.6 million bytes are to be recorded at 1,600 bytes per inch with ½ in. gaps. The following table illustrates the effect of block size on the length of tape required:

Block Length	No. of Gaps	Total Gap Length	Total Tape Length
100 byths	16000	8000 inches	9000 inches
400	4000	2000	3000
1600	1000	500	1500

Increasing block length from 100 to 1,600 bytes reduces total tape length by a factor of 6. Not only does the increased block length decrease the time required to read or write the data but also rewind time and the number of tape reels that must be handled for large files are reduced.

Figure 2-13 illustrates the recorded information within a block. The read/write heads record a byte and a lateral check simultaneously across the tape. The check bit is devised such that the number of magnetic impressions recorded across the tape is always odd. At the end of any block of data, a longitudinal check byte is devised to make the number of bits in each track odd. The check byte has its own lateral check bit. The check bits and byte are called redundant parity data. The conventions described use odd parity. Some tape units use even parity. When a block of data is being read, the redundant information serves as an indication of probable accuracy of sensing. Some tape units record redundant data sufficient to correct most errors detected during reading. The development, recording, and verification of the checking information are completely automatic.

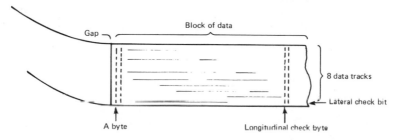

Fig. 2-13   A block of data on magnetic tape.

A tape unit can record a special combination of magnetic impressions called a tape mark. If, when executing a read command, the unit encounters a tape mark, an indication of that event is returned to the computer. Files, parts of files, and labels are usually separated from other data by tape marks. Conventions for the use of tape marks are part of the data organization definition. A possible organization of data is shown in Fig. 2-14. Notice that tape marks are used to segregate volume labels, file header labels, data blocks, and file trailer labels. The two consecutive tape marks will be recognized by I/O system programs as an indication that there are no data beyond that point.

Also shown in Fig. 2-14 is a reflective mark. For some units, reflective foil markers mark the beginning and end of tape. For other units, perforations in the tape are used. The indicators are placed so as to allow a leader of tape beyond the indicated end. A tape rewinds to the beginning reflective mark. If the end reflective mark is encountered during recording, an indication is returned to the CPU so that appropriate programming can terminate recording on that volume.

Though its quality is consistently improving, magnetic tape must be considered an error-prone storage medium. Recovery procedures for magnetic tape can be quite elaborate including features similar to these:

Redundancy Failure During Writing   Backspace and retry the operation once. If the retry fails, erase a few inches of tape and then try the original operation. The philosophy in this situation is that attempts to write on a particular section of tape should be limited. An overly conscientious effort to write might finally create an apparently adequate but marginal block that might cause reading problems later.

Redundancy Failure During Reading   Backspace and retry the operation 10 times. If this is not successful, backspace five blocks and then forward space four blocks and then retry again. The philosophy of the multiple backspace is that any debris on the tape surface might be removed by varying the pattern of motion. Experiments with some tapes show that repeated retries may finally yield success after 50 or more retries.

Noise Blocks   A noise block consists of spurious signals read from an imperfect surface previously erased. If analysis of a redundancy failure during reading indicates that the failing block consists of fewer than 12 bytes, the block should be ignored as a noise block. To ensure that this act does not discard valuable data, all blocks recorded should contain at least 13 bytes.

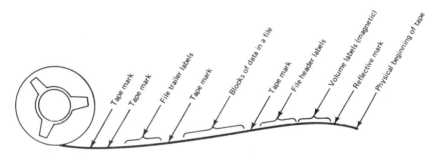

Fig. 2-14   Tape layout.

DIRECT ACCESS STORAGE DEVICES (DASD)

The direct access class of devices includes magnetic disks, drums, strips, and cards. The term *direct access* alludes to the capability of these devices to process data at separate locations on a single volume without passing over the intervening data. Another term sometimes used is *random access devices,* connoting the property that items of data can be stored or retrieved efficiently in a random order. Direct access devices are used for (1) storage of files whose records are processed in an order different from their stored order; (2) storage of libraries of programs including control programs, language processors, and users' programs; (3) storage of files when several files on the same storage volume are to be processed simultaneously.

General Description

Magnetic disk storage units may hold from 5 to 200 million bytes of data with an average storage or retrieval time of 25 to 150 ms for any block of data. The disks themselves constitute a storage volume pack that is removable from most units. The read/write heads shown in Fig. 2-15 do not touch the magnetic surface, but rather, they float on thin air bearings. This design eliminates surface wear and significantly reduces the accumulation of foreign particles that affect magnetic tape reliability.

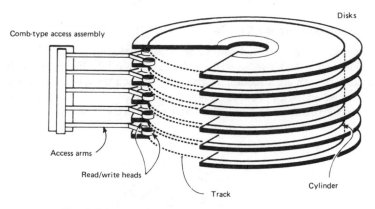

Fig. 2-15   Access arms and read/write heads.

The read/write heads are mounted on a comb of access arms. There is one head for each magnetic surface, and the comb moves all heads simultaneously. With the heads in some fixed position, the continuously rotating disks cause the tiny recording element within each head to describe a circular track on a disk surface. In the illustration, there are 10 heads, so 10 tracks are traversed simultaneously. The tracks in any such set constitute a cylinder of tracks. When the comb moves the heads to another position, another cylinder of tracks is traversed. In the illustration, there are 203 discrete comb positions resulting in 203 concentric cylinders of 10 tracks each. The cylinder idea is useful because all of the tracks in a cylinder are available for reading or recording without physical motion of the comb. Most disk units read or record using only one head at a time. As a result, the bits comprising a byte are strung out linearly along a track with the last bit of one byte adjacent to the first bit of the next.

Magnetic Drums

A magnetic drum has a single cylindrical recording surface. There is a stationary recording element for each data track on the drum, and the drum itself is not removable. The principal advantage of a magnetic drum is the very fast random storage and retrieval capability. A typical drum will hold 5 million bytes of data with an average storage or retrieval time of about 10 ms for any block of data. Larger drums are available with correspondingly longer storage and retrieval times. Typically, drum storage space is more expensive than disk storage space so drums are used for data requiring fast accessibility.

Magnetic Strips and Cards

Magnetic-strip-and-card devices have been designed to achieve some of the economy of magnetic tape as a storage medium while retaining the direct access capabilities of disks and drums. To date, magnetic-strip-and-card devices enjoy much more limited popularity than magnetic tapes, disks, or drums.

Magnetic Recording on DASDs

The two most popular conventions for accommodating data on a track are a sector convention and a self-describing block convention. Figure 2-16 illustrates a disk surface with eight sectors. Each sector of each track will hold a uniformly fixed number of bytes such as 2,048 bytes. When a unit is designed to use sectors, block size for that unit is fixed and equal to sector size.

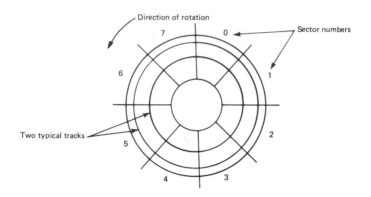

Fig. 2-16   Sectors.

A self-describing block is illustrated in Fig. 2-17. Information is recorded on a track beginning at the index point. The track description information can include an indication of available space on the track or the key of the last record on the track or any other information. A block consists of three recorded areas: (1) the count area of fixed size that includes the block number of this block and also the sizes of each of the other two areas, (2) the key area (optional) that is used in certain searching operations, and (3) the data area that contains the block itself. Because they are self-describing, each block can be of a different size, and the number of blocks on a track is not fixed. Typical use of the device includes reading, modifying, and rewriting an individual block of data. If the modification changes the size of the block, a special form of the write command must be used, and all blocks on the track following the modified block will be erased automatically.

Some DASD units are designed to read or record using more than one head at a time. For example, four heads might be used together as illustrated

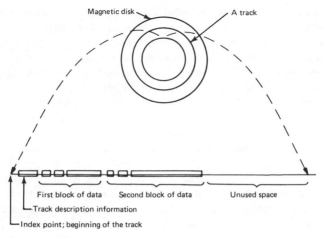

Fig. 2-17   A track with self-describing blocks.

in Fig. 2-18. The four physical tracks traversed by heads 0, 1, 2, and 3 constitute a single logical track; heads 4, 5, 6, and 7 traverse the second logical track. The advantage in using several heads in parallel is not that a particular block of data can be located more rapidly but that, once the block is located, the data can be read or recorded more rapidly.

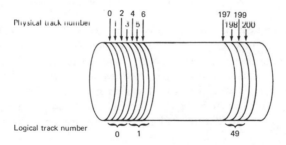

Fig. 2-18   Physical and logical tracks on a magnetic drum.

Direct access device performance can be affected significantly by the combination of physical position of data on the device and the programs that process that data. For example, the time required to retrieve the second block of data of a pair of related blocks might be approximately 1 ms if the block is placed optimally, approximately 20 ms if the second block is placed nonoptimally on the same cylinder as the first, or approximately 100 ms if the retrieval of the second block requires motion of the access comb.

SUMMARY

Data preparation equipment is important as the forerunner to modern computers and as the vehicle for detecting errors in input data. Punched cards are a popular input medium, the 80-column card being most popular. Preparing cards for computer processing involves keypunching, verification, and possibly sorting, collating, or tabulating. The keypunch is widely known for data preparation, the tabulator for accounting without use of a computer. Alternative data-preparation devices record keystrokes on magnetic tape or paper tape.

End-use devices, sometimes termed source/sink devices, include card readers, punches, printers, and manned terminals. Card readers and punches might operate at 1,000 and 300 cards per minute, respectively, interpreting information as 80-character blocks or 960 binary-digit blocks. The binary form allows the greater flexibility in interpretation.

Printers translate information from their main storage form to an image on paper. The image presented typically depends on the timing of a hammer stroke and the engraving on a character chain. Speeds up to 2,000 lines per minute using continuous forms are typical. Printer carriages may be controlled by punched paper tapes. Programming for efficient use of a printer, ensuring that the proper forms are used and recovering when forms tear or jam, is a demanding responsibility.

A terminal that has full-time operator attention requires special system support to cope with operator-imposed delays, to respond promptly to the operator's actions, to enlist the operator's help in some operations, and to keep him informed of activities. Manned terminals incorporating a typewriter keyboard and printer are popular. Other manned-terminal devices include graphic displays, numeric keyboards, card readers, and audio response units. Common carrier transmission lines, half duplex or full duplex leased or dial up are frequently used.

Most magnetic tape units process ½-in. tape in 2,400-ft reels. Characteristics of magnetic tape processing are unpredictable tape length, tape-surface imperfections, no update-in-place ability, and complete variability in block sizes. Data are read and recorded by a set of one- or two-gap heads recording seven or nine tracks along the tape. Data on magnetic tape consist of blocks separated by gaps. Groups of blocks may be segregated by tape marks. Error handling procedures include limited retries to record and repeated retries to read.

Magnetic disk storage devices record information on concentric cylinders with several tracks per cylinder. The recording elements are mounted on a movable comb of access arms. Each element floats on an air bearing and reads or records information serially on a track. Drums are similar to disks, but they usually have smaller capacity, higher performance, and a nondismountable storage volume. Magnetic strips and cards combine storage economy with random access. The information on a DASD track may be formatted in fixed-size sectors or in self-describing blocks.

Exercises

1.(e) How many 8-bit bytes of binary information can be recorded in a 3½ in. high deck of Hollerith cards using all available bit positions?

2.(e) Using an electromechanical sorter that feeds 1,000 cards per minute, how long would it take to sort 10,000 cards alphabetically on columns 1 through 5? Ignore the operator's handling time.

3.(e) Computer output devices include card punches, printers, magnetic tape units, and DASDs. Of these devices, why is the printer least amendable to automatic verification of the result?

4.(e) Suggest why the use of a carriage-control tape on a printer causes an operational problem.

5.(e) If a magnetic tape unit records at 320,000 bytes per second, has a tape-passing speed of 200 in. per second, and a gap size of ½ in., how many inches of tape are required to record 2,000 blocks of 320 bytes each?

6.(m) Calculate the difference in track length of a track 5 in. from the center of a magnetic disk and one 6 in. from the center. Give a plausible reason why a sector on the outer track, being longer, does not hold more information than a sector on the inner track.

7.(m) Assume a magnetic drum has a rotational period of 10 ms and a single physical track can contain 5,000 bytes. What would be the recording rate in bytes per second if a logical track consists of 4 physical tracks? Why would a logical track consisting of 4 physical tracks typically hold fewer 1,000-byte blocks than 4 logical tracks of 1 physical track each?

8.(d) Which recording conventions do you feel provides greater simplicity of programming—a sector convention or self-describing block convention? Give reasons for your answer.

3 Channel Programming

> . . . the input and output facilities of a computer are usually not learned until after all other features have been examined, and it frequently happens that only a small fraction of the programmers of a particular machine ever knows much about the details of input and output. . . . Donald E. Knuth

An I/O channel is an electronic device that transmits information between main storage and I/O devices. All medium and large general purpose computing systems include I/O channels. To control the flow of data, a channel executes a channel program that resembles a CPU program. Most programmers have acquired only modest skill and knowledge in channel programming, a fact that attests to the success of I/O systems in relieving users of I/O programming details.

In early general purpose machines such as the IBM type 701, the central processing unit (CPU) performed both computations and I/O. The productive capabilities of these machines were severely constrained by the relatively slow I/O devices. Not only was the I/O time frequently greater than the computing time, but because the CPU alternately performed both activities, no computation could be performed while input or output was in progress. The channels of later systems were devised to relieve the constraint both by allowing I/O to be simultaneous with computation and by allowing simultaneous I/O processes through multiple channel operation. Figure 3-1 illustrates the effects of channels on productive capability. Execution of a simple repeated read/compute/write sequence is illustrated without any overlap, with one channel, and finally with two channels. For the process, channels improve execution rate by more than 2 to 1.

Figure 3-2 is a conceptual diagram of a computer system. As shown in the figure, the main storage bus is the central electronic trunk in the system; all information entering or leaving main storage must flow along the bus. The CPU, main storage, and the channels are all connected to the bus. In an actual system, some of the units shown separately in Fig. 3-2 might be packaged together. For example, the CPU, main storage, and the main storage bus might be in one package; several channels might share another package; and the device control units might be packaged within the covers of the devices they control.

From a programming viewpoint, a channel resembles a CPU for the following reasons:

1. It has a command repertoire.
2. Its commands have operation codes, main storage addresses, and parameters.
3. A channel fetches commands from main storage for execution.
4. Channel programs are combinations of commands.

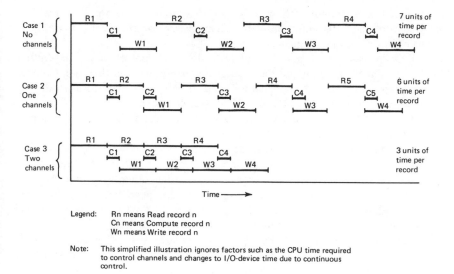

Legend: Rn means Read record n
           Cn means Compute record n
           Wn means Write record n

Note: This simplified illustration ignores factors such as the CPU time required
         to control channels and changes to I/O-device time due to continuous
         control.

Fig. 3-1   Channel/CPU/channel overlap.

The CPU initiates channel program execution, and it may be required to assist the channel during or after the running of the channel program, but it is free to perform other tasks during most of the I/O time. Achieving simultaneous operation of the CPU and the several channels is a significant programming challenge, a challenge that has preoccupied systems programmers for many years.

The channels in the system are independent of each other except that they must compete with each other for use of the main storage bus. This competition is resolved automatically, but the competition affects timing as will

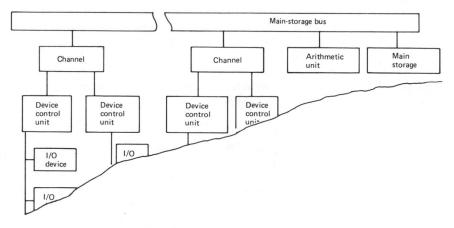

Fig. 3-2   A computer system.

be discussed later. Figure 3-2 shows the logical similarity of the positions within the system of the CPU and each of the channels. A system might contain from one to eight or even more channels.

I/O devices require a variety of individualized control signals depending on their mechanical design and the type of recording medium they use. Control units are placed between the channel and the I/O devices to furnish the specialized control signals and to allow simultaneous operation of several devices attached to a single channel. A single control unit typically controls from one to eight devices.

An example of simultaneous device operation on a single channel is repositioning of the magnetic tape on one tape unit during transfer of data from main storage, through a separate control unit, to another tape unit. Several time-consuming operations, such as magnetic tape rewind, once initiated, can proceed without control from the channel. A special type of channel called a multiplexor channel provides automatic simultaneous handling of several low-speed devices simultaneously. For example, several manual entry keyboard terminals can be controlled simultaneously by a single multiplexor channel. A separate channel program applies to each active terminal. The multiplexor channel is fast enough that it can perform a necessary action for each of several terminals in succession and be ready to perform a subsequent action for each of them while the devices are still occupied with the first actions.

Several of the components shown in Fig. 3-2 are involved in transfer of data to or from a device. An output operation proceeds as follows. The CPU, under control of its program, initiates the operation by selecting a device, a control unit, and a channel and starting a channel program. The channel, under control of its channel program, requests data from main storage and controls the flow of those data to the control unit. The control unit recodes and re-arranges the data as may be required and passes the data to the device, augmenting those data with control signals as appropriate. The device reacts to the control signals and records the information on its recording medium.

Input is accomplished the same way except that data flow in the opposite direction.

The major part of the information in this chapter is in two preliminary sections, "Data Formats" and "Channel Commands," followed by a larger section, "Channel-Programming Examples." A particular system, IBM System/370, is used to make the examples concrete. In all three sections, the hardware information presented is a small subset of the total information that would be pertinent to an I/O system programmer.

DATA FORMATS

There is a reasonable degree of de facto standardization of data storage media throughout the computer industry. The 80-column card is widely used; ½-in. magnetic tape is almost universal; and 14-in. magnetic disks are prevalent. These three media will be used to illustrate channel programming principles. The format of information recorded on these media may differ from one system to another. In the case of cards, the punched-hole representations of

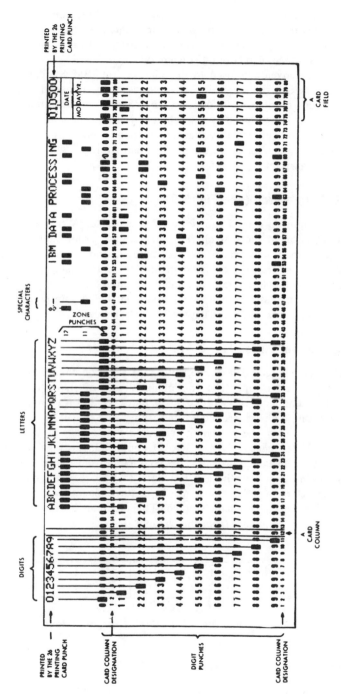

Fig. 3-3 Character coding on an 80-column card.

51

certain characters, particularly the special (neither alphabetic nor numeric) characters, may differ. On magnetic tape, character representations and recording densities may differ. Magnetic disks, being newest of the three media, have the widest range of recording conventions.

The conventions used in this chapter are IBM System/370 conventions, but the actual representation of characters by punched holes or magnetic impression is of minor concern in channel programming. It is usually sufficient to know that if certain characters from main storage are recorded on a medium and subsequently that information is retrieved by the same computer system, the characters returned to main storage will be identical to the original characters.

80-Column Cards (See Fig. 3-3)

Each column on a card can represent a character. When a card is punched, a representation of the first character transmitted from main storage is punched into column 1, the second into column 2, and so forth. If fewer than 80 characters are transmitted from main storage by a single WRITE command, the rightmost columns are left blank; if more than 80 characters are transmitted, the excess characters are discarded. Other interpretations of punched card data are described in Chapter 2, "I/O Devices."

Magnetic Tape (See Fig. 3-4)

A character is recorded on magnetic tape as a combination of magnetic bits in a row across the tape. The continuous stream of characters transmitted by a WRITE command is recorded as a block of information, each lateral row representing a character. Blocks of varying lengths can be recorded. Any block is separated from the preceding and succeeding blocks by unrecorded segments of tape called gaps. Given a READ command, the tape will move forward, transmitting to the control unit the characters from the first block encountered and coming to rest in the gap following that block. The control unit transmits the characters to the channel, which, in turn, places them on the main storage bus for recording in main storage. The tape can be repositioned forward or backward by command from the channel.

Fig. 3-4   A section of magnetic tape.

Direct Access Storage Devices (DASDs)

The information on DASDs is stored on narrow bands of magnetic surface called tracks. A track is traversed by a stationary read/write element as the surface rotates beneath the element. The element is conceptually not unlike a phonograph needle except that the track it follows is a circle rather than a spiral and the information is magnetically recorded and sensed. A track has been cut and straightened in Fig. 3-5.

Fig. 3-5   A section of a DASD track.

The data block itself consists of three recorded areas: count, key, and data. The count area contains an identifier and a description of the block; the key and data areas are available to store the user's data. By command from the channel, the data area, key and data areas, or all three can be recorded. The count area is fixed in size, but the other two areas are flexible; their lengths are recorded in the count area.

CHANNEL COMMANDS

The commands in this section constitute a major subset of the IBM System/370 channel commands. The commands are typical of the commands available in most channels. Several contemporary systems have less flexible commands. Some complex systems, such as the CDC 6600, appear to include more flexible commands. Actually, these systems include small computers called peripheral processing units (PPUs in the CDC terminology) dedicated to I/O functions. The PPUs deal with their assigned devices through channels that have commands not markedly different from those presented here.

The following conventions and clarifications will simplify the presentation:

1. Channel programs consist of "commands"; CPU programs consist of "instructions."
2. The command format is LOC OPER PAR1, PAR2, where LOC is the (optional) symbolic name of the location of this command, OPER is the operation code, PAR1 is the first parameter, and PAR2 is the second. While the commands listed are System/360 commands, the format and operation code symbols used here are not used in any IBM literature.[1] An address of the form L(T) is interpreted "location of T"; the implication is that the quantity T is available at that location.
3. An entire channel program applies to a single I/O device. The CPU program identifies and selects the device to be used, and then it instructs the channel to begin execution of the channel program.
4. A channel program will terminate immediately after execution of a command that does not include the command chaining option. Command chaining is indicated by (C) immediately following the operation code.

[1] The IBM assemblers do not provide a convenient symbolic channel command; the System/370 user must combine appropriate characters to produce the required bit pattern.

5. The commands listed are a subset in two ways: Certain commands are not listed and, for those that are listed, special case details are not complete. In some cases, the examples presented later add detail not presented in the command list.

CHANNEL COMMANDS

COMMANDS			MEANING
LOC	READ	ADDR,N	Read N characters from the device into main storage beginning at address ADDR. The location of this command is LOC.
	WRITE	ADDR,N	Write N characters to the device from main storage beginning at address ADDR.
	TIC	LOC	"Transfer in Channel". Transfer (branch) to the command at location LOC. Command chaining is automatic and need not be specified.
	SEEK	L(T)	Prepare the device to process data on track T. This command applies only to DASDs.
	SIE	L(I)	"Search Identifier Equal." If the identifier with count area of the next data block encountered on the device is identified to I skip the next command. This command applies only to DASDs. It is usually followed by a TIC.
	SKE	L(K),N	"Search Key Equal". If there are N characters in the key area encountered on the device and those characters are identical to K, skip the next command. This command applies only to DASDs. It is usually followed by a TIC.

CHANNEL PROGRAMMING EXAMPLES

Each of the examples in this section illustrates one or more of the principles of channel programming. In every case, the CPU must initiate the channel program by executing a Start Input/Output (SIO) instruction with certain control parameters and addresses set properly. The SIO instruction identifies the device and channel to be used, ensures that both are available, and then starts the channel program. The capabilities of a CPU program are required during channel start-up to effect alternative action if either the device or the channel is unable to respond properly.

A Simple Channel Program

The first example illustrates how simple a channel program can be, and it provides a basis for discussion of some related ideas.

EXAMPLE 3-1

Construct a channel program that writes a 100-character block of data from main storage locations DATA through DATA+99 onto magnetic tape.

Solution

WRITE DATA,100

Single-command channel programs are not unusual, but frequently channel programs will include 5 to 10 commands. It is unusual for a channel program to include more than 20 commands.

Many special conditions can arise during execution of any channel program, even one as simple as that shown in Example 3-1. For instance, what if the device fails to record the data properly, or what if the physical end of the tape is encountered during the process? Most special conditions are not handled directly by the channel program simply because of the limitations of the command set. Rather, when the channel program terminates, the CPU program must inspect the several error and status indicators that are set automatically during channel program execution and take appropriate action. Frequently the action taken will include execution of one or more additional channel programs.

The Interruption Mechanism

Events such as completion of an I/O operation are signaled by the interruption mechanism of the system. In computer terminology, the interruption mechanism causes an *interrupt* rather than an interruption; the latter generic term is not sufficiently explicit. An interrupt causes the CPU to suspend execution of its current program and begin executing a series of instructions designed to investigate the interrupting event. When the investigation is complete and any necessary actions have been taken, the suspended program can be resumed. The interruption mechanism allows the CPU to respond promptly to important events without continually testing for their occurrence.

A DASD Program

Channel program complexity is directly related to the flexibility of the device being controlled. Magnetic tape units, card readers, and many other devices infer that a READ or WRITE command implies "read the next data block" or "write the next card." The random storage and retrieval flexibility of DASDs make their control more complex. Example 3-2 illustrates how a search loop is used to find a particular block on a DASD track.

EXAMPLE 3-2
Construct a channel program to read a 100-character block of data from a DASD into main storage locations DATA through DATA+99. The block of data is on track 000307, and the data block identifier is 03074.*
Solution

	SEEK(C)	L(000307)
SRCH	SIE(C)	L(03074)
	TIC	SRCH
	READ	DATA,100

* The last four characters of a track number are always identical to the first four characters of the block identifiers on that track.

The first command in Example 3-2 causes a recording element to be readied over track 000307. For some types of devices, this may involve physical movement of the recording element, while in others, it involves electronic selection of an element which is permanently positioned over that track. The channel program itself is not affected by that distinction. The second and third commands constitute a loop that inspects each block identifier as it is encountered. The search is terminated when a block identifier of 03074 causes the TIC to be skipped. The READ command will retrieve data from the first data area it encounters.

Channel Program Timing

The execution time for channel commands is dictated primarily by the device being controlled. A channel program may be delayed at certain commands for extended periods while mechanical processes are being accomplished; at other times, the channel program may (and must) proceed at electronic speeds so that mechanical processes that are underway and cannot be stopped abruptly are serviced properly. In Example 3-2, the SEEK command may require several milliseconds if physical movement is required. The SIE command will be delayed until the recording element of the device being used encounters a block identifier. The length of the delay will depend on the distance between adjacent identifier areas, which depends on block size. The TIC command is executed at electronic speeds. The READ command will be delayed until a data area is encountered and 100 characters have been transmitted. All of these timing concerns affect execution speed of the channel program, but do not affect accuracy of the result.

There is a more important timing concern that *can* affect accuracy. Referring again to Example 3-2, after the SIE command has been executed and a block identifier equal to 03074 has been detected, the channel must interpret the READ command and be prepared to accept data before the data area is encountered, or incorrect operation will result. Failure to meet the timing requirements of the device causes a phenomenon called "overrun"; the device has overrun the channel. Overrun occurs whenever a channel fails to retrieve and interpret its next command soon enough, or it fails to furnish output or accept input data fast enough. Overrun is especially difficult to control because of the competition for use of main storage. In the case of the SIE command cited above, overrun is unlikely because the allowable time between the SIE and the READ commands is long compared with the command retrieval and interpretation times. In Example 3-3, a much more stringent timing requirement exists.

Scatter/Gather

Example 3-3 shows how to read information into nonconsecutive storage locations using a single channel program. The computer term for this action is *scatter*. A channel program can scatter information to or gather information from nonconsecutive locations. A special type of chaining called data chaining, indicated by (D) following the operation code READ or WRITE, is available for this purpose. If a READ(C) is followed by another READ, the second command applies to a separate data block. If a READ(D) is followed by another READ, the second command applies to the same data block as the first.

EXAMPLE 3-3

Assume that an 80-character master record and a 50-character detail record are recorded as a single block on a track of a DASD. Read the master record into main storage beginning at location MASTER and read the detail record into main storage beginning at location DETAIL. The data are on track 000204. The block can be identified by the contents of its key area, in this case, JONES.

Solution

	SEEK(C)	L(000204)
LOOP	SKE(C)	L(JONES),5
	TIC	LOOP
	READ(D)	MASTER,80
	READ	DETAIL,50

The SKE/TIC loop in this example resembles the loop in Example 3-2 except that the comparison is based on the key area. The first READ is data-chained to the second READ so that the first 80 bytes of the data area will be sent to one area of main storage and the next 50 to another.

Timing in Example 3-3 is very critical; the second READ must be retrieved from main storage and interpreted in a time interval dictated by the motion of the storage medium. If, because of competition for the main storage bus, the 81st character cannot be recorded in main storage promptly, the relentless flow of data will cause loss of one or more characters. That is, overrun will occur. If this happens, special condition indicators are set; the channel program terminates prematurely; and the interruption mechanism is activated. Although overrun is considered an exceptional condition, it is not ordinarily an uncorrectable condition. Under control of its program, the CPU can detect the overrun condition and restart the channel program properly.

Program Synchronizing

Example 3-4 illustrates how a channel program can be synchronized with a CPU program. The example introduces the interrupt option, which is available on all commands except TIC. The code READ(CI) is interpreted as before, except that the CPU is interrupted during execution of the command. Also introduced in this example is the tape mark. A tape mark is magnetically recorded on a tape by a special channel command. When a tape mark is encountered as a tape is being read, the channel program terminates immediately.

EXAMPLE 3-4

200-character records are recorded as consecutive blocks of data on a magnetic tape. Character positions 10 through 15 of each record are an amount field. The last record in the set is a dummy record, which can be identified by a 0 amount field. Following the last record is a tape mark. Write a channel program and flowchart the related CPU program that will read the records and sum the amount fields. The records need not be preserved in main storage. Assume that the tape is positioned to read the first block.

Solution

The channel program will overlay all of the records into a single main-storage area. After the first 15 characters of record are read, the CPU will extract the amount field and add it to the accumulating total.

Channel Program

LOOP	READ(D)	DATA, 15
	READ(CI)	DATA+15, 185
	TIC	LOOP

Arithmetic Unit

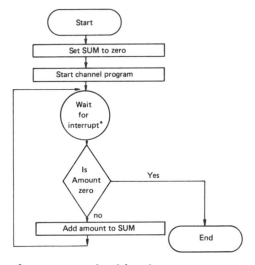

* Or perform some unrelated function.

Notice that the second READ command in the example includes the interrupt and command chaining options. As the channel begins to execute that READ, the CPU program that is being executed is interrupted, and the CPU begins execution of the instructions that inspect the data that have just been read. This inspection and the summing action are accomplished while the remaining 185 characters are being read. The channel program will run continuously until either an error is detected or a tape mark is encountered.

The kind of synchronization illustrated in Example 3-4 can be very important to elapsed job time for some types of devices. For example, a card reader might have a nominal card reading rate of 600 cards per minute and a mechanical clutch that can engage only at the beginning of any 100 ms interval. Using the example of channel programs, 600 cards per minute would be achieved. Using an alternative approach where the channel program had to be restarted after each card had been read, the card reading rate would drop abruptly to 300 cards per minute. More accurately, the reading rate would drop unless the subsequent channel program could be started within a very short time, called reinstruct time. The effect of exceeding reinstruct time for a card reader is illustrated in Fig. 3-6. Reinstruct time differs from one type of device to another. DASD performance can be very dependent on continuous control because failure to read the next consecutive block immediately means that the channel must wait for an entire rotation of the device.

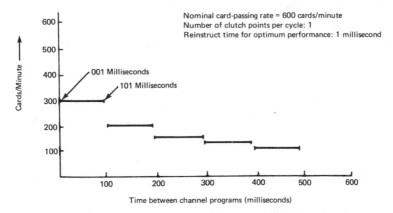

Fig. 3-6   The effect of reinstruct time on I/O device performance.

In an operating system environment, the number of control-program instructions that are executed both following an interrupt and preceding channel program start may exceed the reinstruct time for many I/O devices. From a control program designer's view, the number of these intervening instructions must be kept as low as possible.

CPU Programs versus Channel Programs

The channel programs in an I/O system are complemented by CPU programs that dwarf the channel programs in both size and complexity. Discussion of two points will illustrate why this is true.

The first point is that channel programs such as those presented in examples on the preceding pages do not constitute complete solutions to I/O situations. The I/O system must provide answers to many exceptional-condition questions: What if the device fails to record properly? What if there is not enough room on the tape? What if the device has been made "not ready" by the operator? What if a block identifier known to be present cannot be found? What if the block known to be number 100 in a series is found where number 99 should have been? The programs resulting from these questions are predominately CPU programs; channels simply do not have the necessary logical capability. It is not unusual in operating systems for the exceptional case programming to outweigh normal case programming, and I/O systems are especially concerned with exceptional cases.

The second point indicating why CPU programs overshadow channel programs is the answer to the question, "Who writes the channel programs in an operating system?" The answer is that the vast majority of channel programs are not written by anyone; they are generated. They may be generated by a language translator, such as a FORTRAN translator, or they may be generated by the I/O system as the need arises. Generating channel programs is clearly a CPU program task and, intuitively, the program that generates is more complex than the program that is generated.

Channel Programming Suggestions

As in CPU programming, there are many ways to write a channel program whose only merit is that it works. The suggestions listed below are important to channel program quality:

1. *Consider Error Recovery*   An operating system contains generalized error recovery procedures. Try to write channel programs that can use the generalized recovery procedures. Special recovery procedures are expensive to develop, and they frequently fail to work properly when needed.

2. *Avoid Close Timing Tolerance*   A carefully timed design might provide for the CPU to compute a value a few microseconds before the channel program uses that value. Close tolerance such as that can be upset by competition for use of the CPU, competition for the storage bus, maintenance changes to the CPU program, engineering changes to the equipment, or variations in the speeds of mechanical devices. Other close timing examples would be use of data chaining or of consecutive TICs when controlling a very high-performance I/O device.

3. *Avoid Branching to Unchecked Input Addresses*   For several kinds of I/O devices, the accuracy of input data cannot be checked by the control unit until an entire block has been read. In Example 3-4, input data were accumulated into a partial total, while the remainder of a block was being read. There is no danger in that example; if the data prove to be erroneous, the amount can be subtracted before a retry. However, if the input data had been used as an address for a TIC command, or as a CPU program address, an erroneous branch might have occurred. Such an error in a user's program would ruin the job. Such an error in the control program might cause an entire system failure. If the data must be used before they are checked, the risk can be reduced by using the unchecked value to select an address from a main-storage table. Such an address may be wrong, but it will not be unreasonable.

4. *Do Not Monopolize Equipment*   While continuous control of a channel may yield good performance of a particular device, it may yield poor performance of the system as a whole. A channel program like that used in Example 3-4 might exclude all other use of the channel and any equipment attached to it for several seconds or even minutes.

Whether a monopoly would occur depends on design details of the equipment. (The IBM System/370 channels have a feature, not described here, that allows channel programs to compete for a channel on a moment-by-moment basis. The Burroughs Corporation's B6500 resolves the problem by automatic switching that allows I/O equipment to be reached through any idle channel.)

5. *Don't Ignore I/O Device Performance*   Channel programs that fail to achieve good device performance can ruin system performance. Further, system users will replace or bypass those parts of a system that impede performance (and no one wants his routines replaced).

SUMMARY

Channels provide the ability to perform arithmetic processing and one or more I/O processes simultaneously. Channel programs are initiated by the CPU, but the latter is free to perform other tasks during channel operation. The several channels and the CPU occupy similar positions in a computer system; they all attach to the main storage bus, and they compete with each other for use of that bus. A channel is also connected to one or more device control units, each of which is connected to one or more devices. A control unit furnishes the specialized signals required by the attached devices, and it allows limited simultaneous device operations on a single channel.

Three storage media— the 80-column card, ½-in. magnetic tape, and the 14-in. magnetic disk—are used throughout the computer industry. The recording conventions used in this chapter are respectively one character per card column, a block of characters separated from adjacent blocks by unrecorded tape gaps, and three-area blocks of data on a DASD track. The DASD format is the most complicated; the count, key, and data areas of a block can be separately recorded, and the latter two areas are flexible in length.

A subset of System/370 channel commands, which is useful for programming examples and includes a range of functions not unlike those of most channels, includes:

Command		Meaning
READ	ADDR,N	Read N characters into main storage.
WRITE	ADDR,N	Write N characters from main storage.
TIC	LOC	Transfer to location LOC.
SEEK	L(T)	Prepare to process data on track T.
SIE	L(I)	Search for an identifier equal to I.
SKE	L(K),N	Search for a key equal to K.

A channel program can include as few as 1 command but typically includes 5 to 10. The complexity of a channel program is directly related to the flexibility of the device being controlled. Channel programs can include loops that accomplish searching for particular data or for transferring consecutive data blocks to and from main storage. Two kinds of chaining are optional: command chaining, the absence of which terminates a channel program, and data chaining, which allows a gather-scatter type of data transfer. When a channel program fails to meet the timing demands of an attached device, overrun occurs. Most overruns can be corrected by execution of an appropriate CPU program. The interrupt option uses the system interruption mechanism to synchronize a channel program with a CPU program. Such synchronization can improve I/O device performance dramatically by eliminating reinstruct time.

The CPU programs that complement channel programs are significantly larger and more complex than the channel programs. Two reasons for this are that CPU programs must resolve all exceptional conditions that arise during channel operations and that CPU programs generate most channel programs.

To write channel programs of high quality, one should consider error recovery and, preferably, plan to use a generalized recovery procedure; avoid close timing tolerances that are easily upset; avoid uncontrolled branching that can result from using unchecked data as an address; avoid monopolizing equipment to the detriment of system performance; and ensure that the channel program uses the I/O device efficiently.

Exercises

1.(e) Using the channel logic presented in this chapter, can a single channel program read a record from one magnetic tape and write it on another?

2.(e) Can the following command be the last command in a channel program? Why or why not?
READ(C)   LOC, 100

3.(e) Give a logical reason why SIE and SKE are usually followed by TIC.

4.(e) The channel program in Example 3-1 is for magnetic tape. Why would that program be inappropriate for (1) a card punch? (2) a DASD?

5.(e) Why are some channel commands executed more rapidly than others?

6.(m) Explain what each of the commands in the following program does.
```
            SEEK(C)       L(000404)
LOOP        SKE(C)        L(KEY), 3
            TIC           LOOP
            READ          LOC, 80
```

7.(m) What would be the effect of changing the (C) in the following magnetic tape channel program to (D)?
```
WRITE(C)    LOC, 50
WRITE       LOC+50, 50
```

8.(m) A program must retrieve two consecutive data blocks from a magnetic drum storage device with a fixed recording element for each track. Compare the elapsed times for the following two approaches:
   a. A channel program with two READ commands chained is used.
   b. A channel program with a single READ is executed twice and the reinstruct-time requirement cannot be met.
Assume the first (or only) SIO is executed when the recording element is one-half rotation from the beginning of the first desired block. Assume the rotational period of the drum is R ms and there are 10 fixed-length blocks per track.

9. (m) Describe a situation where two or more of the programming suggestions listed in this chapter would be at odds.

10. (d) An application program is using 100-character blocks of data from a magnetic tape. Devise the channel program and flowchart the CPU program that will retrieve blocks alternately into two 100-character buffer areas. Avoid excessive use of SIO by attempting to extend the channel program in progress. Be sure that the contents of a buffer have been used before the buffer is refilled. You may assume that the CPU repertoire includes an instruction that can test whether a channel is busy.

4 Units of Data

Data are the currency of the Computer. . . . Ivan Flores

In the world outside computers, data are customarily represented by characters, and characters are typically organized into records and
files. A child is taught to recognize the alphabetic and numeric characters at
an early age. Most first-grade students can interpret the records of their own
school accomplishments. Related records are frequently stored together. A
homemaker maintains a file of recipes. Business people maintain files of records
concerning the products they market. We use characters, records, and files in
our everyday lives simply because it is convenient to do so.

The input/output business is vitally concerned with data, a subject that is
surrounded by inconsistent terms and incomplete theory. An expert in the field
wrote in 1969, "We do not, it seems, have a very clear or commonly agreed
upon set of notions about data—either what they are . . . or their relation to
the design of . . . operating systems."[1] The terms are no less confused today,
and the theory of data relationships is not complete. However, many qualified
scientists are at work and, for the first time in the programming industry, theory
is moving ahead of practice.[2] Most of the developing theory relates to the so-
called data based systems believed to be just over the horizon. The terms
entity set, properties, attribute values, and *mappings* suggested by Mr. Mealy
in 1967 and amplified by many others will be essential to an I/O system
description in the 1980s.

In the meanwhile, the industry is particularly confused concerning the
term *record.* In the first place, record can be used as either a noun or a verb
and, when used as a noun, the meaning might be generic (anything recorded
must be a record) or the meaning might be that specifically defined for an
operating system. There is also a problem that the record as seen by a user's
program might differ from the information recorded (that word again!) on a
storage device. Restated in industry terms, a logical record might differ from a
physical record. Current usage varies significantly from system to system.
Common alternatives for logical record are item or, simply, record. Alternatives
for physical record are record or block. In this book, record means logical
record, and block means physical record. That is about the best we can do for
the moment.

---

[1] George H. Mealy, "Another Look at Data," *Proceedings of FJCC,* 1967.

[2] In the authors' opinion, the theory is moving too far ahead of practice. The line
between what is theoretically correct and what is practically possible is always difficult
to define. Our present dilemma is that most proposed practical products are theoretically unacceptable and vice versa.

Terminology problems aside, contemporary I/O systems are concerned with characters, records, and files. Because the nature of these units of data is so fundamental to an understanding of the mechanisms used to process them, each unit will be discussed separately and related to the others. The major topics are:

- characters, character sets, and the binary representations of characters, called bytes
- records, record types, and their physical representations as blocks of data in storage
- files—what they are, how they are organized, and how they are adapted to the physical constraints of I/O devices

CHARACTERS AND BYTES

A character is a symbol usually consisting of adjacent or connected strokes in a spatial arrangement. A character is used to represent data. Characters are frequently printed on pages or displayed on screens. The holes in a column of a punched card can be considered a character, though it is more consistent to consider the holes as representing a character. We acquire great facility in the use of characters early in life. By the time a child is in the second or third grade, he or she not only can recognize the decimal and alphabetic characters, but also can add and subtract using decimal characters and recognizes both uppercase and lowercase letters. It is axiomatic that computers must be able to communicate with people using characters familiar to people. Further, when the computer representation of 2 is added to the computer representation of 3, the result must be the computer representation of 5.

Bytes

The electronic devices that comprise a computer system cannot deal efficiently with images. Inside the computer, all information is represented as patterns of binary digits, frequently called bits. There are 72 or more characters that should be represented:

- 26 uppercase letters
- 26 lowercase letters
- 10 decimal digits
- 10 to 30 special characters including punctuation marks, asterisk, ampersand, the plus, minus, dollar, cent, pound symbols, and so forth

If a fixed number of binary digits is to represent all of these characters, that number must be greater than six. Most, but not all, general purpose computers today use eight binary digits to represent a character. That is, most general purpose computers declare byte size to be 8 bits.

It was not always thus. Some of the earliest stored program computers performed strictly decimal arithmetic. Those machines usually had 4-bit bytes, the minimum number of bits capable of representing the 10 decimal digits. One popular decimal machine had a 7-bit byte. In those early decimal machines, if alphabetic information was handled at all, each alphabetic character was represented by two adjacent bytes. The early binary computers used 6-bit bytes. The early printers could print only a limited set of characters, and 6 bits could represent those characters easily. There are some contemporary 6-bit computers, and large magnetic tape libraries of historical data are frequently recorded in a 6-bit code.

Character Sets

The typical computer users have little reason to care about the binary representations of characters. Their primary requirement is that they expect output from the system in the same set of characters that they used to present information to the system. The users really do not care that the character they presented as an A was represented in a card by a certain combination of holes, was represented in main storage as a certain combination of bits within a byte, was stored on a magnetic drum in another binary representation, and so forth. What they do care about is that if, and when, the original character is printed on a printer, it should have strokes in the arrangement they have come to know as A.

EBCDIC	Bit Configuration	EBCDIC	Bit Configuration	EBCDIC	Bit Configuration	EBCDIC	Bit Configuration
.	0100 1001	a	1000 0001	A	1100 0001	0	1111 0000
¢ [	0100 1010	b	1000 0010	B	1100 0010	1	1111 0001
.	0100 1011	c	1000 0011	C	1100 0011	2	1111 0010
<	0100 1100	d	1000 0100	D	1100 0100	3	1111 0011
(	0100 1101	e	1000 0101	E	1100 0101	4	1111 0100
+	0100 1110	f	1000 0110	F	1100 0110	5	1111 0101
|	0100 1111	g	1000 0111	G	1100 0111	6	1111 0110
&	0101 0000	h	1000 1000	H	1100 1000	7	1111 0111
!]	0101 1010	i	1000 1001	I	1100 1001	8	1111 1000
$	0101 1011	j	1001 0001	J	1101 0001	9	1111 1001
*	0101 1100	k	1001 0010	K	1101 0010		
)	0101 1101	l	1001 0011	L	1101 0011		
;	0101 1110	m	1001 0100	M	1101 0100		
¬	0101 1111	n	1001 0101	N	1101 0101		
–	0110 0000	o	1001 0110	O	1101 0110		
/	0110 0001	p	1001 0111	P	1101 0111		
,	0110 1011	q	1001 1000	Q	1101 1000		
%	0110 1100	r	1001 1001	R	1101 1001		
–	0110 1101	s	1010 0010	S	1110 0010		
>	0110 1110	t	1010 0011	T	1110 0011		
?	0110 1111	u	1010 0100	U	1110 0100		
:	0111 1010	v	1010 0101	V	1110 0101		
#	0111 1011	w	1010 0110	W	1110 0110		
@	0111 1100	x	1010 0111	X	1110 0111		
'	0111 1100	y	1010 1000	Y	1110 1000		
=	0111 1110	z	1010 1001	Z	1110 1001		
"	0111 1111						

Fig. 4-1   Extended Binary-Coded-Decimal Interchange Code (EBCDIC).

Two sets of character representations well known in the computer industry are the Extended Binary-Coded Decimal Interchange Code (EBCDIC) and the American National Standard Code for Information Interchange (ASCII). The most frequently used EBCDIC characters and their representations are shown in Fig. 4-1. The binary-coded decimal pattern can be seen in the representations for the decimal digits, where the rightmost 4 bits count from 0 to 9 in binary. The letters use the same pattern repeatedly beginning with A and again with a. Some of the bit configurations not shown are used to control devices. For example, 0100 0000 is interpreted to mean "space" by devices capable of spacing. Other bit configurations have no special meanings defined. The sequence 0000 1000 does not represent any character in the EBCDIC set of characters. The ASCII character representations are shown in Fig. 4-2. ASCII is a 7-bit code with bit positions numbered $b_7b_6b_5b_4b_3b_2b_1$.

b_7 b_6 b_5 →					0 0 0	0 0 1	0 1 0	0 1 1	1 0 0	1 0 1	1 1 0	1 1 1
b_4	b_3	b_2	b_1	COLUMN / ROW	0	1	2	3	4	5	6	7
0	0	0	0	0	NUL	DLE	SP	0	@	P	`	p
0	0	0	1	1	SOH	DC1	!	1	A	Q	a	q
0	0	1	0	2	STX	DC2	"	2	B	R	b	:
0	0	1	1	3	ETX	DC3	#	3	C	S	c	s
0	1	0	0	4	EOT	DC4	$	4	D	T	d	t
0	1	0	1	5	ENQ	NAK	%	5	E	U	e	u
0	1	1	0	6	ACK	SYN	&	6	F	V	f	v
0	1	1	1	7	BEL	ETB	'	7	G	W	g	w
1	0	0	0	8	BS	CAN	(	8	H	X	h	x
1	0	0	1	9	HT	EM	)	9	I	Y	i	y
1	0	1	0	10	LF	SUB	*	:	J	Z	j	z
1	0	1	1	11	VT	ESC	+	;	K	[	k	{
1	1	0	0	12	FF	FS	,	<	L	\	l	|
1	1	0	1	13	CR	GS	–	=	M	]	m	}
1	1	1	0	14	SO	RS	.	>	N	^	n	~
1	1	1	1	15	SI	US	/	?	O	___	o	DEL

Fig. 4-2   U.S.A. Standard Code for Information Interchange. (By permission of American National Standards Institute, Inc.)

For example, the character K is represented by 100 1011. The nongraphic codes such as NUL, SOH, and so forth, will not be explained here. One can guess the meanings of some of them. To represent an ASCII character in an 8-bit byte, the b_7 bit can be repeated between b_5 and b_6. Thus the sequence would be $b_7b_6b_7b_5b_4b_3b_2b_1$ and K would be represented 1010 1011.

Bits, Bytes, and Words

Because a sequence of 8 bits is inconvenient for humans to use, a byte is frequently represented as two hexadecimal digits. The relationship of binary digits to hexadecimal digits is shown in Fig. 4-3. Referring to Fig. 4-1, the EBCDIC code for the character M is 1101 0100 or, in hexadecimal, D4. A good notation in common use is to write hexadecimal D4 as $(D4)_{16}$.

Many computer systems identify a subdivision of main storage called a word. Typically, a word might consist of 4 bytes. Word size is of concern to the designer of the I/O system for a particular computer because many operations may be constrained by the design of the computer to deal with whole words, half words, or multiples of words. In the world outside computers, a word is a combination of characters, and words vary in length. Successful computers have been built using variable-length words where a word can begin at any byte and is terminated by a byte that has a particular flag bit on. The current design trend is to use fixed-length words but to reduce the significance of word boundaries as much as possible. Figure 4-4 shows how bits, hexadecimal digits, bytes, and words are related in one series of computers.

Hexadecimal Digit	Binary Equivalent	Decimal Equivalent
0	0000	0
1	0001	1
2	0010	2
3	0011	3
4	0100	4
5	0101	5
6	0110	6
7	0111	7
8	1000	8
9	1001	9
A	1010	10
B	1011	11
C	1100	12
D	1101	13
E	1110	14
F	1111	15

Fig. 4-3   Hexadecimal equivalents.

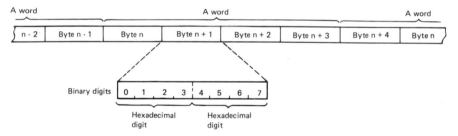

Fig. 4-4   Word structure (IBM System 360).

Fields

A computer program that processes the data within a record usually deals with fields, each of which consists of consecutive bytes with the record. In Fig. 4-5, for example, bytes 1 through 5 contain employee number, 6 through 26 contain employee name, and so forth. Frequently, all of the records in a file will have identical field formats. In other cases, a file might contain records with several different field formulas. In such a case, a certain byte such as byte 0 might be identified as a type-code field used to identify the field format that applies to the record. Sometimes a field such as employee number serves the special purpose of ordering records within a file. Such a field is called a key field or record key.

Contemporary I/O systems have little concern for fields, preferring to leave field definition and all field-related processing to the user's program. In the future, I/O systems will be required to shoulder this responsibility.

Removing field definition from the user's program is essential to a quality called data independence, the quality that allows changes to the form and content of stored records without changes to users' programs. Data independence is discussed in Chap. 20.

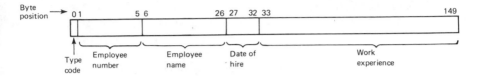

Byte position

Type code | Employee number | Employee name | Date of hire | Work experience

Note: Byte positions could be defined as beginning with 1 instead of 0. The convention shown has the advantage that the address of any field is the address of the record plus the byte position of that field.

Fig. 4-5 Fields within a record.

RECORDS AND BLOCKS

Just as a student's record is a collection of characters, a record in a computing system is a collection of bytes. The term *block* as used in I/O systems has no good real-world counterpart. In an I/O system, a block is a collection of bytes handled as a unit. A block of data might be recorded on an auxiliary storage volume and separated from other blocks by interblock gaps. The information transmitted to a printer by a single write command is a block. Frequently, a block contains one or several whole records. The relationships between records and blocks will be clarified soon, but first we should understand more about records.

Records

A record is a collection of bytes. From the standpoint of an I/O system, an important question is "How many bytes?" To answer this question in a way that is useful to the I/O system, the records of a file are identified as being of one of the following types:[3]

> *Fixed (F)* All records within the file have a single uniform length. An I/O system can handle F records conveniently because the I/O system is aware in advance the number of bytes to be moved and the amount of space required to store a record. Examples include records that represent line items of a purchase order, punched cards used for gas and electric service billing, payroll check vouchers, additions or withdrawals of parts from inventory, votes in an election, and individuals in a census.
> *Variable (V)* The length of each record is explicitly stated within the record. Fig. 4-6 illustrates a V record. Records that contain descriptive information not subject to arithmetic calculation or records that include

[3] The three types of records to be described are identified by most operating systems; the F, V, and U designations are less universal.

a variable number of fixed-length fields are sometimes set up as V records. For many years, there was a controversy about whether it would be better to represent data in both of these cases as a variable number of fixed-length records. That controversy has apparently been settled in favor of variable-length records.

Undefined (*U*) The length of each record is not known to the I/O system. The records have not been identified as either F or V. U records do not conform to any length convention that the I/O system recognizes. It is the responsibility of the user's program to determine what constitutes a record. Undefined-length records could occur in situations where (1) variable-length records produced by one operating system might be declared as type U for processing by another operating system if the record descriptor conventions for the two systems are not identical, or where (2) records representing different transaction types in a commercial process might be identified by transaction-type codes that imply specific lengths. Such records are of type U according to the I/O system definition because the I/O system is not aware of the transaction codes or their meanings.

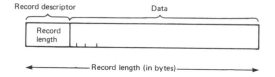

The record descriptor consists of 2, 3, or 4 bytes (fixed for any one system). The record descriptor includes record length and may include other information.

Fig. 4-6 A variable-length record.

A question asked is: "How can an I/O system deal with records of undefined length?" The answer is that the records are not really of undefined length. The distinction between F, V, and U records has to do only with the source of the length specification. For F records, the length can be placed in a table where both the I/O system and user's program can find it for use in processing all of the records of a file. V records are self-describing. If an I/O system is required to process records of type U, the user's program must furnish the length specification for each record as that record is processed.

The three types F, V, and U include all possible cases. In the universe of all records, some records conform to type F and others to type V, and by definition, all other records are of type U. One might observe that F and V are not essential; all records could be considered type U. The rationale for the three types, proven by experience, is this: If records are known to be of fixed uniform length, significant processing efficiencies and flexibilities accrue. Failing that, if each record is self-describing, a lesser but still significant advantage obtains. When record length is not known, an I/O system must proceed blindly and cautiously; some efficiency is lost, and some functional conveniences available for the other classes of records may be unobtainable. The advantage of types F and V can be illustrated for reading data from magnetic tape. For F records, blocks can be of uniform length, and block length can be checked automatically by the computer system to ensure that no information has been lost. For V records, block length may vary, but because the records are self-describing, the I/O system can perform the check. For U records, the user's program must be involved if length is to be checked at all.

Blocks

A block is a collection of records or pieces of records. Blocks are a concession to the hard realities of I/O devices. They are designed to adapt records to the physical constraints of a device, to achieve efficient use of auxiliary storage space, and/or to achieve a desirable storage and retrieval rate. The next few sentences illustrate some appropriate uses of the word "block." Records are blocked to form a block. Conversely, a block can be deblocked to separate the records. When there is exactly one record in each block, records are said to be unblocked; otherwise, they are blocked. If there are always five records per block, the blocking factor is 5.

For our present discussion, the important thing about a block is its relationship to records. Consider the records that constitute a file to be placed end to end to form a continuous string of bytes as shown in Fig. 4-7. The following relationships of records to blocks can be identified:

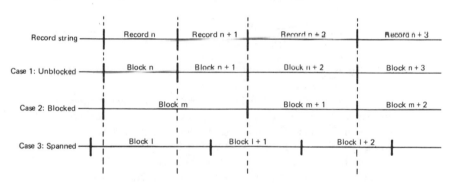

Fig. 4-7   Relationships of records to blocks.

Case 1. Unblocked   A block contains exactly one record.
Case 2. Blocked   A block may contain one or more complete records.
Case 3. Spanned   A block may contain consecutive bytes from the string of bytes without regard to record boundaries. This type of block may begin with part of a record, span several complete records, and end with part of another record. The case is general enough to include records that are much larger than a block.

Figure 4-8 illustrates a situation in which a record spans several blocks.

To understand why the three blocking cases are individually useful, we must first understand the motivations for blocking at all. The principal motivations that influence blocking are listed in the following:

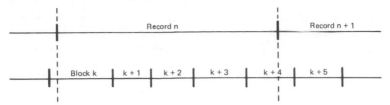

Fig. 4-8   A record spanning several blocks.

1. There is a significant base cost involved in storing or retrieving a block of data. By combining records, the cost per byte of storing or retrieving is reduced. This effect is illustrated in Fig. 4-9. If cost per byte of storing or retrieving blocks were the only consideration, an entire file would be stored as one block.

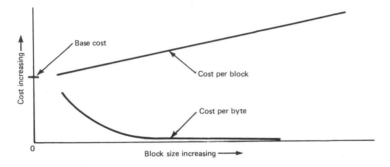

Fig. 4-9   Prorated cost per byte stored or retrieved.

2. The existence of large blocks is detrimental to performance when the records in the blocks of a file are processed in an order different from their stored order. For example, the cost of retrieving a single record when the blocking factor is 10 would be significantly greater than the cost with a blocking factor of 1, because the entire block will be retrieved in either case. This effect of the blocking factor is illustrated in Fig. 4-10. If the cost of storing or retrieving an individual record were the only consideration, records would always be unblocked.

3. A large block requires a significant quantity of main storage space. This is a particularly important concern if a file is to be processed on several systems, some of which may have limited main storage resources.

4. A small block may be excessively wasteful of auxiliary-storage space. If a magnetic tape unit records 1,000 bytes per inch of tape and creates a ½-in. interblock gap, waste becomes excessive when block size drops below, say, 500 bytes.

5. Most I/O devices require that block size must not exceed a particular value. For example, a printer may be unable to accept a block larger than a print line, and many DASDs require that a block must not exceed the length of a track.

6. Some I/O devices require that a block have precisely a certain length. For example, some magnetic drums require that blocks contain precisely 256 bytes.

7. Block size affects recoverability. Recording media such as magnetic tape contain minor imperfections. When data are recorded on an imperfect medium, there is a small but significant probability that any character recorded will be found to be illegible at some later time. As block size is increased, the probability that any particular block contains an illegible character increases. If blocks were large enough, it would be virtually certain that every block would exhibit legibility problems during retrieval.

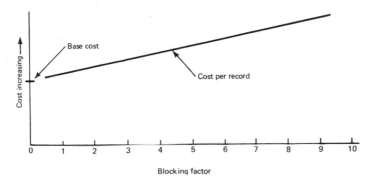

Fig. 4-10   Cost of storing or retrieving individual record.

Combinations of Records and Blocks

Three record types (F, V, and U) and three blocking cases (unblocked, blocked, and spanned) have been described. Theoretically, all combinations of record types and blocking cases could be used. As Fig. 4-11 indicates, each combination has some utility. However, because each combination requires a certain amount of individual programming support in the I/O system and because an unnecessarily large number of combinations complicates interchangeability of data between programs, most I/O systems recognize a limited set of combinations. Figure 4-12 indicates the general availability of support for each combination.

Notice particularly that, according to Fig. 4-12, spanning is not widely supported. Why? Because from an I/O system standpoint, spanning is inherently undesirable. As an example of the kinds of problems that can occur in processing spanned records, consider what must happen to update a record using a single magnetic tape unit if the record spans a block boundary so that part of the record is on tape reel 1 of the file and the other part is on reel 2. The first reel must be demounted and the second mounted to allow retrieval of the blocks, and the first must be remounted to allow recording of the first part of the updated record, and so forth. Not only is the operational problem annoying, but the amount of programming required to cope with this kind of problem makes spanning undesirable.

Record Type	Blocking	Comments
Fixed	Unblocked	Useful when card readers, printers, and punches are used directly and for records processed in a random order and for large records.
Fixed	Blocked	Particularly useful when short fixed length records are processed in order.
Fixed	Spanned	Useful when records are larger than the I/O device can accommodate.
Variable	Unblocked	Has some utility, but variable/blocked is frequently preferable because the latter provides less variability in block size.
Variable	Blocked	Very useful. Provides a fairly uniform block size while accommodating variable record length.
Variable	Spanned	Very useful when maximum record length is large.
Undefined	Unblocked	Very useful. Can be used by a utility program to copy a file without concern for its content.
Undefined	Blocked	Useful. Allows processing of blocked records that do not conform to I/O length conventions.
Undefined	Spanned	Possibly useful because it is the most general case but awkward to define. Not provided in any major system.

Fig. 4-11   Record types.

	Unblocked	Blocked	Spanned
	Fixed/unblocked	Fixed/blocked	Fixed/spanned
Fixed-length records	•••	•••	•
	Variable/unblocked	Variable/blocked	Variable/spanned
Variable-length records	•••	•••	••
	Undefined/unblocked	Undefined/blocked	Undefined/spanned
Undefined records	•••	••	

Code = ••• means available in most systems

•• means available in some systems

• means available in at least one major system

(blank) means not available in any major system

Fig. 4-12   Availability of combinations of record types and blocking cases.

Figures 4-13, 4-14, and 4-15 illustrate the most frequently used cases of blocking and spanning. In the F blocked case, the record length and block length are not recorded in the block, but rather are held in a table during file processing and are recorded in the file label if a label exists. The V blocked convention includes a block descriptor containing block length and, of course, each record carries its own descriptor. In the V spanned case, an unused byte in the record descriptor can be used as a segment control code to indicate whether a segment is a complete record or part of a record.

Designing Records and Blocks

The descriptor information included in V records and blocks raises some design questions. Should a descriptor be considered part of a record and therefore be created and modified by the user's program or should a descriptor be considered auxiliary to the record, to be attached by the I/O system? In most systems, the record descriptor is considered part of the record and, though that answer is esthetically repugnant, there are sound practical reasons for it.

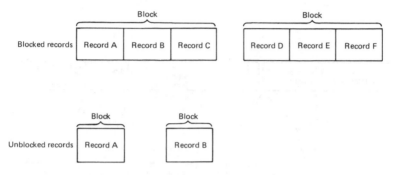

Fig. 4-13   Fixed-length records.

A related question concerns records destined to be printed, punched, or displayed graphically. Such records are frequently augmented by an extra control byte that controls vertical spacing on a printer (single, double, suppress, etc.), stacker selection on a card punch, or line position on a graphic display.

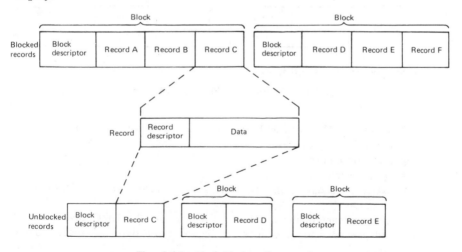

Fig. 4-14   Variable-length records.

If a "best answer" to these questions exists, that answer is not known to the authors. A detailed analysis would require one or more chapters and then might be inconclusive. A few concerns, offered without explanation, are as follows:

Segment Codes (GCOS-III)

Code	Meaning
00	Complete record.
01	First segment of a multisegment record.
10	Neither first nor last segment of a record.
11	Last segment of a multisegment record.

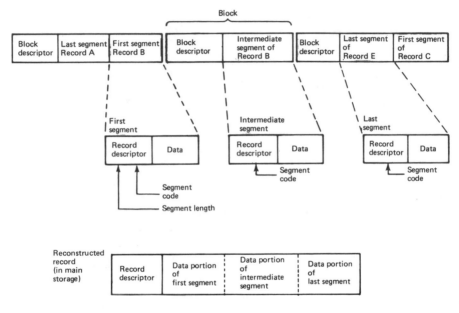

Note: Not all segment and block combinations are represented

Fig. 4-15　Spanned variable-length records.

- alignment of record and field boundaries with word boundaries
- confusion of the user about main storage space requirements for records and blocks
- system performance due to extra moving of data
- exposure to data if the user furnishes or accidentally modifies control information
- independence of the user's program from details of I/O device control
- independence of the user's program from type of record being processed
- design of language processors

Unless the designers are prepared to analyze these matters in great depth, they might be well advised to simply copy the record and block conventions of some major system. That strategy has the advantages that the conventions are at least workable, and one can accept full credit for whatever elegance they have while disavowing responsibility for their weaknesses.

FILES

A file is a collection of records. Usually the records within a file have some logical relationship to each other. For example, the records of a file might represent the invoices in an accounts receivable file, the parts in an inventory file, or the employees in a personnel file. However, it is not necessary that the records of a file have any logical relationship. If a collection of records is treated as a file, it is a file. Because the records of a file are grouped into blocks for the physical I/O process, there is no contradiction in considering a file to be a collection of blocks of records.

A file is a very definite collection of records. That is, when a file has been identified, any particular record either is or is not included in that file. One might expect, then, that the term *file* would be rigorously defined. The definition above, i.e., a file is a collection of records, does not say very much, but there is not much more that can be said correctly. The American National Standard[4] definition, notably, "a collection of related records treated as a unit," is of doubtful help. The records of a file need not be related in any way other than that they do belong to the same file, and "treated as a unit" has no discernable meaning. Another definition, used by two major systems,[5] terms a file "a named collection of related records." That definition adds very little insight.

The definitions used by yet another operating system is just as dubious: "An original collection of data stored in such a manner as to facilitate the retrieval of each individual datum."[6] The trouble with "a file is a collection of records" is that it is a necessary but not a sufficient definition; not every collection of records is a file. The crux of the matter is that the term *file* is only meaningful in the sense that an operating system gives it meaning. In short, a file is a collection of records that is treated as a file. Short, concise, and not very helpful.

File Identification

A file is often identified by its location. Some examples of files are:

- all of the records on a particular reel of magnetic tape
- all of the records between the second and third tape marks on a particular reel of magnetic tape
- all of the records on tracks 10, 11, and 117 of a particular magnetic drum
- the records represented in a deck of punched cards
- the records printed as a report on a particular printer

[4] American National Standard Institute, Inc., document X3. 12-1970.

[5] "Data Management System Reference Manual for Time Sharing Operating System," document DJ-001-2-01 (RCA). A definition that is identical is used for OS/360 (IBM).

[6] "Programmers Reference Manual for EXEC-8," document UP-4144 (Sperry Rand).

Just as with files maintained by a clerk, a computer file is usually given a name. If a file has labels, the name of the file is recorded in the labels. An I/O system can inspect a label when searching for a particular file or when verifying that the operator has made the proper file available on a particular I/O device.

File Organization

As has been stated, a record either does or does not belong to a file depending on whether that record is contained within the space that belongs to the file. Thus, the records of a file naturally have some physical relationship to each other. That is, the records within a file will conform to some rules of organization. There are several basic concepts that are modified, combined, and embellished to become the file organizations supported by a particular I/O system. Some widely used organizations are as follows:

> *Sequential Organization*   The physical order of records corresponds to the chronological order of acceptance of those records by the I/O system.
> *Indexed Organization*   Indexes to the file are maintained so that when any particular record from the file is required, a search of the indexes will indicate the storage location of the record.
> *List Organization*   Groups of related records are included on lists. As an example of the use of such lists, if records for all female employees are on one list and records for all professional employees are on another list, then records for female professional employees can be identified by matching the two lists.
> *Direct Organization*   Records can be stored so that the location of any record is related in some consistent way to an identifying key of that record. For example, a record for an employee could be stored at the storage address that is equal to the employee's identification number. The record for employee number 1234 would be stored at address 1234 of a particular storage volume.

The first three organizations are used frequently outside of computers. The sequential organization results in a chronological file such as a diary. A mail-order catalog has an indexed organization. The index to this book contains a short list for each key word. A person might match the list of pages that discuss records with the list for blocks to determine what pages might mention the relationship of records to blocks. The direct organization is peculiar to computers. It exists because computers have an exceptional ability to calculate rapidly and accurately. Humans, lacking this capability, are more likely to combine physical dexterity and visual searching in their file organizations.

Logical Files and Physical Files

A file as described in the preceding sections may occasionally be called a physical file to distinguish it from a different record collection, a logical file.

Frequently, a user may wish to process more or less information than the physical file contains. For example, if student records for an academic year constitute a physical file, one might be interested in processing logical files such as (1) a logical file of the student records for a particular class for last year and (2) a logical file of the student records for all classes for the last five years. In the first case, the logical file is contained in a physical file; in the second case, the logical file consists of several physical files.

If mechanisms can be arranged so that users' programs process logical files and that logical files are only loosely related to physical files, the usability of a user's program is extended. In future systems, the distinction between logical files and physical files is expected to increase. For example, in a class of systems called *data base systems,* a logical file may contain records whose field arrangement is significantly different from the records of the physical file. Recognizing the future importance of distinguishing between logical files and physical files, we note that a few operating systems use the term *data set* for physical file, reserving the word "file" to mean logical file. Most contemporary systems do not make the distinction formal. In this book, *file* is used to apply to both, and where a distinction is required, logical file or physical file is used.

Collections of Files

Most operating systems assume some responsibility for maintaining administrative information about files in the form of a file catalog. A file catalog might contain the following information for each file:

> file name
> location
> date of creation
> owner's name

The principal value of the catalog is that it provides a continuously current location of a file. Before operating systems included catalogs, each user was required to know the locations of the files. When several users process the same files, knowing file locations can be difficult. File catalogs are described in Chap. 16, "Catalogs and Space Allocation."

SUMMARY

In the world outside computers, characters are organized into records and files. Inside computers, a character is represented by a byte, and bytes are combined into records, blocks, and files. A great deal of confusion surrounds the definition of the fundamental units.

Bytes are usually declared to be 6 or 8 bits long. Historically, 4-, 6-, and 7-bit bytes were used. Byte size is determined principally by the number of distinct characters that must be represented. Two widely used standards for representing characters in bytes are EBCDIC and ASCII. In some computers, a fixed number of bytes is defined as a word.

Within a record, bytes are logically grouped into fields. A field used to order records within a file is called a key field. Fields are of limited concern to contemporary I/O systems.

The records of a file can be of three types:

Type F   All records are of fixed uniform length. When it can be used, this type allows greatest system efficiency.

Type V   Each record includes a record descriptor that declares the length of that record. This type of record allows the flexibility of variable record length while retaining good performance.

Type U   Record length can be determined only by the user's program. This record type can be used when neither F nor V applies.

The records of a file are combined into blocks for handling by a channel program. Records in a file can be:

Unblocked   There is exactly one record per block.

Blocked   There are one or more complete records per block.

Spanned   A block may contain parts of records.

Blocking for a file, often determined for efficiency, may be affected by I/O device requirements or by concern for recoverability. All combinations of record types and blocking cases are useful, but in most systems, spanned records are limited to type V. Records and block design should ensure that the record descriptor and control byte sometimes appended to records are treated in a consistent and practical manner.

A file is a collection of blocks of records, usually related to each other. A file may be identified by its location or by a file name. The records within a file can be arranged in one of several organizations:

- a sequential organization, in which the physical order of records is dictated by the chronology of their acceptance by the I/O system
- an indexed organization, in which the physical location of each record is maintained in an index
- a list organization, in which the location of each record is maintained on one or more lists
- a direct organization, in which each record is stored at a location that is related to the value of a key field within the record

Sometimes a distinction is drawn between a logical file and a physical file. A logical file might be a segment of a physical file, or it might include several physical files. Most operating systems maintain file catalogs that contain the current location and other information about files.

Exercises

1.(e) Explain why byte size is defined as 8 bits in many systems.

2.(e) If bytes representing EBCDIC characters are sorted to ascending binary value, which will come first, lowercase letters, uppercase letters, or the decimal digits? Answer the same question for ASCII.

3.(e) What are the hexadecimal equivalents of the EBCDIC representations of A and of 5?

4.(e) Must all of the records of a file have identical field formats? Explain.

5.(e) Which of the three record types F, V, and U is most universally usable? Why?

6.(e) What record type and blocking case would be most appropriate for a file of records whose lengths vary from 50 to 500 bytes with an average length of 70 bytes? Assume a magnetic drum with a fixed 256-byte block length will be used to store the records.

7.(e) Using the segment codes in Fig. 4-15, is it possible that a block could consist of two segments, the first segment having code 01 and the second having code 00?

8.(e) Which three of the four file organizations listed in this chapter might be appropriate for a file whose records are to be retrieved individually in an unpredictable order?

9.(m) When a computer has a word length of 4, the block descriptor for V records is usually defined to be 4 bytes even though 3 or even 2 bytes might be adequate. Why?

10.(m) Assume you are to devise a general purpose utility program that copies a file, changing its block size. Which combinations of record type and blocking case cannot be allowed for the input file? Why?

11.(m) Define the terms *character, byte, field, record, block,* and *file.*

5 Control Statements

The I/O system controls two major classes of resources for system users: files to be created or used, and devices to store and retrieve the files.

The reasons for controlling the use of files and devices are among the fundamental reasons for having operating systems; the controls are essential to efficiency, accountability, privacy, equitability, and so forth. Just what administrative procedures should be established for controlling use of files and devices are a matter of design. Contemporary system designers have universally chosen to employ control statements in the control process. Under most circumstances, the would-be users of files and devices must furnish control statements declaring their requirements.

From the users' viewpoint, control statements are at best a nuisance and at worst an outrage. There was a time not too many years ago when computer users simply took their magnetic tape under their arms, their card decks in their hands, walked into the computer room and used the equipment they needed. Frankly, it is much easier for a user to know what is required than to describe it.

The use of control statements is analogous to reserving a table at a restaurant. The maitre d' is the I/O system. You inform him of your needs: table for four, near the window. Frequently, your requirements can be met immediately, though heavy demand for similar or identical resources can result in delays. Delays can become lengthy if some customers are given preferential treatment or if others dawdle over their meal. If your requirements are limited, you can bypass the maitre d', taking a seat at the counter. In so doing, you tacitly agree to restrict your choice of fare to the short-order menu. The I/O system users are required to announce their requirements by control statements in advance of need. A significant queue of users may build up if many require identical resources. Waiting time can be particularly long if some users have credentials allowing them to bypass the waiting line or if some jobs being processed are particularly lengthy. Some systems allow users to bypass the control statement procedure if their requirements are modest. Such requirements might be limited to the creation and use of small, temporary files to be stored on any available DASD.

THE CONTROL STATEMENT

The mechanism used to communicate resource requirements from the user to the I/O system is the control statement. Control statements are not part of the user's program. Rather, they are an adjunct to the user's program, used to communicate to the system and to the user's program information describing the processing that is to be accomplished. Because most of this information controls the system or the user's program in some way, the name control statement is appropriate.

The control statement is conscientiously separate from the user's program logically, chronologically, and physically.

Logical separation is the result of careful classification of information that must be furnished by a user. Information that describes how records should be processed is included in the user's program. Information that describes the environment in which the user's program should be run is included in control statements. This classification allows a user's program to be largely unaffected by changes in its environment, thereby extending its usability.

Chronological separation results from system conventions that require a user's program to be compiled before it can be executed, while control statements are interpreted for execution in an essentially unprocessed form. Figure 5-1 describes the chronology of development of a user's program. Notice that the user's program is specified at stage 1, while the control statements for the run are submitted at stage 4.

Stage	Activity	User's Program	Control Statements	Input Data	Result
1	Program writing				Source program
2	Compilation	Compiler	Used to control the compiler	Source program	Object program
3	Program testing	Object program	Denote test data and limited device complement	Test data	Test results
4	Production run	Object program	Denote actual data and full device complement	Actual data	Actual results

Fig. 5-1   Chronology of user's program development.

Physical separation of the user's program and its control statements is entirely a matter of convenience for the system. As described above, the user's program is introduced to the system separate from its control statement. Maintaining the control statement information separate from the user's program allows the former to serve as a concise advance notification to the system of device and file requirements to be used in job setup.

The collection of I/O control statements and other control statements that an operating system may require for a particular job can be visualized as a deck of cards submitted as part of a job request. (See Fig. 5-2.) In practice, the statements might not be submitted as part of the job request, but, rather, might be prestored in system libraries. A prestored collection of control statements can be called into use by a single control statement that identifies the collection. Especially in time sharing systems, control statements may not make up a deck, but, rather, may be entered into the system directly from a keyboard. Some operating systems, and particularly EXEC-8, allow the user's program some ability to create or modify its own control statements.

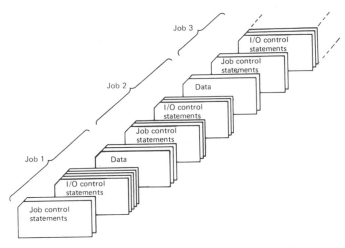

Fig. 5-2   Control statements in a stack of jobs.

Syntactic rules for control statements differ from system to system. A control statement usually has some identifying character pattern in the first or first and second character positions as illustrated in Fig. 5-3. The identifying characters are used by the operating system to detect control statements that are intermixed with data records. The user must be warned to avoid use of the identifying pattern for other purposes. That warning causes users some legitimate concern; it is sometimes difficult for them to know when data records might contain the identifying pattern accidentally. Following the identifying characters are a few fields whose presence is required and whose form and position in the statement are rigidly specified. Beyond that are optional fields, usually separated by commas. In some systems, the meanings of optional fields are implied by their position within a control statement. If any such field is not specified, its absence must be indicated by consecutive commas. The GCOS example in Fig. 5-3 illustrates that convention. Other systems use self-identifying option fields as illustrated for OS/360. The conventions for some systems, such as EXEC-8, are highly coded, cryptic, and concise. Others tend to be self-explanatory. Their "everyday English" appearance belies their rigid rules of spelling, allowable symbols, and punctuation.

One of the most significant merits of control statements is also a cause of user frustration. As mentioned earlier, control statements are not compiled with their related applications programs, but, rather, are submitted in an essentially unprocessed form when the compiled programs are run. The merit lies in the ease with which control statement parameters can be changed from run to run. The frustration lies in the frequency of human errors that result. A glance at the examples in this chapter reveals something of the number of alternatives and syntactic complexities that can be presented to the system untested at the time of a run. A single job typically requires 5 or 10 control statements, but may sometimes require 50 or more. Operating systems are becoming more comprehensive in the diagnostic screening of control statements, but an incorrect or missing control statement usually means an unsuccessful run and a disappointed user. One of the major advantages of time sharing systems is their ability to analyze control statements as they are created so that corrections can be made promptly.

System		Symbol	Meaning
EXEC-8	@ASG,C USER1*F1,T/1,N43	@	Control statement identifier
		ASG	Statement type, notably assign
		C	Catalog the file
		T/1	Magnetic tape, one unit
GCOS	$ TAPE F1,X1D,,N43,,USER1F1	$	Control statement identifier
		TAPE	Statement type; notably assign magnetic tape
		X1	Configuration control, use any unit
		D	Dismount reel after use
OS/360	//F1 DD DSNAME=USER1.F1,UNIT=(TAPE,1),DISP =(NEW,CATLG),VOL=SER=N43	//	Control statement identifier
		DD	Statement type, notably data definition
		DSNAME	Data set name, i.e. file name
		DISP	Disposition
		NEW,CATLG	File to be created and cataloged
		VOL=SER	Volume serial number

The above statements have similar meanings in three separate systems. They apply to a file the user's program is designating F1. They cause allocation of a magnetic-tape unit to record the file on reel N43. The newly created file has a name consisting of USER1 and F1 combined.

Fig. 5-3   Sample control statement.

Connecting a User's Program to Its Data

It is important to understand how the information from a control statement completes a circle of relationships. The following items refer to the circled numerals in Fig. 5-4. The items are logical connections, not necessarily chronological steps.

1. A GET instruction within the user's program identifies a main-storage location LOC, where a record should be placed after it is retrieved.
2. The GET instruction identifies a table, TABLE1, that contains information about a file, including the control statement name CNAME.
3. The user has furnished a control statement with the statement name CNAME. That control statement specifies a file name FILE1.

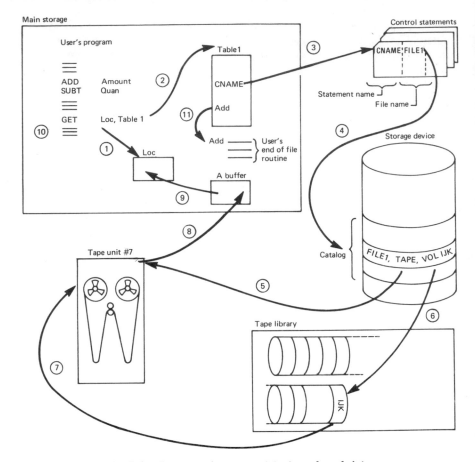

Fig. 5-4   From service request to transfer of data.

4. The I/O system searches a catalog that associates file names with device type and volume identification codes. FILE1 happens to be on magnetic tape volume IJK.

5. The I/O system allocates a device of the proper type, in this case, a magnetic tape unit. Unit number 7 happens to be available.

6. The I/O system instructs the operator to retrieve volume IJK from the library end.

7. To place the tape on unit 7.

8. Under control of a channel program furnished by the I/O systems, unit 7 transmits a block of data to a buffer area in main storage.

9. The I/O system extracts the required record from the buffered block of data.

10. The user's program resumes execution at the instruction following the GET instruction.

11. If, in attempting to retrieve a record, the I/O system finds that no

records remain in the file, the system causes the user's program to be restarted at an address specified in TABLE1, in this case, address ADD.

Notice that if the control statement CNAME had identified some file other than FILE1, the circle would have been completed, but an altogether different record would have been furnished to the user's program.

Formal mechanisms have been established for communicating information across the interfaces that separate a user, the user's program, and the control program. Four interface mechanisms are shown in Fig. 5-4. The GET instruction is a system call; TABLE1 is a table; CNAME is a control statement; and ADD is a system exit. Only the control statement mechanism is used for the interfaces described in this chapter; the other three mechanisms are used in Chaps. 7 and 8.

As mentioned earlier, the 11 items listed are not chronological. The actions shown in steps 3 through 8 are usually performed before the GET instruction is executed; they need not be performed for every record-retrieval request.

RESOURCE REQUIREMENTS: FILES

As stated earlier, the user's resource requirements fall into two categories: requirements for files and requirements for devices. Of the two, files are the more directly related to the user's program. A user's program processes records or blocks taken from files. It is really the file, rather than the user's program, that requires the device.

One of the most fundamental concepts used in data processing systems is that programs should be reused repeatedly, but the data processed should be changed for each reuse. A common method of changing the data is for the user to identify a different file for each processing run. The control statement is almost invariably used to identify files to the system because it allows the user to change a specification for each run of a program.

If the reader will imagine himself or herself in the position of an I/O system designer, he or she can guess rather easily the kinds of information about a file the I/O system would need from a control statement. Included should be information the user might want to change from run to run. Excluded should be information that, if changed, would require changes in the user's program. First, the I/O system would need a precise, unambiguous identification of the file. There must be no doubt as to what file is being described. Next, if a new file is being created, the I/O system would need to know how it should be organized and where it should be stored. And finally, the I/O system would need to know what restrictions to place on the use of this new file; or, if the file is not new, by what authority this user expects to gain access. In summary, the control statement information about a file should include file identification, storage-utilization instructions, and file-security specifications. The control statement aspects of these three major topics are discussed on the following pages.

File Identification

A popular philosophy of great importance is that a file should be identified by a file name. Naming a file has the same advantages as naming a person; the name can be constant, though nearly all other distinguishing attributes may change. The use made of a file name depends on whether the file is a new file or an existing file. When a file is about to be recorded on a storage medium as a *new* file, the name may serve several purposes:

1. If the file is to have a machine readable label, the name will be recorded in the label for later use in identifying the file.
2. If the I/O system maintains a catalog of volume identification numbers for files, the file name serves as the argument for indexing the new file's volume identification numbers or other descriptive information into the catalog.
3. If the storage volume is demountable, the system may give the file name to the operator so that the operator can affix to the volume a visible label containing that identifying name.

When a file is an *existing* file recorded on a storage medium, the file name can be used for the following purposes:

1. If the I/O system maintains a catalog of volume identification numbers, the file name serves as the indexing argument for retrieving those numbers from the catalog. The volume identification numbers can be used by the I/O system in instructing the operator to provide the appropriate storage volumes.
2. If the I/O system does not maintain a catalog, or if the particular file name is not included in the catalog, the file name can be given to the operator with the mounting instructions. In this case, the operator is required to identify the volumes either from personal knowledge or by labels, attached to the volumes, displaying the file names.
3. If the file has machine readable labels, the I/O system can compare the file name from the control statement with the file name from the label to verify that the operator has furnished the proper volume.

In cases where a labeled storage medium is not involved (for example, when a file is to be printed or a deck of cards is to be read), the file name serves only for visual identification. Recognizing that control statements are an annoyance and a source of errors, system designers have tried to reduce the amount of information that control statements must contain. The popular goal, achieved surprisingly well, is to identify a file by a name and to require no other file-related information whatever. This is accomplished for existing files by retaining all other file-descriptive information in a combination of a file catalog and machine readable labels. For new files, the absence of descriptive information in a control statement may imply that a standard default definition is intended. A defaulted definition could perhaps result in a half-million-byte file, organized sequentially, and stored on any convenient DASD. Another possible interpretation is that the descriptive information missing from a control statement may be supplied by a user's program.

File-Name Structure.   The most important requirement placed on a file name is that it be unique. To ensure that the name chosen by one user is not identical to the name chosen by another, arbitrary rules can be set up. For example, each user might be assigned a two-character code that might be used as the first two characters of each file name invented. Another alternative in common use requires the system to combine the user's identification code and the file name specified on the control statement to form a "qualified name." For example, if a certain user has been assigned code ABC that is used for accumulating that user's computer system costs, and if the file name DEF is specified, then the qualified name for that file would be ABC.DEF. If a user wishes to refer to a file that was created by another user, the qualified name must be used. Thus user ABC would identify file R created by user S as S.R.

In addition to being unique, file names may be required to comply with some simple restrictions. For example:

1. A maximum number of characters may be allowed. The file name must fit within the space assigned to it in a file label, and the design of system tables may further restrict the length.
2. There may be restrictions on the characters used in the name. For example, if names were qualified as suggested above, the character "." might not be allowed for any purpose other than to separate the qualifier from the simple file name.

File names are usually chosen to indicate file contents. Examples might be ACCOUNTS and INVNTRY.

The name-qualifier idea can be generalized and extended to many levels of qualification. A name such as A.B.C.D used in a generalized system could consist of (class of file).(owner's department).(owner's name).(file name). Nearly all general purpose I/O systems have multilevel catalogs that accommodate qualified file names. Figure 5-5 illustrates how a catalog can be used to identify the storage volumes that contain any particular file. Each subcatalog has a name of its own and contains the names of the subcatalogs related to it.

The use of subcatalogs eases the problems of achieving uniqueness among file names. If one system user is instructed to use subcatalog A and another is instructed to use subcatalog J, there is no possibility that the file names of files established by these two users will be identical. Catalog structure is discussed in more detail in Chap. 16.

File Identification Without File Name.   Quoting Ivan Flores, a popular author in the programming field, "Files do not come from nowhere."[1] The location of a file must be known to the I/O system either because that location is recorded somewhere within the system or because it is furnished by the user. The control statement conventions used to describe file location are presented later in this chapter. Ideally, location information should be used for its natural purpose only: to find an existing file or to control placement of a new file.

[1] Ivan Flores, *Data Storage and Management,* 1970.

However, there can be cases in which a file has no name and, in those cases, an I/O system can be designed to identify the file by its location. Great care must be exercised in such a design to protect the privacy and integrity of data. For example, assume that an existing file recorded on a magnetic tape without labels is required for processing. The user identifies the file by its volume serial number and its position relative to other files on the magnetic tape, and the operator places the tape volume on a device as instructed by the I/O system. Although it is impossible to determine whether the magnetic tape presented is the correct tape, a well-designed I/O system should attempt to determine that the tape presented for processing is not some identifiable tape other than the desired one. If, for example, the I/O system should find that the tape volume presented does have labels, then it is not the proper volume, and it should be rejected.

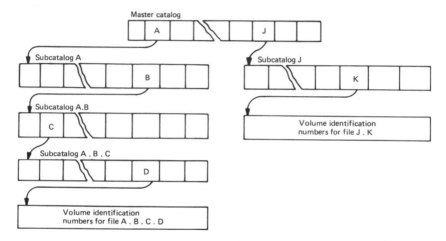

Fig. 5-5   A multilevel catalog.

Concatenation.   It is frequently convenient to consider two or more files to form a single file. For example, each department of a large company might have its own personnel file that is used for daily processing. At the end of each month, all of the department files combined might serve as a single file for developing company-wide statistical reports. To allow this kind of flexibility in processing, a file is recursively defined as a file or the concatenation of a file and a file.[2]

Some conventions that have been used successfully to indicate that a file is concatenated are as follows:

- two or more control statements having the same statement name but different file names
- one or more unnamed control statements following a named control statement, each control statement naming a separate file
- two or more file names included in a single control statement

[2] The statement above is a literal interpretation of a definition in Backus normal form, notably: (A file):: (A file) | (A file) U (A file).

It is not essential that an I/O system provide for concatenation of files. But concatenation is one of those luxuries that, once experienced, can become a near-necessity. Figure 5-6 illustrates how files can be concatenated. If an operating system does not provide concatenation ability, the user may be required to run a separate program to combine files.

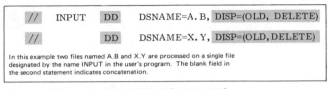

In this example two files named A.B and X.Y are processed on a single file designated by the name INPUT in the user's program. The blank field in the second statement indicates concatenation.

Note: In this figure and throughout the book, shading covers parts of program statements that are not pertinent but that must be included to be correct.

Fig. 5-6   Data set concatenation (OS/360).

Storage Utilization

The user may want to make or be required to make several specifications concerning the way storage should be used to accommodate a file. These specifications can include:

file organization
block size
labeling conventions
space requirements
volume identification

All five of these specifications must be made when a new file is being created and, depending on system design, they may have to be respecified when a file is to be used.

File Organization.   When a new file is being created, the user must specify which of the file organizations offered by the system should be used. Chapters 11 through 14 of this book describe four organizations in detail. Current operating systems do not have good nonredundant methods for declaring file organization. Typically, they require a user program specification for all file organizations and a control statement specification for certain organizations.
The most appropriate mechanism for the file organization specification is the control statement, for at least two reasons. The user's program that furnishes the records to be recorded as the new file is frequently a general purpose utility program. The usefulness of such a program extends to files of any organization if file organization is specified by control statement. The system may need to know the file organization choice before the user's program is ready for execution. Specifically, certain organizations may require that portions of the storage space be cleared or preformatted for indexes of directories. Such an operation can require as much as several minutes of elapsed time. Preformatting should be avoided if possible, but where it is necessary, it should be accomplished before main storage and devices are allocated to the user's program.

However, the kinds of system calls and the sizes of tables in the user's program may depend on file organization, making it essential that file organization be known when the program is being compiled. If at some future date I/O systems can be designed to make the user's program completely independent of the choice of file organization, then all indications of file organization should be removed from the user's program.

For existing files, it is theoretically unnecessary to specify file organization; the I/O system should be able to detect file organization by inspecting the file labels. There are two reasons why that solution is not workable for all situations. As mentioned earlier, the file organization specification must be available when the user's program is being compiled. The file itself may not be available at that time. The file may not contain a label and, hence, the required information may not be ascertainable from the file itself. Figure 5-7 illustrates a file organization specification.

```
FUNCT     ALLOCATE

FILE          NAME=FILEBB, ORG=IND

SIZE          ITEM=. . .


The above control statements specify an indexed organization.
```

Fig. 5-7   File organization specification (Honeywell Series 200/OS).

Block Size.   The information in files is stored as blocks of bytes for several reasons:

1. For many types of storage devices, there is a relatively fixed amount of space wasted in unusable gaps whenever one or more bytes are recorded. When blocks of bytes are recorded, the gap-space overhead per byte is reduced.
2. For many types of storage devices, data must be recorded in blocks of arbitrary fixed size. For example, Sperry Rand Corporation's Fastrand® Magnetic Drum records information in 168-byte blocks.
3. For many types of storage devices, storage or retrieval of a single byte of data requires a relatively large interval of time. Storage or retrieval of several bytes adds very little time per byte.

Figure 5-8 illustrates the effects of increasing block size on storage space utilization and data retrieval time.

Because the choice of block size depends on the physical characteristics of the device to be used, block size should be specified by control statement. However, a change in block size may affect the user's program directly for either or both of the following reasons:

1. A user's program may be designed to process blocks of data as if they were individual records. For example, a general utility program might copy a file without deblocking and reblocking.

2. Even when a user's program is designed to process records rather than blocks, some I/O systems buffer blocks of data temporarily in main storage space provided by the user's program.[3] An increase in block size would increase the amount of space the user's program must provide.

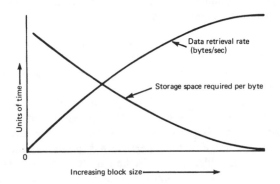

Fig. 5-8   The effects of block size on storage device performance.

The result of these considerations is that block size is customarily specified by the user's program just as file organization is. Figure 5-9 illustrates a convention for specifying block size by control statement.

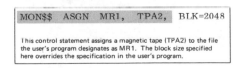

MON$$ ASGN   MR1,   TPA2,   BLK=2048

This control statement assigns a magnetic tape (TPA2) to the file
the user's program designates as MR1. The block size specified
here overrides the specification in the user's program.

Fig. 5-9   A control statement specification for block size (Honeywell Mod 4 Operating System).

Labeling Conventions.   Ideally, every file would be labeled with a uniform set of standard labels. However, an operating system can enforce a mandatory label standard only if the flexibility to process data with other labels is not required. Most operating systems allow several different file-labeling and volume-labeling conventions. The result is chaotic and regrettable. Not only do label standards differ from one computer vendor to another, but standards change from time to time for any one vendor.

When a new file is being created, the I/O system must know the label convention to be used. The two alternative sources of the specification are, of course, the user's program and a control statement. Some contemporary systems use one vehicle and some, the other. The control statement seems the preferable vehicle because

---

[3] A design that buffers blocks in the user's area of main storage has several disadvantages and should be avoided if possible. Its principal advantage is reduced system overhead, an advantage not easily ignored.

1. File labels have nothing to do with a user's program; a label specification in a user's program is logically out of place.
2. Languages such as COBOL and FORTRAN, used for specifying user's programs, have no capability to stipulate label conventions.
3. The I/O system should have the label specification available before the user's program is loaded into main storage so that file labels can be prepared in advance of need.

For existing files, the label convention specification may be made by control statement, or it may be available from catalogs maintained by the system. The user's program should not supply this specification. To do so would limit the user's program usability unnecessarily.

One might think that a good I/O system should be able to inspect an existing file to determine label type without a separate specification. Experience has proven that such a design is hazardous when several alternatives are involved. For example, suppose the operator has presented the wrong storage volume, that volume has illegible labels, and the channel program attempts to read from that volume using commands designed for a recording density different from the recorded density. The results can be hopelessly ambiguous.

The best source of the label convention specification for an existing file is the file catalog. Next best for existing files and best for new files is the control statement. Fig. 5-10 illustrates such a specification.

FILE   U3.F1, LINK=ABC, DEVICE=TAPE,   LABEL=NSTD

This control statement allocates a magnetic tape unit for use
with a file named U3.F1. This file is designated ABC by the
user's program. The tape has non-standard labels. STD
would indicate standard labels. Lack of a specification implies
STD.

Fig. 5-10   Label convention specification (TSOS).

Storage Space Requirements.   I/O systems usually allow or require the user to estimate the space required for a new direct access storage file. This estimate, made by control statement, allows an operating system to provide space in a more efficient way than would otherwise be possible.

There are several units of space that can be used: number of cylinders, tracks, half tracks, or sectors; and number of blocks, records, or bytes.

The first four are natural subdivisions of space for most DASDs. A user can make a meaningful estimate in terms of those natural subdivisions if it is known what type of device will be used. Fifty tracks of 10,000 bytes each is far different from 50 tracks of 100,000 bytes. Specification of storage space in terms of blocks, records, or bytes has the advantage that the specification is not affected by choice of I/O device. This is important because, as will be discussed later in this chapter, the user may not want to be specific about the type of device that should be used for any particular file. Most systems allow specification of DASD space in either of at least two units.

The user may not know how large a file will be initially or how large it may become later. Most operating systems accommodate this problem by allowing the user to specify two space quantities: a primary quantity, which is assigned initially, and a secondary quantity, which is assigned repeatedly whenever the space already assigned is exhausted. For some data organizations, the user may be required to specify a third quantity of space that is to be used for a special purpose, such as an index or an overflow area. Such special purpose specifications are regrettable because they are a serious annoyance to the system user; where possible, systems should strive to avoid them.

If a user does not request contiguous storage space, a system might assume that a combination of small extents can be used to fill the user's requirements. There are at least two special situations in which the user may want to specify that storage space be contiguous:

1. Such a requirement could occur when a user's program calculates device physical addresses. An example is calculation of the address where the record with next higher key can be found. Address calculation would be complicated unnecessarily by having discontiguous space assigned. (Note, however, that such calculations in a user's program are undesirable and should be discouraged or even forbidden.)
2. If a file is to be used with great frequency, the normally modest performance differential resulting from discontiguous space could become significant.

It is probably unrealistic to require that the space acquired to fulfill a secondary quantity be contiguous with the primary space. Figure 5-11 illustrates how the storage space can be specified.

```
/ALLOCATE FILENAM=TEST, SPACE=(TRACK,30,10)

This specification is for 30 tracks initially plus an increment
of 10 tracks wherever the already-allocated space is exhausted.
```

Fig. 5-11   Direct access space requirement specification (TSOS).

Storage-Volume Identification.   The computer operator must be able to identify demountable storage volumes such as magnetic tape reels and disk packs. To provide visible identification, gummed labels can be attached either to the volumes themselves or to the protective covers. A visible label might include such information as:

- date when the data on the volume were recorded
- owner's name
- file name(s)
- date when the data on the volume can be discarded
- volume identification code

At present, we are concerned only with the volume identification code.

When a new file is to be created, the user may have important reasons for choosing a particular volume: It may be a volume that the user personally owns, or it may contain other related data that should share a volume with the file for convenience in mailing. Volume identification codes for new files must be specified by control statement so that they can be changed easily.

For existing files, volume identification codes are frequently available in catalogs within the system. If an existing file is not cataloged, some systems require that it be cataloged before it can be used. Other systems employ a completely opposite philosophy, allowing a control statement specification of volume identification codes to override cataloged information.

In general, the user should not be encouraged to specify volume identification codes. A system frequently can achieve improved volume handling efficiency by placing new files on volumes that are already available on I/O devices. This is especially true for new files that are of temporary use. For example, files used during program compilation frequently can be placed on storage volumes maintained by the system for that kind of use. Such volumes are called public volumes. Even if a file is to be saved for an extended period, an operating system can sometimes assign a volume that is readily available but not in use. Such volumes are called *scratch volumes,* a colloquial expression where scratch has the same connotation as it has in scratch paper. Figure 5-12 illustrates volume identification code specification in a control statement.

@ASG,TEL FILEY ,6C/2 , N432/N433

Fig. 5-12   Volume identification code specification (EXEC-8).

File Security Specifications

File security involves many factors, including protection from fire and water, protection from magnetic fields, and protection from accidental or malicious physical damage. Additionally, the privacy of data can be compromised by inadequate library controls, inadequate shielding against electronic surveillance, and dishonest operators. Chapter 19 is devoted to these topics. Some aspects of security are beyond the control of an operating system, but there are several important security aids that systems can provide:

- scratch control for security against accidental destruction of data by premature reuse of storage space
- copying of files and journaling of transactions to allow recovery of the contents of a file after erroneous processing
- access control to avoid unauthorized modification or disclosure of data

These three topics will be discussed briefly below. Our concern at this time is control statement syntax; the more detailed and philosophical discussion of security is deferred to a later chapter.

Scratch Control. The cost of storage media is such that a storage volume is reused whenever the data it contains are no longer of value. Some files are valueless immediately after use. An example of such a file is a temporary file created during compilation. Such a file is created simply as an extension to main storage to hold information temporarily. Another file may have value until an updated version is created or even beyond that time as a basis for recovery if the updated version is accidentally destroyed. In data processing terms, the updated version is called a newer generation, and the older generation is called a father, grandfather, or great grandfather. For some files, a grandfather may be preserved, and for others, a great grandfather; the decision is delegated to the owner of the file.

Operating systems can furnish control over storage space scratching in two ways: by generation and by date. To control space reuse by file generation, the system must maintain awareness of generations. The mechanisms that can accomplish this awareness and control are discussed in Chap. 16, where the file catalog is described. To control by date, a system can accept a control-statement specification of the date when a file can be scratched. As a minor variation, a system might accept a specification of the number of days the file is to be preserved. Such a specification has the advantage that it need not be changed as time passes. A scratch date for the file label can be calculated from the number specified and the current date, assuming the latter is available within the operating system. Some forms of a date specification are shown in Fig. 5-13.

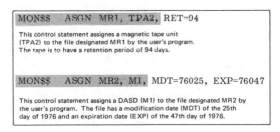

Fig. 5-13 Scratch control specification (Honeywell Mod 4 Operating System).

Copy and Journal. Most general purpose systems include a checkpoint/ restart capability that allows a user's program to be restarted from an intermediate checkpoint rather than from the beginning in the event of erroneous or incomplete processing. However, when a program updates an existing file, it may be impossible to restart from a checkpoint or even from the beginning of the user's job.

Every system has the ability to run a utility program for the user to create a backup copy of a file. As illustrated in Fig. 5-14, TSOS has a special control statement that makes a backup copy. The example causes the file named CLARK.LOGA to be copied, resulting in a new file CLARK.LOGB. Most major systems do not have special statements for this purpose, possibly because it is almost as convenient for the user to run a preliminary process to accomplish the copy.

```
/COPY CLARK. LOGA, CLARK, LOGB, DOG. LITTER
```

Fig. 5-14   Control statement to copy a file (TSOS).

For large files, copying can be an extravagance because of time and storage space required. Under such conditions, it is preferable to require the system to copy a file infrequently and create a journal of all changes to a file as they occur. If a journal exists, an old copy of the file can be updated with all changes up to the time of an erroneous operation, and then the erroneous operation can be rerun correctly. The ability to create a journal is new to general purpose systems, but it has been used in special purpose systems for several years.

Access Control.   In recent years, the problems in protecting data from accidental or malicious destruction or disclosures have become complex. Major factors that contribute to that complexity are as follows:

1. Large DASD capacity exposes a great volume of data to potential mischief.
2. Multiprogramming makes it impractical to have only a single user's data available to the system at any one time.
3. Communications-based systems allow a degree of anonymity to the user, making it easier for an interloper to use the system without fear of apprehension.

There are two principal mechanisms used to control access to files:

Passwords   A password is a secret combination of characters that must be furnished to gain access to protected data.
Permissions   A permission is a certification made by the owner of a file granting a particular user of the system access to that file.

The creator of a file may have a sincere interest or even a moral obligation to restrict the use of that file. Secret passwords established by control statements can be used for this purpose. Usually two passwords are allowed for any file: one that authorizes the user to use but not modify the data and one that authorizes the user to both use and modify the data. These two are illustrated as RDPASS and WRPASS, respectively, in Fig. 5-15. A few systems have experimented with a third class of password that allows a user to modify but not inspect data in a file. Such a facility might be useful to a clerk who is authorized to make changes to monthly salary figures in a payroll file but is not authorized to know salaries other than those that are being changed. The clerk could be required to furnish employee identification, old salary, and new salary. The would-be user of a password-protected file must furnish the password. In most systems, the password is furnished by a keyboard-terminal operator in response to a message from the I/O system.

/CATALOG FILENAME=. . . , RDPASS=C(1234), WRPASS=C(5678) , . . .

This control statement establishes 1234 as the password for reading and 5678 as the password for modifying the file.

Fig. 5-15 Password specification (TSOS).

GCOS-III includes a system of permissions illustrated in Fig. 5-16 that augment the password mechanisms. A permission is an authorization for a user to either inspect or modify a file. Permissions can be either positive or negative; they can either include or exclude a user or all users from access to a file. Permissions have the advantage that they require no special action on the part of the user; the user either is or is not permitted to use the data.

---

1. FCREAT   CLASS021/PROB1INPUT, READ

The creator of the file named CLASS021 is giving read-permission to all users.

2. FCREAT   CLASS022/PROB1INPUT, WRITE/JONES

The creator of the file named CLASS022 is giving permission to a user named JONES to both read and write.

Fig. 5-16 Permissions specifications (GCOS-III).

RESOURCE REQUIREMENTS: DEVICES

The preceding pages have discussed the requirements of files including file identification, storage utilization, and security specifications. The other physical resources that a user's program requires are devices; specifically, devices to read, write, and modify the files discussed earlier. Device requirement specifications along with the file specifications already discussed constitute the I/O system's major uses of control statements.

One might think that it would be unnecessary for the users to declare their device requirements; the I/O system should be able to perceive the user's device requirements from file requirements. To some extent, that is true. But there are many things the users know about their needs that allow them to make a better specification than the system could make unassisted. For example, users frequently have a preference or even a requirement that their new files should be recorded on a particular type of device. The users may also know that their programs make heavy concurrent demands on certain files, or they may have other information that should influence the configuration of the system components allocated to their programs. Further, the users know whether records will be processed in a natural sequence or whether random processing will require all volumes of a file to be simultaneously available. The specification of these kinds of device requirements are discussed in the next three sections entitled "Device Type," "System Configuration," and "Storage-Volume Handling."

Device Type

I/O systems usually allow a user to specify device type with one of three degrees of precision as follows:

Actual Device Type (See Fig. 5-17, line 1.) The I/O system can recognize a distinct code for each type of device attached to the system. A user might specify a particular device type because he or she wants the stored file to be processable on another system that has the specified type of unit.

Line	Control Statement	Meaning
1	@ASG, C FILEY, 6C	User is requesting a unit of type 6C, a particular type of magnetic tape unit.
2	@ASG, C FILEY, T	User is requesting a unit of class T, the class of all magnetic tape units.
3	@ASG, C FILEY	User has not specified an I/O device type or class.

In all three lines above, @ASG indicates a control statement for assigning devices, C indicates that the file is to be cataloged, and FILEY is the file name.

Fig. 5-17 Device-type specifications (EXEC-8).

Device Class (See Fig. 5-17, line 2.) Several related types of devices can be treated as a class. When the class name is specified, the I/O system will assign a device of its own choosing from the class. A user might specify the class of all DASDs if random-processing capability is required or the class of all printers is required if the printing requires no capabilities unique to one type of printer. Some systems invite users to invent their own device class groupings and designations. Such special groupings would be appropriate, for example, when certain units have an optional feature not available on all units of that type.

Any Device Chosen by I/O System (See Fig. 5-17, line 3.) Most I/O systems will furnish a device type chosen accordingly to a published rule if the user fails to indicate a preference. The system's choice typically will be a DASD because DASDs can tolerate interleaved use by several programs. If the file is an existing file, the I/O system must choose a unit that can accept the particular storage volume already in use. The proper choice must depend on other information in the control statement or on information available within the system.

System Configuration

The performance of a hardware-software system can be affected significantly by inappropriate assignment of files to devices. For example, a user's program that processes one input file to create one output file might require 2 min of elapsed time when the two files are stored on two separate devices on two separate channels. The same problem might require 5 min if the two devices share a channel, and as much as 20 min or more if the files share a single storage device. On the other hand, spreading files unnecessarily across devices is disadvantageous for the following reasons:

1. It complicates system resource scheduling by wastefully tying up equipment.
2. It complicates the operator's job by requiring that volumes be mounted and demounted unnecessarily.
3. It exposes the user's job to a higher probability of equipment mal-function.
4. It increases the logistics problems of storing and shipping storage volumes.

In theory, a language processor could analyze the flow of a user's pro-gram to determine some aspects of acceptable configuration. Alternately, an I/O system could determine an acceptable configuration from experience in serving a particular user's program. Both of those solutions are beyond the state of today's art. Presumably, the user knows whether certain files will be processed concurrently and which files will be processed heavily, so the user can make judgments affecting the system configuration. Several of the specifi-cations the user might care to make are as follows:

Number of Units If the records of a file will be processed in a random order, it will be necessary to have all volumes of the file available to the system simultaneously. If records are processed in the order of storage within the file, only one volume need be available at a time, but system efficiency may be improved by using two units alternately. The use of two units, properly supported by I/O system programming, allows over-lap of such activities as magnetic tape rewind, volume mount and dis-mount, and device warm-up time. Figure 5-18, line 1, illustrates a request for two units.

Line No.	Control Statement	Meaning
1	//DD1 DD DSNAME=X,Y,DISP=OLD,UNIT=(.2)	Allocate 2 units
2	//DD2 DD UNIT=(2311,SEP=(DD1)), SPACE=(TRK,(200, 10)	Allocate a unit of type 2311, the unit to be distinct from the units allocated in statement DD1 above.
3	//DD3 DD UNIT=AFF=DD2	Affinity is indicated.
4	//DD4 DD DSNAME=W.X, DISP=OLD, UNIT=182	Allocate unit number 2 on control unit 8 on channel 1
5	//DD5 DD DSNAME=STEP, UNIT=2311, DISP=OLD, VOLUME=(PRIVATE,,,SER=123)	Use the storage volume with serial number 123 as a private volume.

Fig. 5-18 System configuration specifications (OS/360).

Unit Separation If two major files are to be processed simultaneously, they should be mounted on separate devices, if possible. Figure 5-18, line 2, illustrates a request for a device separate from the devices on line 1.

Unit Affinity   Figure 5-18, line 3, illustrates a request to share a device with another file. A user might indicate device sharing simply to reduce the number of devices used by his program or to consolidate several files onto a single volume for convenience in shipping.

Absolute Device Assignment   Figure 5-18, line 4, illustrates a request for specific unit. A user may want to designate that a specific unit should be used for a particular file for one or more of several reasons:

1. The unit may have a special feature not available on other similar devices.
2. The user's program may be a diagnostic program being run to test a specific I/O unit.
3. The physical location of a particular unit may be important operationally. For example, a particular card reader may be in a room separate from the computer center itself.

Public/Private Volumes   A user may want a storage volume assigned exclusively for his or her use because the user wants to move the file from system to system freely or because he or she intends to store the data in a vault to be removed only with the user's permission. In such cases, the user can indicate that the file should be placed on a private volume as indicated in Fig. 5-18, line 5. Unless a user has a reason to want a file placed on a particular storage volume, the user should be encouraged to let the system assign a convenient nonprivate volume. Some of these public volumes are always mounted on devices and are available for files that have only temporary value. Most operating systems distinguish between public and private requirements implicitly. If the user identifies specific volumes or if the file is to be preserved, the system assumes "private"; otherwise, the system assumes "public."

Storage-Volume Handling

Assuming a file has been identified and I/O devices have been allocated, we still have these questions: For a multiple-volume file, in what order should the volume be made available for processing? Where will the file come from and what should be done with it when the user's program is completed? These questions are discussed in the next two sections.

Volume Mounting Order.   An I/O system responsibility is to instruct the operator to mount storage volumes on units at appropriate times. Most cases require no guidance from the user, as the following cases show:

1. For new files, i.e., files being created, volume 1 should go on the first I/O device allocated, volume 2 on the second, and so forth. If there are fewer devices than volumes, the devices should be reused in rotation as processing moves from one device to the next.
2. For existing files when there are equal numbers of volumes and I/O devices, the volumes should simply be mounted in a convenient order.

The only case requiring guidance is the case of an existing file with more volumes than devices. In this case, the system must know whether the user intends to process the file from the beginning, the end, or some other point. Statistically, the best guess would be the beginning. Lacking information to the contrary, a system can assume a natural sequential process. If the user intends a different order, he or she should be required to indicate that fact. Figure 5-19 illustrates an acceptable method.

Control Statement	Volume-Mounting Order
/FILE LINK=. . . , MOUNT=FIRST	Use the natural order; if no specification is written MOUNT=FIRST will be used by default
/FILE LINK=. . . , MOUNT=LAST	Use volume in reverse of the order indicated by the volume serial number for this file
/FILE LINK=. . . , MOUNT=0003	Mount the third volume of the file only

Note: In TSOS, these instructions apply to magnetic-tape files only.

Fig. 5-19   Volume mounting order specification (TSOS).

File Routing.   Figure 5-20 lists some sources and destinations of files. In a few cases, an I/O system can deduce the appropriate alternative. For example, the actual presence of data records following the control statements in the job stream, as shown in Fig. 5-2, is ample evidence that a file is being "furnished herewith." An I/O system could go further, deducing a source as follows: If the file name in a control statement matches a file name in the catalog, the file is available elsewhere and, incidentally, the catalog indicates that location. If the file name is not in the catalog, the I/O system could assume that a new file will be created by the user's program. In practice, such a deduction is risky. A more advisable policy requires the user to specify whether a file is OLD or NEW. This redundant information can be used by the I/O system to detect inconsistencies in file naming, a common source of error. Notice in Fig. 5-20 that an alternative destination can be specified. The alternative specification applies only if the user's program fails to run satisfactorily. A user might want a temporary file destroyed if the program runs successfully but saved for analysis if the program fails. File routing is specified by the DISP (disposition) parameters in a control statement. The convention is DISP=(source, normal destination, alternate destination).

SMALL-SYSTEM SUBSETS

All general purpose operating systems include a control statement mechanism of some kind. However, the syntax of specification and the number of alternatives for any specification can be significantly restricted. The syntactic rules for the control statements of the operating systems used in the examples of this chapter would impose a significant processing burden on a small computing system. This burden could be reduced by restricting the syntax to a more rigid and more highly coded form, or by altering the processing conventions of the system to provide preprocessing of control statements. The latter alternative has the advantage of maintaining language compatibility with larger systems.

The determination of what kind of specification and what alternatives might be eliminated profitably depends on system design and on the intended use of the system.

Sources	Control Statement Parameter	Comments
Furnished herewith	none required	The I/O system detects this condition without specification
To be created	NEW	
Available elsewhere	OLD	
Destinations		
Return to user	none required	All cards and printed material are returned to user
Destroy	DELETE	
Store permanently	CATLG	Catalog and preserve the file
	KEEP	Preserve the file
	PASS	Leave volumes mounted, disposition will be specified later.

Sample control statements

//FILE1 DD DSNAME=D99. . . , DISP=(NEW, CATLG, DELETE) , . . .

//FILE1 DD DSNAME=XX2. . . , DISP=(OLD, DELETE, KEEP) , ...

Fig. 5-20   File routing (OS/360).

File Name   A simple file name restricted to the size that will fit in the fields provided by the file labels may be adequate. Name qualifications are required only if multilevel catalogs are maintained.

Labeling Conventions   If a system can be restricted to processing files that conform to a single basic label standard, a very significant reduction in complexity will result.

Storage-Space Requirements   Some small systems require the user to specify the actual address of the space intended to be used. Such a convention results in very significant savings in system programming and processing time.

Security/Privacy   The responsibilities for security and privacy of data can be assumed by the owner of the files and the operators of the system. Passwords, permissions, scratch control, and copying/journaling can all be replaced by manual controls, particularly in systems that do not provide multiprogramming or time sharing.

Device Assignment   Small systems may require that the user identify each file with a specific device. Further, the user can give written volume handling instructions to the operator, probably using a preprinted form. These simplifications eliminate all device allocation, all device scheduling, and much of the operator-interaction programming.

The programming required to support the interfaces described in this chapter is very complex, more complex than an inexperienced person might imagine. Systems with all of the features described are difficult to design, difficult to correct, difficult to document, difficult to learn, and even difficult to use. Clearly, most of the interfaces described in this chapter are candidates for elimination in minimum-system design.

SUMMARY

Control statements communicate requirements for file and I/O devices. They are advantageous for the purpose because they are separate logically, physically, and chronologically from the user's program. The control statements and new data necessary for several jobs can be visualized as a deck of cards. A control statement is a vital link connecting a program and a file. A major advantage of control statements is the ease with which files, parameters, and devices can be changed from run to run. A disadvantage is the user's difficulty in getting them right the first time. Syntax and style vary significantly from one system to another.

The information related to files that should be communicated by control statements can be categorized as follows:

File Identification A file can be identified by its name recorded in a machine readable label, in a file catalog, and on a visible label. Uniqueness can be ensured by a hierarchic name structure. Files without names must be identified by their locations. A concatenation ability allows two or more files to be treated as a single file.

Storage Utilization For new files, file organization, block size, labeling conventions, space requirements, and volume identification must be specified, explicitly or by default. Control statements frequently contain the information.

File-Security Specifications Control statements can be used to specify scratch control (by generation or by date), copy and journal requirements, and access control. The latter is usually based on passwords that qualify would-be users, or on permissions that grant access to certain users by names.

The I/O device specifications communicated by control statements can include the following:

Device Type A user may be allowed to specify a particular device type, or a device class. By default, some systems would assign a DASD.

System Configuration A user may be encouraged to specify the number of I/O units required, whether or not files can share a unit, whether a specific unit is required, and whether a private storage volume is required.

Storage-Volume Handling A user's specifications may include volume processing order, and source and destination of the file.

Examples of the specifications listed can be found throughout the chapter. The interfaces described in this chapter are complex in every respect. Most of them can be eliminated for small-system design by requiring the system user to control system resources and to instruct the operator directly.

Exercises

1.(e) Why are the control statement name and the file name usually different?

2.(e) Give two reasons why a block might be made large enough to contain several records.

3.(e) What is the advantage of specifying storage-space requirements in terms of blocks rather than in terms of tracks?

4.(e) Using file disposition as shown in Fig. 5-20, why might a user specify DISP=(NEW, KEEP, DELETE)?

5.(m) Why should block size be specified by control statement rather than by the user's program?

6.(m) If storage space requirements are specified in the manner illustrated in Fig. 5-11, describe a situation that would justify a small primary and large secondary quantity.

7.(m) It has been stated that the execution time for a program that processes one input file to create one output file might increase from 2 to 5 min because of a change in system configuration. How is it possible that execution time could increase more than double?

8.(m) List at least three reasons why absolute device assignment requests are undesirable.

9.(d) If the mechanisms and specifications described in this chapter are difficult to design, correct, document, learn, and use, why do they exist? Limit your answer to 100 words.

6 Device Allocation

Device allocation is the process of determining which device will be used to fill each of a set of device requirements. In most systems, device allocation is a job-scheduler activity. The reason for including it in this book is not to crusade for enlargement of I/O system scope, but rather to acquaint students of the I/O system with allocation problems and techniques. After all, if device allocation is not an I/O system function, it is at least a very close relative.

There are two major alternative philosophies that can be adopted regarding the use of I/O devices:

Philosophy No. 1 Any job can request and expect to get the I/O equipment it requires up to the total complement of devices attached to the system. In a system so designed, device allocation is a complex problem that is resolved by systematic application of allocation strategies. This fully general approach is exemplified by OS/360, and it is the major topic described in this chapter. Its primary advantage is generality; its disadvantage is complexity.

Philosophy No. 2 Any job can request I/O devices as it sees fit, but under all but the most exceptional conditions, data will be staged between those devices and DASDs by system programs. The user's program will store and retrieve DASD data only, and the requested devices are not usually allocated to the user's program. This approach avoids most of the complexity of general allocation and provides excellent execution time for the user's program. The primary disadvantage is the cost and elapsed time required for the extra handling of data during staging. The staging approach is exemplified by EXEC-8. Its principal techniques are described in Chap. 10, "Data Staging."

Compromises between these two philosophies are often used. In fact, EXEC-8 will perform general allocation when required, and OS/360 utilizes staging in significant degree. The purpose in presenting the most general allocation techniques is not to advocate the general approach, but rather to provide insights and ideas that can be adopted, adapted, or discarded in the design of a system.

To understand device allocation, we must understand a little about job scheduling, the activity that precedes device allocation. The job scheduler reviews users' requests for services, giving particular attention to the priority, the expected running time, the amount of main storage required, and the kind and number of I/O devices required. The objectives of the scheduler are to allow efficient use of equipment while providing acceptable elapsed time for each service request. In some environments, efficient use of equipment is emphasized; in others, the most important consideration is recognition of priorities. To establish the gross order of execution of programs, the scheduler refers to tables that indicate availability of resources such as main storage space and I/O devices. The scheduler might maintain its own tables for this purpose, or it might use information maintained by the supervisor and I/O system. In either case, the scheduler matches the resource requirements of outstanding service requests with the inventory of resources available and applies its own algorithms, weighing efficiency against priority. At some point, this analysis yields a decision that the system is ready to run a particular job.

We shall assume that the scheduler's analysis is basically sound but somewhat coarse. For example, if the selected job requires two magnetic tape units on separate channels, the scheduler will have determined that two or more tape units are available, but it may not have determined whether they are on separate channels. Or, if the job requires direct access storage space, the scheduler will have determined that a DASD is available, but it will not have determined whether the storage volume on it has space adequate to fill the requirement.

This chapter concerns the methods an I/O system can use to allocate devices. Four major topics are discussed: (1) maintaining the inventory of devices, including classification of devices and the status of each device; (2) static allocation of devices, including allocation in situations where alternative allocations are possible; (3) dynamic allocation of devices in response to a device requirement that arises during execution of a user's program; and (4) automatic volume recognition wherein the system recognizes volumes that the operator mounts on devices at the operator's own choosing, thereby bypassing static allocation.

DEVICE INVENTORY

During the system generation process that tailors an operating system for use with a particular computer system, the inventory of I/O devices available to that system is established. That inventory can be represented in tables and bit masks as described below.

I/O Unit Tables

During system generation, a table or section of a table is constructed for each I/O device attached to the system. Such a table or table section, illustrated in Fig. 6-1, can be called an I/O unit table, a term used throughout this book. The unit table for a particular device contains the channel and unit addresses, a device type code, device-status indicators, and other information about the device. Examples of status indicators are whether the device is in normal operating condition, whether it is in use, and whether an operator action is in process. A unit table can be considered a main storage representation of an I/O device.

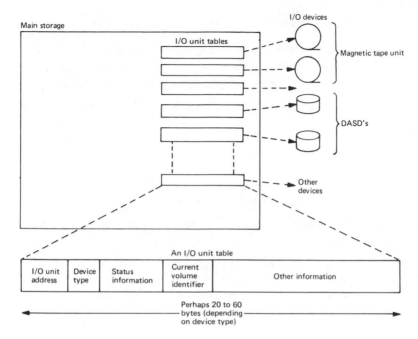

Fig. 6-1 I/O unit tables.

Bit Masks

A convenient representation of the inventory of each type of device is a bit mask devised as follows. If a system includes n I/O devices, let each unit be represented by a bit position in a string of n bits. A bit mask for units of type ABC will have 1s in the positions representing units of type ABC. Bit masks can be used conveniently to represent devices belonging to a particular class, devices currently inoperable, or devices currently allocated. Using logical AND and OR operations on the bit masks, one can ascertain quickly which units of type ABC are in operating condition and not currently allocated. Such information is essential to the allocation process. Examples of bit masks and their use are shown in Fig. 6-2. A cross-reference table such as that shown in Fig. 6-3 can be used to relate bit positions to unit tables.

Device Status

Several special conditions that may apply to a particular I/O device affect the allocation process. Some of these are:

- availability of the device to the system, e.g., a device might be unavailable because of malfunction
- special assignment within the system, e.g., a device might be serving as the operator's console
- current activity, e.g., a magnetic tape drive might be currently in use.

These special conditions affecting allocation are described in the following paragraphs.

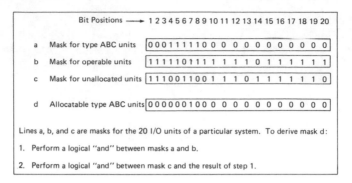

Fig. 6-2   Bit masks.

Availability of the Device.   A device may be unavailable to the system for one of the following reasons:

1. It is being repaired or is awaiting repair.
2. It is undergoing routine periodic inspection or testing.
3. It is being used for a purpose not related to the system.

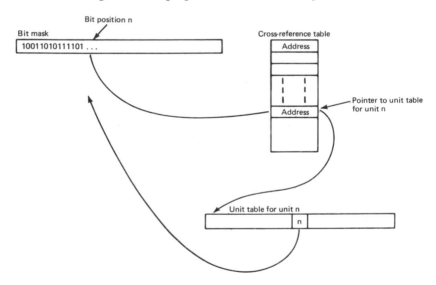

Fig. 6-3   Relating bit masks to unit tables.

An I/O system can assume that all devices identified during system generation are available at all times unless specific action has been taken either by the system or by the operator to make a device unavailable. Some systems, particularly symmetric multiprocessing systems, include extensive self-diagnosing capabilities that can result in a spontaneous decision to declare a device unavailable due to malfunction of the device. In a more typical case, the operator may command the system to relinquish a particular device. Figure 6-4 illustrates commands for a system to relinquish a device and to accept a device being returned to the system.

Relinquishing a device is complicated slightly if the device is in use. It is not reasonable to require the operator to issue the command only when the device is not in use, because a device can become free and be reallocated in just a few seconds. The best design allows the operator to issue the command at any time. If the device is in use when the command is received, the unit table is marked to indicate that the device should be relinquished as soon as its current allocation is terminated. This results in the three possible states of availability mentioned earlier: (1) fully available to the system, (2) scheduled to become unavailable, and (3) unavailable.

VARY 263, OFFLINE	This command takes the device at channel and unit address 263 out of system control.
VARY 263, ONLINE	This command returns the device to system control.

Fig. 6-4 Operator commands affecting device availability (OS/360).

Special Assignment within the System. A device might be serving some special long-term assignment within the system that restricts its general usability for users' files as these examples illustrate.

Operator's Console A device that has been assigned as an operator's console must have its other possible uses severely restricted so that operator messages are not intermixed with users' data.

System Residence A device that is storing libraries of programs or data essential to the moment-by-moment operation of the system must have its other possible uses restricted. The volume mounted on such a device cannot be demounted and, furthermore, overall system performance would be affected seriously by unnecessary competition for use of the device.

Permanently Mounted Volume If a particular data volume is to be used frequently over an extended period, a system might provide for the volume to be permanently mounted. Commands requesting rescinding permanent mounting are illustrated in Fig. 6-5.

a	MOUNT 263, VOL = (SL,1234)
b	UNLOAD 263

Line a causes the volume with a standard label (SL) and serial number 123 to be permanently mounted on the device with channel and unit address 263. Line b causes the mounted volume to be released.

Fig. 6-5 Operator commands to mount a volume permanently (OS/360).

Current Activity. A device may not be available for allocation because of transitory conditions. For instance, the device may already be allocated. When a device with serial capabilities has been allocated, it is not available for allocation. Direct access storage devices such as magnetic disks and drums can accommodate simultaneous allocation to fill several requirements. Or possibly the device has direct access capability, but a private volume is currently in use. If a storage volume is owned by a particular user, it may not be available for general use.

STATIC ALLOCATION OF DEVICES

Static allocation is performed in anticipation of the actual need for devices. The definition of static needs of a job is contained in the control statements for that job. Static allocation is completed before the user's program begins execution, and it is in effect until the user's program terminates or the user's program indicates that the device is no longer required. Dynamic allocation, a process that allocates devices as they are required during execution of the user's program, is discussed later in this chapter.

The I/O system is usually asked to allocate several devices at the same time. As each requirement is analyzed, the I/O system will discover that it falls in one of four classes.

1. There is only one way the requirement can be satisfied. For example, the user may have requested a certain type of device of which there is exactly one available for allocation. Such requirements are filled by the demand-allocation routines.
2. There are several ways the requirement can be satisfied. For example, the user may have requested one unit of a certain type of which there are two available for allocation. Such requirements are filled by the decision-allocation routines.
3. The requirement can be satisfied by use of generally available space on a direct access storage device. Such requirements are filled by public-space allocation routines.
4. There is no apparent way the requirement can be satisfied. For example, the user may require a particular device whose unit table indicates it is not available. Such requirements are filled, if possible, by the allocation recovery routines.

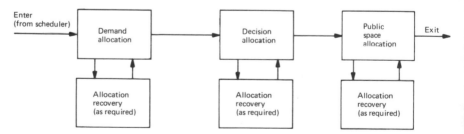

Fig. 6-6   Static allocation.

The overall static allocation process is shown in Fig. 6-6. The order of processing is very important, and that order is established by the following rule: Requirements should be filled in order of increasing alternatives. For example, if two devices, D1 and D2, are available and requirement R1 can be satisfied only by D1 while R2 can be satisfied by D1 or D2, then requirement R1 should be filled before R2 is filled. The problem that can arise if R2 is filled first is amply evident. R1 was a demand situation, while R2 was a decision situation. Notice, however, that R2 becomes a demand situation as soon as R1 is filled. This phenomenon is not unusual. It requires that allocation be done a step at a time, reviewing the effects of each step on the remaining unfilled requirements.

Demand allocation, decision allocation, public space allocation, and allocation recovery are discussed on the following pages.

Demand Allocation

The demand allocation routines work with all of the user's requirements, gathering information from tables and from the file catalog and processing each requirement to the point where that requirement has been filled or until it is determined that the requirement does not pose a demand allocation situation. Remember that a demand allocation situation exists when there is one and only one way a particular requirement can be filled. Each of the following cases requires slightly different handling:

1. A specific device identified by its channel and unit address is required.
2. A particular storage volume is required, and that volume is already mounted on a device.
3. One or more devices of a particular type are required.
4. One or more devices of a particular class are required.
5. Space on any storage volume is required.

The cases listed above are discussed in the following paragraphs.

Specific Device.   If the user's control statement has requested the device at a particular channel and unit address, that device must be allocated. This case is the simplest one to handle. (It is also the most restrictive case, and its use should be discouraged.) Assuming the job scheduler has done its work properly, the required device should be immediately available. Exceptions can occur if the I/O device is taken from the system by operator command, or it is allocated for some other purpose subsequent to the job scheduler's analysis. If the required device is not available, the allocation recovery routines can attempt a recovery.

Specific Already-Mounted Volume.   Sometimes a particular already-mounted volume is required. This can happen when a user intends to create a new file, and the user has explicitly stated the volume identification code of a permanently mounted volume or intends to use an existing file that was used in an earlier process. To determine that the user's condition applies, the demand allocation routines must search the appropriate unit tables comparing the required volume identification code with the codes of available volumes. If a match is found, the device is allocated; if not, the requirement is processed as discussed in the next paragraphs.

Devices of a Particular Type.   When one or more devices of a particular type are required, two determinations must be made: how many units are available and how many are actually required. The number available can be determined readily using bit masks. The number required may have been stated explicitly by the user. If not, the number required must be inferred. When a file is to be processed serially by a single user, one device would be enough. When records from a file are to be processed in a random order or when a file is to be processed by two or more users' programs simultaneously, each volume of the file requires its own device.

If the number of units required equals the number available, a demand situation exists, and the available units should be allocated. If the number required is less than the number available, a decision situation exists, and the requirement should be set aside for later handling. If the number required exceeds the number available, the allocation recovery routines should be called to attempt to remedy the problem. Allocation recovery is discussed later in the chapter.

Devices of a Particular Class.   This case is essentially the same as the preceding case, but it is listed separately because it should be processed after the preceding case. The requirement for devices of a class may not reveal its true nature as a demand situation until other demand situations are satisfied. For example, if magnetic tape units T1 and T2 are of different types but both belong to class C, a requirement for a device of class C appears to be a decision situation until a requirement for a device of type T2 has been filled.

Decision Allocation

The procedures described in the preceding section allocated devices only in those cases where there were no alternatives. In a few instances, alternatives seemed to exist but, as other requirements were filled, the apparent alternatives proved to be illusions. The decision allocation programs are used to allocate devices in cases where alternatives exist. Examples of such alternatives are as follows:

1. When a requirement could be filled by an available device on channel 1 or by an available device on channel 2, which device should be selected?
2. When a requirement for a device of class A could be filled by an available device of type a or one of type b, which device should be selected?
3. When there are two or more requirements that could be filled by a certain device, which requirement should be chosen?

There are two important reasons why such alternatives should be analyzed carefully:

1. Arbitrary allocation could result in reduced system performance. For example, arbitrary allocation might produce a very uneven distribution of I/O activity to channels.

2. Arbitrary allocation could result in an inability to satisfy all requirements in cases where careful allocation would be successful. Example 6-1 illustrates this point.

EXAMPLE 6-1

Assume there are two unfilled requirements for magnetic tape units, R1 and R2. R1 specifies two units from the class of all magnetic tape units. R2 specifies one unit of type T1. Assume further that there are three tape units available, two of type T1 and one of type T2. Notice that neither R1 nor R2 is a demand allocation situation.

Arbitrary allocation

Allocate both T1 units to R1. The result is that R2 cannot be filled.

Decision allocation

Allocate a T1 unit to R2 and the other two units to R1.

The problem that faces the decision allocation program is complex, and many of the parameters are not known. With some simplifying assumptions, such as the assumptions that all I/O devices are equally capable, all channels are equally capable, all files will be equally active, and each device can be reached by only one channel, the problem could be reduced to a linear-programming problem. That approach is not useful because the assumptions are not correct and because the solution to the linear-programming problem is too costly.

The goal in designing a decision allocation process should be to achieve a good compromise between the quality of allocation performed and the resources required to perform that allocation. Decision allocation can be performed reasonably well using a series of simple decisions repeatedly. The process to be described includes most of the features of the OS/360 decision allocation process. Clearly, other approaches are possible. Figure 6-7 illustrates the major steps performed. The steps in that process are discussed separately in the sections that follow.

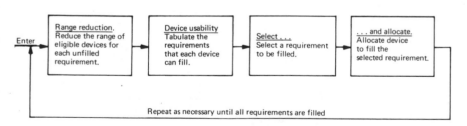

Fig. 6-7   Decision allocation.

Range Reduction.   The requirements not filled during demand allocation have the common characteristic that there are more than enough devices eligible for each requirement. The objective of the range reduction process is to reduce the number of eligible devices by eliminating those that are the least desirable. For example, if the class of all magnetic tape units includes a few low-performance units, those units can be eliminated at this time. An argument could be made as to whether a unit separation specification expresses a requirement or a preference. If it is considered a requirement, it may have been considered during demand allocation; if a preference, it should be handled at this time.

If, during range reduction the number of eligible devices for any requirement equals the number required, those devices should be allocated. Then the entire process described in Fig. 6-7 should be restarted with the reduced number of unallocated devices. Alternatively, if the number of eligible devices exceeds the number required for all requirements still unfilled, the next step in Fig. 6-7 should be taken.

Device Usability.   Up to this point, the allocation processes have consistently considered the number of devices that are eligible to satisfy each individual requirement. The point of view switches abruptly now, and a tabulation should be made showing for each eligible device what requirements it can fill. An example of this tabulation is shown in Fig. 6-8. This tabulation is an aid in the decision making that must follow shortly: Whenever a requirement can be filled by two or more eligible devices, the device that can fill the fewest requirements should be chosen. That strategy fills a requirement with only modest reduction in the alternatives available for the still unfilled requirements.

If it should happen that any device is usable by only one requirement, that allocation can be made at this time. In Fig. 6-8, device D1 should be allocated to fill requirement R1. The effect of this act must be incorporated into the ranges of eligible devices for other requirements. Even though none of those requirements could have been filled by this device, the list of eligible devices for those requirements may be affected because of a unit separation specification.

Assume:			Then:			
Devices eligible for each requirement are:			Requirements fillable by each device are:			
R1	R2	R3	D1	D2	D3	D4
D1	D2	D3	R1	R1	R2	R1
D2	D3	D4		R2	R3	R2
D4	D4					R3

R1, R2, and R3 are requirements for 1 device each.

D1, D2, D3 and D4 are I/O devices.

Fig. 6-8   Requirements fillable by each device.

Select and Allocate.   The reader may believe that allocation is nearly complete now, so a good strategy would be to assign devices arbitrarily and finish the job. Actually, only the trivial cases have been handled so far, and the most important part remains. The remaining unfilled requirements are such that the next allocation that should be made is not apparent. The point has been reached where judgment rather than fact must be used. From this point until allocation is complete, the process involves two steps used repeatedly: selecting an unfilled requirement and allocating an eligible device (or devices).

The following rules can be used to select an unfilled requirement in a rational, though possibly not optimal way. If two or more requirements are equally qualified under the first rule below, the tie is broken by the second rule, or failing that, by the third rule or, failing that, by the fourth.

1. Select the unfilled requirement that has the fewest eligible devices. Filling any other requirement first would have a high probability of making this requirement unfillable.
2. Select a requirement that is mentioned in a separation specification. Separation requirements can be satisfied best only while a relatively large selection of devices is available.
3. Select a requirement that is mentioned in a volume-affinity specification. Allocating for such a requirement has the advantage of satisfying two or more requirements with only modest reduction in the number of devices available for the remaining unfilled requirements.
4. Select a requirement arbitrarily.

The next step is to allocate devices to fill the requirement selected by the preceding rules. The following rules, used singly or in combination, can be applied to restrict the set of devices eligible to fill the selected requirement:

1. Select the devices that would be least usable in filling other requirements. The table of requirements fillable by each device, described in Fig. 6-8, can be used in this selection.
2. Eliminate all eligible devices except those on one selected channel. The selected channel should be the one that has the greatest number of available devices of the type required. This choice tends to leave a flexible arrangement of unallocated devices.
3. Eliminate all eligible devices except those that fall on a lightly loaded channel. Channel load might be estimated by the number of files allocated to devices on each channel. Such an estimation is probably worthwhile only if the channel-load information serves some additional purpose.
4. Select devices that already have mounted volumes that can be used. For example, sometimes a requirement for a magnetic tape volume can be satisfied by a tape volume that is already mounted on an eligible device. Selecting such a device reduces the amount of operator activity required.
5. Select devices in any order. This alternative has the advantage of simplicity.

Filling one requirement affects the alternatives available for the unfilled requirements. In Fig. 6-7, these effects are incorporated by the return path that restarts the entire demand allocation process. In practice, it may be possible to streamline the process by modifying existing tables rather than reconstructing tables as the flowchart indicates. One note of caution: Before each repetition of the decision-allocation process, any eligible devices eliminated by range reduction during the previous pass should be made eligible again. The decision process is such that a device considered undesirable on one pass may become the only eligible device on the next.

Public Space Allocation

Direct access storage devices can be used simultaneously by two or more unrelated programs with reasonable efficiency.

In EXEC-8, some direct access storage space is reserved for the system itself, and some is reserved for program libraries. All of the remaining space is considered to be public space that can be used to fill static or dynamic requests for storage space. The control program monitors the use of public space. If available public space is in short supply, the control program moves files that have had no recent activity to magnetic tape. If a user's program requests a file that has been moved to tape, the control program moves that file back to the public space.

When a system includes an adequate number of direct-access storage devices, it should be possible to satisfy a user's requirements at any time without advanced warning. Using this assumption, the scheduler can assume that requirements for public space need not be considered in scheduling users' programs, and the I/O system can perform both demand and decision allocation before considering requirements for public space. Should the public space available prove inadequate, the allocation recovery routines can attempt to provide an additional public volume.

Allocation Recovery

The allocation recovery routines solicit the operator's assistance to accomplish allocation when the requirements of a job cannot be met. Allocation recovery should be required infrequently because device allocation is attempted only after the job scheduler has determined that the requirements can be met. The only cases that will require allocation recovery are the following:

1. The scheduler's analysis was not detailed enough. For example, the scheduler's analysis might have ignored channel separation requirements.
2. The inventory of available devices changed after scheduler analysis and before device allocation. Reduction in available inventory could result from device failure or from dynamic allocation of devices from the available inventory.
3. Unusually large requirements for public storage space cause that space to be in short supply.

An attempted allocation might fail for lack of a specific device, devices of a certain type, or devices of a certain class. The appropriate action for the allocation recovery routines is to request operator assistance. Alternatives that can be offered to the operator include the following:

1. Make a device available. This might be done by canceling a low-priority program already running or by returning a device that had been undergoing routine maintenance to the system.
2. Change the requirement. The operator might decide that a channel separation specification should be ignored or that the requirement for

a particular device type should be changed to indicate a different device type.

3. Wait for a device to become available. If the operator knows that the requirement can be filled within a short time, waiting might be the best alternative.

4. Cancel the entire job. If the user's requirements cannot be met, canceling the job may be the only alternative.

Most enterprises can tolerate an occasional allocation-recovery situation. Intolerably high frequency of allocation recovery situations can be reduced by improving job-scheduler analysis, reducing the time between scheduler analysis and device allocation, limiting the use of dynamic allocation, and/or discouraging the use of devices that are in chronically short supply.

DYNAMIC ALLOCATION

The term *dynamic allocation* applies to the allocation of devices at the time of need without advance notification of expected need. The distinction between static and dynamic allocation can be illustrated by a simple example. Assume the control statements for job A specify that two magnetic tape units are required. Two appropriate units will be allocated before job A begins execution. That is static allocation. During execution of job A, assume a condition arises requiring some DASD space, possibly to contain a table that has grown to an unexpected size. At that time, job A could request allocation of a device; or more specifically, job A could request dynamic allocation of a device. From a control program viewpoint, dynamic allocation is significantly different from static allocation because the latter implies availability of information that can be used for scheduling work.

Dynamic allocation has several advantages:

1. Dynamic allocation reduces the period of time for which a device is allocated. Static allocation requires that a device be allocated for some time before its actual use.

2. Dynamic allocation can reduce the number of devices required by a user's program. The advance notification required for static allocation sometimes results in allocation of devices that may not be used at all.

3. Dynamic allocation used in conjunction with dynamic deallocation can further reduce the time period or the number of devices required.

4. Dynamic allocation allows scheduling of work on a strict priority basis, a simpler and more defensible basis than scheduling by availability of devices.

Completely general dynamic allocation would allow a user's program to request devices of any type at any time. The problems in filling such requests are apparent; there is little that can be done to plan for an unforeseeable requirement. Consequently, dynamic allocation facilities of most systems are limited or nonexistent.

EXEC-8 includes a dynamic allocation capability, so it will be used for illustrations. Figure 6-9 shows the sequence of instructions a user's program would execute to cause dynamic allocation. A system call, such as that illustrated, is a formal request by a user's program for some control program service. (System calls are very important to discussions in later chapters, but we shall not examine them thoroughly here because our immediate concern with them is limited.) The system call illustrated simply presents a control statement to the control program. That control statement is identical in form and content to an EXEC-8 control statement that would be presented for static allocation. The ability of the EXEC-8 control program to accept a control statement in this way is quite unusual. The less structured and coded forms of control statements in many other systems would mitigate against such a capability.

Location	Operation/operand	Interpretation
	LA A0, LOC	Load the address (LOC) of the control statement into register A0
	ER CSF$	Executive request (system call) for Control Statement Format service
	(next instruction)	
LOC	@ASG,T FILE1, 8C	Assign (ASG) a magnetic tape unit of type 8C for a temporary (T) file named FILE1

Fig. 6-9   A dynamic request for an I/O device (EXEC-8).

Deadlock

If a unit of the type required is available, it can be allocated immediately. If not, the I/O system has no choice but to delay the user's program until such a unit becomes available. The principal challenge in designing a dynamic allocation feature is to provide a useful feature while keeping the enforced delays to a reasonable level. Delays that arise during dynamic allocation are particularly serious for two reasons:

1. The resources already allocated to a user's program are idled during the waiting period. This reduces overall productivity of the system.
2. A combination of dynamic allocation requests can result in a condition called *deadlock* where two or more users' programs experience permanent delay. A deadlock can occur quite easily as the following example suggests. If program 1 is using device A and program 1 requests device B, but program 2 is using device B, program 1 will have to wait. Now, if program 2 requests device A, program 2 will also have to wait.

Deadlocks can be quite complex, involving several programs and a variety of resources. It is often difficult to detect a deadlock and, furthermore, the alternatives available for resolving deadlock are all unattractive. To detect an impending deadlock is more difficult still and is not within the state of the programming art.

Avoiding Deadlock. Fortunately, there are several known techniques for avoiding deadlock. An excellent practical discussion of the subject was presented by Mr. James Havender in 1968.[1]

One deadlock-avoiding technique was inherent in the static allocation process described earlier, though it may have passed unnoticed. The technique is an all-or-nothing technique as follows: If all of the resources required for a user's program are available, they should be allocated. If one or more resources are not available, all resources already allocated should be freed. The philosophy in the all-or-nothing technique is simply that a program that has all the resources it needs cannot be involved in a deadlock, nor can a program that has no resources at all.

Dynamic allocation is exposed to deadlock because it tends to violate the all-or-nothing philosophy. A technique involving a pool of resources can avoid the threat of deadlock. All of the I/O devices allocated to a user's program can be considered the user's facility pool. The pool is created by the static allocation routines. Whenever a user's program dynamically requests a device, the system assigns a device from the user's device pool if possible. By ensuring that the pool includes appropriate devices, a user can avoid the delays and deadlocks that might otherwise result. Figure 6-10 illustrates two forms of a system call that can be used to free a device. One form is used to make the device available within the user's device pool, and the other is used to deallocate and free the device completely.

Location	Operation/operand	Interpretation
	LA AO, IADD	Load the address (IADD) of the control statement into register AO
	ER CSF$	Execute request (system call) for Control Statement Format service
or { IADD	@FREE,S F1	Free the device that has been used with file F1 but retain it in the device pool
IADD	@FREE F1	Free and deallocate the device that has been used with file F1

Fig. 6-10 Freeing a device (EXEC-8).

Another technique for avoiding deadlock is to limit dynamic requests to those resources that are available in virtually unlimited supply. The best, and possibly the only good example of such an I/O resource, is public direct access storage space. If a user's dynamic requirements are limited to the use of public space and if reasonable bounds are placed on the amount of public space available to each user, dynamic allocation can be highly useful and efficient. The dynamic request shown earlier in Fig. 6-9 can be used to request public space simply by changing the device-type parameter appropriately. A

[1] J. W. Havender, "Avoiding Deadlock in Multitasking Systems," *IBM Systems Journal*, No. 2, 1968.

virtually infinite supply of public DASD space can be maintained by staging inactive files off direct access storage devices onto magnetic tapes as suggested early in this chapter.

A final alternative technique for avoiding deadlock is to consider all dynamic allocation requests to be refusable. That is, to require the user's program to be capable of accepting "no" as an answer. In practice, a "no" answer probably means that the user's program would prematurely terminate processing, necessitating a rerun later. If the odds are such that "no" occurs infrequently, rerunning may be acceptable. After all, if a user feels the rerun cannot be afforded, the risk can be avoided by using static allocation only.

AUTOMATIC VOLUME RECOGNITION

The methods of allocating devices usually accepted as standard are the static and, to a lesser extent, the dynamic methods described earlier. A feature usable with either static or dynamic allocation that allows the operator to mount volumes on any available I/O units can be called *automatic volume recognition*. The justifications for the feature are the following:

1. It improves system efficiency by allowing the operator to mount volumes considerably ahead of need.
2. It simplifies the operator's job by allowing the operator to mount volumes without detailed instructions.

An incidental result is that the operator either consciously or unconsciously makes device allocation decisions for the system.

Automatic volume recognition is fundamentally simple. Some of its principal features are as follows:

1. The operators understand that they should mount volumes appropriately for the programs that will be executed soon. The system must keep the operator informed of expected running order.
2. Whenever the operator mounts a volume on an available device, his or her manipulation of the device controls causes the interruption system to be activated. The I/O system responds to the interrupt and records the operator action appropriately. Automatic volume recognition is readily practical only for devices that activate the system interruption system during the mounting process.
3. The automatic volume recognition routines periodically search the unit tables, looking for indications of operator activity. When an activity is detected, the label is read from the mounted volume and recorded in the unit table. By implication, automatic volume recognition can be used only with volumes having standard labels.
4. When device requirements of a job are being processed by the static allocation routines, many of the required volumes will be found already mounted, and the associated devices can be allocated at that time.

5. If some of the required volumes have not been mounted in advance, the static allocation routines can allocate devices for them in the usual way.

SUMMARY

The control program maintains the inventory of all I/O devices, using bit masks and unit tables. The inventory information includes the number of devices of each type and of each class attached to the system and the status of each device. Status information that affects allocation of a device includes whether a device is available to the system, whether it is serving a special purpose within the system, and whether it is currently allocated.

Static allocation is performed at the instigation of the job scheduler before a user's program begins execution. Static allocation is performed in stages as follows:

1. Demand allocation that allocates devices for requirements that can be filled in only one way. Examples include a requirement for a specific I/O unit for a particular already-mounted volume or for a number of units that happen to match exactly the number available.
2. Decision allocation that allocates devices when available devices exceed requirements. A rational process is used repeatedly filling one requirement on each repetition.
3. Public space allocation that allocates generally usable space on direct access storage devices. Public space is allocated last because, under proper constraints, it is available in virtually infinite supply.
4. Allocation recovery that solicits operator assistance when available resources fall short of requirements.

Dynamic allocation routines are used to satisfy requirements presented by a user's program during the latter's execution. If a dynamic request cannot be satisfied immediately, the user's program must be delayed. A combination of interlocking requests can cause permanent delay or deadlock. Using a facility pool or limiting dynamic requests to public space on direct access storage devices can reduce or eliminate both problems. Still another technique is to consider dynamic requests to be refusable.

Automatic volume recognition is an allocation feature that allows the operator to mount volumes at his convenience and, in so doing, to improve system efficiency and, incidentally, to make allocation decisions for the system. The feature requires an interruption system that is activated by the volume mounting procedure, and it requires standard volume labels.

Exercises

1.(e) Using the operations AND, OR, and NOT, describe how the bit masks in Fig. 6-2 could be used to develop a bit mask indicating which devices are both type ABC and allocated. Display the resulting mask.

2.(e) All systems identify the two device states, available and unavailable. Why do some systems include a third state—scheduled to become unavailable?

3.(e) Why would a strategy of allocating the device that can fill the fewest requirements be inappropriate during demand allocation?

4.(m) Devise a simple example in which demand allocation of devices to satisfy one requirement would cause another unfilled requirement to become a demand allocation situation.

5.(m) When a control statement specifies two units of a certain class, why might it be unacceptable to allocate units of differing types?

6.(m) What possible disadvantage can you envision if public space allocation is accomplished before the other steps in static allocation?

7.(m) It was stated without explanation that control statement forms that are not rigidly structured might be impractical vehicles for communicating dynamic allocation requirements. Suggest why this is so.

8.(m) A technique for avoiding deadlock not mentioned earlier uses an arbitrary but fixed ordering of I/O units. Every job is constrained to request dynamically only those units that are farther down the list than all other units they currently hold. Devise an example that illustrates why jobs using the rule cannot deadlock.

9.(m) While dynamic allocation is appealing from a user's point of view, it has aspects that detract from system performance. Aside from the possibility of delay due to unavailability of requested devices, what performance problems could you envision from widespread general use of dynamic allocation?

7 Opening and Closing Files

There are two major categories of information that must be communicated between a user and the I/O system: resource requirements and processing specifications. Resource requirements were discussed in Chap. 5, "Control Statements." This chapter and the next describe the portions of the I/O system that respond to the user's requests to prepare files for processing and to store and retrieve data. (See Fig. 7-1.) These interface portions of the I/O system are sometimes called the *logical input/output control system* (*LIOCS*) or *the access methods*. LIOCS (pronounced lie-ox) was coined to distinguish that part of the I/O system that interacts with the user's program, from the *physical input/output control system* (*PIOCS*). PIOCS is the part that schedules and initiates channel activity and responds to the computer interruption system. The term LIOCS and PIOCS are going out of style; *the access methods* and *the I/O supervisor* are more current terminology.

Before discussing the actual processing specifications, we shall examine the mechanisms available to the user's program for communicating these specifications.

COMMUNICATION MECHANISMS

From the application programmer's view, all interfaces to the operating system may be described in a language manual for, say, COBOL. In actuality, the COBOL manual describes a comprehensive I/O interface that is only indirectly related to the I/O system interface. The COBOL user's statement of the I/O parameters is actually a statement to the COBOL language processor. The latter converts the user's statements to a combination of system calls, tables, and exits that are the real interfaces to the I/O system. Figure 7-2 illustrates the process. Notice that the COBOL processor itself uses calls, tables, and exits. These three mechanisms, system calls, tables, and exits are described in the following three sections.

System Calls

The system call is a sequence of one or more instructions resulting in transfer of CPU control from the user's program to the I/O system. The instructions may be augmented by parameters placed in registers or in locations having predefined positions relative to the instruction sequence. The final instruction

in the sequence is frequently an instruction that activates the system interruption mechanism, but it may be a simple branching instruction. A system
call usually includes one or more return points predefined as the points where
the user's program should resume execution; the choice of return points depends
on the outcome of the service requested by the call. Frequently, the normal
return point is the instruction following the call.

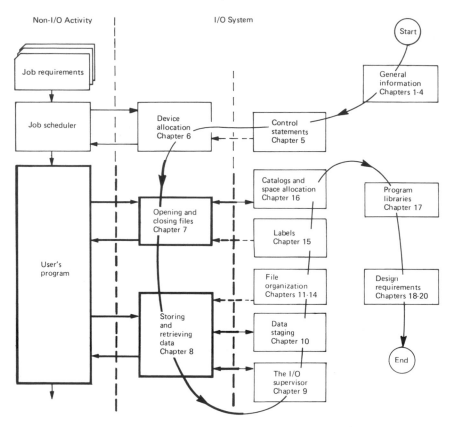

Fig. 7-1   The user's program and I/O system interfaces.

In the instruction manuals for most current systems, the system call is
described as a macro instruction. This designation is a little misleading because
the real interface is a combination of bit settings, instructions, and return
conventions. The use of a macro statement for this purpose presupposes the
use of a macro assembler. A few years ago, that supposition was valid: Many
early language processors converted source language to assembler source
language, and a separate process converted assembler language to object-
program form. Most modern language processors avoid the inefficiency of this
cascading procedure. However, the macro form probably will continue to exist
both because the system designer is typically expert in assembler language
and because no better alternative has been discovered. Some examples of the
macro form of system calls are shown in Fig. 7-3.

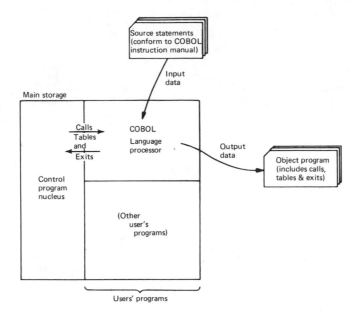

Fig. 7-2   A language processor creates calls, tables, and exits.

System		
TSOS	GET TAB,LOC	
	Literal meaning:	GET the record that is next in sequence from the file identified by the table named TAB, and place it in main-storage location LOC.
EXEC-8	OPEN 'OUTPUT' TAB	
	Literal meaning:	OPEN the file related to the table named TAB and prepare to OUTPUT data.
SCOPE	CLOSE FILE1, UNLOAD	
	Literal meaning:	CLOSE the file named FILE1 and UNLOAD the storage volume.

Fig. 7-3   Examples of the macro forms of system calls.

Tables

The second mechanism available for the I/O system interface is the table. The term *table* should be interpreted as "a condensed enumeration of items" rather than the more familiar "an arrangement of items in rows and columns." Other terms sometimes used with the same intent are *control block* and *list*. There are no formal rules that govern table size or information content. Typically, a table might contain 50 to 500 characters of information. One kind of table, a unit table that contains information about a particular I/O unit,

Common Segment

UNIT CONTROL BLOCK

0 (0) SRTEJBNR Internal job no.	1 (1) SRTECHAN Allocation channel mask	2 (2) UCBID Identifier	3 (3) SRTES Status
4 (4) UCBCHA Channel address and flags	5 (5) UCBUA Unit Address	6 (6) UCBFL1 Flag byte 1	7 (7) I Index
8 (8) UCBETI Error routine ID	9 (9) UCBSTI Statistics table index	10 (A) UCBLCI Logical channel word table index	11 (B)
12 (C) UCBWGT Flags and mask	13 (D)		
16 (10)			
20 (14)			

Offset		Bytes and Alignment	Field Name	Field Description, Contents, Meaning
0	(0)	1	SRTEJBNR	Internal job identification.
			xxxx	Job protection key − set if the mounted volume is to be retained or contain a passed data set.
			.... 00..	Zeros
			....1.	Set during device allocation if the volume is to be demounted and is retained or contains a passed data set. Causes job name in demount message.
			1	Set during device allocation if the volume to be mounted is to be retained or contain a passed data set.
1	(1)	. 1	SRTECHAN	Allocation channel mask.
2	(2)	.. 1	UCBID	UCB identification − Hex FF.
3				(not shown above)
4	(4)	1	UCBCHA	Channel address.
			1.......	Halt I/O.
			.1......	Status modifier.
			..xx x...	(Reserved bits)
			xxx	Channel address − binary number.
5	(5)	. 1	UCBUA	Unit address.
6	(6)	.. 1	UCBFL1	Flag byte 1.
			1.......	Busy − Device status.
			.1......	Not-ready − Device status.
			..x.....	Post flag.
			..0.....	No channel program is being executed using this device.
			..1.....	A channel program using this device has not yet been posted as having completed.
			...1....	After a channel end status a separate device end status occurred with an error indication. (IOB-Intercept flag.)
			.... 1...	Busy − Control unit status.
			.... .xx.	Direct access storage devices:
			.... .01.	Stand-alone channel program of I/O supervisor is being or was executed. (Arm seeking.)
			.... .11.	User's channel program is being executed. (Data transfer.)
			.... .01.	Telecommunications devices: Inhibit HIO instruction because the line is in receive status.
			 1	I/O error routine is in control of this device. No other I/O operations are permitted on this device.
7	(7)	... 1	UCBDTI	Index to the Device Table.
8	(8)	1	UCBETI	A binary number used by the exit effector routine to complete the 8 byte name of an IBM-supplied error routine for this device.
9	(9)	. 1	UCBSTI	Increment which, when multiplied by 10, becomes an index to the Statistics Table (STATAB).
10	(A)	.. 1	UCBLCI	Increment which, when multiplied by 8, becomes an index to the Logical Channel Table (LCHTAB).
11	(B)	... 1	UCBATI	Index to the Attention Table (ANTAB).
12	(C)	1	UCBWGT	Flags and channel mask.
			1.......	SYSIN.
			.1......	SYSOUT.
			..1.....	Assumed that this device will be allocated for a public volume request.
			...1....	Rewind command has been addressed to this magnetic device by I/O support.
			 xxxx	I/O Supervisor path mask. (Used where there are two or more paths to a device):
			.... 1...	Primary path to the device is inoperative.
			.... .1..	Optional path 1 to the device is inoperative.
			..... .1.	Optional path 2 to the device is inoperative.
			1	Optional path 3 to the device is inoperative.

Fig. 7-4   An actual table definition from OS/360.

was described in the preceding chapter. A detailed description of a portion of a unit table is shown in Fig. 7-4. That depth of detail is not pertinent for our purposes; the sample is presented to illustrate the amount of detail actually required.

The really important characteristic of a table is that it is formally and meticulously described. Interface table definitions must be carefully devised because they will be used widely. The expense resulting from a change to a table definition will be high, and, even more important, the extent of the effects will be difficult to determine. Two examples illustrate this point. The first concerns timing. Interface tables contain values that are set by the I/O system for use by the user's program. The table definition should indicate just when the values are set or modified. If not, the user's program may experience intermittent problems very difficult to analyze. The second example concerns unused fields. Tables frequently include space that is intended for use at some undefined later time. If the table description simply labels such fields "not used," an ingenious user might find a good use that will cause a problem later. A more precise labeling would say "reserved for control program use." Table names become an important part of the everyday vocabulary of system programmers, a vocabulary that evolves as systems are designed, developed, and replaced.

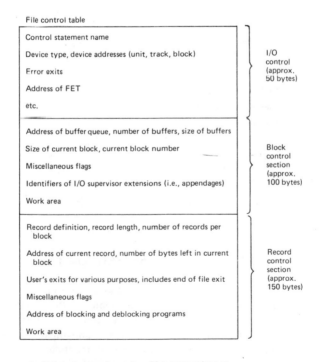

File control table

Control statement name	
Device type, device addresses (unit, track, block)	I/O control (approx. 50 bytes)
Error exits	
Address of FET	
etc.	

Address of buffer queue, number of buffers, size of buffers	
Size of current block, current block number	Block control section (approx. 100 bytes)
Miscellaneous flags	
Identifiers of I/O supervisor extensions (i.e., appendages)	
Work area	

Record definition, record length, number of records per block	
Address of current record, number of bytes left in current block	Record control section (approx. 150 bytes)
User's exits for various purposes, includes end of file exit	
Miscellaneous flags	
Address of blocking and deblocking programs	
Work area	

An FCT can be as small as perhaps 50 bytes or as large as 300 bytes, depending on options used.

Fig. 7-5   A file-control table (FCT) simplified.

The table is a convenient complement to the system call. When the number of parameters being passed to the I/O system by a system call becomes large or when the same parameters apply to several situations, the use of a table to hold that information is convenient and efficient. Of the illustrations in Fig. 7-3, two explicitly contain the names of tables, and the third contains a parameter that is used to identify a table.

Examples of tables are shown in Figs. 7-5 to 7-7. The three shown are not just casual examples; they are present in nearly every contemporary operating system, and they are fundamentally important to understanding I/O systems. The examples are simplified by the omission of a great amount of detail. As a case in point, the OS/360 version of the table in Fig. 7-4 is the data-control block (DCB). That block, in its various forms, requires 66 full-size pages for its definition.[1] The names *file-control table* (*FCT*), *file-extent table* (*FET*), and *I/O unit table* (*UT*) are not taken from any particular system, though they may be found in some contemporary systems. The abbreviations FCT, FET, and UT are worth remembering. They are used throughout the remainder of the book.

File extent table

Address of FCT
Address of UT
Addresses of I/O supervisor extensions (i.e., appendages)
Extents (beginning and ending addresses)
File protection information
Processing priority of this file
Addresses of access method programs
Number of volumes in file
Current volume number
etc.

An extent is a portion of a file discontiguous from other portions of the file on a single DASD volume.

An FET can be as small as perhaps 50 bytes or as large as several hundred bytes, depending on device type and number of extents.

Fig. 7-6   A file-extent table (FET) simplified.

The FCT (Fig. 7-5) is a table within the user's main storage space. It contains information about a particular file. Some of the information in the FCT is kept up to date by the I/O system whenever the file is open. Other fields within the FCT are used by the I/O system and must be maintained by the user's program. The table itself and some of the fields initially within it are created by the user's program. As mentioned earlier, that usually means that a language processor must generate an object program that has one or more FCTs, one for each file to be processed.

[1] "IBM System/360 Operating System: System Control Blocks," form #GC28-6628.

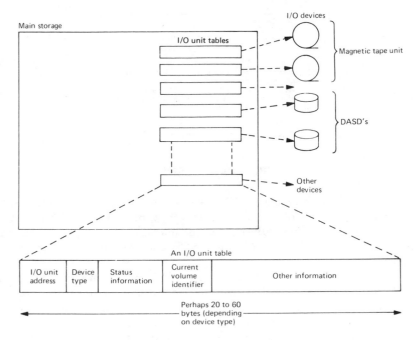

Fig. 7-7   I/O unit tables.

The OPEN macro constructs an FET (Fig. 7-6) as a convenient storage place for information about the file being opened. An FET contains information that is of no interest to the user's program or that must be protected from the user's program. An example of data that must be protected is the extent information that gives the table its name. The extents indicate the boundaries of the file. If the user's program were capable of changing the extents, the user could gain unauthorized access to other files.

Figure 7-7, I/O unit tables, is a duplicate of a figure from the preceding chapter, repeated here for convenience.

Exits

An exit is a mechanism that allows the I/O system to relinquish control of the CPU to the user's program under certain prearranged circumstances. For example, the user's program might include a procedure for dealing with illegible records. If the I/O system encounters a data record that it cannot retrieve correctly, the I/O system causes the CPU to begin executing the user's special procedure. The existence and location of such a procedure must be communicated by one of the other mechanisms. The address of an exit can be communicated as a parameter in a register during a related system call, or as an entry in a table, or an exit address can be communicated by a system call expressly for that purpose. The latter method is illustrated in Fig. 7-8. Exits are sometimes termed *system exits* and sometimes *user exits;* the choice depends entirely on point of view. An exit from the control program is an exit to the user's program.

Operation	Operands
EXLST	OPENX=LOC1,NOSPACE=LOC2

This system call communicates a list of exits. LOC1 contains the first instruction of a user's routine that must be executed during file opening and LOC2 begins a routine to be executed if the system is unable to furnish the storage space required by the user's program.

Fig. 7-8   A list of system exits (TSOS).

FILE PROCESSING

The major contemporary I/O systems require the user's program to notify the I/O system of an intent to process a particular file by issuing a system call named OPEN. OPEN, and its antithesis, CLOSE, constitute the file-related processes. Most of our discussion concerns OPEN; it is the more complex macro.

OPEN and CLOSE are carry-overs from the manual processing of records. Records in a manual system are paper documents that are stored in a file cabinet. If a record is to be stored or retrieved, the cabinet must be opened. If one were planning to process many records in a limited period of time and if opening the cabinet required special authority, one might open the cabinet as a separate operation and, for convenience and efficiency, leave it open but guarded during the record processing period.

Carrying the clerical analogy one step further, there is no reason that opening the cabinet should be required as a separate operation. Clerks frequently open and close filing cabinets as an incidental action in processing of individual records. As operating systems tend toward individual transaction processing, the formal use of the OPEN macro becomes less desirable.

Even in batch processing, the requirement to OPEN a file is a nuisance. FORTRAN, the most widely known of all programming languages, has no OPEN statement. FORTRAN programs simply begin to READ or WRITE files without ado. This characteristic presents a serious challenge to the language processor because the object program must include an OPEN for each file to be processed. Nor can the language processor simply search a source program serially to detect the first activity for any file because there is no assurance that program statements will be executed in that order. The solution is this: The object program can include an I/O coordinating subroutine that monitors all use of files for that object program. When an unannounced READ or WRITE occurs, the coordinating subroutine must issue the required OPEN.

As the example in Fig. 7-3 suggests, the OPEN macro conveys no essential information from the user's program that could not be conveyed by other means. In the future, I/O systems will probably not require the user's program to issue an OPEN request, but, rather, will assume that the file should be opened when the user's program requests the first record. The activities ascribed to OPEN on the next several pages would apply whether OPEN were explicit or implied.

Before discussing details of OPEN and CLOSE, it may be worthwhile to clarify a confusing point of terminology. OPEN is the name of an assembler language macro instruction, and it is the name of a particular type of system call. But OPEN is also the name of all of the code in the I/O system that exists for the purpose of preparing a file for processing. To make matters even worse, in the spoken system programming vocabulary, all three or any one of them may be called *the OPEN macro* to distinguish OPEN from the identically pronounced English-language verb "open." The same terminology conventions apply to CLOSE.

The OPEN Macro

Depending on system design, OPEN can be a minor operation consisting of little more than the volume positioning abilities described below, or it may be one of the most extensive and intricate parcels of code in the I/O system. The major responsibilities of OPEN are to get the file ready for processing, initialize system tables as required, and generally check on dozens of details to ensure that the subsequent record and block processing can be performed correctly and efficiently. The activities accomplished by OPEN usually include:

- volume mounting
- volume label verification
- volume positioning for file access
- file label processing
- initializing tables and table values
- preparing system programs as required
- initial filling of buffers (possibly)

Each of these seven activities is discussed as a separate topic on the next several pages.

One factor that complicates OPEN is that some of the processing that OPEN is prepared to accomplish may have been accomplished before the OPEN call was issued. For example, if a particular file has been opened and closed earlier by the same user's program now requesting an OPEN, volume mounting, volume label verification, and volume positioning may not be required. It is characteristic of OPEN that a great many minor actions must be performed, the specific actions depending on clues that may be found in several tables.

The flowchart shown in Fig. 7-9 indicates a few of the alternatives and also indicates the approximate sequence of activities. Logically, activity 1 must precede 2 and, unless one would risk positioning the wrong volume, 2 must precede 3. Activities 4 and 5 must use the file label and, therefore, cannot precede 3. Activity 5 could precede 4 but, because 4 might terminate the process prematurely, it makes sense to do it first. Activity 6 could be done at any time. Number 7 must be done last because it uses connections established in the earlier activities; it constitutes preliminary file processing.

Connecting a User's Program and Its Data.   The activities of OPEN are so varied and intricate that one could easily miss the essential point. The essence of OPEN is to connect a user's program and its data.

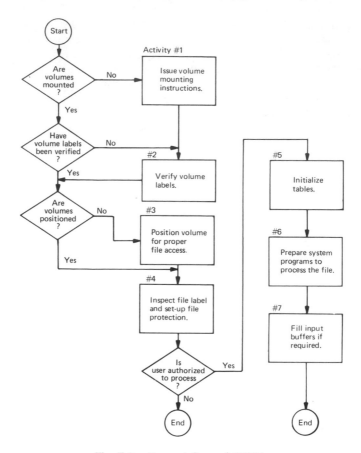

Fig. 7-9   General flow of OPEN.

The FCT, FET, and UT were chosen as table examples earlier because the three of them have very important relationships. Figure 7-10 shows the FCT in the user program's area. It contains information useful to the user's program and to the I/O system. It serves as a repository for static information about a particular file and as a place where the user's program and the I/O system can leave messages for each other. The FET resides outside the user's program area where it is protected from the user's program by computer-imposed addressing restrictions. The FCT contains the address of the related FET and vice versa. These addresses can be seen in Figs. 7-5 and 7-6. The FET contains information that, if changed accidentally or intentionally by a user's program, might cause problems in continued operation of the I/O system or compromise of data not related to the user's program. The FET contains the address of the UT, and the UT identifies a particular I/O device. These addresses establish the chain shown in Fig. 7-10, which relates a particular file to a particular device. Link number 1 in that chain is established by the language processor that prepares the user's program. Link number 4 is established permanently by the system generation process. Links 2 and 3 must be established by OPEN.

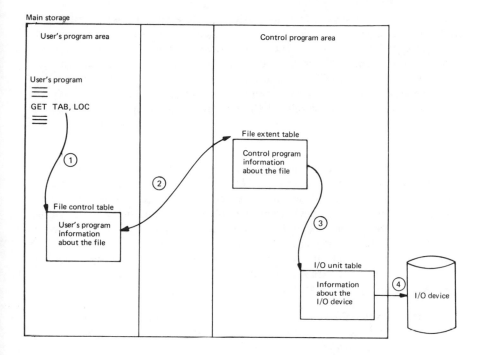

Fig. 7-10   Connection between an I/O request and an I/O device.

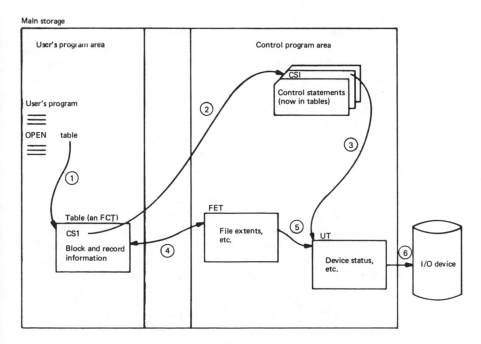

Fig. 7-11   OPEN uses a control statement name.

The vital piece of information necessary to establish links 2 and 3 is, of course, the control statement name included in the FCT. This idea was explained earlier in Chap. 5, but its importance justifies repetition. Refer now to Fig. 7-11. Link 1 is established by the language processor. Link 2 exists logically, but it is OPEN's responsibility to search the names of the control statements, by now firmly encoded in main storage, to locate the one named in the FCT. Link 3 was established during device allocation. Now OPEN can establish links 4 and 5 as it creates the FET. Link 6 is, of course, the permanent link of a UT and the device it represents.

Volume Mounting. Frequently, the file that is being opened resides on demountable storage volumes. In many cases, the volume mounting instructions to the operator are issued during device allocation before the user's program is initiated, but there are cases when the volume mounting instructions will not have been issued. For example, if a single magnetic tape unit is used to process two different magnetic tape files for a single user's program, the OPEN related to the second file will surely find that the volume has not been mounted. A few of the questions that must be answered and actions that must be taken by OPEN are as follows:

1. Are volume identification codes available? These codes may already be in tables as a result of control statement processing. If not, they must be retrieved from the file catalog.
2. In what order will the volumes be processed? In most cases, volumes will be processed in their natural order. Exceptional cases include the intent to extend an existing multivolume file and the intent to process a file in reverse order. These cases are identified by combinations of parameters furnished with the OPEN macro and in control statements.
3. Are the necessary volumes already mounted? In many cases, volume mounting is not required because the volume either is permanently mounted or already has been mounted for this or some previous operation or because the user has indicated no preference for a particular volume.
4. If volumes are not already mounted, have mounting instructions been issued? In many systems, mounting instructions are issued to the operator as soon as a device has been allocated. But because the appropriate operator action may take several minutes, an indicator is set in the UT to indicate that instructions have been issued and verification of the action is delayed as long as possible, notably until opening. If mounting instructions have not been issued, OPEN must issue them. If instructions have been issued but mounting has not been accomplished, OPEN should relinquish control of the system, asking to be notified when the operator has complied.

Volume Label Verification. Storage volumes are usually, though not always, identified by labels that can be inspected or modified by the I/O system just as can any other data recorded on a volume. Such labels may be called machine readable labels when it is necessary to differentiate them from the visible labels that are an aid to the operator. The form and content of volume labels are described in Chap. 15; those details need not concern us here.

It is possible that the volume labels of the volumes containing a particular file have been verified to ensure that mounting instructions were executed correctly. Volume labels will have been verified if the volumes have been used in previous processes and have not been demounted. In many computers, the operating system can determine when the operator demounts one volume and mounts another because that action activates the interruption system.

Volume label verification is usually a simple process; the label is read, and critical information, including at least the volume identification code, is compared against the expected value. Comparison failure is followed by appropriate operator instructions.

There are several unusual cases that must be accommodated or disallowed. Common sense dictates that one will disallow all of the following cases unless one's audience demands them:

1. The expected volume is labeled with a label whose format is foreign to the I/O system. One method for handling this case is to utilize a system exit to let the user's program accomplish label verification. If this is done, the user's exit program should perhaps be required to accomplish volume positioning and file label handling as well; foreign labels might imply foreign volume formatting conventions as well. The responsibilities of the user's program and the tools available for its use must, of course, be documented in a user's manual.

2. The expected volume is unlabeled, but it is legible. OPEN should verify that the volume does not have a standard label. There is not much that an I/O system can do to protect the data on unlabeled volumes from accidental or intentional compromise, but protection of labeled data cannot be guaranteed unless every volume is checked for recognizable labels.

3. The expected volume is unlabeled, and it is illegible. Sometimes operating systems are required to tolerate processing of stored data that do not conform to I/O system conventions. An example might be engineering test data recorded on magnetic tape without interblock gaps. Philosophically, OPEN should attempt to verify that the volume does not have a standard volume label. In practice, such an attempt might yield incomprehensible results and might result in improper positioning of the recorded medium. If such data must be processed by the system, a good design might require the operator to confirm that the volume has been mounted properly. The confirmation would imply that the operator is personally aware that the intended processing is appropriate.

4. The expected volume is legible, and it is either labeled or unlabeled, but one or more of the recording parameters is not known. An example might be a parameter that identifies one of several character representations for magnetic tape. This case is mentioned because it is a hazardous case. A system designer might conclude that OPEN should be coded to try all possible parameter values systematically

until trial and error reveals the proper combination. Experience has shown that because the proper combination of parameters occasionally may fail to produce correct results, such a design should be avoided, at least for devices with a relatively high error rate.

Volume Positioning.   If there is programming required to position the medium for processing, OPEN may be required to accomplish the positioning. One example is positioning to a fresh page on a printer. A more difficult example for media currently in use is magnetic tape. This seemingly trivial function is actually quite complex. Some of the concerns are as follows:

1. For unlabeled tape, there is no way to verify that the desired position has actually been reached. Positioning may require execution of several channel programs. In cases where the tape itself is not in excellent condition, there is a significant possibility that the final position may not be correct.
2. For tapes with labels foreign to the I/O system, positioning is complicated by the unknown format of the labels. If a convention can be designed for accommodating the unknown label format, positioning is conceptually possible, and proper positioning can be verified by the user as the (foreign) file labels are verified. As suggested earlier, a better solution may be to require the user's program to position the tape.
3. Positioning depends on the nature of processing intended. If the user's program intends to either extend an existing file or read an existing file backward, the volume must be positioned differently from the normal forward processing position. Clues that affect positioning can be parameters furnished with OPEN either alone or in combination with control statement parameters.

File Label Processing.   Filing cabinets and the drawers in them are often labeled for quick and certain identification. In the same way, storage volumes and files may have labels that can be read and written by an operating system. Volume labels serve primarily to identify volumes. File labels serve to identify, and they contain some very important descriptive information. Some of the items of file label information that OPEN uses to identify and protect a file are as follows:

File Name   The use of a file name to identify a file protects data from accidental damage. In the case of magnetic tape, OPEN can use the file name to verify that the medium has been positioned correctly. For DASDs, OPEN can use the file name to identify the label and thereby to gain access to the contents of the label.

Expiration Date   The expiration date recorded in a file label is a date set by the creator of the file. If that date has not yet passed, OPEN should set a flag indicating that no output activity should be allowed. The OPEN shown in Fig. 7-3 indicates the user's intent to perform output operations. If the expiration date has not passed and the user's program indicates an intent to perform output, OPEN can perform the following functions:

1. Terminate the user's program. This has the disadvantage that it is too severe, possibly costing rerun of a large amount of work.
2. Request the operator to either override the expiration date or terminate the user's program. This alternative has the disadvantage that it asks the operator to make a judgment, probably without adequate information.
3. Set the flag mentioned earlier and let the I/O system deal with the problem when and if output is actually attempted. This may be the best alternative. It has the advantage that it defers action on a condition that may not materialize. Language processors frequently generate programs that indicate an output intent, but that may not actually accomplish output.

Passwords and/or Permissions   It is OPEN's responsibility to confirm that the user is authorized to use the file being requested. The file label will indicate whether passwords and/or permissions apply to this file. This subject is discussed in detail in Chap. 18, "Operating Characteristics."

Most of the above discussion applies to the processing of existing labels. When a new file is being opened, the OPEN macro must create the file labels. Information to be included is available from the FCT and the control statement.

Table Initializing.   OPEN is responsible for initializing certain main storage tables indicating the status of the file and arranging parameters for convenience in file processing. Examples include a flag indicating that the file is open, counters for the records and blocks processed, record and block sizes, and many others. There are at least three possible sources for many of these parameters, such as record length:

A Table Entry   The user's program may have specified record length by entry in an FCT. Such a specification is typically made in the user's source program, but may have been made by computation within the user's program at any time before OPEN.
A Control Statement   Sometimes parameters such as record length are stated in the control statement that is related to the file being opened.
The File Labels   If the file was created at some earlier time (as opposed to being created at this time) and the file has labels, the record length specification will be in the file labels.

When a user's program is creating a new file with labels, several of the parameters describing records and blocks must be recorded in the labels. Clearly, the values recorded should be the ones that were actually used. When an existing file is being modified, the decision is more difficult. For example, if new blocks added to a file are of one size and old blocks are of another, there are potential problems with either choice. At the very least, OPEN should issue a message to the user (not the operator, but the user) indicating what has been done.

Preparing System Programs.   The occurrence of an OPEN serves as a warning that record and block processing are about to begin. Record and block processing can be accomplished by any of several programs, such as the READ macro or the GET macro. Which programs will be required is determined by the kinds of requests the user's program will make and the way the file is organized. A collection of programs that can provide a particular class of services for one particular file organization is called an access method. If system design is such that the access method programs are not always available at fixed locations in main storage, OPEN must cause the required programs to be placed in main storage and establish table entries identifying them. Figure 7-5, illustrating an FCT, includes addresses of blocking and deblocking programs. Figure 7-6, an FET, includes other access method programs. Access methods are the subject of the next chapter.

Initial Filling of Buffers. If a file is to be read sequentially using an access method and buffers have been provided, the access methods will be responsible for keeping the buffers filled. Normally, buffers become available for filling one at a time as the user's program works its way through the buffered records. At OPEN time all buffers are empty. The process of filling the buffers initially is called buffer priming. Buffer priming can be accomplished by OPEN, or it can be accomplished by modest extension of the access method programs. The primary advantage in designing OPEN to accomplish buffer priming is that some code is removed from the access method programs, thereby improving the performance of those frequently used programs. The disadvantages are as follows:

1. Buffering and buffer control are appropriate concerns of an access method. It is architecturally undesirable for the details of buffering and buffer control to affect OPEN.
2. The amount of code that must be added to OPEN to perform this function is usually more than would be required in the access method programs. Careful design of the access method programs might furnish buffer priming with very few added instructions.
3. There are times other than OPEN when buffers require priming. For example, the user's program might occasionally instruct the access method to discontinue the current sequence and begin a new sequence of records at some arbitrary point in the file. Because the access method programs must be prepared to handle these other cases, it is quite natural to have them handle the OPEN time case as well.

The better choice leaves buffer priming to the access methods. Contemporary systems are split on this question.

The CLOSE Macro

The CLOSE macro is used to terminate processing of a file or section of a file. Its two major variations are illustrated in Fig. 7-12. CLOSE 'FILE' is used to terminate processing of the entire file. CLOSE 'REEL' is used to terminate processing of the portion of a file contained on the volume currently being processed and to automatically prepare the next volume of the file for processing. The term CLOSE "REEL" used in EXEC-8 implies the use of magnetic tape. OS/360 uses FEOV (force end of volume), which is more general but less phonetic. A better term might be CLOSE VOLUME, the term we shall use in this book.

```
CLOSE 'FILE'TAB,L

CLOSE 'REEL'TAB,N


TAB is the address of the table containing file parameters,
L means rewind and unload the magnetic tape reel, and N means
no rewind.
```

Fig. 7-12   The CLOSE macro (EXEC-8).

CLOSE must be prepared for a variety of situations. Besides the FILE and VOLUME alternatives, there are differences between input and output files, differences between CLOSE instigated by the user and CLOSE triggered by exhausting data or storage space, differences between sequential and non-sequential files, and differences between storage devices. Despite the number of variations, the principal concerns of CLOSE are rather easily listed:

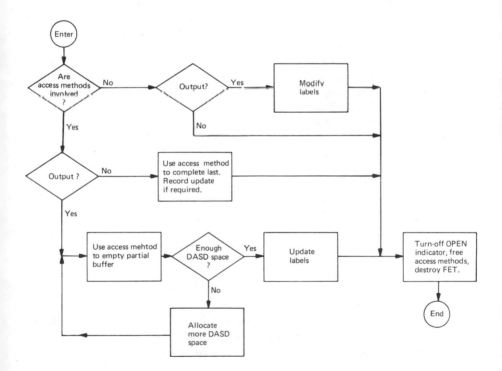

Fig. 7-13   CLOSE FILE for a DASD sequential file.

1. Deal with the last few records or blocks. On output, filled or partially filled buffers must be stored. On input, unprocessed data in buffers can be discarded.

2. Modify or create labels in accordance with applicable conventions.
3. Reposition volumes in accordance with parameters or default options.
4. Prepare the next volume of the file for processing if appropriate. This activity is very similar to the OPEN activity that prepared the first volume for processing. Carefully designed, OPEN and CLOSE can use common programming for these two activities.
5. For CLOSE FILE, reverse several of the actions of OPEN by resetting flags, releasing the main storage space required for tables, and releasing any access method programs that were loaded to process the particular file.

Figure 7-13 shows how these activities are organized for a limited set of alternatives.

End-of-File Conditions.   The occasions for execution of OPEN are obvious; the user's program executes the OPEN call before data can be stored or retrieved. The occasions for executing CLOSE are varied and worthy of examination.

CLOSE FILE is the counterpart of OPEN. The user's program usually can be expected to execute a CLOSE FILE when file processing has been completed. As Fig. 7-14 indicates, the user's program often is aware of the condition naturally. For example, when all records have been stored in an output file, the user's program will be aware because it has no more records to store. The only case where the user's program requires a signal that file processing is complete is when a sequential input process has exhausted the file. The conventional mechanism is an end-of-file exit provided by the user in the FCT. When the user requests a record and all records have been processed, the end-of-file exit will be taken. The user typically will execute CLOSE FILE in the exit routine.

	All records being processed in sequence	Random or incomplete sequential processing
Input	The I/O system is aware that the file is exhausted.	User's program is aware naturally.
Output	User's program is aware naturally.	User's program is aware naturally.

Fig. 7-14   Conditions triggering CLOSE FILE.

Closing a File under Unusual Conditions.   If a user's program terminates leaving one or more files open, the I/O system must take some action to close those files. Why? Because a file left open causes several problems:

1. Tables constructed in the nucleus by OPEN will not be discarded. If a system runs for an extended period with no provision for recovering such space, the loss of main storage could be significant.
2. Labels for the files involved may be incorrect or missing. Subsequent attempts to process those files may produce unpredictable results.

3. Operator instructions may not be issued appropriately. This may result in storage volumes not getting proper visible labels and, depending on system design, may result in I/O devices becoming permanently tied to files that are not in use.

Some systems include a special routine that can be used to cause abrupt and immediate closing of a file. The routine can be executed during abnormal termination of a user's program. Executing CLOSE file under such circumstances might be hazardous. For example, use of a system exit provided by a program that has been abnormally terminated would be inadvisable because the condition causing termination may have damaged the user's exit routine or the table entry identifying the exit routine.

End-of-Volume Conditions. CLOSE VOLUME is generally not understood. Confusion arises from this source: While the CLOSE VOLUME macro is closely related to CLOSE FILE, CLOSE VOLUME applies only to sequential processing of multivolume files. CLOSE FILE applies to all files; CLOSE VOLUME applies in very special circumstances only. Even further, CLOSE VOLUME is usually implicit; the call is rarely executed by a user's program.

	Condition detected by I/O device	User spontaneously executes CLOSE VOLUME
Input	Data on the volume is exhausted. I/O system does label processing, volume switching, etc. Exits are used if available. (A very useful case.)	Data in buffers is discarded. I/O system does label processing, volume switching, etc. Exits are used if available (Not a very useful case.)
Output	Space on the volume is exhausted. I/O system does label processing, volume switching, etc. Exits are used if available. (A very useful case.)	Data in buffers is recorded. Then I/O system does label processing, volume switching, etc. Exits are used if available. (A useful case.)

Fig. 7-15 CLOSE VOLUME situations.

The various uses of CLOSE VOLUME are tabulated in Fig. 7-15. Notice that the device-detected conditions can be handled automatically by the I/O system. The user's program is involved only if an end-of-volume exit has been provided. CLOSE VOLUME on output is very useful in some commercial applications. For public utilities customer file, splitting the file into separate volumes by geographic area allows an individual volume to be processed on each day of the month, thereby spreading the processing load. Customer billing, conducted this way, is called cycle billing.

SUMMARY

There are three mechanisms used in communication between a user's program and the I/O system:

1. System calls whereby the user's program executes a sequence of instructions resulting in a transfer of control to the I/O system. The

file processing facilities of an I/O system are activated by OPEN and CLOSE. The terms are carry-overs from manual opening and closing of file cabinets.

2. Tables wherein information is deposited by the user's program for use by the I/O system and vice versa. The file-control table (FCT), file extent table (FET), and I/O unit table (UT) are of immediate interest.

3. Exits whereby the I/O system transfers control to a prearranged point in the user's program under certain conditions.

The major responsibility of OPEN is to connect a user's program and its data. This responsibility entails readying a file, preparing tables, and ensuring that conditions for valid and efficient file processing are met. OPEN is a very complex function. Not only must it cope with labeling conventions that differ from device to device, but it must cope with environmental situations such as operator error, illegible labels, previously mounted volumes, special volume positioning requirements, and file protection as well as other more routine activities such as table initialization, access method preparation, and, possibly, initial buffer filling.

CLOSE has two major variations, CLOSE FILE and CLOSE VOLUME. Both varieties deal with final records or blocks, modify labels and position volumes. CLOSE FILE is used to terminate processing of a file. In addition, CLOSE FILE reverses several of the actions of OPEN, releasing tables and communicating with the operator. CLOSE FILE is typically triggered by an explicit system call. If a user's program fails to close its files, the I/O system must close them. Special care is required if the user's program has terminated abnormally.

CLOSE VOLUME is used only with multivolume sequential processing. In most instances, it is used implicitly to switch volumes.

Exercises

1.(e) Is OPEN a macro? Explain your answer.

2.(e) In Fig. 7-10, why isn't the FET designed to be physically part of the FCT?

3.(e) It was stated that CLOSE VOLUME is applicable only to sequential processing of a sequential file. If that is so, why do you suppose CLOSE VOLUME is characteristically described with OPEN and CLOSE FILE than with the sequential access method?

4.(m) As illustrated in Fig. 7-4, each field of a table is usually given a name. The names illustrated are clearly not for human conversation; they cannot be pronounced. What purpose do they serve?

5.(m) Why aren't links 4 and 15 in Fig. 7-11 established at static allocation time?

6.(e) There are two possible situations under which a file should be positioned at the end of the last existing volume. One of these is in preparation for backward read, a process useful in sorting. What is the other situation?

7.(m) Assume that, on detecting an expiration date not passed, OPEN sets an indicator for use later if the user's program attempts output. Should that indicator be in the FCT, the FET, or the UT? Give reasons for your answer.

8.(m) Several systems accommodate a form of OPEN that identifies two or more files to be opened. What advantages might such a convention have?

9.(m) File parameters can be furnished from any of three sources. Which source is the most source of record length in each of the following situations?

a. A general utility program is used to create a new DASD file.

b. A specially written program is used to create a personnel file.

c. A general utility program is used to read a file for the purpose of copying it.

10.(d) OPEN is a notoriously slow process. Suggest some shortcuts or efficiencies to improve that performance.

8 Storing and Retrieving Data

An I/O system exists for one reason—to provide a service. The control statements and file processing macros described in the preceding chapters provide services that are, at best, indirect. In a sense, they require the user to serve the system, and they would rank low on a user's popularity scale. The interfaces to be described in this chapter allow the system to serve the user. A homely analogy exists in travel reservations. Control statements inform the system of an impending requirement for physical resources much as a traveler might reserve facilities at a hotel. OPEN announces the intention to begin use of resources as does registration at the front desk. Up to that point, no real service has been provided for either the user's program or the traveler, but from that point forward, both expect service worthy of the preceding nuisance.

Now, just what service would a user like? In 1965, the late John Haanstra[1] said, "The user wants to say 'WRITE' and his record goes away, and he wants to say 'READ' and it comes back, and that's all the user wants to do about input and output." Specifically, the user does not want to write control statements, nor does the user want to call OPEN, but those were the subjects of previous chapters, and we cannot help those problems here. Finally, we are going to say READ and WRITE.

ACCESS METHODS

The I/O system programs that interpret and fulfill the user's requests for storage or retrieval of data can be called *access methods*. The access methods are the user's friend. They are the culmination of labels, staging, libraries, passwords, file organizations, concatenations, and countless other contrivances. In the popular idiom, the access methods are where it is at!

Consider the problems in designing the READ and WRITE programs. One bound is the user's interface, notably, READ and WRITE. At the other extreme are the files. The access methods fall in between these bounds as shown in Fig. 8-1. The I/O supervisor, on the right, is not a bound but, rather, a filter. It imposes certain rules on channel program users.

---

[1] In 1965 John Haanstra was president of IBM's Data Systems Division. The quotation is approximate; it was not recorded at the time.

146

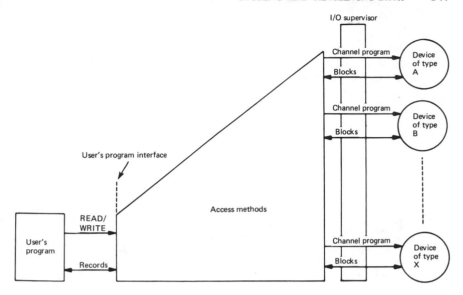

Fig. 8-1   Access method interfaces.

To reduce the user's concerns to READ and WRITE, the access methods must excel in three ways:

Buffering   The execution of READ and WRITE should appear to be instantaneous, else the users must be concerned whether their requests have been executed or whether completion is pending. The desired effect can be accomplished by delaying the user's program until the record is removed (WRITE) or the record is available (READ). A system of buffers can reduce the delay to an acceptable level. The buffers can be filled from an I/O device in anticipation of need or emptied to an I/O device as time allows.

Blocking   If the block of data to be moved by a channel program is not a record, the access methods must convert blocks to records and records to blocks without the user's participation, else the user must be concerned about blocking factors and blocking conventions.

Device Independence   All characteristics of individual·I/O devices must be absorbed so that the user has no concern for device idiosyncracies. In fact, the user wants to deal with an idealized device that has no limitations or devicelike characteristics whatever.

Now, the casual observer might expect that because access methods are designed independently by unrelated enterprises, no two would have similar internal organization. In actuality, all access methods are organized in a roughly common way that, once described, is readily justified. The common convention is the vertical split shown in Fig. 8-2. The dividing line is defined by blocks of data in main storage. Programs to the left of the line furnish the buffering and blocking suggested earlier. Programs to the right deal with devices to furnish device independence. This division of labor may not be inevitable, but it is at least quite natural. A few of its merits are as follows:

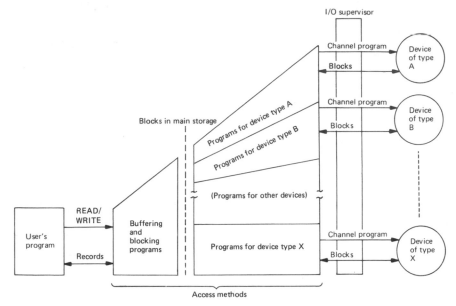

Fig. 8-2   Segregating access method activities.

1. It clearly separates independent programs. Blocking and buffering are closely related, particularly when a spanning convention is allowed. However, blocking and buffering programs have little in common with programs that control devices.
2. It localizes the device-dependent programs, thereby reducing the cost of adding programs for new I/O devices.
3. It avoids duplication of effort by allowing a common buffering and blocking routine to be used with many different device-dependent routines.

In the practical world of data processing, what the user would like is tempered by what the desired service costs. The compartmentalized access methods of Fig. 8-2 invite the user to consider three levels of service. The three levels are identified in Fig. 8-3, and they are described as follows:

Channel Program Level   At this level, the access methods furnish no service at all. The user's program undertakes most of the I/O responsibility. The I/O supervisor, to be described later, furnishes a small measure of assistance and a good measure of control. At this level, the user's program utilizes the same interface to a file that the access methods use. This level of service might be selected by a user because his or her requirements make greater efficiency possible when the access methods are bypassed or because the requirements cannot be met completely at either of the other two levels. An example of the former situation might be a requirement to read only the first 100 bytes of each block of data. An example of the latter is the use of an I/O device that is foreign to the access methods.

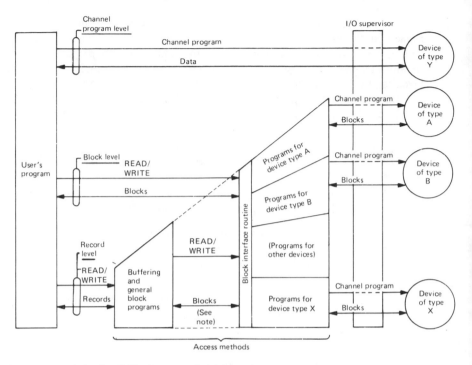

Note: In some systems, the interface dividing the access methods is informal.

Fig. 8-3   Levels of service.

Block Level   At this level, the users must do their own buffering and blocking, but the access methods furnish channel programs and perform other device-related activities. By selecting this level, a user avoids the intricacies of channel programming, a very important advantage. This level might be selected in preference to the more automatic record level because the user's program expects to deal with blocks of data rather than records or because the blocking conventions in the file do not conform to the I/O systems' conventions. READ and WRITE are the names usually given to the principal system calls at this level. They are distinguished from the record-level macros by conventions that differ from one system to another.

Record Level   At this level, the user executes a system call when a record is required and another system call to dispose of a record, and the user wants everything else done for him or her. This level uses the full services of the access methods. Unless a user has a requirement that makes this automatic service impossible or inefficient, this level is expected to be selected. In some systems, the principal macros at this level are designated GET and PUT; in other systems, READ and WRITE. We shall use the latter for reasons to be discussed later.

The services at the various levels usually cannot be intermixed in the processing of a single file. For example, if a user has been processing data at the channel program level, the access methods would be unprepared to accept a request at the record level. The reason is that the user's program might not, and in some systems, it cannot set up the addresses and prepare buffers as required by the access methods. An intermixing of the block level and record level might be possible, but such an intermixing may be hazardous. The following quotation using the terms *Physical I/O* and *Logical I/O* for block and record levels, respectively, is taken from an operating system manual:

> The use of Physical I/O in place of Logical I/O removes the user from the Data Management Subsystem rules and conventions. All such users should be careful to follow the data management conventions if they want to use the same volume with Logical I/O. . . .[2]

The body of programs called the access methods provides service in a variety of circumstances. The principal variables are

- the user's choice of service level; record or block
- the type of I/O device involved
- the organization of the file; sequential, indexed, list or direct

Our discussion so far has avoided reference to file organization. The access methods shown in Fig. 8-3 presume a common file organization. When other organizations are involved, a third dimension is introduced. In some systems, the access methods for different file organizations share common code. In some systems, the access methods for different file organizations are almost totally distinct. These latter systems use the singular term access method to designate the programs for a unique combination of service level and file organization. The access method names for one system are shown in Fig. 8–4.

	Sequential Organization	Indexed Organization	Direct Organization
Block level	BSAM (Basic sequential access method)	(not available)	BDAM (Basic direct access method)
Record level	QSAM (Queued sequential access method	BISAM (Basic indexed-access method) QISAM (Queued indexed-sequential access method	(not available)

Notes: The term queued implies automatic buffering.

The list organization is not used in OS/360.

Fig. 8-4   Access method names (OS/360).

A primary objective of the originators of the access method idea was that a program which uses an access method should be unaffected by choice of device. That is, the user's interface to an access method should be device-independent. Device independence for the user's program implies device dependence within the access method itself. One of the principal challenges in the design of an access method is to cope with a variety of devices in such a way that they all appear to the user as if they were the same device.

[2] Operating System/200 and Extended Mod 1 (Honeywell).

An additional objective that has not been achieved completely is that the user's interface to the access methods should be independent of file organization. Referring to Fig. 8-4, we note that while BSAM is at the same level as BDAM, their macros are not identical. Some, but not all, QSAM macros are identical to QISAM macros. The principal value in making such macros and the related tables identical would be extended applicability of a user's program. They differ because the file organizations place slightly different requirements on the user for information.

The introduction to the access methods is now complete, and we must turn our attention to more detailed matters. The next three topics describe the three levels of service already introduced. The discussion proceeds from least to most comprehensive level so that each description can build on its predecessor.

The Channel Program Level of Service

The channel program level of service is particularly interesting because it is a service level available to a user's program and to the access methods. That fact, illustrated in preceding figures, is shown in more detail in Fig. 8-5. The access methods are capable of processing only those files that conform to specific rules of organization and that use devices whose characteristics they recognize and accommodate. These restrictions are simply recognition that no program, access method or other, is capable of magic. The channel program level of service has no similar restrictions because the user's program furnishes the accommodations to file organization and device characteristics.

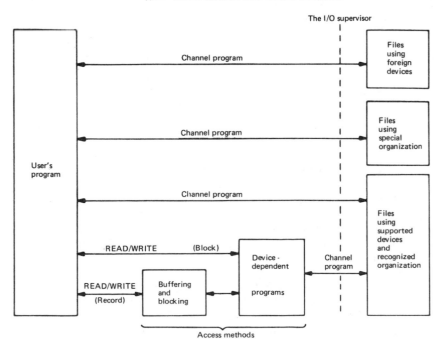

Fig. 8-5   Uses of the channel program level.

The channel program level of service represents a compromise. Some systems, such as the CDC SCOPE System, do not provide this level of service to users' programs. EXEC-8 includes the channel program level for use with "arbitrary devices." OS/360 allows the channel program level with no restrictions. Whether, and to what extent, it is desirable for a system to provide the channel program level interface for users' programs are debatable and much debated questions. Eliminating the channel program level reduces the amount of checking required of the I/O supervisor by eliminating opportunities for errors and security violations in channel programs. On the other hand, the channel program level offers the user the greatest possible freedom to design a program that is efficient or that accomplishes some unusual process.

The Input/Output Supervisor.   In many computer systems that use general purpose operating systems, certain instructions called privileged instructions are reserved for use by the control program only. One of the restricted instructions is invariably the one that causes a channel to begin executing a channel program. This restriction ensures that the control program will be aware of all channel activity so that it can impose appropriate priority and data-protection rules. Figure 8-6 illustrates how a user's program can request execution of a channel program. The user's program executes a call to the control program supervisor. The latter analyzes the parameters furnished with the call and, because this is an I/O request, branches to the I/O supervisor. The I/O supervisor checks the validity of the request and, at an appropriate time, starts execution of the user's channel program. The I/O supervisor provides similar services for the access methods. The fundamental importance of the I/O supervisor justifies devoting an entire chapter, Chap. 9, to it.

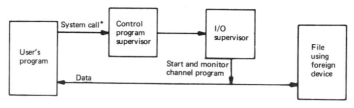

*See Chapter 9, figure 4 for examples

Fig. 8-6   A user's program requests channel program execution.

I/O Devices and Channel Programs.   That channel programs are affected by device characteristics is abundantly evident. Channel commands that are required for one device may be unacceptable by another. Consequently, part of the definition of the channel program level interface is contained in the manuals that describe specific devices.

1. Does the device have critical timing requirements?
2. Does the device require specialized operator instructions?
3. For storage devices, what are the geometric parameters, including track length, tracks per cylinder, etc.?
4. Are addresses consecutive binary, nonconsecutive decimal, or other?

5. How are unusual conditions reported by the device?
6. Is it possible to recover from some failure conditions and, if so, how is recovery accomplished?
7. Is validity checking of data possible?

Satisfying these concerns is difficult and expensive. Further, a program that meets the requirements of a particular type of device will not operate correctly with any device whose requirements differ. Such a program is called device-dependent. The desire for device independence is an important motivation for using the next higher service level.

The Block Level of Service

At the block level the access methods are involved. They furnish the channel programs, and they interact with the I/O supervisor, the file, and the I/O devices just as described previously for the user's interface at the channel program level.

The user's interface at this level includes several system calls; the principal ones are READ, WRITE, and CHECK.[3] To acquire a block of data, the user executes a READ. The access methods interpret this call, perform such necessary actions as constructing or modifying channel programs, and finally, they request service from the I/O supervisor. At that point, although the requested service may not be complete, the user's program may be allowed to continue execution. The user's program can issue a CHECK call when it has reached a point where the requested block is required. Upon execution of CHECK, the control program will suspend execution of the user's program until the I/O system has fulfilled the READ request. The CHECK serves to ensure that the user's program does not erroneously attempt to process a block before the channel program has completed its work. Figure 8-7 illustrates this chronology in greater detail.

Varieties of Block-Level Macros.   Examples of macros typically available at the block level are shown in Fig. 8-8. Some of the variations are as follows:

1. Read or write the next physical block as illustrated in lines 1 and 2.
2. Read or write a particular physical block on a magnetic disk or drum as illustrated in line 3.
3. Read or write a block as in any of the preceding examples, but do not return control to the caller until the action is complete. An example is shown in line 4.
4. Check for completion of a read or write activity, as described earlier. Line 5 is an example. The user's program is delayed until the I/O operation is complete.

In some systems, the execution of a second READ or WRITE to the same file implies a CHECK for execution of the preceding macro. For example, the sequence READ,READ has the same effect as READ,CHECK,READ. A few systems allow the user to execute several READs or WRITEs for a single

---

[3]Approximately half of the contemporary general purpose systems name this macro WAIT, rather than CHECK.

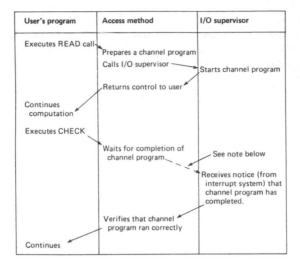

User's program	Access method	I/O supervisor
Executes READ call	Prepares a channel program	
	Calls I/O supervisor	Starts channel program
	Returns control to user	
Continues computation		
Executes CHECK		
	Waits for completion of channel program	See note below
		Receives notice (from interrupt system) that channel program has completed.
	Verifies that channel program ran correctly	
Continues		

Note: In a multiprogrammed system, a wait such as that noted above
yields control of the CPU to the Control-Program supervisor
for use as it sees fit.

Fig. 8-7   A READ-CHECK chronology.

Line No.	System Call	Meaning
1	PAM TABLE1,RD'LOC=AREA	Read(RD) the next consecutive block into location AREA
2	PAM TABLE1,WRT,LOC=AREA	Write(WRT) the next consecutive block from location AREA
3	PAM TABLE1,WRT,HP=27	Write block number 27 (Half Page=27) from the area identified in the file control table
4	PAM TABLE1,RDWT	Read the next block and wait for completion (RDWT). Use the area identified in the file control table.
5	PAM TABLE1,WT	Wait (WT) until the previous I/O operation using TABLE1 has completed

Notes:

(1)   In all of the above, PAM (primitive access method) is the name
of the system call.

(2)   Using PAM, the specific intention, such as read or write, is
indicated by a parameter, RD, WRT, etc.

(3)   TABLE1 is the name of the file control table.

The use of the single macro name, PAM, is unusual. Most systems
use distinct names such as READ, WRITE and CHECK. The
unusual form is presented here to illustrate an alternative.

Fig. 8-8   Macros at the block level (TSOS).

file before checking for completion of the first. This capability allows the caller to achieve extensive semiautomatic buffering, and it provides the I/O system a list of requests from which it can schedule I/O activities intelligently. Examples of such scheduling are sorting of requests and combining of channel programs to improve DASD efficiency. Figure 8-9 illustrates how an additional parameter on READ allows CHECK to refer to any of several outstanding requests. WRITE and CHECK can be used similarly.

```
User's program
_____

READ CP1,SF,FCT1,AREA1

_____
_____

READ CP2,SF,FCT1,AREA2

_____
_____

READ CP3,SF,FCT1,AREA3

_____
_____

CHECK CP1

In the above example CPn is the name of a table used to allow
CHECK to identify a particular occurrence of READ, SF is a code
meaning sequential forward, FCT1 is the file control table name,
and AREAn is the main storage area that is to receive the block
```

Fig. 8-9   Multiple outstanding READs (OS/360).

Figure 8-10 shows the internal flow of a READ macro. The process is quite simple though some of the activities shown entail significant numbers of instructions. Further, each variation, each type of device, and each organization of data either adds complexity to the flowchart shown or requires development of a similar but different program. The internal flow of WRITE is not different in any significant way.

Processing Order.   READ and WRITE tend to be sequential operations. That is, unless the user has indicated to the contrary, a READ macro will retrieve the block that is next in sequence following the block most recently retrieved. WRITE will store a block physically beyond the last one written. Such sequential operations are useful for sequential files, but frequently are not useful for indexed, direct, or list organizations. In these exotic organizations, sequences of records may be identifiable, but blocks that are physically in sequence may contain records in an unpredicted order. For such organizations, sequential block READs might encounter indexes, empty blocks, and control data that would not be meaningful to a user's program. If block operations are to be furnished for the exotic organizations, interpretations that match the sequential file interpretation as nearly as possible seem appropriate. Such an interpretation could be useful for such routine activities as copying a file.

Variations of READ and WRITE shown earlier in Fig. 8-8 provide the ability to break an old sequence and begin a sequence from a new point. Some systems include NOTE and POINT macros for this purpose. NOTE is a macro that collects enough information about a block just recorded so that at any subsequent time, the POINT macro, furnished with the collected information, can reestablish the earlier position. Used in combination, NOTE and POINT allow a user to build an index to individual blocks or to sequences of blocks in a file.

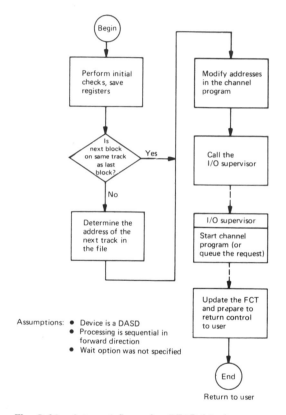

Fig. 8-10   Internal flow of a READ block macro.

Another positioning macro usually provided is a backspace macro, sometimes coded BKSP. The ability to backspace over a record or a block is a deceptively difficult service to provide. For one thing, many devices such as card punches and printers are incapable of backspacing. For another, backspacing can be difficult when it involves crossing a volume boundary. Consider what must happen if a magnetic tape has been recorded for its full length, rewound, and removed from the drive, another tape reel has been readied for processing, and then the user's program requests a backspace. As a further complication, backspace record is very complex for spanned and undefined record types.

There is, however, one very important reason why backspace is essential in any complete I/O system: The FORTRAN language allows the user to specify backspace. The problem cannot be resolved simply by maintaining information about the immediately previous record or block within tables related to each file because the user's program is allowed to issue backspace as often as it will. The best advice regarding design of a backspace macro is to restrict its applicability as much as possible. Some contemporary systems restrict backspace to single-volume sequential files only. Others allow multivolume files but without the ability to backspace across a volume boundary. Still others have no restrictions at all.

The Record Level of Service

The most comprehensive level of access method service is the record level. In some systems, this is the only level provided. This level relieves the user of concern about storage and retrieval of data to the greatest possible degree. At this level, the user is concerned only with records, never with blocks, and only in the following way: When the user issues a READ, a record should be presented to him or her, when the user issues WRITE, a record should be stored and, in both cases, the service should appear to be immediate. In practice, these objectives have been met almost completely.

There are several important aspects of record-level service that must be discussed. One aspect, buffering, requires such extensive coverage that it will be deferred until later in the chapter so that its size does not obscure other important concerns.

Record-Level Macro Name.   Approximately half of the contemporary I/O systems use GET and PUT as macro names for sequential record processing. However, to keep GET and PUT easy to use, designers have not seen fit to provide for the use of CHECK with either GET or PUT. This lack forces an I/O system to use a combination of buffering and user program delay to eliminate timing problems, a good solution when records are processed in sequence. However, if GET were used for retrieving records in an unpredicated sequence, where anticipating the user's requests is impossible, the delays in user program execution would be unacceptable. Consequently, systems that use GET and PUT for sequential record processing use READ, WRITE, and CHECK for random record processing. The resulting alternatives are as follows:

1. Use READ and WRITE for all record moving macro names.
2. Use GET and PUT for sequential record processing. Use READ and WRITE for random record processing. Use READ and WRITE for block processing.

Alternative 1 seems less confusing, and it is the alternative used in this book. Neither choice has a clear, practical advantage over the other.

Macro Variations.   Figure 8-11 illustrates some variations of record-level macros. Lines 1 and 2 illustrate the simplicity of the basic macros. The only parameter required simply indicates which file is involved. As is conventional with READ and WRITE, the user's program may resume execution before the requested service is complete. Line 3 illustrates a CHECK macro that can be used to ensure that a READ or WRITE has been completed and completed properly. Line 4 illustrates how READ can include an operand forcing an automatic delay awaiting completion. An identical convention is available with WRITE. Lines 5 and 6 illustrate operands that provide for a record to be moved from its buffer into a user's work area. Some implications of such a move will be discussed shortly. Line 7 illustrates how a record with a certain key value can be retrieved. The reading and writing of individual records identified by their keys are restricted to DASD files whose organizations were designed for that purpose. Specifically, an indexed, direct, or list organization would be appropriate.

Macro	Meaning
M:READ TABLE1	READ the next sequential record from the file identified in TABLE1 into the main storage area indicated in TABLE1.
M:WRITE TABLE1	WRITE the record presently in the area identified in TABLE1 as the next consecutive record in the file identified by TABLE1.
M:CHECK TABLE1,ABN,EOFLOC	CHECK for completion of the I/O operation pending against TABLE1. When the operation is completed normally, continue with the next instruction. On ABNormal completion, branch to EOFLOC.
M:READ TABLE1,WAIT	READ the next consecutive record and WAIT until that operation is complete before executing the next instruction.
M:READ TABLE1,BUF,LOC	READ the next record from the file represented by TABLE1 into the BUFfer area named LOC.
M:WRITE TABLE1,BUF,LOC	WRITE as above.
M:READ TABLE1,KEY,KEYLOC	READ the record whose KEY is found in location KEYLOC into the main-storage location indicated by the BUF field of TABLE1.

In all of the above, TABLE1 is the name of a file control table (FCT).

Fig. 8-11   Record-level macros (Xerox BPM).

In addition to the forms shown, a typical system might include macros or macro parameters to do the following:

1. Terminate processing of the current block and move automatically to the next block.
2. Terminate the current block and begin at any other block.
3. Insert, update, or delete records in an existing file.
4. Process sequentially in a reverse direction.

Each of these alternatives is worthy of discussion. However, to avoid excessive preoccupation with the external features of the I/O system, we shall leave off this discussion, suggesting to the interested reader that the users' manuals of any major system can be consulted for further information.

How a Record-Level READ Works. The internal logic of a record-level READ depends very much on the alternative parameters offered, the organization of the referenced file, and the block buffering scheme used. As an illustration of this point in OS/360, there are 16 separate programs for sequential retrieval of records from a sequential file. Using OS/360 terms, there are 16 separate programs for QSAM GET—not 16 program modules, but 16 alternative programs.

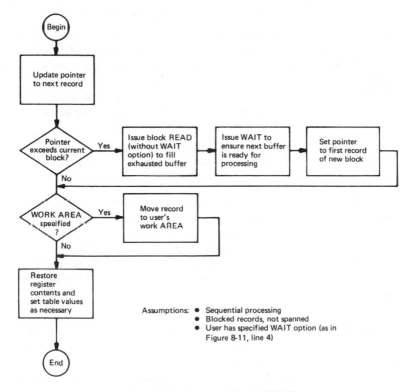

Fig. 8-12 A record-level READ.

Figure 8-12 illustrates the internal flow of a record-level READ program. Notice that, if the next record is within the current block, the process is very simple. That simple process does not involve input or output activity, and it does not require supervisory authority. Careful design can allow entry to that process by a simple branching instruction. Because that path is frequently used, the number of instructions in it should be minimal.

When the updated pointer indicates that the current block is exhausted, a block-level READ is executed so that the I/O system can begin the necessary channel program scheduling. There is no need to wait for that READ to be completed; rather, there is a need to determine whether the next buffer is ready. That next buffer was scheduled for filling at some earlier time.

The Move and Locate Modes.   The access methods typically fill or empty a set of main storage areas called buffers according to a systematic buffering plan. If the user's program accepts a record for processing right in the record's buffered location or if it delivers a record for output right to the appropriate buffer location, the access method is said to be working in locate mode. If, alternatively, the user's program identifies its own work area where records are to be delivered or accepted by an access method, the latter is said to be working in move mode. In locate mode, the access method simply locates the next record for the user; in move mode the access method moves the record to or from a work area.

The two modes are justified by the following opposing factors:

1. Moving a record to a work area makes subsequent addressing of fields within the record easier. The unchanging addresses within a fixed work area simplify the user's program. The move mode can be almost essential when a record spans a block boundary.
2. Moving a record to a work area is fundamentally wasteful of computer resources; it accomplishes no useful work. Addressing complexity is one thing, but processing efficiency is another.

Recognizing these factors, most systems include both modes.

At first glance, the two modes seem simple enough to require no explanation. Three of the four cases are simple, but the fourth is not:

READ/move   The user identifies a work area by macro parameter of table entry. The access method keeps track of buffer location and performs the required move simply.

WRITE/move   Very similar to the above.

READ/locate   The access method identifies the record position by placing that address in a table or in a register according to preestablished conventions.

WRITE/locate   This case is a problem.

The problem in WRITE/locate is that, if record moving is to be avoided, the record must have been placed in the proper buffer location before the macro is executed. This raises a question as to how the user can determine the correct location for the record before the WRITE macro is issued. Each of the following usable resolutions has its own disadvantages:

1. Design WRITE/locate to accept the current record and to return the location to be used for the next record in a register or table. This solution has the disadvantage that OPEN must be required to furnish the location to be used for the first record. Involving OPEN in this access method matter is undesirable, if for no other reason than it requires the users to declare in advance their intention to use WRITE/locate.
2. Design WRITE/locate so that the user issues it before the related record is processed rather than after. This alternative has the disadvantage that if it is used with READ/move, as would seem to be natural, the WRITE for a record must be issued before the READ for

the same record. Not only is that sequence unnatural, but if the READ of a WRITE/READ pair encounters an end-of-file condition, the user will be unable to deliver a record for which a WRITE has already been issued.

3. Do not include a WRITE/locate capability in the I/O system. This alternative has the disadvantage of lack of symmetry.

On balance, this last alternative seems most desirable. The second alternative is clearly the worst.

End-Use Device Control.   A principal function of an I/O system is to furnish records to and accept records from users' programs. In one circumstance, the users may not care what the I/O system does with a record except that it should be retrievable at some later time. In another circumstance, the users care a great deal about the disposition of the record. The users may not want the record stored at all, but rather, they may want it printed. These two cases include two fundamentally different services: data storage and input/output.

If the system users were asked at the time they presented their records to the I/O system, "Will you want this record back later?" they could answer the question readily. If they answer yes, the request is for data storage; if no, the request is for output. The users are disciplined to this distinction because the form of a record they would present for storage is usually not acceptable for use outside the system and vice versa. In recognition of this fact, the user-oriented languages such as COBOL, FORTRAN, and PL/I provide special language conventions for use when I/O service is intended.

Operating systems usually combine the storage and I/O services obscuring their differences for several important reasons:

1. User's interface requirements for the two types of services have much in common. For example, the READ and WRITE macros can be used for both types of service.
2. System mechanisms for the two types of services have much in common. For example, tables that identify files, control statement relationships to programs, I/O supervision, and buffering mechanisms are applicable to both types of service.
3. The services should appear identical to the user's program whenever possible because in many cases the system intends to perform an I/O service indirectly using a storage service as an intermediate step. Such staging of input and output is described in Chap. 10, "Data Staging."

Data are stored on devices such as magnetic tape and DASDs. I/O data, in the non-storage-data sense, are intended for end-use devices such as card readers and printers.

End-use devices require control information that is of concern to the user. Card readers and punches may require stacker selection or card printing control. Printers and graphic display devices require spacing control, heading information, page numbering, and line formatting.

In designing an I/O system, someone must decide what kinds of device control services should be made available to a user's program. Two rules that can be used as a design policy are these:

1. Any end-use device control that is implied by capabilities in the principal source languages should be available, usually at the record level. The access methods should accommodate these device control requests in such a way that end-use data can be staged.
2. Any other end-use device control should not be furnished by the I/O system. Users' programs that must utilize end-use devices in such special ways should have the devices allocated to their programs during execution and should use the channel program level interface.

These two rules place an upper and lower bound on the I/O system requirements. The second rule is as important as the first because an overzealous design can result in complexities that limit ability to support a wide range of current and future devices.

There are two widely used techniques for providing end-use device control. Most systems provide both. The first technique designates the first character of an output record as a control character to be used for device control. This convention results from a feature common to several models of printers and card punches that a variation of the standard print or punch command will cause the device to interpret the first byte as a control character. Figure 8-13 presents a standard set of character meanings. The user's program is customarily responsible for inserting the control byte into each record and also for informing the access methods, by way of an entry in the FCT, that the special command variation is to be used. If the user's program furnishes a character from the standard set and, as is often the case, the device expects a character from its own unique set, the access method must convert to the acceptable code.

The extended American National Standard Code for Information Interchange (ASCII) is as follows:

Code	Action Before Writing Record
b	Space one line before printing (blank code)
0	Space two lines before printing
—	Space three lines before printing
+	Suppress space before printing
1	Skip to channel 1
2	Skip to channel 2
3	Skip to channel 3
4	Skip to channel 4
5	Skip to channel 5
6	Skip to channel 6
7	Skip to channel 7
8	Skip to channel 8
9	Skip to channel 9
A	Skip to channel 10
B	Skip to channel 11
C	Skip to channel 12
V	Select punch pocket 1
W	Select punch pocket 2

These control characters include those defined by ANSI FORTRAN. If any other character is specified, it is interpreted as 'b' or V, depending on the device being used.

Fig. 8-13   Printer and punch control.

The second technique for providing device control uses one or more macro forms such as that displayed in Fig. 8-14. An access method can respond to such a macro by executing a separate channel program to accomplish the request, by modifying an existing channel program to accomplish the requested action along with some other activity, or by appending an appropriate control byte to a record in the manner of the preceding paragraph. This last alternative is useful for files that are to be staged on a DASD to be printed or punched later.

Macro	Meaning
@SKIP TABLE1,xx	Advance the forms on the printer according to code xx. TABLE1 is the FCT.

Fig. 8-14 A macro for controlling printer forms (OS/200).

Another more elaborate technique for furnishing device control uses an I/O editor. An editor can furnish not only the types of controls already discussed but also such editorial services as character conversion, number base

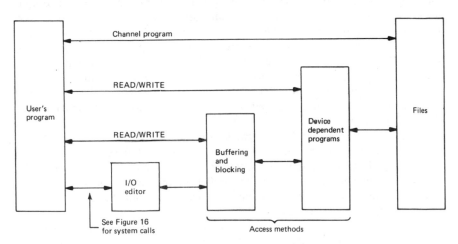

Fig. 8-15 I/O editor interfaces.

System Call	Comments
CALL IOEDIT	This call establishes repetitive patterns such as printed-page headings.
CALL RDREC	Read an input record and convert it to a standard form.
CALL WRTEC	Insert device-control information into a record and write that record to a print or punch file.
CALL EPRINT	Edit a line for printing and write that line to a printer file.

Fig. 8-16 I/O editor calls (GCOS).

conversion, and appropriate propagation or suppression of zeros. Such an editor can be provided as an extension to the access methods serving the user as if it were part of the access methods and using the access methods in providing that service. Figure 8-15 shows how an I/O editor can be placed in a system, and Fig. 8-16 lists some of the system calls available in one such editor.

BUFFERING

A buffer is a cushion against the shock of fluctuation in activity. During data storage and retrieval, shocks come from two sources. (1) The user's program furnishes data to the I/O system in short bursts. During any instant in time, a complete record either is or is not being presented. When a record is being presented, the I/O system is accepting data from the user's program at an extremely fast rate. For example, a 100-byte record is delivered to the system in a few microseconds. The transaction is really a transfer of ownership and does not necessarily involve movement of the record itself. During that instant in time, the inventory of data owned by the I/O system is increasing at a rate approaching 100 million bytes per second. A high-performance output device accepts data at a much slower rate, usually about 1,000 times slower. (2) The user's program provides no advance warning that it will request transfer of ownership of data. To provide efficient operation of the entire system, the data should be accepted by the I/O system immediately upon request. Most I/O devices require advance notice of a few milliseconds or more before data can be transferred to them. The latter period is about 100 times longer than the time required by the I/O system to accept the data from the user's program.

An I/O system cushions against the shocks of such fluctuation in activity by managing an inventory of main storage buffer space to hold data temporarily. Data for output are accepted into a buffer at the request of the user's program and released from the buffer to the storage device when the latter is ready to accept it. Input data are accepted from the input device as rapidly as the device can furnish it, provided only that buffer space is available and the data are provided to the user's program at the latter's request. Provided the amount of data to be transferred over a given period is within the capability of the device, the inventory of data in buffers will grow and shrink, while the user's program continues its work unobstructed.

The Value of Buffering

Buffering furnishes only one important advantage—improved performance. The following are some of the performance implications of buffering, which are not as obvious as those just discussed:

1. Buffering reduces the elapsed time for a user's program by allowing the user's program to run at times when, without buffering, it would be forced to wait. Elapsed time is an important aspect of performance.

2. By improving elapsed time for a user's program, buffering results in freeing all of the resources allocated to the user's program sooner.

3. Buffering improves the individual performance of many types of I/O devices. For example, under certain circumstances, it might require 30 ms of direct access device time to get ready to retrieve a block of data and 3 ms to actually retrieve it. If a second block is to be retrieved immediately after the first, the get-ready time for that second block will be avoided, thereby reducing channel, control unit, and device time very significantly.

In some ways, multiprogramming is an alternative to buffering. Multiprogramming can improve system performance by utilizing devices that might otherwise be temporarily idle. But the overhead cost of multiprogramming is high in main storage, channel time, and storage device time, so multiprogramming is somewhat self-defeating. Notice that for the three items listed in the preceding paragraph, multiprogramming has an effect opposite from the buffering effect. Why, then, does any system use multiprogramming? One important reason is that buffering has the following limitations: (1) If a user's program furnishes or requires more data than an I/O device can accommodate over an extended period, buffering capabilities are exceeded, and no further gain in performance is possible. Adding more buffers will not help unless there are fluctuations in activity. (2) For some I/O requirements, buffering is not possible. For example, when a user's program is requesting records from a certain file in an unpredictable sequence, there is no way that an I/O system can anticipate a request. In such a case, the extra handling of data implied by buffering can be detrimental to performance.

Figure 8-17 illustrates the advantages and limitations of buffering in some typical situations. The cases are simplified by ignoring the effect of continuous control on I/O device performance. For such simple cases, one can conclude correctly that two buffers yield the maximum gain. A single buffer causes alternating I/O and compute; two buffers cause either continuous computing or continuous I/O; and three or more buffers yield no advantage beyond that achieved by two buffers.

Are there situations where three or more buffers are justified? Yes, and they occur frequently as indicated by these examples:

Variable Computing Time   If computing time per block varies from block to block, a large number of buffers can achieve a smoothing effect furnishing input blocks or accepting output blocks rapidly for a time. A user's program might exhibit variable computing time because it processes only certain classes of records from a sequential file.

Variable I/O Time   As in the above case, a large number of buffers can achieve smoothing. The I/O time can vary from block to block either because blocks are being retrieved at random or because of the continuous control phenomenon to be discussed in a moment.

Environmental Effects   In a complex environment, there are possible advantages in accomplishing whatever one can whenever one can. For example, filling several input buffers furnishes a supply of data that is beneficial if the input channel is usurped by a competing activity. Filling several output buffers will allow continuous operation of an output device, while the CPU is usurped by a high-priority activity.

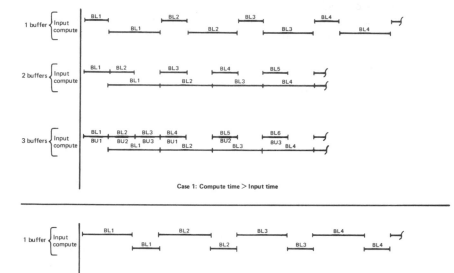

Fig. 8-17   Buffering in simplified situations.

An attempt to illustrate all of the above would be more complicated than the benefit a reader might derive. However, the "variable I/O time" case as it applies to rotating storage devices is too important to pass so easily.

Using conventional DASDs, data transmission must begin at the beginning of a block. If that instant is missed, an entire rotation is wasted. We shall limit our concern to four parameters: the rotational period R, the input or output transmission time I/O, the compute time C, and the number of buffers n. Figure 8-18 contains cases analogous to those in Fig. 8-17. In case I, two buffers achieve an I/O limited condition because the contents of a buffer can be processed in less time than the data-transmission time. Notice that the penalty for an insufficient number of buffers is much greater than before because the rotational period R is usually long relative to either I/O or C.

Figure 8-18, case II, is the more interesting case because C is greater than I/O; the best that can be hoped for is a compute-limited case. Further, we must expect to allow an occasional nonproductive rotation so that computing can catch up with the somewhat faster I/O. As one can observe from the charts, the compute-limited condition will be reached when enough buffers exist to support computing for a period slightly greater than R. Specifically, we require n large enough so that $nC > R + I/O$.

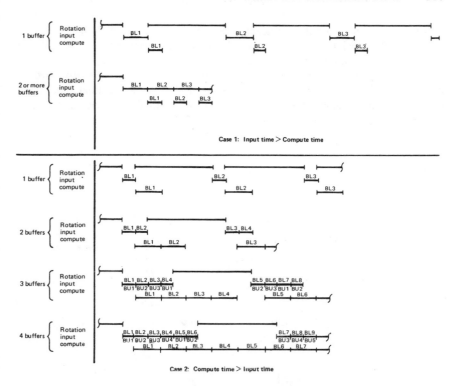

Case 1: Input time > Compute time

Case 2: Compute time > Input time

Fig. 8-18   DASD buffering.

Buffer Pools

Surprisingly, little has been written about buffering. A few articles in and around 1960 gave a false indication of a developing science of buffering. One article, by Owen Mock and Charles Swift, described buffering in the SHARE 709 System for the IBM Type 709.[4] Figure 8-19, reprinted from their paper, displays the buffer-pool idea very well. The pool of inactive buffers is a collection of segments of main storage reserved for use as buffers. The PUT routine, analogous to our record-level WRITE, gradually fills buffer after buffer. Whenever a new buffer is required, the B4 program selects one from the inactive pool. Filled buffers enter a quiet-buffer pool awaiting availability of a channel and control unit. The buffer is emptied with deliberate speed, and the empty buffer is returned to the inactive pool. A similar sequence on the left side of the diagram accommodates input.

It is not necessary to have a formal buffer pool to accomplish buffering. A simple and commonly occurring example is the use of two buffers with a single file. Such buffers, alternately serving an I/O and processing activity, do not constitute a pool because they lack the selectivity essential to pooling. Specifically, a collection of buffers should be considered a pool only if the assignments given to the buffers is not completely predetermined. Notice,

[4] Owen Mock and Charles J. Swift, "The SHARE 709 System: Programmed Input-Output Buffering," *Journal of the ACM*, April 1959.

however, that the two buffers assigned to a single file could have been selected from a buffer pool for use while the file is open and returned to the pool for other assignment when the file is closed.

Buffer pools are used in many contemporary systems. Usually, two or more files are allowed to share a pool only if they have identical block size. One can readily imagine the fragmentation problem that would occur if buffers of varying sizes were required from a single pool.

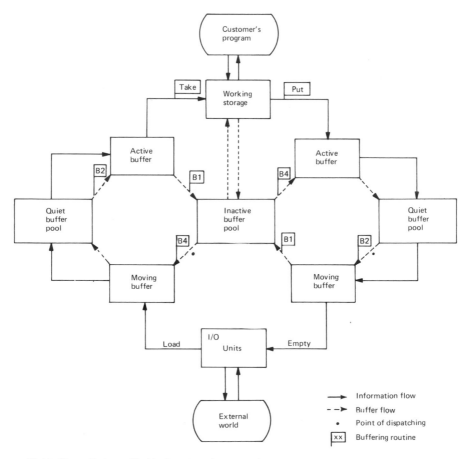

Working Storage: That area utilized by the customer for program data, intermediate and final results.

Active Buffer: A buffer unit to or from which the customer's program is in the process of transmitting data.

Moving Buffer: A buffer unit currently being operated upon (read into or out of) by one of the channels of the DSU.

Quiet Buffer: A buffer unit containing current information coming from or destined to one of the input-output units but which is currently awaiting activity.

Inactive Buffer: A buffer unit not currently employed.

Fig. 8-19   Buffer pools. (Reprinted from Journal of the ACM, April 1959.)

A pool of buffers can be constructed by the language processor that compiles the user's program, or it can be constructed by the I/O system during execution of the user's program. Figure 8-20 illustrates both methods. There is little advantage of one alternative over the other, though some small processing time advantage may accrue from using the compile-time alternative when that alternative is applicable. Notice, however, that use of compile-time alternative implies that block size is fixed at compile time.

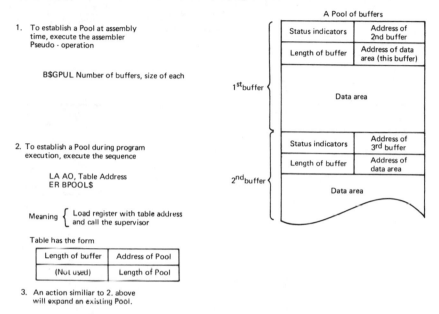

1. To establish a Pool at assembly time, execute the assembler Pseudo - operation

   B$GPUL Number of buffers, size of each

2. To establish a Pool during program execution, execute the sequence

   LA AO, Table Address
   ER BPOOL$

   Meaning { Load register with table address and call the supervisor

   Table has the form

Length of buffer	Address of Pool
(Not used)	Length of Pool

3. An action similiar to 2. above will expand an existing Pool.

A Pool of buffers

1st buffer {
| Status indicators | Address of 2nd buffer |
| Length of buffer | Address of data area (this buffer) |

Data area

2nd buffer {
| Status indicators | Address of 3rd buffer |
| Length of buffer | Address of data area |

Data area

Fig. 8-20   Constructing a buffer pool (EXEC-8).

Buffering Techniques

Some techniques that have been used successfully in the process of buffering are described in the next several paragraphs.

Simple Buffering.   The simplest form of buffering consists of using two buffers alternately. For input, one is being filled while the other is being processed, and then the roles are reversed. The technique is readily extended to any number of buffers used on a rotational basis. Such a scheme, illustrated in Fig. 8-21, is called simple buffering.

Several items in Fig. 8-21 are worth noting. As shown, input stages 1, 2, and 3 fill all buffers before the user's program begins using data. In practice, that phenomenon is characteristic of systems where OPEN does buffer priming. Systems where the access methods accomplish priming would be characterized by the user's program becoming active at stage 2. Notice also that simple buffering is cyclic. Input buffers are filled in the order 1,2,3,1,2,3,1, etc. The user's program processes buffer contents in the same cyclic order. The programmed controls ensure that the filling cycle does not overrun the using cycle and vice versa. Another aspect, illustrated in output stages 4 and 9, is that either the user's program or the I/O system may be inactive from time to time. The output cycle is similar to the input cycle 1,2,3,4,1,2, etc.

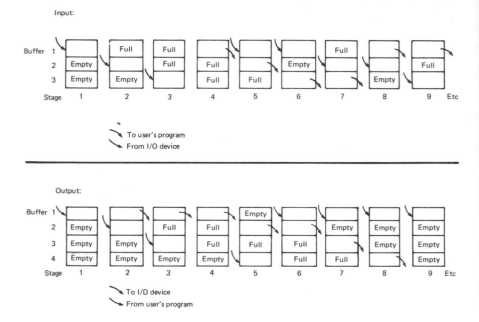

Fig. 8-21   Simple buffering.

Exchange Buffering.   A procedure that is very common in commercial batch processing creates a new master file by updating some or all records of an old master file. If a user's program processes each record in a work area rather than in a buffer, this procedure requires two nonproductive moves of records in main storage: one move to the work area and one to the output buffer. Using the READ/locate described earlier in the chapter eliminates one of these moves. A technique called exchange buffering can be used to eliminate the remaining move. The READ macro identifies a work area just as in a READ/move. However, in exchange of buffering, a record is not moved; rather, the roles of the work area and the segment of the buffer containing the desired record are switched. The work area becomes part of the buffer and vice versa. When the record has been processed completely, a WRITE macro causes a similar exchange of areas with the current output buffer.

Exchange buffering is illustrated in Fig. 8-22. Notice that as records are processed, the segments that compose the input buffer and the segments that compose the output buffer get separated and reordered. The important attribute of exchange buffering is, of course, that data records stay in a fixed location during processing. Notice that record 22, for example, stays in a fixed location, while the identification of that location changes from input segment to work area and then to output segment.

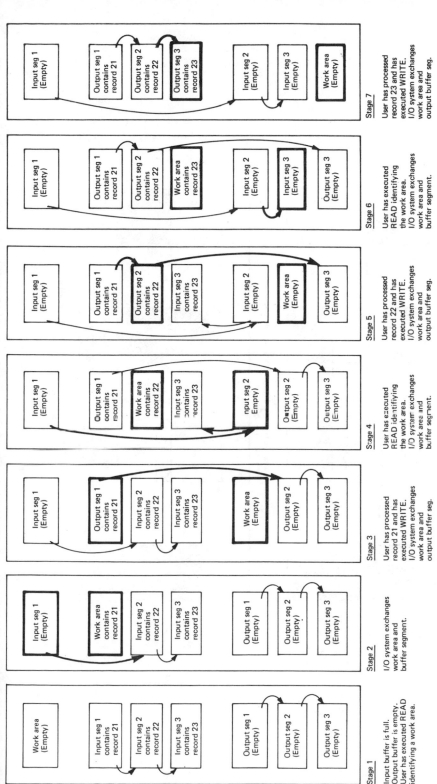

Fig. 8-22 Exchange buffering.

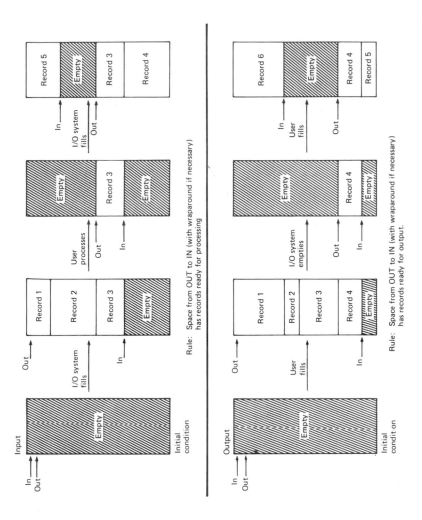

Fig. 8-23 Circular buffering.

172

Exchange buffering is not a completely satisfactory technique. It has been described here because the reader should know that the technique exists and that it is available in a major commercial system. It has two shortcomings:

1. It causes fragmentation of each buffer and, consequently, requires use of a scatter/gather feature of the input and output channels. As already described in Chap. 3, scatter and gather have certain undesirable limitations.
2. It is too complex, both in its internal workings and in its external description, to be appealing.

In short, the burdens probably outweigh the advantages.

Dynamic Buffering.   Dynamic buffering is another technique that is mentioned here more for completeness than for its past commercial value. The principle in dynamic buffering is that a user's program might execute a large number of READ requests referring to random records or blocks. These requests would enter an I/O supervisor queue awaiting channel program execution. Such a queue could be sorted by the I/O supervisor to achieve efficient use of I/O devices or to expedite requests of highest priority. At the time a request is selected from the queue for execution, a buffer can be assigned to it. Assignment at an earlier time would mitigate against a large queue. The queue, queue sorting, and the opportunity for dynamic buffering are all discussed in Chap. 9, "The I/O Supervisor."

Circular Buffering.   The SCOPE System uses a technique that differs somewhat from all of the preceding techniques. A circular buffer is a contiguous segment of main storage that is at least as large as the largest block to be processed. In most systems, such a block would be structured into a pool of buffers. In SCOPE, the segment is not so structured. Rather, the space within the segment is used as if it were endless; the end of the segment is treated as if it were followed by the beginning. Figure 8-23 illustrates a circular buffer being used for input and for output. The IN and OUT pointers, stored in a table available to the user's program and to the system, are used in a tail-chasing manner readily understandable from the diagrams.

SUMMARY

The access methods allow the user to say WRITE to dispose of a record and READ to retrieve it. The access method programs lie between that macro interface and the I/O supervisor. To furnish READ and WRITE efficiently, access methods accomplish buffering, blocking, and device independence. These accomplishments, common to most I/O systems, result in fairly uniform organization of access method programs, allowing users to select from three service levels:

Channel Program Level   At this level, the user's program bypasses the access methods, furnishing its own channel program conforming to I/O supervisor, I/O device, and file organization rules. Some systems restrict or eliminate this service level.

Block Level   At this level, the access methods store and retrieve blocks of records, shielding the user's program from most I/O device characteristics. READ and WRITE furnish block handling, and CHECK synchronizes I/O activity with the user's program. Macro variations allow storing or retrieving of random or consecutive blocks with or without automatic synchronization. NOTE, POINT, and BKSP (backspace) provide modified sequential block processing.

Record Level   At this level, READ and WRITE furnish buffering, blocking, and device independence. Apparent instantaneous service is provided by automatic synchronization. Macro variations provide sequential, modified sequential, reverse sequential, or random record processing. The latter usually implies the use of CHECK rather than automatic synchronization. The move and locate modes of READ and WRITE allow processing in a work area or within the input or output buffer. End-use device control, such as printer forms control, is furnished by a control byte on each record or by control macros such as SKIP. An I/O editor can furnish device control as well as record editing.

Buffering can be performed using several alternative techniques. In most systems, a main storage area is structured into a pool of buffers either before or during program execution. A simple buffering technique assigns buffers consecutively as required when the user executes READ or WRITE. Dynamic buffering defers assignment of input buffers till the last possible moment to conserve buffer space. Exchange buffering fragments individual buffers to avoid movement of records within main storage. Circular buffering uses contiguous main storage as an endless buffer. The I/O system and the user's program pursue each other around the circle.

Exercises

1.(e) Buffering is a means to a goal. What is that goal?
2.(c) Why is device independence of a user's interface to an access method valuable?
3.(e) What two parameters, used in combination, determine a particular access method?
4.(e) List at least three reasons why a user might select the channel program service level.
5.(e) Why is the POINT macro not usable as a substitute for BKSP?
6.(e) Assume a user's program is creating a new master file by updating old master records and inserting new master records. Why is GET/move with PUT/locate not a useful combination?
7.(e) Describe a simple case in which three buffers would provide faster execution of a user's program than would two buffers.
8.(e) What is the advantage of assigning buffers dynamically?

9.(m) At the block level, some I/O systems infer CHECK and then READ when the user's program issues a second READ. This design limits the user's alternatives. Why is it done?

10.(m) Explain in your own words the problem peculiar to PUT/locate.

11.(m) An I/O system might require the user's program to declare at OPEN time that the forms control macro, such as that illustrated in Fig. 8-14, will be used. Why might such a specification be required?

12.(m) What is the principal difference between simple buffering and circular buffering?

9 The I/O Supervisor

Supervisor: An administrative officer in charge of operations.
. . . Webster's Seventh New Collegiate Dictionary

The I/O supervisor is the police officer that controls traffic at the intersection of arithmetic-unit programs and their channel programs. As a police officer, it both directs traffic for greatest efficiency and guards against infractions of the rules. The responsibilities of both the human traffic officer and the I/O supervisor are primarily administrative. Neither is concerned with the reasons for the traffic; they are concerned only with efficiency and fair play. For either type of traffic, the administrative role is very important.

Its position of authority allows the I/O supervisor of most systems to accomplish the following objectives:

1. Ensure efficient use of I/O devices and channels.
2. Establish the sequence of execution of I/O activities.
3. Protect data and programs from accidental or intentional damage or compromise.
4. Detect I/O operation failures and correct those failures when possible.
5. Accumulate and record statistics of I/O activities as a basis for device maintenance, user billing, and system-performance analysis.
6. Accomplish the above goals with modest cost in main storage space and CPU time.

Before the advent of operating systems, each user of the computer system typically presented his or her program and data to an operator whenever a job was to be run. At the conclusion of that job, both data and program would be returned to the user's office. There was little need for an I/O supervisor under such circumstances. The entire system, including the attached I/O devices and the data available through them, was considered the rightful domain of one user's program. In that primitive environment no policing action was required, nor is it required on the smaller computer systems of today.

During the mid-1950s, a large computer was typically supported by two or more small computers called peripheral computers. Peripheral computers performed routine services such as printing reports from magnetic tape. Peripheral computers were a serious burden because of their cost and the problems of scheduling their work to match the requirements of the large computer. For a period of time around 1960, one frequently heard the term SPOOL, an industry contraction for simultaneous peripheral operations on line. In SPOOLing, the peripheral CPUs were eliminated, and the I/O devices from those peripheral systems were attached directly to the larger computer. One

176

computer, the Honeywell 800, was designed to perform simultaneous operations of this kind without major programming support. However, it soon became apparent that ease of operation, flexibility, and efficiency could be achieved best by some form of programmed supervision. Some reasons that SPOOLing and the other more general forms of multiprogramming that came later require an I/O supervisor are as follows:

1. Multiprogramming makes it impossible for any one user to ensure efficient use of the system. For example, a single user might achieve maximum efficiency for his or her program by monopolizing completely two I/O channels to make a copy of a file on magnetic tape. However, the system would perform more efficiently if those channels were freed occasionally so that another user's program could use them to retrieve the new parameters it might require for an extensive arithmetic operation.
2. Multiprogramming removes some of the operator's ability to enforce job priorities. In a non-multiprogrammed system, the operator can enforce priorities by controlling the sequence of running programs. In a multiprogrammed system, several programs run simultaneously, and the operator cannot enforce priorities for the moment-by-moment interactions between such programs.
3. Multiprogramming exposes data to accidental or intentional damage or compromise because the data for several programs must be simultaneously available to a multiprogrammed system.
4. Multiprogramming makes a supervisor necessary to identify the results of each I/O operation with the program that has been served. The situation resembles that where a customer requesting a service is given a number and asked to wait. When the service is complete, the supervisor effectively calls out the customer's number to reestablish the relationship between the customer and his or her request.

In today's systems, the historic multiprogramming requirements for an I/O supervisor remain strong. But it is worth noting that, even without multiprogramming, a modern system would require an I/O supervisor. The reason is that existence of large volumes of data on auxiliary storage devices makes continuous enforcement of the rules of access essential.

A GENERAL DESCRIPTION OF THE I/O SUPERVISOR

I/O supervisors are composed of two essentially separate parts: (1) an I/O request handler that responds to requests from programs that require channel program execution and (2) an I/O interrupt handler that responds to the interruption mechanism of the computer, analyzes the results of an I/O activity, schedules corrective action, and posts completion of service requests. The separation of the two parts is a fundamental aspect of an I/O supervisor, and it is the natural outgrowth of the computing machinery. A CPU program requests execution of a channel program at one instant in time, and the channel program completes its execution at an unpredicted later time. This separation in time and the differences between the actions required at those times result in two pieces that have only a few shared instruction sequences. The two parts do share tables and queues, as will be discussed later in this chapter. The two parts are so natural that they can be identified in virtually all I/O systems. They can even be detected in the Master Control Program for the Burroughs Corporation, B6500—a rather remarkable fact when one considers the unique stack organization that characterizes the B6500.[1]

The I/O Request Handler

Figure 9-1 is a simplified flowchart of an I/O request handler. The process is started by a request for service. The request may have originated directly from a user's program or from some other part of the control program. After checking that the request is valid, the I/O request handler must determine whether the required device and a channel that can communicate with the device are available. If so, the I/O activity is started; if not, the activity is queued for later initiation. In either case, there is nothing further the I/O request handler can do, so the CPU is relinquished to the control program supervisor. The latter will determine whether the user's program should be resumed or whether some other activity is more appropriate. The procedure of the I/O request handler is so simple that it requires little explanation. Some of the details and implications are not so obvious, and they are discussed later in this chapter. But first, we shall review the flow of the other half of the I/O supervisor, the I/O interrupt handler.

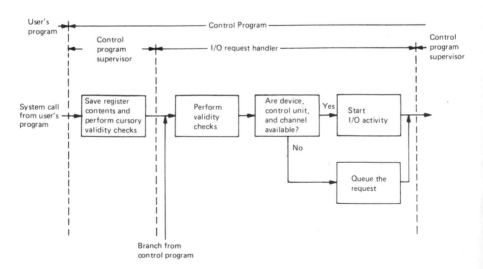

Fig. 9-1   The I/O request handler.

[1] An excellent paper is by Rajani M. Patel, "Basic I/O Handling on Burroughs B6500," *Proceedings on the Second Symposium on Operating System Principles,* ACM, October 1969.

The I/O Interrupt Handler

Whenever the computer interruption system signals an I/O interrupt, the I/O interrupt handler is entered. Just how this is effected will depend on details of the interruption system. In most systems, entry to the I/O interrupt handler is indirect with control going first to the control program supervisor. This allows the latter to preserve information that will be required when the interrupted program is restarted. The occurrence of an I/O interrupt signals two things: that an I/O activity is complete and that some I/O equipment that was busy is now free. These two facts are the basis for the processing that must be accomplished in the I/O interrupt handler. Figure 9-2 illustrates the process.

In reaction to the completed I/O activity, the I/O interrupt handler must check status indicators as may be appropriate for the particular computer system. If no errors are indicated, it simply posts the activity complete. Posting an event, as you probably know, has the effect of allowing another program that is dependent on that event to continue execution. If an error is indicated, the I/O interrupt handler activates an error correction routine. One might have thought that the analysis of the completed I/O activity should have been delayed until after some new activity had been started using the newly freed equipment. The reason for the apparently inefficient order of processing is that error correction is usually given higher priority than any queued I/O request. If other I/O activity were started before the already-completed activity had been checked, the equipment required for error correction would not be immediately available.

Having checked the completed activity for accuracy, the I/O interrupt handler must determine whether the newly freed equipment can be used to satisfy any of the service requests that could not be started by the I/O request handler. If the devices required by any of the requests on that queue are now available, the I/O activities for those requests are started. It is possible that more than one I/O activity can be started at this time. Some reasons for this are in the following:

1. The I/O activity just completed may have been more demanding of channel capability than those pending. For example, the completed activity may have monopolized a sharable channel due to high data transmission rate, while several of the pending activities might share that same channel. (Not all channels are designed to be shared in this way.)
2. In a complex device configuration, one I/O activity might be utilizing a channel required by a second activity and a device required by a third. Figure 9-3 illustrates one such possibility. If the activity just completed was using device A and channel 1, then an activity that uses device B on channel 1 and an activity that uses device A on channel 2 can both be started.
3. It is possible that during handling of an I/O interruption, a second I/O activity may have been completed freeing more I/O equipment.

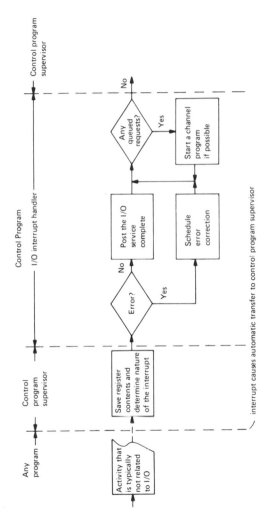

Fig. 9-2 The I/O interrupt handler.

180

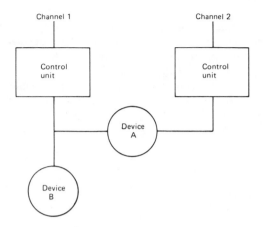

Fig. 9-3   A shared I/O device.

When all possible I/O activities have been started, the I/O interrupt handler has completed its work, and it must relinquish control of the CPU. There is no possibility that any more of the I/O activities that are still awaiting devices can be started until another I/O interrupt is received. In most systems, control is relinquished to the control program supervisor so that it can determine whether to resume the program originally interrupted or to take some other action.

SOME IMPORTANT DETAILS OF THE I/O SUPERVISOR

The preceding paragraphs described the principal activities of the two major pieces of an I/O supervisor. The next several topics add some details to items already mentioned and add some new ideas. The topics discussed are:

- Interaction of the user and the I/O supervisor
- I/O supervisor use of the system
- The I/O request queue
- Error conditions

Interaction of the User and the I/O Supervisor

In this section, we are concerned with using the I/O supervisor. The users are identified, their calling sequences are discussed, and the exits that allow close cooperation between user and the I/O supervisor are described.

Origin of the Request.   A request for I/O supervisor service may come from a user's program or from the control program itself. In some cases, the calling program will not have supervisory authority and in other cases it will. An example of the latter might be the OPEN macro requesting execution of a channel program that will retrieve a volume label. In any event, the I/O request handler receives control. The form of the request might depend on its origin as illustrated in Fig. 9-4. A user's program must issue a system call but OPEN might save time by using a more direct subroutine linkage. Whether a shortcut such as this is desirable is a question that should be decided for the entire control program. An important consideration in this case is that the I/O handler might eliminate some validity checking for requests that originate in the control program itself. This is a fundamental philosophical question that should be resolved early in the design of an I/O system. Stated succinctly, the question is, "Must the I/O handler treat all requests as if they had equal validity?" The issue is fundamentally important for these two opposing reasons:

The GCOS-III terms 'slave mode program' and 'master mode' correspond to 'user's program' and 'supervisory authority'. The I/O request handler of GCOS-III has several entry points including entry points named INOS and LINK illustrated below.

Calling Program	Calling Sequence	Effect
Slave Mode	MME GEINOS (I/O command) ZERO P1,P2 ZERO P3,P4	Master Mode Enter giving control to the INOS entry point of the I/O request handler. The existing contents of CPU registers will be saved for the calling program. The request will be validity checked.
Master Mode	.GINOS (I/O command) ZERO P1,P2 ZERO P3,P4	Branch to the INOS entry point of the I/O request handler. The CPU registers are assumed to contain certain parameters. Contents of CPU registers will not be preserved for the calling program. The request will be validity checked.
Master Mode	.LINK	Branch to the LINK entry point of the I/O request handler. The CPU registers are assumed to contain certain parameters. Contents of CPU registers will not be preserved. A queue element is ready for linking into the I/O request queue. The request will not be validity checked.

Legend: P1 -- Pointer to the file control table
P2 -- Pointer to the channel program
P3,P4 -- Addresses of caller's routines to be executed
under special circumstances

Fig. 9-4   Calling the I/O request handler (GCOS-III).

1. Any unnecessary action by the I/O handler delays the earliest possible start time for a channel program. That delay could reduce the effective performance of a device such as a magnetic drum. A delay of a few microseconds might require an extra rotation during a critical activity such as program loading.
2. If the validity of requests from certain programs is assumed, then those programs must be as rigorously tested and as carefully protected from tampering as is the I/O handler itself.

The best answer probably is a compromise such as that illustrated in Fig. 9-4. Some requests from within the control program need not be scrutinized as thoroughly for violations in their form or content as requests from users' programs, but all requests probably should be screened thoroughly for violations of security rules. This matter must be studied very carefully to achieve an effective design. A basic problem is that a part of the control program that has been surreptitiously modified might attempt to bypass or destroy the validity-checking instructions or it might even replace the entire I/O supervisor. This matter is discussed more fully in Chap. 19, "Privacy and Security."

Request Validation.   One responsibility of the I/O supervisor is to protect data and programs from accidental or intentional damage. A large number of tests of validity can be made, but efficiency requires that some compromises be made. Most of the validity checks that are made in current systems consist of verifying that the addresses furnished in registers and tables are acceptable. Some examples are as follows:

1. Are the tables established by OPEN being used? OPEN plays a key role in establishing access to files and in protecting files. That role can be effective only if I/O supervisor calls are checked for compliance. For example, the I/O supervisor should check whether the file-control table identified in the user's calling sequence (see Fig. 9-4) was previously identified by OPEN. Such a check must rely on information stored in protected tables.
2. Are main storage addresses furnished by the user within legitimate bounds? For example, does the main storage area that will be used to furnish or receive data belong to the user?
3. Is the channel program acceptable? This kind of check applies principally to DASDs. A good example is the check that auxiliary storage addresses are within the bounds of the file.

The nature and extent of checking that must be performed depend on the degree of protection desired and the automatic capabilities of the computer system itself. If the computer system exercises very little control over channel programs during their execution, the I/O supervisor may have to perform a detailed analysis of the channel program to furnish the desired degree of security.

I/O Supervisor Interaction with a Caller's Program.   There are several points during the processing of an I/O request when special actions by the caller's program might be appropriate:

● Just before the channel program is started. An example of a special action at this time is the assigning of a dynamic buffer to the channel program. Dynamic buffers were discussed in Chap. 8.
● When a channel program command with an interrupt option is executed. An example of a special action is modifying the channel program to continue or terminate its execution.
● When a channel program is terminated by an unusual condition. An example of a special action is modification and restart of the channel program to begin processing records in an area of a file that is not contiguous with the area just processed.

Programs that perform such special actions can be called I/O supervisor appendages or, simply, appendages. An appendage is executed whenever the caller's program has indicated that an appendage exists and the special condition requiring it arises. The actions performed by appendages could be accomplished by system exits, were it not for the following two problems:

1. The action to be performed is frequently trivial, and the linkages to and from a system exit program would require too much time for reasonable efficiency. In some cases, the action must be performed rapidly so that a running channel program will be controlled properly. (Good design disciplines require that occasional failure to execute an appendage soon enough must be anticipated by the caller's program.)
2. The action to be performed frequently requires the abilities to inspect and modify information that belongs to the I/O supervisor and is protected from the ordinary user's program.

To resolve these two problems, most I/O supervisors simply branch to an appendage, thereby giving the appendage all of the authority of the control program itself. Appendages in most systems are identified by file-control table entries. In EXEC-8, an appendage is called an interrupt routine, and it is identified in the I/O supervisor calling sequence.

Very careful design is required so that appendages can accomplish their work unencumbered but without freedom to accidentally or intentionally subvert the data protection features of the system. One satisfactory design, widely used, requires that appendages be stored in protected system libraries, and they are treated as if they were part of the control program. The caller's program identifies the appendages that will be used, but those appendages are not part of the caller's program. This design limits the caller's flexibility, but it potentially provides several alternatives selectable by any caller.

I/O Supervisor Use of the System

Having discussed interactions between the I/O supervisor and a calling program, we move now to interactions between the I/O supervisor and the computer system.

Availability of the I/O Device, Control Unit, and Channel.   Both the I/O request handler and the I/O interrupt handler have occasion to test for availability of I/O equipment. This determination is simplified by the nearly universal convention that an appropriate I/O device will have been identified by OPEN before the caller issues request for I/O supervisor service. The device that will be used is identified indirectly by a sequence of pointers that was described in Chap. 7, "Opening and Closing Files." Figure 9-5, a duplicate of a figure presented in that earlier chapter, illustrates a typical pointer sequence.

The pointer chain convention raises two interesting questions. What if OPEN has not been executed? How can OPEN itself call the I/O supervisor? (In effect, who "opens" OPEN?) The answer to the first question is that in most systems the I/O supervisor simply rejects any call affecting a file that has not been opened. There is no compelling reason why such a call must be rejected. Rather, the I/O supervisor could infer that OPEN should be executed whenever an I/O request is received and the pointer chain is not complete. There is good justification for such a design, a matter that was discussed in Chap. 7.

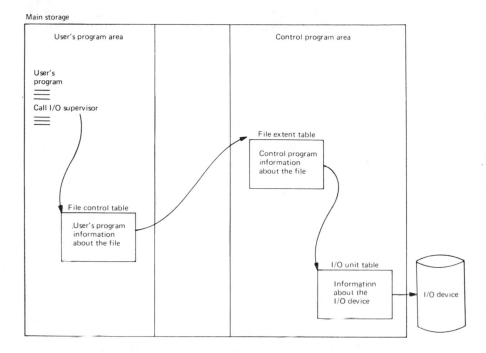

Fig. 9-5   Connection between an I/O request and an I/O device.

The second question was, "Who opens OPEN?" The answer is that OPEN, having the full authority of the control program, can simply create the required tables and the pointer chain. For example, before calling the I/O supervisor for the purpose of reading a label from a particular magnetic tape, OPEN can (and does) construct a file-control table and all other appropriate tables and pointers. The I/O supervisor can treat the subsequent call in a completely normal way.

Assuming that the I/O device has been identified and it is available for use, there is still the question whether a channel and a control unit are available. Because control units and channels are heavily shared and because their activities are quite independent of the CPU, it is impractical to tabulate their moment-by-moment status. Rather, the I/O supervisor can test for availability of a particular channel/control unit/device combination, or it can simply attempt to start a channel program using those components. Some systems, such as the Burroughs B6500, assist such an attempt by automatically selecting any available path to the I/O device. In other systems, the I/O supervisor can systematically try the limited number of possible paths to the device.

Starting an I/O Activity.   For most kinds of I/O devices, it is a simple matter for the I/O supervisor to start the channel program, verify that the start actually occurred, and proceed to other matters. However, auxiliary storage devices require special considerations.

First, if the combination of the storage device, control unit, and channel allow complex channel programs such as those described in Chap. 3, then the I/O supervisor must take appropriate steps to condition those devices to prevent unauthorized action. For example, if a particular file has been opened for reading only, the I/O supervisor should condition the equipment to reject output commands. Similar conditioning can limit the range of auxiliary storage addresses accessible to a channel program. In systems where channel programs are limited to one or two commands, the I/O supervisor can protect data by simply inspecting the channel commands.

Secondly, for direct access storage devices with movable read/write elements, efficiency of channel use can be improved by systematically prepositioning the elements in advance of starting channel programs. Doing this properly can overlap the motions of several elements, thereby avoiding lengthy delays during channel program execution. Using the channel commands described in Chap. 3, an I/O supervisor can preposition an element by removing the command chaining flag from the first SEEK in a channel program and then starting that one command program. A channel can complete its responsibility for a SEEK quickly, and it is free to execute other channel programs while the I/O device accomplishes movement of the read/write element. Later, when the complete channel program is executed, the reexecuted SEEK will be accomplished almost immediately.

Disabling the Computer Interruption Mechanism.   In Chap. 1, the subject of reenterability was discussed. There may be critical points throughout a control program where reentry cannot be tolerated and the I/O supervisor may include several such points. For example, the sequence of instructions that finds a channel available and starts a channel program may not be reenterable. The reason is that reentry might cause a second channel program to preempt a channel causing confusion later when a channel thought to be available is actually in use. There are several "mays" and "mights" in all of this because careful design could eliminate nonreenterable instruction sequences, sometimes with only modest performance loss. A practical alternative to eliminating a nonreenterable sequence is to disable the interruption mechanism during execution of the sequence. Without interruption there will be no reentry.

The interruption mechanism of a computer is designed to provide quick reaction to a condition that may be urgent. Disabling temporarily eliminates that reactive ability. Disabling for short periods may be acceptable, but the periods should be kept short for the following purposes:

1. The system must be responsive. For example, a user entering data directly from an attached keyboard terminal usually requires response within a few seconds.

2. The system can accommodate devices with tight timing requirements. For example, a reader sorter for sorting paper documents might require response to an I/O interruption within a few milliseconds.
3. The limit of the computer's ability to stack interrupts is not exceeded. If too many interrupts occur while the interrupt mechanism is disabled, some interrupts may be permanently lost.

The I/O Request Queue

The I/O request queue contains those requests for which I/O activity could not be immediately started. The logic employed in managing this queue establishes I/O priorities for the entire system.

There are several important ideas involved, including

queue structure
channel sets
queueing techniques
logical and physical devices
shared devices

I/O Request Queue Structure.   There are many techniques that can be used in structuring the I/O request queue. At one extreme, the queue could be completely unordered. Such a queue is easy to maintain, but, of course, it is time-consuming to determine what request should be activated when I/O equipment becomes available. At the other extreme, the queue could be ordered so that the request to be activated can be identified immediately upon receipt of an I/O interrupt. The structure that would allow the greatest economy in CPU burden probably lies between the extremes, and a good approximation to it would require analysis of alternatives by simulation. In practice, the choice is simplified by an overriding requirement that I/O activity should be started as soon as possible after receipt of an I/O interrupt. The reasons are readily apparent: (1) For some types of devices, device performance is improved by continuous or near-continuous control by a channel. (2) All other things being equal, it is better to do I/O queue servicing while channels are busy than while a channel is waiting. In short, the I/O request queue should be structured and queue analysis should be done principally at the time a request enters the queue rather than at the time a request is taken from the queue.

An I/O interrupt indicates that a channel has completed an activity. Sometimes but not always, a control unit and device complete an activity at the same time. To decide properly which queued request should be activated, the I/O supervisor must consider all requests that can be satisfied using the now available channel. A queue that has been structured into subqueues, one for each channel, is shown in Fig. 9-6. A table of pointers is used to identify the first queued request for each channel, and that request identifies another request requiring the same channel, and so forth. A series of request elements and pointers is sometimes called a chain or a linked list.

A Channel Set.   One of the complicating factors in maintaining subqueues of I/O requests is that there may be more than one channel by which a particular device can be controlled. In Fig. 9-7, device A can be controlled only by channel 1, but device B can be controlled by either channel 2 or channel 3, and device C can be controlled by 1, 2, or 3. The set of channels that can control a device can be called the channel set for that device. The channel set for a device usually consists of one or two channels.

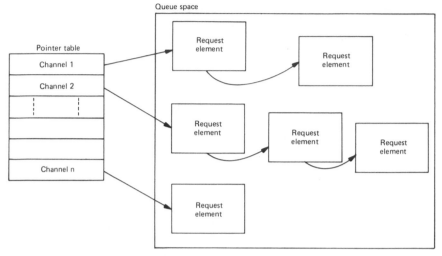

Fig. 9-6   Channel subqueues.

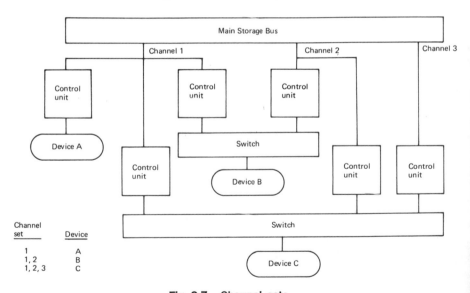

Fig. 9-7   Channel sets.

The channel set idea can be used either of two ways:

1. The request queue can be structured into subqueues with one subqueue for each channel. If this is done, a request that uses device C

in Fig. 9-7 must be placed on three subqueues, one subqueue for each channel in device C's channel set. This alternative is used in GCOS-III using linked lists.

2. The request queue can be structured in subqueues with one subqueue for each channel set. If this is done, requests on several subqueues may be candidates for activation when a channel becomes available. This alternative is used in OS/360.

Queuing Techniques.   Of the possible philosophies of ordering the requests on a subqueue, the following have been used successfully:

First In, First Out (FIFO)   This philosophy is the easiest to implement, and it is least costly in CPU execution time.

Priority   The requests within a subqueue can be ordered according to the priorities of the programs issuing the requests. This philosophy has the advantage of the ability to expedite critical work.

Ordered Seek   This philosophy orders the requests for a particular direct access storage device in a way that is optimal for that device. For example, requests using a magnetic disk storage device with a movable read/write element can be ordered so that motion of the element is minimized.

Regardless of other considerations, recognition must be given to any ordering requirements specified in the caller's program. The sequence "Rewind a tape, then read a block" has an effect different from "Read a block, then rewind the tape."

In designing either the priority or the ordered-seek philosophies, considerable care is required to ensure acceptable results. A danger with priority ordering of the I/O request queue can be illustrated using two programs, H and L. Program H has high priority, and it uses one I/O device heavily and very little else. An example might be a program that searches a complete file for records of a particular type. Program L has lower priority; it requires a great deal of main storage space and CPU time, and it uses a file stored on the same device as the file for program H. Using priority ordering, program L will not run at all until program H completes. One device is used continuously, but the remainder of the system is eventually idled. A technique that has been used successfully to overcome this problem is to raise the indicated priority for each queued request by one unit whenever some other request is selected from the queue. With this increasing priority, every old request will finally achieve a priority greater than any newly arriving requests. When that happens, the old request will be selected.

A danger with the ordered-seek philosophy is that a low-priority program might monopolize a device required by a high-priority program. Assume program HP has high priority, and it makes occasional reference to a file. Program LP has lower priority, and it makes heavy use of a file. Assume further that the two files occupy areas widely separated from each other on a single DASD. During the execution of these programs, if the situation ever arises where there are no requests in the queue for program HP, then program LP can monopolize the shared device to the total exclusion of program HP.

The I/O supervisor has effectively raised the priority of program LP to be higher than program HP. An effective technique for resolving this problem is to order the requests so that the read/write element begins at one extreme position and moves steadily toward the other extreme satisfying all possible requests as it goes. Then the element is returned to the original position ready to begin its next sweep, and so on.

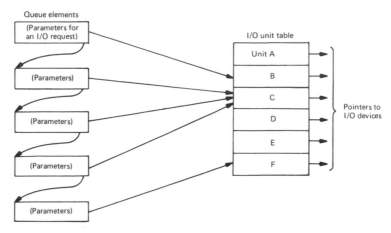

Fig. 9-8   I/O request-queue elements and a convention unit table.

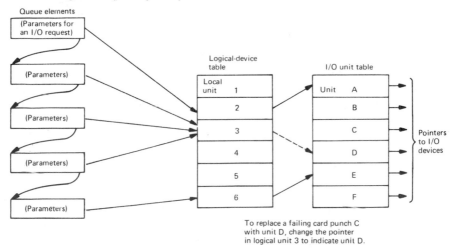

Fig. 9-9   Using a logical-device table.

Logical Devices and Physical Devices.   For convenience, the queue element that represents an I/O request on the I/O request queue will contain pointers and other relevant data. A pointer to the unit table indicating the I/O device that will be used is typically included. Figure 9-8 illustrates these unit-table pointers. A logical-device table included in GCOS-III has an important advantage. Figure 9-9 illustrates how this feature allows automatic redirection of requests in the event of I/O device failure. Notice that the same effect cannot be achieved in Fig. 9-8. Changing the entry in the conventional unit table would destroy that entry's primary purpose, notably to consistently represent a particular I/O device.

Error Conditions

The term *error*, used in an I/O system context, means lack of success in performing an action. A more accurate word would be failure. However, we shall conform to the industry term, error, in this book because that usage is universally accepted and because failure has an extreme connotation. Computer systems and baseball players commit errors.

In the early days of computers, error handling programs were simple and, frequently, ineffective. If an error occurred while reading cards, the operator could be instructed to reposition the cards for a retry. In so doing, the operator could inspect the failing card and, if damage was apparent, replace it. Where magnetic tape was involved, the standard procedure was to backspace the tape and retry reading. If 10 retries failed, the job was abandoned. Today's procedures rely heavily on retry, but the variety of devices is great and the pattern of actions is frequently complex.

Modern computer systems have checking circuitry that detects errors in channel program execution. The indicators for these errors are usually bit patterns in a particular main storage byte permanently reserved for that use. A computer system will have indicators for all or most of the following:

I/O Device Check   Checking circuits in the I/O device indicate a malfunction.

Program Check   The channel program included an invalid command.

Wrong Length   The number of bytes of data transferred was either greater or fewer than the channel program specified.

Protection Check   The channel program attempted to violate a protection mechanism. For example, the channel program may have attempted to write on a storage device conditioned for read only.

Chaining Check   An overrun condition affecting accuracy of data transfer has occurred.

Data Check   Checking circuits indicate that the transferred data contained one or more errors.

Just as the instruction set of one computer differs from another, the precise meaning of any indicator differs from one computer to another. More important, the meaning of a specific indicator on a specific computer may differ from one I/O device to another. Even further, indicators may occur in combinations implying simultaneous occurrence of two or more error conditions. In consequence, the error handling routines are varied, complex, and subject to change as I/O devices are added to the system or optional features are added to devices.

Error Handling.   Figure 9-10 expands the error handling control section of the I/O interrupt handler. The essence of Fig. 9-10 is this: Once an error indication has occurred, the appropriate error routine should get control, and it should continue to get control after each retry of the failing activity. In most other respects, the system should continue as if no problem existed.

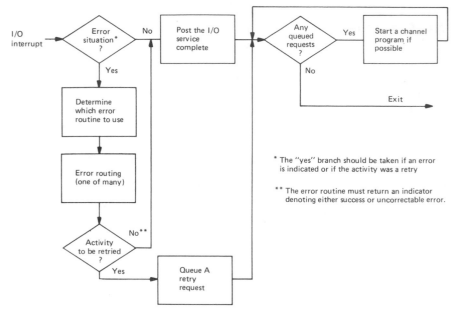

Fig. 9-10   Error handling in the I/O interrupt handler.

Error Routines.   The error correcting procedures used depend on the type of I/O device. A backspace and rewrite procedure is sensible for a magnetic tape, but it is not appropriate for a card punch. Good procedures must be determined by engineering analysis of circuits and media and by statistical analysis of actual failure cases. Without such analysis, one would be hard pressed to say whether there is any justification for retrying for a tenth time, or a twentieth time, or whether there is any justification for retrying at all. Figure 9-11 illustrates the kinds of actions that can be used in a magnetic tape error routine. Though that procedure is only illustrative, it is realistic. Notice that steps 1 through 5 include 40 reread attempts, and even then the procedure is not complete. It would be folly to design such a procedure without intimate knowledge of the device. Ideally, correction procedures should be part of the engineering specifications for each device.

Error correction procedures in most systems consist principally of retrying the operation, preceded by repositioning of the medium if appropriate. There are two good reasons why retry is used. Both engineering analysis and experience prove that a retry will be successful for many kinds of errors. There are not many practical alternatives. A philosophical point that must be recognized is that a highly complex procedure might have a limited chance of success particularly when applied to a device known to be failing. One procedure that has been used successfully is an alternate path procedure. I/O device errors are frequently baffling even with detailed analysis using engineering test equipment.

Occasionally attempting the same process using a different channel and different control unit will yield success even when the original channel and control unit seem to be in good operating condition. An error routine can accomplish methodical use of alternate paths using the channel set information discussed earlier.

Another usable procedure is to substitute an identical I/O device to replace the failing unit. This process requires operator assistance, of course.

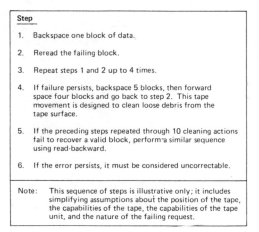

Step

1. Backspace one block of data.

2. Reread the failing block.

3. Repeat steps 1 and 2 up to 4 times.

4. If failure persists, backspace 5 blocks, then forward space four blocks and go back to step 2. This tape movement is designed to clean loose debris from the tape surface.

5. If the preceding steps repeated through 10 cleaning actions fail to recover a valid block, perform a similar sequence using read-backward.

6. If the error persists, it must be considered uncorrectable.

Note: This sequence of steps is illustrative only; it includes simplifying assumptions about the position of the tape, the capabilities of the tape, the capabilities of the tape unit, and the nature of the failing request.

Fig. 9-11   Error procedure for data check while reading magnetic tape.

Permanent Errors.   If the error correction procedures fail to correct an error condition, the error must be considered noncorrectable or permanent. In some cases, the user may have furnished an exit for this eventuality. When the user has specified no alternative, the running of that program must be terminated. The I/O supervisor can cause that termination by giving a proper indication to the control program supervisor.

Packaging of the Error Routines.   Whether the error routines should be considered part of the I/O supervisor or whether they should be a separate entity is a debatable point. This matter is discussed generally in Chap. 19, "Privacy and Security." Briefly, the concern is that the responsibilities and authorities of the I/O supervisor can be fulfilled best by small and stable programs. Clearly, their variability dictates that the error routines should be modular. In most cases, their size and infrequency of use dictate that they should not occupy main storage permanently. Rather, they are usually stored on auxiliary storage volumes and are moved to main storage as required using the program loading facilities of the system. One special case must be considered—the error routine that corrects errors in loading the error programs. Unless that routine is kept in main storage, the occurrence of error during error program loading will pose an insurmountable problem to the I/O supervisor.

Error Statistics.   The continued improvement of error correction procedures makes the recording of error statistics more and more important. The reason?

The error routines may disguise equipment problems that should be fixed before they interfere with system operation.

Error statistics for each device can be accumulated by the error routines in a convenient table, such as the I/O unit table. The information that is collected might include

- the number of correctable errors that have occurred
- the number of retries required for success for each correctable error
- the number of permanent errors that have occurred
- conditions of various indicators at the time of each permanent error
- the number of service requests processed (without this number, the items above are of limited value)

When a table containing the information is filled to capacity, the information can be moved to auxiliary storage. It might be appropriate to notify the operator of this action; if the tables overflow with increasing frequency, the operator may wish to alert computer maintenance personnel to the gradually deteriorating situation.

SUMMARY

The I/O supervisor is a collection of programs that

ensure efficiency
establish the sequence of I/O activities
protect data
correct I/O errors
accumulate statistics

Multiprogramming is a principal factor creating the requirements for an I/O supervisor.

An I/O supervisor is composed of two parts: (1) the I/O request handler that validates I/O service requests and, if the required equipment is available, starts the I/O activity and (2) the I/O interrupt handler that checks a completed I/O activity for errors, posts the related I/O request, and starts I/O activities for waiting requests.

The primary user's interface to the I/O supervisor is a system call. The I/O request handler inspects the addresses furnished to validate the call. In some systems, alternative entry points allow properly qualified programs to bypass these preliminary actions. The caller can identify appendages to be executed at appropriate points during I/O request processing. Appendages can improve operating efficiency, but improper design can jeopardize the data protection features of a system.

The I/O supervisor can inspect a chain of pointers established by OPEN to determine what I/O device is required to satisfy a particular request. Availability of the device is usually indicated in the I/O unit table. Availability of an appropriate control unit and channel can be determined by systematic tests of the equipment. When the I/O device is an auxiliary storage device, some preconditioning by the I/O supervisor may be appropriate. Preconditioning can prepare the equipment to reject unauthorized action by the channel program, and for devices with movable read/write elements, it can improve efficiency by positioning the elements near the data to be processed. The interruption system may be disabled for short periods during the execution of nonreenterable sequences of I/O supervisor instructions.

I/O requests that require equipment not immediately available are placed in a queue. The queue element representing an I/O request typically identifies the unit table of the required I/O device. Alternatively, the element could identify a logical-device table. In general, the queue should be structured so that the effort required to select a request from the queue for processing is small. This might be done by organizing requests into linked lists, one list for each channel or channel set. The requests within each list could be arranged for processing FIFO, in priority order, or in the order allowing most efficient operation of the I/O device. These last two alternatives require particularly careful design. In any case, the callers might dictate the order of execution of their own requests.

When the I/O supervisor detects an error condition, an error routine appropriate for the particular I/O device gets control and should continue to get control after each retry. An error routine should be designed according to engineering specifications for the device. The probability of successful error correction may be improved by systematically using alternative channels, control units, and I/O devices for retries. If an error proves uncorrectable, a user exit can be used or, lacking an exit, the user's program must be terminated. Error routines are usually stored on DASDs to conserve main storage space. The I/O supervisor should accumulate error statistics so that deteriorating device conditions can be detected.

Exercises

1.(e) Which part of the I/O supervisor is more likely to have alternative entry points, the request handler or the interrupt handler? Give reasons for your answer.

2.(e) Under certain circumstances, the I/O supervisor may have to check the addresses used in channel commands. Is it possible that an address in a channel command might be modified after the I/O supervisor check and before the command is executed? If so, how?

3.(e) Why might it be inadvisable for OPEN to place appendages in a user's main storage area?

4.(e) In this chapter, only one circumstance was described where the I/O supervisor modified a channel command.
   a. What was that circumstance?
   b. What purpose did the modification serve?
   c. Which of the two major parts of an I/O supervisor would accomplish this action?

5.(m) Which, if any, of the I/O supervisor objectives listed early in this chapter apply exclusively to multiprogramming systems?

6.(m) Assume two programs are being executed in a multiprogrammed environment. Is it possible that circumstances might allow all channel programs for these two CPU programs to be started by the I/O request handler and none by the I/O interrupt handler?

7. (m) In an environment where a single user's program is being executed and the control program is requiring no I/O activity, could the circumstances arise where the I/O interrupt handler would be required to start an I/O activity?

8. (m) Assume all I/O equipment is idle when an I/O request requiring device C in Fig. 9-7 is received.

   a. Why would channel 1 be an undesirable choice for filling the request?

   b. What channel would be most desirable?

9. (m) Describe a situation where FIFO ordering in the I/O request queue would cause inefficient use of an I/O device.

10. (m) It was stated that I/O error correction is usually expedited. One possible design would start no other channel program until a channel program using the failing device has been started. What is the basic problem with that design?

11. (m) Assume a magnetic tape unit is failing in such a way that tape positioning is occasionally incorrect and that the Fig. 9-11 error procedure is being used. Describe a sequence of events that would yield an apparently successful read though the desired block of data is permanently illegible.

10 Data Staging

Staging area: an area in which troops are assembled and readied prior to a new operation or mission. . . . Webster's Collegiate Dictionary

Data staging is the activity of moving data from one location to another to prepare them for processing or the reverse activity of moving data from a location where they were stored temporarily during processing to a more permanent location. Staging is not directly productive, but rather it is an auxiliary activity that allows the actual processing of data to be more efficient, more responsive, or less exposed to failure. During the staging process, the data being moved might be rearranged or edited methodically. For example, blocking factors might be changed or character representations might be translated from one code to another.

If you think carefully about the definition of staging, you will observe that all I/O activity is, in a sense, staging. Conventional central processing units are able to process only the data that reside in main storage, and any activity that moves data to main storage or removes data from main storage is staging according to our definition. However, because we do not want to include all I/O activity in our present discussion, we shall exclude from our definition of staging that I/O activity immediately surrounding the actual processing of data. Figure 10-1 clarifies this point. The distinction is not really rigorous, of course. For example, the staging on the left side of Fig. 10-1 might be accomplished by a utility program. The activities of moving data from the tape reel to main storage and from main storage to the magnetic drum are simple I/O activities relative to that utility program, but they are staging relative to the central user's program.

Staging is not directly productive, nor is it accomplished without cost. In fact, there are several costs inherent in staging:

1. Staging uses devices, control units, channels, main storage, and CPU time.
2. Staging before a process requires time thereby delaying, or at least potentially delaying, start of the intended process. Similarly, for staging after processing, the start of the printer, punch, or other end-use device is delayed.
3. Staging exposes data to accidental damage or disclosure just as any other handling does.

Staging is profitably used only when its advantages offset these costs. There are three general circumstances where staging is used, and the principal reason for using staging is different in each one:

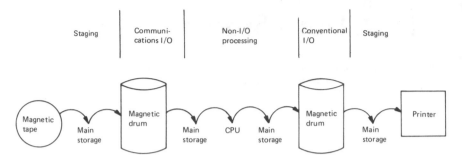

Fig. 10-1   Data staging and other activities.

1. Staging of data entering or leaving the system is done principally for flexibility in scheduling. With staging, data can enter or leave the system at the convenience of the terminal operator, and it can be processed at the convenience of the system.
2. Staging of data files is done principally for economy in storage. With staging, data files can be stored on low-cost media with high volumetric density of data and be processed from high-performance, sharable devices such as magnetic disks or drums. Were it not for the relatively high cost and low volumetric efficiency of disks and drums, all data could be stored permanently on those devices.
3. Staging of work in process is done primarily to provide responsiveness of the system to externally imposed demands. For example, a staging technique called rollout can be used to suspend processing of one program to allow execution of a higher priority program. Time sharing systems use techniques called paging or swapping to stage work in process for a large number of users' programs so that their execution can proceed in parallel.

The three circumstances listed above are sufficiently different to require special staging techniques for each circumstance. In the sections that follow, each circumstance is defined more fully; the reasons for staging in that circumstance are detailed; and some of the techniques that have been developed are described.

DATA ENTERING OR LEAVING THE SYSTEM

Data entering the system consist of control statements and data. The input device might be a card reader, magnetic tape, direct access device, or keyboard. Data entering the system are called *system input data,* SYSIN. In the case where the device is a keyboard and the keyboard operator expects diagnosis or processing of each unit of data as it is entered, a more descriptive term might be *interactive input data.*

Data leaving the system consist of lines for printing or punching. The output device might be a printer, card punch, paper-tape punch, magnetic tape, or any other output device. Data leaving the system are called *system output data,* SYSOUT.

In some systems, SYSIN and SYSOUT might be limited to end-use devices in order to reduce system implementation cost, but SYSIN and SYSOUT are characterized more by the nature of the data involved than by the kind of device. All major systems stage SYSIN and SYSOUT.

Justification for SYSIN and SYSOUT Staging

Some of the most important reasons for staging SYSIN and SYSOUT are listed below:

1. Staging of input and output data allows the system to process requests in an order that gives proper recognition to priorities while utilizing equipment efficiently. If staging is not done, requests must be processed in order of their presentation through any one input device, and the output device must be available during processing.
2. Staging can make a user's program less dependent on I/O device availability. For example, a single program might produce three output reports simultaneously on a system with only one printer if output is staged. Further, that one printer need not be available during execution of the user's program. Even further, several such programs can simultaneously have the effect of multiple printers.
3. Staging allows the frequently slow processes of communicating data to terminal devices to be accomplished independent of the user's program. This reduces the period of time that resources are required by the user's program.
4. Staging can improve end-use device utilization. A printer might achieve 1,000 lines per minute of printed output when output is staged, while performance during direct use might be 100 lines per minute or even less depending on characteristics of the user's program.
5. Staged input data are reprocessable. This is especially important when input is accepted directly from a keyboard terminal. If such input data are processed directly by a user's program and no machine-processable copy is made, that data would have to be rekeyed in the event of system or program malfunction.
6. Staged output data are reprocessable. Staged output data can be reused several times to produce multiple copies of results. They can be transmitted over communication lines so that printing can be done at several locations. They can be reprocessed to recover from printer problems such as torn forms without rerunning the user's program. They can be saved as a compact, permanent, machine-processable record of processing results. They can be used as input for a subsequent process.

Restated, staging can break up the sequential dependency of SYSIN and SYSOUT while providing a reprocessing capability.

SYSIN Processing

SYSIN is a stream of service requests consisting of control statements and data records. SYSIN is staged by a control program routine called one of these: a symbiont (EXEC-8), a load control (MCP), or a reader (OS/360). The staging routines can either be started automatically by the control program, or they can be started by the operator. In EXEC-8, devices that will be used for SYSIN are identified during system generation. Whenever one of these identified devices is readied by the operator, the control program automatically initiates symbiont activity for it. The operator can temporarily override this automatic action if the device is to be assigned other functions. In OS/360, the operator initiates the staging operation. As SYSIN is being staged, the records within it are examined, and certain records serve to control the staging process. For example, an EXEC-8 symbiont detects the following records:

@RUN   Denotes the beginning of control statements for a user's request.
@FILE   Denotes beginning of data records to be processed by the user's program.
@ENDF   Denotes the end of a collection of data records.
@FIN   Denotes the end of SYSIN records related to a user's request. This record is optional; the occurrence of another @RUN is an acceptable indication that the preceding request is complete.

All of the information is placed on the staging device, typically a magnetic drum or magnetic disk device. The control statements for any request are stored separate from the data record.

The control statements will serve as an input data file for the control program routines that schedule work, and the data records will become an input file for the user's program. To read an input file that has been staged, the user's program calls upon a symbiont (EXEC-8), a pseudo-card reader (MCP), or an access method (OS/360).

The mechanisms used to process an input file can be essentially the same as for any other file. In OS/360, the user's program must issue an OPEN system call referring to a DCB, which refers to a data definition control statement, and so on, just as for any other file. In this case, the data definition statement has been modified by the SYSIN reader to identify the staged file. After processing the input file using the sequential access method, the user's program issues a CLOSE system call just as the user would for any other file.

SYSOUT Processing

SYSOUT is the name given to that output from a user's program that should be presented to the user. Such output is usually printed, punched, or displayed. The user's program can create one or more SYSOUT files in much the way it would create other files using the system calls and conventions related to a symbiont (EXEC-8), a pseudo-card punch or printer (MCP), or an access method (OS/360).

SYSOUT files are staged just as SYSIN files. The staged output is recorded on an output device by a symbiont (EXEC-8) and a SYSOUT writer (OS/360). An output file may contain control records or control fields attached to the data records that define device control actions such as forms control for printers or stacker select for card punches.

Remote Job Entry.   The term *remote job entry* (*RJE*) is used to describe the use of SYSIN or SYSOUT devices attached to the computer system through common carrier communication lines. RJE is not fundamentally different from what has been discussed. The two facets most affected are in the following:

1. The actual coding of the RJE package is affected by requirements of dialing and other communications conventions.
2. The computer-system operator cannot personally intervene to manipulate the device. Messages affecting operation of the device must be communicated to the device itself.

OS/360 furnishes a separate package of RJE programs that serve the reader and writer functions. EXEC-8 furnishes the RJE capabilities as part of the symbiont package.

Communications-Based Systems

The philosophy and design of communications-based systems could easily be subjects of another book. In this section, mention is made of a few ideas and terms used in programming for communications systems.

Conversational Remote Job Entry.   When keyboard terminals with either graphic display or typewriter output are used, RJE can be extended to become conversational process. In conversational RJE, the control program and the terminal operator work cooperatively to develop a valid service request or to print output. For example, as the keyboard operation completes each control statement, the conversational RJE program can analyze that statement and either accept it or request that it be rekeyed correctly. Or the operator might want to rekey all lines beginning 20 lines back. For output, the system can request that tab stops be set appropriately and that the proper forms be placed in the printer. Or the keyboard operator may want to interrupt output, key some input, and then resume output.

Conversational RJE requires that data, particularly SYSIN data, be readily available for inspection and rework. To provide conversational service effectively, EXEC-8 modifies its staging strategy to keep as much SYSIN and SYSOUT data in main storage as possible, using magnetic drum space only when data volume requires it.

Time Sharing.   In time sharing, not only are SYSIN and SYSOUT performed conversationally, but the user's program is also used interactively. After a small amount of SYSIN data has been collected, the user's program should process those data, and the output data created should be sent back to the user. The major difference between time sharing and conversational RJE in the handling of SYSIN and SYSOUT data is that the input staging is not complete before the user's program begins processing, and the output files are not closed before output staging begins.

STAGING OF DATA FILES

Many data files are stored on magnetic tape principally because tape is inexpensive and easy to handle, and it provides a high density of data per cubic foot of storage space. Sometimes, users' programs can be organized to process a magnetic tape data file directly with excellent efficiency, but frequently greater processing efficiency would be possible if the files were stored on a disk or drum storage device.

Justification for Staging Data Files

There are three alternatives available. Data can be stored and processed on the medium most efficient for storage. Data can be stored and processed on the medium allowing most efficient processing. Data can be staged.

The costs of storing data on the two media are easily calculated, and they can differ significantly, particularly if the file is large and the higher-performance medium is not dismountable from its device. The difference in processing efficiency is not so easily calculated. Some factors affecting processing efficiency are as follows:

1. Good staging devices offer excellent nonconsecutive processing capability. When applicable, that capability can reduce the execution time of a user's program, thereby reducing the period of allocation of resources to that program.
2. Good staging devices can be used by several programs simultaneously reducing the total number of I/O devices required. This can be particularly important in time sharing where many users' programs are simultaneously executed.
3. Staging provides an opportunity to change the blocking factor from a large factor efficient for storage to a small factor efficient for non-consecutive processing.
4. Staging provides an automatic back-up copy of a file.

Data File Staging

The most natural combination of devices for data file staging is a high-performance magnetic disk or drum and magnetic tape. This combination has been used in special purpose systems, and it is used effectively in EXEC-8.

EXEC-8 uses its extensive direct access storage capacity for three purposes:

● System's residence—that is, storage space for the program comprising the operating system.
● Working file space—that is, space that can be used for scratch files that are created during a program run and can be scratched immediately afterward.
● Staging space for permanent data files.

The major portion of all space is in the third category above, and that is the part of interest to us.

EXEC-8 maintains the user's data files in the data file space, staging files to magnetic tape as necessary to provide room for additional files. Files are moved to tape automatically whenever available space drops below a fixed amount specified at system generation time. Files are also moved to tape when a user's program unexpectedly requires more space than is available.

To determine which files should be moved to tape, control information maintained for each file is analyzed, and files that have not been used recently are selected. Files moved to tape are placed consecutively on a reel assigned for system use. Typically, a reel stays mounted and is not rewound until it is completely filled.

When a user requires a file that has been staged to tape, that file is staged back to a direct access device for the user. If necessary, other files will be staged to tape to make room available.

STAGING OF WORK IN PROCESS

For our purposes here, work in process consists of data, tables, and programs temporarily in main storage in connection with the processing of some user's service request. There are three separate techniques that are used to stage work in process: rollout, swapping, and paging. They will be discussed in the following sections.

Rollout

Work in process might be staged temporarily to auxiliary storage to make main storage space available for a high-priority service request. Such staging is called rollout, and its counterpart is called rollin. The value of rollout is limited by the fact that devices allocated to the rolled-out program are idle but not available for reallocation. Some alternatives to rollout are in the following:

1. Cancel a running program and rerun it later. The principal disadvantage of this alternative is the variability of rerun cost.
2. Reserve enough main storage space to satisfy a high-priority request at any time. This alternative has two principal disadvantages: The unused main storage is a significant cost. A second high-priority request cannot be satisfied quickly.
3. Schedule work in such a way that at any instant in time, the processing for one or more service requests is nearly complete. The problems inherent in this alternative are apparent.

Rollout seems to be the best alternative.

The design of rollout includes no particular problems. One suggestion worth considering is this: Rollout should be limited to very high-priority service requests that are constrained to utilize sharable I/O devices and modest main storage space.

Swapping

On a preplanned basis, several users' programs can utilize a single area of main storage, each accomplishing limited processing before relinquishing to the next. Staging under these circumstances is called swapping. One set of data, tables, and programs can be swapped out from main storage, and the next set swapped in in rapid succession to furnish a modest but continuous level of service to many requests using limited main core resources. Swapping is used in general purpose time sharing systems. Justification for swapping is justification for time sharing, a complex justification indeed. Time sharing may be a fundamentally inefficient use of equipment, but is justified by improved productivity of the system users themselves.

Paging

A system can furnish the effect of unlimited main storage size by moving segments of programs or data in and out of main storage. To accomplish this, programs and data are arbitrarily broken into segments called pages, and "pages are turned" by staging old pages to auxiliary storage replacing them with pages that are currently required. Using the computer interruption system appropriately, the control program can detect an attempt by any program to execute an instruction or to store or retrieve data outside the pages that are available in main storage. When such an attempt is detected, the control program can retrieve the required pages from the staging device, suspending execution of the interrupting program until paging is complete. Such a system is called a virtual storage system, an industry term meaning a system in which users' programs have the effect of virtually unlimited main storage space. The justification for paging requires justification for virtual storage systems. Virtual storage systems can be used for time sharing, so that is a justification in many cases, and they simplify the planning required for users' programs, thereby improving effectiveness of people.

Paging systems operate in a conditionally stable manner. As long as certain critical operating parameters stay within limits, acceptable performance can be achieved. However, when a limiting condition is met, a phenomenon called thrashing occurs, and the useful work produced by the system may drop suddenly by a factor of 2, 3, or even more. To understand thrashing, we must know a little about page size, working sets, and page replacement algorithms.

Page Size.   In choosing an appropriate page size for a paging system, the objective is to choose the smallest size that is large enough to yield an acceptable average amount of processing supported by each page. Figure 10-2 shows three situations. When pages are used for a file of data that is processed sequentially, the amount of processing supported by a page of data is directly proportional to page size. Such pages yield a straight line. If the records of a file are processed randomly, increasing the page size would increase the number of records processed from each page very little. The most interesting case is the case where pages contain programmed instructions. The amount of processing supported by a page increases linearly with page size until a page is large enough to contain a small loop. Then processing per page increases rather rapidly until page size is large enough to contain a modest-sized program. The payoff from increasing page size beyond that point is less because large pages simply include unused space. In IBM's DOS/VS, page size is 2,048 bytes; in OS/VS1, it is 2,048 bytes; and in OS/VS2, it is 4,096 bytes. Smaller pages require that too many pages be moved to and from main storage, while larger pages simply require too much main storage space.

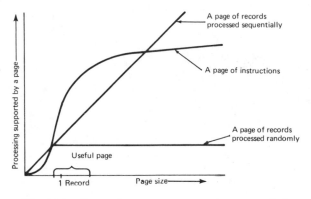

Fig. 10-2   Page size versus processing supported.

Working Sets.   A user's program is contained in a collection of pages. During execution, instructions from one page and then another are executed and, finally, all pages will have had some part in the execution. Now, if one were planning to keep all pages in main storage, paging would have no advantage. The question is, "How many pages are required in main storage to yield a reasonably low probability that when instructions from a certain page are to be executed, that page will still be available because of its previous use?" The answer depends in part on the algorithm used to page inactive pages out to auxiliary storage. But, regardless of that algorithm, it has been shown that programs characteristically conform to the pattern shown in Fig. 10-3. There is a very abrupt point where the probability changes from a very small number to a value approaching 1.0. Decreasing the number of pages allotted to a number less than the working set has a disastrous effect; the required page will almost never be present.

Another term sometimes used for working set is parachor. Parachor is typically expressed in bytes rather than pages. Every program has a certain size and a certain parachor. Unfortunately, there is no simple method to determine parachor short of simulation or measured execution.

Page-Replacement Algorithms.   Whenever a page not already available is required, some page currently in main storage must be replaced. One could undoubtedly concoct many different algorithms for deciding which page to remove from main storage. Two usable algorithms are:

First In, First Out (FIFO)   Whenever a new page is required, the page that has been in main storage longest is removed. This algorithm has the advantage of simplicity.

Least Active   A queue of pages in main storage is maintained. Whenever a page is used, it is moved to the head of the queue. Whenever a page must be replaced, the one at the bottom of the queue is paged out. This algorithm presumes that pages used most recently in the past will be used most immediately in the future.

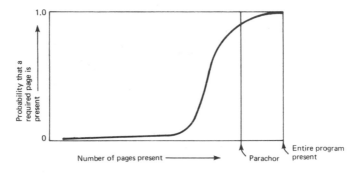

Fig. 10-3   The parachor phenomenon.

Thrashing.   Assuming that a paging system has been designed so that the storage devices used to store and retrieve pages can accommodate the expected paging rate, one should assume that a paging system will run smoothly and efficiently. Whenever a page required by one program is not available, another program can be executed while the required page is being retrieved. Some factors that can cause thrashing are these:

1. Excessive multiprogramming is attempted. If too many programs are in an executing state, it will be impossible to allot parachor for all of them.
2. The page replacement algorithm is faulty. One fault of the simpler algorithms is that a page required by one program might replace a page from the working set of another program. This action would cause excessive paging for the latter program without reducing the paging requirements of the former.
3. Main storage is too small. A relatively large main storage is required so that several programs with large parachors can be in execution simultaneously. Otherwise, one can expect delays while paging is being accomplished.
4. The auxiliary storage devices used for paging are not of sufficiently high performance. Thrashing tends to be self-supporting. That is, a system cannot move freely in and out of a thrashing condition. If, for example, the auxiliary storage devices can furnish only four pages per second and the system is designed to require three pages per second, a minor departure from the averages will cause thrashing. Much better

operation would result from devices that can furnish 40 pages per second with a system designed to require 30.

The Future of Paging Systems.   There is something very fascinating about paging systems. The bitter experiences of the past should teach lessons not easily ignored. Still, many of the best designers believe that paging has been demonstrated as fundamentally sound. It is safe to predict that paging will not disappear from the systems designers' bag of tricks, at least not in the foreseeable future.

SUMMARY

Data staging is the process of moving data from one location to another in preparation for processing or following processing. Data can be rearranged or edited during staging. Costs inherent in staging include system resource time, delay in the start of actual processing, and exposure of data to damage or disclosure.

Data entering or leaving a system, called SYSIN and SYSOUT data, are staged principally to provide flexibility in scheduling. More specifically, staging SYSIN or SYSOUT provides

- flexibility to schedule users' programs to utilize system resources efficiently while recognizing priorities
- flexibility to run a user's program while output devices such as printers are not available
- efficiency of transmitting data to or from terminal devices without tying up resources required by the user's program
- efficient use of end-use devices
- reprocessable SYSIN and SYSOUT data

During SYSIN staging, control statements are separated from data intended for users' programs processing. Routines variously called a symbiont, a pseudo-card reader, or an access method perform the staging. Staged SYSOUT data can include information to be used to control the end-use device. Some special forms of SYSIN and SYSOUT staging used in communications based systems are called remote job entry, conversational remote job entry, and time sharing.

The principal justification for staging data files is to provide compact economical storage of data on one medium and high-performance, flexible, nonsequential processing on another. Data file staging can be provided in such a way that users' programs effectively experience unlimited quantities of direct access storage space. To accomplish this, the control program monitors file and space usage. Dormant files are staged to magnetic tape to make room for new files as they are created or old files that must be restaged from tape.

Work in process, consisting of a user's programs, data, and tables residing in main storage, can be staged to provide main storage space under several circumstances. To make main storage space available for a high-priority service request, a rollout may be used suspending one program while another is executed. Swapping is a systematic rollout-like process that allows several programs to share a single main storage area to achieve processing in parallel. Swapping is used in time sharing systems.

Paging is systematic processing of segments of data by segments of programs. Whenever a required segment, that is, a required page, is not already available in main storage, that page is staged in overlaying some dormant page. Paging can provide the effect of virtually unlimited main storage. Page size and the page replacement algorithm affect the rate of paging that must be accomplished. If actual requirements exceed that rate, thrashing can occur, and system performance will drop markedly.

Exercises

1.(e) Define data staging.
2.(e) What properties of a magnetic drum make it an excellent staging device?
3.(e) How does SYSOUT staging ease problems resulting from torn forms on a printer?
4.(e) State two facets of RJE that distinguish it from other SYSIN and SYSOUT staging.
5.(e) List two or more aspects of conversational RJE that distinguish it from nonconversational RJE.
6.(e) If page size is 1,024 bytes and the working set for a particular program is 10 pages, what is parachor for that program?
7.(m) Assume the records of a certain file are to be processed in their natural order as they exist on magnetic tape. Describe conditions that would justify staging the file to a magnetic drum for processing.
8.(m) Describe in about 25 words how time sharing can improve the effectiveness of people.
9.(m) Write a sentence that distinguishes the techniques of rollout from swapping. Write another sentence distinguishing swapping from paging.
10.(d) In view of the fact that the CPU is concerned with only a few main storage locations at any time, why is main storage so large? Describe some of the primary considerations that determine optimum main storage size.

11 The Sequential Organization of Data

> The principal problem of human memory is not storage but retrieval. The key to retrieval is organization, or, in even simpler terms, knowing where to find information that has been put into memory. . . . Jerome Bruner

Before starting sequential organization of data, we should first consider some preliminary remarks about the organization of data.

THE ORGANIZATION OF DATA

One of the most interesting challenges in the management of data within a computer system concerns the organization of stored records. The organization of records has to do with physical relationships. Records may be organized according to simple or complex rules depending on the capabilities of the I/O devices used and the requirements of anticipated use of the records. As a simple illustration, records might be stored on magnetic tape in the order of their presentation to the I/O system by a user's program. A file of such records is said to have a sequential organization. In another situation, records might be stored on a direct access storage volume in an order determined by relative values in a key field of each record. Such an organization might be called an indexed, list, or direct organization depending on the organizational rules employed. The burden of storing according to complex rules of orgnization must be justified by the efficiency or, in some cases, the very feasibility of intended later use.

There is a growing base of formal writing that is developing formal definitions for organizational ideas such as multilists, inverted trees, and bifurcating arborescences. In keeping with that trend toward formality one of the authors began to develop the rules that define data organizations. The results of his efforts are presented below.

Rules for the Sequential Organization of Data

Rule 1 Units of data: The sequential organization is concerned with blocks of data only.

Rule 2 Succession of blocks: Block b is the successor to block a if the most natural physical motion of the recording medium on the device causes block b to be encountered immediately following block a.

Rule 3 First block: The first block in an extent is the only block in that extent which is not the successor to some other block in the extent.

Rule 4 Last block: A block is the last block in an extent if the block that succeeds it is a file mark.

Rule 5 Extent succession: A sequential file is composed of one or more extents coupled by considering the last block of one extent to be succeeded by the first block of the next extent.

It is quite easy to recognize that these rules are not complete or rigorous. Even more damaging, they are not particularly useful, and attempts at more rigor make them less useful. A more useful, though less scientific approach, is to discuss each organization thoroughly but without attempts at mathematical precision. This is the approach taken in this and the next several chapters.

Quite probably, the data organizations described in Chaps. 11 to 14 do not exhaust all possible organizational concepts. Clearly, they do not exhaust all possible variations of all possible organizational concepts. However, they do illustrate most of the principles in use throughout the industry. A sequential organization similar to that described in this chapter is included in the systems offered by most major computer vendors. The list organization described in Chap. 14 is available in only a few systems. Not all computer systems support all the types of file organizations.

SEQUENTIAL ORGANIZATION OF DATA

The sequential organization of data is a magnetic-tape-like organization. That is, when an I/O system is creating, interrogating, or modifying a file organized according to the sequential organization conventions, the effects on the file and on the user's program are the effects one would expect from taking the same action directly on an idealized magnetic tape. An example will help to clarify this frequently stated sequential organization/magnetic tape analogy. Assume that a user's program has been periodically requesting blocks of data from a sequential file that is stored on a magnetic drum. If the user's program changes its pattern of I/O requests and it requests that a block of data be stored, what would you expect the effects of this request to be? The answer is, "The effects are the same as if the same sequence of actions had been applied to a magnetic tape."

The preceding answer is not satisfying, and it raises several other questions:

Question How can the effects be the same as if magnetic tape has been used?

Answer The sequential access method routines, which are part of the I/O system, take whatever actions are necessary to effectively simulate a magnetic tape reaction to the user's requests.

Question Why would one want a magnetic-tape-like reaction?

Answer The reasons are partly historical and partly rational. In the early 1960s, magnetic tapes were the only storage devices commonly used and, because operating systems were not available, most programmers had to be very familiar with magnetic tape processing. A magnetic-tape-like reaction was widely understood. That historical reason is less valid today. To many readers of this book, the magnetic tape analogy just explains one unknown in terms of another. Rationally, magnetic tape device capabilities represent a reasonable compromise of the capabilities of a wide range of devices. If one chose to make a data organization card-reader-like, the utility of that organization would be severely limited. Alternatively, a magnetic-drum-like organization could be achieved for only a few types of devices.

Question   How can one simulate a magnetic tape reaction using a device such as a printer?

Answer   The simulated effects are limited to what one can reasonably expect without resorting to magic. For example, because a printer is an output-only device, simulation is attempted only for output activities.

Question   Can one assume that the term *sequential file* means a file that is organized according to the sequential organization conventions?

Answer   In this book, yes. However, not all operating systems observe that special meaning.

USES OF THE SEQUENTIAL ORGANIZATION

Batch processing is a way of life in data processing systems, possibly a vanishing way of life. But, while the chroniclers of the future describe data base systems and event driven systems, much of today's processing is still largely batch processing. And no aspect of current systems is more batch related than the sequential organization.

The manual systems that preceded automatic data processing were not strictly batch systems. A clerk could pull a ledger card from a file and post an individual transaction. Admittedly, the clerk could be more efficient when transactions were batched. But processing of single transactions was practical. The advent of automatic data processing shifted the balance. Batch processing rapidly became more efficient, and processing of individual transactions became more difficult. While automatic data processing consisted of card operations (sorting, punching, collating, and tabulating), individual records could be modified manually. Card handling equipment is called unit record equipment for that reason. With magnetic tape, batch processing reached its zenith. Individual records could not be detected visually. To locate a particular record required excessive time using expensive equipment, and even if a record could somehow be identified, it could not be updated.

Before about 1960, most general purpose systems did not include direct access devices for auxiliary storage. Magnetic drums were commonly used in systems, but they served as main storage rather than as auxiliary storage. Most systems included only one type of auxiliary storage device—magnetic tape. In fact, the more fully developed systems of the early 1960s were described as tape-to-tape systems. All input data for several jobs were placed on a magnetic tape by special purpose equipment. The typical computerized application sorted the input transactions to the order of the master file, processed the transactions against the master file creating a new master and one or more reports on magnetic tape. The records on the report tapes were then sorted to the proper order for printing. The report tapes were removed from the system for printing, using specialized equipment. Though the sequential organization was not known by that name, the tape-to-tape operation involved many files having sequential organization:

input transactions
sorted input transactions
master files

updated master files
report tapes
sorted report tapes

Direct access storage devices have two principal advantages over magnetic tape: (1) Individual blocks of data can be stored or retrieved in any order efficiently. (2) A block can be updated in place. Don't be misled. Magnetic drums have a sequential bias that is inherent in their physical motion. However, their nonsequential capabilities are an extreme contrast to magnetic tape.

The sequential organization is the workhorse of data organizations. It is the only organization described in this book whose use is not restricted to direct access storage devices. It is the simplest of the organizations described, and it has the widest applicability. In a typical enterprise, the number of sequential organization blocks processed might be 1,000 times the number from all other organizations combined. In most systems, the sequential organization is applied to magnetic tape drives, direct access storage devices, card readers, card punches, and printers.

Some familiar examples of sequential files illustrate the extent of use of the sequential organization:

1. The one, two, or three temporary files created during program compilation are sequential files.
2. A printed inventory status report is a sequential file.
3. A deck of cards representing accounts receivable transactions is a sequential file.
4. A library of programs in source or object form may be a sequential file.

Because the alternative organizations are more expensive in terms of storage space and CPU time, the sequential organization is used whenever its capabilities meet a user's requirements. An alternative might be chosen either because the I/O system does not include sequential organization support for the I/O device that is to be used or because magnetic-tape-like capabilities will not fulfill the user's requirements. One magnetic tape characteristic that limits the use of sequential files is the inability to update in place.

ORGANIZATION CONVENTIONS

The magnetic-tape-like definition of the sequential organization assumes an idealized magnetic tape. An idealized magnetic tape has a definite beginning point, but it is infinitely long, and it has no surface defects. To read or write a particular block of data, the intervening blocks must be passed over. Any block of data can be retrieved, but blocks cannot be inserted into an existing file. If an existing block is updated, all blocks following it become unretrievable.

The sequential organization deals with blocks of data only. Two alternative techniques allow record processing using a sequential organization: (1) The access methods can block and deblock records for the user's program. (2) The file specifications can force one record per block. Using this alternative, we note that block processing and record processing become synonymous.

Objectives

The objectives of sequential organization are simplicity, applicability, and utility.

Simplicity.   The sequential organization should be easily understood by its users, and the access methods that complement it should impose a minimum of burden to the computer system. Minimizing both main storage space requirements and CPU time requirements is important because the sequential organization is intended for heavy use over a wide range of computer systems.

Applicability.   The sequential organization should apply to a wide range of I/O devices uniformly. That is, the sequential organization should allow the sequential access methods to furnish device independence. Device independence has been mentioned several times in earlier chapters. It is the quality that allows a user's program to be unaffected by I/O device characteristics. The applicability objective, fully met, would limit the sequential organization and the access methods that use it to those capabilities common to all pertinent I/O devices. In practice, some concessions are made and, consequently, some of the services provided by the sequential access methods are device-dependent.

Utility.   The simplicity and applicability objectives are restrictive. However, the sequential organization should have great utility; it is intended to serve all but the most specialized requirements. Surprisingly, there is a single functional capability whose inclusion would violate the simplicity and applicability objectives but whose exclusion still allows great utility. That functional capability is the storage and retrieval of records at random, based on key values within the records. One might observe that random accessing capability receives more than its share of attention. In this book, three chapters are devoted to organizations providing random accessing capability, while only the present chapter applies to the nonrandom case. A more realistic view is that where the ability to store and retrieve records based on key values is applicable, that ability has far-reaching or even fundamental importance.

Organization Conventions for Several Device Classes

The conventions for the organization of records in a computer system and the conventions that a secretary uses for filing paper records are logically similar. In general, the rules for filing allow timely disposition of records in such a way that the record retrieval requests anticipated can be satisfied without embarrassment. The sequential organization is required to fill one type of requirement that is not imposed on the secretary's filing system: For some classes of devices, the records to be retrieved were not previously stored, and for other classes of devices, the records being stored will not be retrieved. An example of the former class is a card reader, and an example of the latter is a printer. The sequential organization conventions for several classes of devices are described in the following sections.

Magnetic Tape.   In the simplest case, a sequential file on magnetic tape is a sequence of blocks terminated by a tape mark. The blocks in such a file are in the physical order that matches the chronological order of their acceptance by the I/O system. The first block of a file is usually preceded by a tape mark, though, in some I/O systems, the tape mark is omitted for the first file on an unlabeled tape.

In some systems, information that is not part of a sequential file can be stored within the file's boundaries. In OS/360, no such information is allowed. DOS/360 allows checkpoint records, identified appropriately, to be embedded. GCOS-III allows special information of any kind to be embedded. In the latter system, any single-character block is interpreted as a file mark. A file mark whose value is $(17)_8$ is interpreted as a file delimiter. A file mark whose value is $(00)_8$ indicates that checkpoint information follows. File marks with other values indicate to the sequential access methods that special information follows and that a system exit should be taken to allow the user's program to process that data in some special way.

A sequential file can extend to two or more reels of tape. Each volume has its own tape-mark delimiters, and the sequence of volumes is indicated by control cards, the file catalog, and/or the file labels. In some systems, a single reel of a multireel file can be processed as if it were a file, and that is a useful capability rather easily provided.

A variety of record and block forms, typically including F, V, and U records unblocked, and F and V blocked, are allowed. Some of the considerations involved in blocking and spanning were discussed in Chap. 4. The important point here is that the widest selection of record and block alternative forms offered within any particular operating system will typically be offered for magnetic tape sequential files.

The character codes and record formats used to represent data on magnetic tape are simple accommodations to the engineering specifications of the tape device. That is, the information being recorded on magnetic tape is not translated by the access method from one character code to another, nor are characters rearranged within a record. Rather, the access methods simply move information from main storage to the magnetic tape. If the character codes for magnetic tape and main storage are different, as they usually are, the translation from one code to another is an automatic feature of the computer system rather than the access methods.

Some of the principal capabilities furnished by the sequential access methods for magnetic tape files are listed in Fig. 11-1. Figure 11-1 will be used for comparison of magnetic tape files with other sequential files.

• Read forward one block
• Read backward one block*
• Write one block
• Forward space one block
• Backward space one block
• Forward space to file delimiter
• Backward space to file delimiter
*Read backward is not available in all systems.

Fig. 11-1   Magnetic tape processing capabilities.

Whether a function such as read backward should be offered is a very difficult question. The principal arguments are as follows:

1. If the magnetic tape devices of the system are capable of backward reading, that capability will be practically inaccessable to the user unless the sequential access method furnishes backward read.
2. Simulating read backward using double backspace and read forward is very inefficient. Effectively, a user's program that requires read backward cannot be executed if the magnetic tape devices allocated cannot read backward.
3. The use of read backward limits device independence. Simulating read backward for a card reader would be very inefficient.
4. Read backward can be simulated using a direct access storage device, though the problems are more complex than one might expect.

Magnetic tape devices are not designed to allow update in place. Whenever a block of a sequential file is written, that block automatically becomes the last block of the file. Until it is closed, a sequential file that is being created, modified, or extended will not have a delimiting tape mark. Spacing forward to the file delimiter can be performed properly only if the tape mark exists.

Direct Access Storage.   In the simplest case, a sequential file on a direct access storage volume is a sequence of blocks stored on tracks with consecutive addresses. Blocks may or may not conform to sector or track boundaries, depending on the operating conventions of the device. The last block of the file is usually followed by a file mark. The use of this delimiting file mark is a debatable issue.

Positive   A file mark is a convenient file delimiter because it can be detected automatically by the computer system.

Negative   Under some conditions, a file mark may not fit within currently available space. Such a condition would cause unjustified allocation of added space and, possibly, the mounting of a new volume. An extreme case might result in premature termination of a user's program. The address of the last block in the file must be available in the file label to allow extending an existing file. That address can serve as a file delimiter.

OS/360 resolves this issue by using a file mark if and only if a file mark will fit on the last track containing a block of data.

Most of the conventions described for magnetic tape apply to direct access volumes. An operating system should allow information that is not part of the file to be stored within file boundaries to the same extent that it is allowed for magnetic tape. A file can extend to multiple volumes just as it does with magnetic tape. In addition, a sequential file on a direct access storage volume is usually allowed to occupy a number of discontinuous extents. Record and block format alternatives are usually identical to the magnetic tape alternatives, and the comments made regarding character codes and record formats apply equally to direct access storage volumes.

The processing capabilities provided for direct access storage files might not include read backward even if read backward is furnished for magnetic tape.

However, an update-in-place capability is usually provided. Use of update in place will make a user's program device-dependent. However, that disadvantage is clearly outweighed by the efficiencies update in place provides. One can rationally argue that a process using update in place is device-dependent for good reason. Figure 11-2 compares the principal processing capabilities usually offered for sequential files on magnetic tape and direct access devices.

Capability	Availability	
	Magnetic Tape	Direct Access
Read forward one block	Yes	Yes
Read backward one block	Yes	Maybe
Write one block	Yes	Yes
Forward space one block	Yes	Yes
Backward space one block	Yes	Yes
Forward space to file delimiter	Yes	Yes
Backward space to file delimiter	Yes	Yes
Update a block	No	Yes

Fig. 11-2 Sequential file processing capabilities: magnetic tape and direct access devices.

Punched Cards.   A sequential file on cards consists of a variable number of consecutive cards, each card representing a block of data. Blocks are essentially fixed in size, though a system might allow the user to specify block size less than total card capacity. If that is done, the last several card columns are simply ignored. For example, if block size for a card input file were specified as 60, blocks would consist of the first 60 characters from each card.

If a card file has labels, the label cards serve as file delimiters. An unlabeled card file really has no delimiters, and the extreme limits of a file are recognized by operating conventions. Some typical operating conventions are described in the following examples:

1. The end of a card file in the input stream is indicated by the occurrence of a control statement. The sequential access method routines that read cards from an input card reader must check every block of data to detect a control statement.
2. If a card file is read using a card reader allocated exclusively for that purpose, the end of the file is indicated by the card reader itself. A command to read a card after all cards have been read will result in a special identifiable response from the card reader.
3. When cards are being punched, files in the punch stacker can be separated by blank cards or by cards with a peculiar pattern of punching that is easily detected visually. Separator cards can be punched by the CLOSE routines.

Printers.   If you felt that the description of a card file in terms of magnetic tape processing capabilities stretched reality, then your reaction to tape-like processing using a printer may be complete consternation. A review of the motivation for such tape-like processing may forestall that reaction:

Observation   Printers have some very important capabilities. They are able to present information on paper for use outside the computer system.
Observation   Printers have some very bad characteristics from a system efficiency viewpoint for the following reasons:
1. Printers are slow compared to most storage devices.
2. Printers require significant operator assistance for aligning forms, replacing ribbons, and so forth.
3. Recovery from failures of any kind is complicated when the failing process includes printer operation.
4. Printers are expensive, and they are not sharable by two or more users simultaneously.

Challenge   If the capabilities of a printer can be described as a subset of the capabilities of a storage device, then the operating system can substitute a storage device for a printer whenever it is advantageous to do so.

We must recognize, of course, that the required printing must be accomplished sooner or later. Nevertheless, a substitution can pay off handsomely. The desirability of substituting a storage device for a printer applies so generally that many systems never allocate printers to users' programs.

A wide variety of record formats and blocking alternatives can be allowed on cards. In practice, only a few are offered in most systems. Several systems consider card files to consist exclusively of 80 character, unblocked, fixed-length records. Whether alternatives are really required or even understood by potential users is doubtful.

The conversion between the character representations on cards and in main storage is furnished by the computer system automatically. For many card devices, two-character modes are possible. One mode recognizes each card column as containing a single character. Cards punched by a keypunch conform to this mode. The other mode, usually called the column binary mode, reproduces the binary contents of main storage directly into a card. By using these two modes, sequential files on cards can be represented in standard character codes or in binary.

Another alternative offered in several systems is the control character illustrated in Fig. 11-3. The control character is not punched into a card, but, rather, is used to control stacker selection, offset stacking, or printing on the card. This feature introduces a lack of symmetry between reading and punching cards that is probably confusing to the system user. If a file is punched using the control-character feature and then that file is moved to a card reader and the cards are read, the information returned to main storage will not match the original information. The control characters will have disappeared.

Many of the principal processing capabilities furnished for magnetic tapes are not possible for card files. Figure 11-4 illustrates the usual limitations. Some systems in the past have simulated the capabilities requiring backward motion by instructing the operator to reposition the cards appropriately. Systems today do not do that. A better alternative is to copy the information from a card file to a storage device before processing that requires backward positioning is attempted. Figure 11-4 also indicates that spacing forward to the file delimiter is not offered for card files. The reasons are readily understandable.

First, if a file is being punched, no delimiter exists. Furthermore, such a file is always positioned at its extreme limit. A magnetic tape file might be positioned at the delimiting tape mark as a preliminary step to extending the file by adding blocks. Card files are not extended that way.

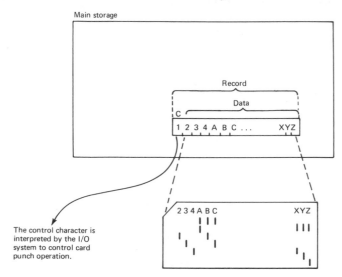

Fig. 11-3   A record containing a control character.

Capability	Availability			
	Magnetic Tape	Direct Access	Card Readers	Card Punches
Read forward one block	Yes	Yes	Yes	No
Read backward one block	Yes	Maybe	No	No
Write one block	Yes	Yes	No	Yes
Forward space one block	Yes	Yes	Maybe	Maybe
Backward space one block	Yes	Yes	No	No
Forward space to file delimiter	Yes	Yes	No	No
Backward space to file delimiter	Yes	Yes	No	No
Update a block	No	Yes	No	No

Fig. 11-4   Sequential file processing capabilities: magnetic tape, direct access, and card devices.

Secondly, if a file is being read, forward spacing could be accomplished by passing cards, ignoring their contents, but it is difficult to devise a justification for such spacing. When a file in a card reader is positioned as if the last card had been read, no further processing of that file is possible. The file cannot be extended because the card reader is incapable of punching cards, and reading backward is impossible.

A sequential file on a printer consists of printed lines. Each line is a block. Lines are printed in the order of their presentation to the I/O system. The beginning of a file is usually delimited by a page that is blank or that contains a recognizable pattern of printed information. The identifying page can be printed by OPEN, and it can serve as a final delimiter for the previous file. As an alternative, a final delimiter page can be created by CLOSE. At the user's option, the pages of a file might include top and/or bottom headings that are inserted by the I/O system and are not really part of the file. Page headings usually include page number and date and might include such items as file name and information from the control statement identifying the user's service request.

The form of a printed file is important. Form is the result of two kinds of controls, line editing and line positioning. Line editing involves character-by-character inspection of a record, rearranging and separating fields so that they will appear as columns, replacing leading zeros by blanks, converting from the existing number base to decimal, and so forth. The editing of a line is the responsibility of the user's program in most systems. That is, when the record is presented to the I/O system, it has already been edited.

Capability	Availability				
	Magnetic Tape	Direct Access	Card Readers	Card Punches	Printers
Read forward one block	Yes	Yes	Yes	No	No
Read backward one block	Yes	Maybe	No	No	No
Write one block	Yes	Yes	No	Yes	Yes
Forward space one block	Yes	Yes	Maybe	Maybe	Maybe
Backward space one block	Yes	Yes	No	No	No
Forward space to file delimiter	Yes	Yes	No	No	No
Backward space to file delimiter	Yes	Yes	No	No	No
Update a block	No	Yes	No	No	No

Fig. 11-5   Sequential file processing capabilities: all devices.

Line positioning can be controlled by the first character of a block of data as illustrated for card punching in Fig. 11-3. The control character is not printed, but, rather, it is interpreted by the I/O system to cause actions such as single, double, or triple spacing, space suppression, or skipping to the next page.

The processing capabilities offered to the user for creating a sequential file on a printer are shown in Fig. 11-5. You may notice they are identical to the capabilities offered for card punching, though that fact has no special significance.

SEQUENTIAL FILE PROCESSING

Sequential files are usually manipulated by the sequential access method programs. The user's interfaces to the access methods were described in Chap. 4.

That information, together with the sequential organization descriptions just presented, describes implicitly what the sequential access method must do. Many of those activities are sufficiently simple that no description is necessary. Some of the not-so-obvious activities and techniques are described under the topic headings that follow.

File Positioning

The GET, PUT, READ, and WRITE macros of the sequential access methods imply nextness, either the next record or the next block. Nextness is relative; its use implies that the current position is established.

For many I/O devices, the act of storing or retrieving a block of .data leaves the recording medium properly positioned for a subsequent action. Reading a card leaves the card deck positioned to read the next card. Writing a block of data on magnetic tape leaves the tape positioned for writing the next block. The sequential access method routines maintain a tally indicating the current position of a file. The tally is useful for repositioning a file under special circumstances, such as NOTE/POINT, and a final tally is usually required for the labels created by CLOSE.

Direct access storage devices are unusual in that the recording medium is in constant motion even when the device is idle. For such devices, a static relationship between the device and the medium cannot exist, so the current position is completely defined in tables. Whenever a block of data is to be stored or retrieved, the current position is extracted from the table and is used in the search portion of the channel program.

OPEN establishes the initial position of a file. The proper initial position depends on the kind of processing to be performed and the type of I/O device used. Figure 11-6 presents the alternatives. Establishing the initial position implies physical positioning of the medium for all devices other than direct access devices, and it implies appropriate setting of tallies or addresses mentioned above. CLOSE VOLUME performs a similar positioning activity for each volume or extent of a file.

Process to be Performed	Device Type				
	Magnetic Tape	Direct Access	Card Reader	Card Punch	Printer
Create a file	Beginning	Beginning	NA	Beginning	Beginning
Retrieve data from an existing file	Beginning	Beginning	Beginning	NA	NA
Extend an existing file	End	End	NA	NA	NA
Retrieve data backward from a file	End	End	NA	NA	NA

NA means not applicable
Beginning means before the first data block
End means after the last data block

Fig. 11-6   Initial positioning of a sequential file.

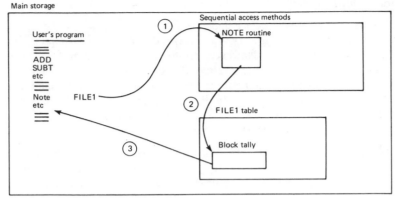

1. The user's program issues the NOTE request.
2. The NOTE routine extracts the current position from the table, and
3. Returns it to the user's program.

Fig. 11-7 NOTE uses the block tally.

The block tally or address that indicates position is used by the NOTE macro as shown in Fig. 11-7. The exact form and meaning of the information returned to the user depend on the type of device being used. Figure 11-8 illustrates POINT.

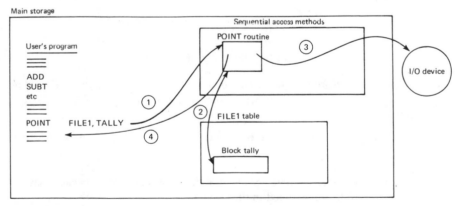

Magnetic Tape Devices

1. The user's program issues a POINT request.
2. The POINT routine subtracts the current position from TALLY;
3. Causes the magnetic tape to be repositioned, and
4. Returns to the user's program.

Direct Access Storage Devices

1. The user's program issues a POINT request.
2. The POINT routine replaces the current position with TALLY, and
3. (No I/O device action required),
4. Returns to the user's program.

Fig. 11-8 POINT reestablishes a file position.

Device Independence

A collection of services is device-dependent if its use is not limited or altered by choice of I/O device type. Device independence is a very popular quality advertised by most systems. However, critics point out that most systems include so many device-dependent alternatives intermixed with their device-independent services that a user's program is almost certain to be inadvertently device-dependent. The fault causing this criticism may lie with the systems designers because they have not analyzed the users' requirements clearly and, as a result, have not described device independence properly.

Device-Independence Requirements.   In most cases, the user's program deals with files on direct access storage devices. To demonstrate that statement, all situations have divided into three mutually exclusive and exhaustive cases:

> *Case 1*   The user's program expects to interact with a direct access storage device.
>
> *Case 2*   The user's program expects to interact with a device of a type selected by the system.
>
> *Case 3*   The user's program expects to interact with a specific type of device that is not a direct access storage device.

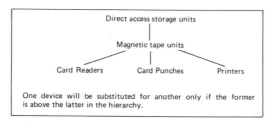

Fig. 11-9   Hierarchy of devices.

Case 1 clearly conforms to the claim made above. In case 2, the I/O system must choose a device type. The best choice will provide most of the following advantages:

- low cost per unit of time or, if a device is sharable, a prorated low cost per unit of time
- high performance
- high availability either because the device is sharable or because several identical units are included in the system
- operational superiority in that it requires little operator interaction, its failure rate is low, its recording medium is reusable, and/or it has superior ability to recover from failure

The best choice in case 2 is almost certainly a direct access storage device. Presented with a case 2 situation, most, if not all, contemporary systems will select a direct access storage device. The predeliction to direct access storage devices is illustrated in Fig. 11-9.

There are very few cases that are properly case 3. For example, card files and printed reports are handled most efficiently by staging to and from a direct access storage device. Contemporary systems furnish staging automatically unless the user specifically obstructs it. One clear situation where staging is not the best alternative is when a large file resides permanently on magnetic tape because of the low cost of shelf storage using magnetic tape. Other examples are quite rare.

If users' programs usually interact with direct access devices, why is device independence so important? The complete answer is not a simple desire to allow any program to interact with any type of device, though that is desirable. Other important answers are these:

1. Families of similar devices should have a common interface to allow flexibility in device allocation and to allow improvement in a computer system as improved devices become available. For example, a program written to use a magnetic drum should operate correctly with any direct access storage device.
2. A common interface to several devices eases the education burden.
3. A common interface simplifies language processors by standardizing the access method interface for object programs.

While all three of these are important, probably only the first two have been properly recognized.

An Alternative Approach to Device Independence

The system manuals for most contemporary systems describe device independence in terms of facilities that perform uniformly for several different classes of I/O devices. The system users understand that staging of data might or might not occur, but that they need not be concerned provided they use device-independent facilities.

Recognizing the advantages of direct access storage devices to both the system and the system user, the EXEC-8 designers elected to provide an alternative approach to device independence. The EXEC-8 users understand that a collection of system programs called Symbionts will accomplish staging and, consequently, the users can assume that their programs will interact with a direct access storage device. In this way, the users' programs will be independent of the limitations of the less flexible devices. For example, the user's program in EXEC-8 can request backspace or update in place for a file that is to be printed because the staging device is acknowledged to be in use. EXEC-8 does not identify a sequential organization of data that is magnetic-tape-like.

The distinction between EXEC-8 and other systems in this device-independence issue is primarily one of emphasis, but the differences from the user's viewpoint are quite dramatic.

Channel Program Scheduling

What the sequential processing of data lacks in elegance, it must make up in performance. The sequential access methods should be coded carefully to avoid unnecessary use of time-consuming system services and the less efficient computer instructions. But far more important than the performance of the access method programs is the effect the access method programs have on the performance of the I/O devices themselves. All of the types of I/O devices considered in this chapter are electromechanical; physical motion is involved. With physical motion involved, one of the following must apply:

1. Data must flow across the channel at a rate dictated by the physical motion of the device.
2. The motion of the device is linear, and the device must be stopped and restarted frequently.
3. The motion is rotational, and further transfer of data must wait while an idle rotation is being completed.

For a great many combinations of I/O devices and CPUs, data can flow across a channel at the rate dictated by the physical motion of the device only for the duration of a single channel program. That is, the time consumed by the CPU, the supervisor, and the I/O supervisor in starting a new channel program exceeds the limits dictated by the physical motion of many I/O devices.

One solution to this problem is to use a single channel program to move several consecutive blocks of data whenever possible. If several main storage buffers are being used, the access methods can delay until two or more are available before a channel program is scheduled.

Another fruitful, though more complex, technique has the objective to link a new channel program to one that is either in an I/O supervisor queue awaiting initiation or is already being executed. Each time a successful linking is accomplished, a channel program initiation is avoided. The basic steps involved in programming the technique are as follows:

1. Find the existing channel program.
2. Attach the new channel program.
3. Test to determine whether the attachment was accomplished early enough.

The order of steps 2 and 3 is important. If one tests first and then attaches, the test results may become invalid before the attachment can be completed.

SUMMARY

The sequential organization of data is designed to provide a magnetic-tape-like reaction file processing activities regardless of the characteristics of an I/O device. The similarities are provided by the combination of sequential organization conventions and access methods. They are limited to what one might reasonably expect.

The sequential organization is tied closely to history; the predominance of magnetic tape devices and batch processing of the 1960s influenced it substantially. It is still used much more heavily than all other organizations.

The objectives of the sequential organization are simplicity, applicability to a wide range of devices, and the capability to serve all but the most specialized requirements. The conventions governing the organization require separate interpretation for each applicable class of device. Magnetic tape conventions set the standard, and the conventions for direct access devices, card equipment, and printers represent the best compromises for magnetic-tape-like processing. The sequential organization on tape allows the following capabilities:

1. Read forward or backward one block.
2. Write one block.
3. Space forward or backward one block.
4. Space forward or backward to file delimiter.

The capabilities for card equipment and printers are significantly less than the above. The sequential organization for direct access storage devices usually allows all magnetic tape capabilities plus update in place.

OPEN initially positions the first volume of a sequential file, and CLOSE VOLUME positions subsequent volumes. Positioning will be at the beginning or end of the file. During file processing, position is established by a combination of physical positioning and a tally maintained in main storage. The tally is useful for repositioning during NOTE or POINT, and it may be recorded in the file labels.

Device independence is usually provided as a set of capabilities common to several classes of devices. Device independence serves four purposes:

1. It allows a program to interact with any of several classes of devices.
2. It provides flexibility in allocating devices, and it allows evolutionary changes in the computer system.
3. It eases the education burden.
4. It simplifies language processors by standardizing an object-program interface.

An alternative approach to device independence is offered in EXEC-8. Users of that system are assured that their programs will be interacting with files on direct access storage devices. When necessary, the system will use Symbionts to stage files to or from other classes of devices. This emphasis provides independence from device limitations, a form of device independence not available using the common subset of device capabilities.

An important aspect of sequential processing performance is I/O device performance. To allow devices to perform well, sequential access method programs must meet the natural demands of the physical motion of the devices. Moving several blocks of data with a single channel program can be accomplished by delayed scheduling of a channel program or by linking new and existing channel programs.

Exercises

1.(e) Which of the magnetic tape processing capabilities are provided for printers? For direct access storage devices?
2.(e) Give two reasons why single transaction processing on magnetic tape is so inefficient.
3.(e) Under what circumstances would a file be initially positioned after the last data block?
4.(e) For which class of devices discussed in Fig. 11-8 would you expect POINT to be the more time-consuming?

5.(c) What reasons are given for providing read backward capability for magnetic tape devices, even though other classes of devices cannot simulate that capability?

6.(m) The first page of this chapter describes the I/O requests of a user's program. Give a more explicit answer to the question, "What would you expect the results of this request to be?"

7.(m) Suggest how an I/O system might simulate backspace one block for a card punch.

8.(d) List at least five of the most important factors a system designer should consider in choosing between the two alternative approaches to device independence described in this chapter.

12 The Indexed Organization of Data

An indexed organization allows individual records to be inserted into a file at any time; it allows retrieval of individual records identified by their keys; and it allows retrieval of sequences of records that have ascending key values. The organization includes structures of data records and hierarchic indexes. An indexed organization requires a direct access storage device.

Indexed organizations are offered in several contemporary systems, usually with the name indexed sequential organization. The related access methods are called *basic indexed sequential access method, BISAM* and *queued indexed sequential access method, QISAM* or, generically ISAM. The word "sequential" used in this connotation means in order by key value, an entirely different meaning from "sequential" as used in the preceding chapter.

An indexed organization is designed for the combination of individual record processing and logical sequence processing. Some alternative requirements and alternative organizations are as follows:

- Sequential processing only. A sequential organization is a more efficient alternative.
- Individual record processing only. A direct organization may be more effective.
- Individual records retrievable on the basis of either of two or more key values within the records. A list organization offers this capability.

The principal advantages and disadvantages of the indexed organization are shown below:

ADVANTAGES	DISADVANTAGES
Can support both random and sequential processing	Access method routines that process indexed data arc large and complex
Requires relatively minor amounts of planning and analysis in advance of creating the file	Performance for processing individual records is only moderately good Performance deteriorates as file expands
	Structures do not allow natural extension to satisfy the requirements of the data base systems of the future

The development of indexing techniques got a slow start. In the early 1960s, the direct organization was popular and promising. The development of

227

the indexed sequential access methods for the IBM/360 Computer Systems seemed to be the turning point. In the late 1960s, the requirement to store and retrieve individual records from a file was usually satisfied by an indexed organization.

Throughout this chapter, organizational ideas are usually presented with two alternatives, reflecting first the OS/360 mechanism and then the EXEC-8 method. The reasons for illustrating from those two systems and in that particular order are as follows:

1. The OS/360 indexed organization is effectively an industry standard. Several other systems offer variations of the OS/360 organizations with from minor to major limitations.
2. The design of the EXEC-8 indexed organization differs significantly from the OS/360 design. The two designs should give the reader a broader view of indexing possibilities.

AN INDEXED ORGANIZATION EXAMPLE

The latter pages of this chapter contain detailed design information. Before you begin studying those details, you should understand generally what the parts of the indexed organization are and how they work together. The example that follows is illustrative rather than realistic. The number of records in the file is impractically small, and the organization of records is not precisely that of any contemporary system.

A Personnel Records File

Figure 12-1 is a list of the personnel records of a certain enterprise. Each employee is represented by a 1,000-character fixed length record in an indexed file.

Name	Employee Number	Date of Hire	Num Def
Arnold, Helen J.	2156	0524	
Barnes, Jack B.	1319	02	
Carlson, Ronald C.	3604		
Carhles, Edith F.	2791		
East, Walter T.			
Enders, Samuel J.			
Fox, Thomas W.			
Fulmer, Harold			
Gordon, Dwight L.			
Heath, John A.			
Hogan, Don J.			
Irwin, Linda			
Jones, Janet			
Kent, Douglas			
Larsen, Rex			
Perry, Ber			
Sanders, S			
White, Jo			

Fig. 12-1   Personnel records for an indexed-organization example.

A programmer in the Personnel Department presented the service request that created the file. The programmer's storage space estimates, included in a control statement, caused the allocation of space identified for three purposes: a prime data area to contain the records for personnel employed at that time, an overflow area to contain records for new employees, and an index area that would contain information to be used in finding individual records in the file. When the initial service request had been fulfilled, the file had the form shown in Fig. 12-2.

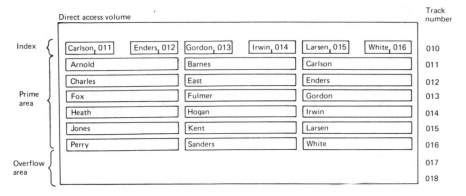

Fig. 12-2   The initial form of the personnel file.

The index is used primarily to find individual records in the file. To find the record for Kent, the access methods search the index for the first entry not less than Kent. That entry, Larsen, shows that the record for Larsen and for several other persons alphabetically preceding Larsen can be found on track 015. A search of track 015 yields Kent's record. That record can be inspected, or it can be modified and returned to the file.

After a few weeks, the enterprise hires a new employee whose last name is Kiley. Kiley properly belongs between Kent and Larsen, but there is no space available there. The access method programs will place Kiley's record in the overflow area, track 017 block 1, and they will indicate in Kent's record that Kiley's record follows logically. The result of these actions is shown in Fig. 12-3.

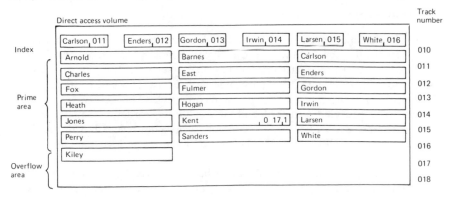

Fig. 12-3   The personnel file including Kiley's record.

Now, to retrieve Kiley's record, the access methods proceed just as previously described for retrieving Kent's record. In searching track 015, the access method programs discover the desired record falls between Kent and Larsen. The overflow location indication in Kent's record yields Kiley's record. If another record, Kramer, is added to the file between Kiley and Larsen, that record would be noted within Kiley's record as shown in Fig. 12-4.

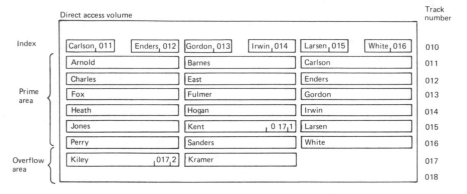

Fig. 12-4   The personnel file including Kiley and Kramer.

STORAGE AREAS

The preceding example mentioned three storage areas for an indexed file:

- a prime area where most of the data records of the file are stored
- an index area containing blocks of information useful in locating any particular data record in the file
- an overflow area that can accommodate data records that do not fit within the prime area

Descriptions of the organizations of data in three areas and the relationships of the three to one another constitute a description of the indexed organization.

The Prime Area

Keys.   Each data record in an indexed file must have an associated key. In most systems, the key for any record is included within that record. An alternative, used in EXEC-8, considers the key to be separate from the record but associated with it. Figure 12-5 illustrates both ideas. The key in the alternate definition could be repeated within the record itself. The key serves the dual purpose of identifying a record and of establishing ordering among records. The order among records is such that record a precedes record b if the compare instruction of the CPU indicates the key of record a is less than the key of record b.

The records in an indexed file might be fixed, variable, or undefined length conforming to the F, V, or U format conventions. However, the embedded keys must be of uniform length throughout the file, and the positions of embedded keys cannot vary from record to record. The indexed organization assumes that a key identifies a unique record. That is, no two records can have identical keys.

Throughout this chapter we shall be discussing records and keys. To simplify examples, we shall use the graphic conventions shown in Fig. 12-6. The conventions depict keys as being numeric values occupying the leftmost bytes of each record. In practice, keys are not so constrained.

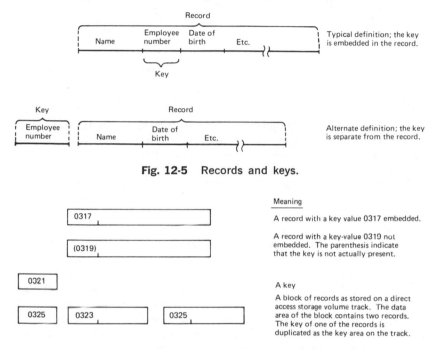

Fig. 12-5   Records and keys.

Fig. 12-6   Conventions for depicting records and keys.

Record Sequence. When an indexed file is being created, records are accepted from the user's program in key sequence and stored in the prime area. Records are frequently blocked for economy of storage space. Because the records are in key sequence, all of the keys in one block are less than all of the keys in the next block and greater than all of the keys in the preceding block. Two alternative block formats are shown in Fig. 12-7. The first alternative is a simple grouping of consecutive records with the highest key in the block used to identify the block. The second alternative identifies the block in the same way, but the records within the block are arranged differently. Such a block is constructed by working from both ends, storing a key and its related record at opposite ends of the block. This alternative includes pointers that are useful within the block form shown, but are included primarily for use with overflow records.

The highest key in each block is recorded separately as an aid in retrieving individual records. Using either of the conventions shown in Fig. 12-7, the block containing the record with key 0319 is the first block in the prime area whose key is 0319 or greater.

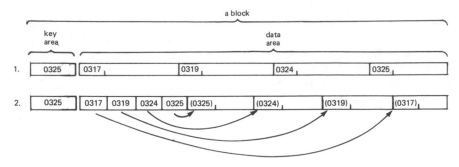

Fig. 12-7   Prime-area block formats.

Indexes

As data records are being combined into blocks and the blocks are being stored in the prime area, information describing the prime area is being abstracted to form indexes. The index built from the abstracted information is hierarchic. That is, it can consist of two or more levels. The lowest level contains the abstracted keys mentioned above. The next level contains information abstracted from the lowest level. That second level serves as an index to the lowest-level index. The next higher level is an index to the level below it, and so on. These relationships are illustrated in Fig. 12-8.

While Fig. 12-8 is incomplete, it illustrates clearly the most fundamental ideas of an indexed organization. To find a record with key value 0319, begin at the highest level and search for the first key that is not less than 0319. Associated with each key in an index block is the address of a block in the next lower level. Using the not-less-than rule at each level, one arrives easily at the appropriate prime-area track and at the appropriate block on that track. The value of the index is that it allows one to arrive at the appropriate prime-area block very quickly with only modest demands on the I/O equipment.

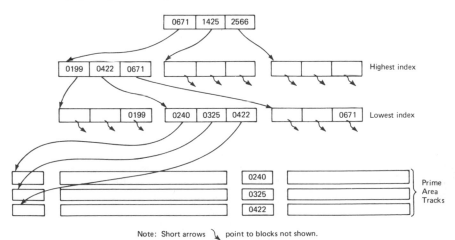

Note: Short arrows ↘ point to blocks not shown.

Fig. 12-8   Relationships between index levels.

Pointers.   Figure 12-8 shows arrows pointing from one block to another. Arrows cannot exist inside computer systems; they are replaced by addresses called pointers. Pointers can be either absolute or relative.

An *absolute pointer* is the address of an area of storage. An absolute pointer might refer to a particular cylinder, track, sector, or block. The bytes of an absolute address can be decimal, hexadecimal, octal, or other, depending on the particular I/O device being used. Absolute pointers have the advantage that they are ready for use immediately without computation.

A *relative pointer* is a simple number R. A relative pointer might refer to the Rth track of the space allocated to a particular file or to the Rth block of data or to the Rth cylinder. Relative pointers have the advantage that they are unaffected if a file is moved from one location to another.

The kind of pointer used in any particular situation is a design decision. The OS/360 and EXEC-8 indexed organizations offer an interesting contrast. OS/360 uses absolute addresses of tracks, while EXEC-8 uses relative addresses of blocks.

Index Blocks.   Index blocks contain keys and pointers. Figure 12-9 shows two alternative index block structures. The OS/360 index block shown is designed to allow a multilevel search by a single continuous channel program. The channel program uses a search loop to find an appropriate key value. When the desired value is found, the channel program reads the related pointer into a main storage location where it is used as the argument for a SEEK in the still-running channel program. It is easy to understand that a pointer that is to be used in this way must be absolute.

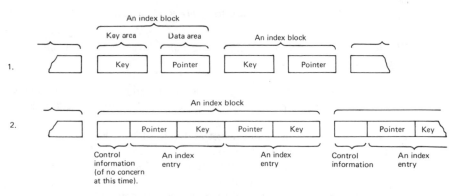

Fig. 12-9   Index blocks; two alternatives.

The EXEC-8 index block is intended for processing in main storage; the desired index block is moved to main storage where it is searched. When a key that is not less than the argument is found, the corresponding pointer is the relative address of the next block that must be retrieved. That block is either in index block of the next lower level or a data block.

Index Levels.   As was mentioned earlier, index-block entries are developed while data are being prepared for storage in the prime area. An index entry is created whenever a new pointer is rquired in an index. Because EXEC-8 pointers refer to blocks, the EXEC-8 routines create an index-block entry whenever a prime block is filled. The process goes as follows: When the first prime block has been filled, an entry pointing to that block is created for the lowest-level index. When the second prime block has been filled, another lowest-level entry is created, and so forth. At such time as any index block is full, an entry pointing to that index block is created for the next higher index level. The situation that would exist after a few records had been stored is shown in Fig. 12-10.

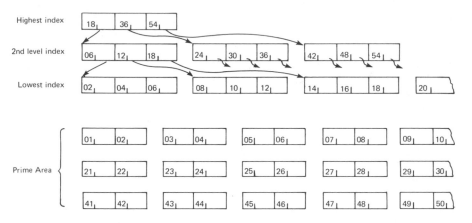

Assume 2 records per data block and 3 entries per index block.

Fig. 12-10   Index levels during file loading (EXEC-8).

The logic that creates index entries and index levels in OS/360 differs in the following ways:

1. An index entry is created for a prime track rather than a prime block. This difference simply reflects the fact that OS/360 pointers refer to tracks.
2. An entry is made in the level just above the lowest level whenever the last prime track on any particular cylinder has been filled. This level of index effectively breaks the entire range of key values into a smaller range identified with each prime-area cylinder.
3. An entry in a still-higher-level index is usually made whenever an index track is filled.

Index Density.   The lowest-level index usually has one entry for several records. To locate any particular record, the search must extend beyond the index to be completed by a limited search of data records. Such an index is called a range index or sparse index. An indexing scheme featuring an entry for every data record could be devised. Such an index, called a dense index, would have certain merits. For one thing, it would eliminate special provisions for locating overflow records because the location of every record would be available in the index. But dense indexes have several disadvantages as well:

1. A dense index is larger than a range index. Size is important because indexes are frequently stored on very high-performance devices where space is quite expensive.
2. A dense index must be modified whenever a new record is added to the file. By contrast, a range index is modified rarely.
3. Retrieval time using a dense index may be greater than for a range index because dense index may require more levels than a range index.

A range index is possible only when the order of the records themselves can be controlled. The keys of the records in a block (EXEC-8) or on a track (OS/360) serve as a final stage of the index.

The Overflow Area

The ability to accept new records into a file without recopying the entire file is one of the important features of an indexed organization. When possible, new records are accommodated in the prime area just as if they had been included in the initial complement of records. When the appropriate position in the prime area is already occupied by another record, an overflow results. Overflowing records are stored in the overflow area. Overflows are a normal phenomenon in an indexed organization; they do not constitute error conditions, nor are they cause for alarm.

Presented with a new record to be stored in an indexed file, the access method programs use the file indexes to determine the prime-data position where the record should be stored. Finding this position serves two purposes. It allows the access method programs to determine whether the record is, in fact, new. If the file already contains a record with the same key, the "new" record must be rejected. It also allows the new record to be stored in or near its natural prime-data position.

If the prime-data position is already filled, an overflow results. To explain the overflow mechanisms, we shall explore three questions: Which record actually overflows? Where is the overflowing record stored? What extensions of the index allow the overflow record to be found when required?

Which Record Overflows?   In EXEC-8, the new record that does not fit in the appropriate prime-data block becomes an overflow record. This choice results in a minimum disturbance to already stored records. The personnel records file described earlier accommodated new records in this way. Kiley's record in Fig. 12-3 was such an overflow record.

The OS/360 design provides for every prime-area track to contain consecutive records. If a prime-area track contains 10 records, those 10 are always in key-value order, and there is no other record in the file whose key value falls within the range represented on that track. Adding Kiley's record to the file displayed in Fig. 12-2 would cause Larsen's record to overflow, so that the records on track 015 would continue to be consecutive. The result is shown in Fig. 12-11. Adding Kramer's record would not further affect track 015; Kramer does not fall within the range of keys on that track. Kramer's record would be an overflow record. However, adding another new record, Kessler, would force Kiley's record to overflow.

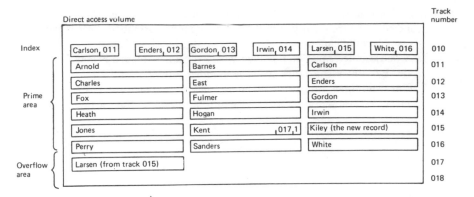

Fig. 12-11   The personnel file with Kiley displacing Larsen.

Maintaining consecutiveness on prime tracks has some advantages and some disadvantages:

ADVANTAGES

Sequential retrieval performance is improved.

The requirement for pointers within the prime area blocks such as that shown for KENT in Fig. 12-4 is eliminated.

DISADVANTAGES

The time required to insert new records into a file is increased. Inserting a new record may force a rippling effect moving records along an entire track.

Moving already-stored records exposes them to accidental damage. Rippling is particularly hazardous because of the special recovery problem it creates.

Moving already-stored records limits extendability of an indexed organization to accommodate alternate indexes. The reasons are discussed later in this chapter.

Where Is the Overflowing Record Stored?   The creator of an indexed file must specify by control statements how much space should be reserved for overflow records. In many systems, the creator is allowed to specify whether the overflow area should be a continuous area or whether a small part of the overflow area should exist on each cylinder that has prime area. Distributing the overflow area decreases the physical-motion time for devices that have movable read/write elements. An overflowing record is stored in the first unused space in the overflow area or in the portion of the overflow area on the same cylinder as the overflowing track.

The records on an overflow track have no predictable order among their keys. To establish logical order among overflow records, sequences of key values are indicated by pointers. A series of records each containing a pointer to the next record in the series is called a chain, and the individual records are said to be chained together. Figure 12-12 shows several chains in an overflow area.

What Extensions of the Index Provide for Overflow Records?   The EXEC-8 design provides that the indexes need not be changed when records overflow. The lowest-level index in that system points to prime-area blocks. If a prime-area block has an overflow record, that fact is discovered during inspection of the block itself after that block has been moved to main storage.

The OS/360 design is quite different. In that system, overflows always occur from the end of a prime-data track. One possible design would have had a pointer on each prime track pointing to an overflow chain. That design possibility was discarded in favor of an indexed-overflow design that completely avoids use of the prime track when an overflow record is being retrieved.

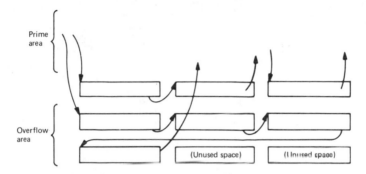

Fig. 12-12   Overflow-area chains (EXEC-8).

Figure 12-13 illustrates an indexed-overflow structure. In such a structure, the low-level index has pairs of entries; the first of each pair includes a pointer to a prime-area track, and the second of each pair has a pointer to the beginning of an overflow chain for that track. In the low-level index of Fig. 12-14, key 046 has a prime-area pointer, but because the prime track has not overflowed, there is no overflow pointer in the next index entry. The next index-entry pair indicates that records with keys larger than 046 but not exceeding 077 are on the prime track indicated. That track has overflowed, so that records with keys greater than 077 but not exceeding 081 are in an overflow chain. When a file is newly created, the keys within each index-entry pair are equal, and the overflow pointer is blank. If a record is inserted into a prime track forcing a record to overflow, the key for the index entry pointing to that track is reduced to reflect the true situation on that track. In Fig. 12-13, the low-level index entry with key 077 originally had a key 081. That key value was reduced to 077 when record 081 was forced off the track by a new record.

As one further enhancement to performance, the lowest-level index can be distributed so that index entries reside on the same cylinder as the prime tracks they reference. This arrangement can result in reduced motion time of a movable read/write element. However, distributing the index has disadvantages that may outweigh its apparent advantage:

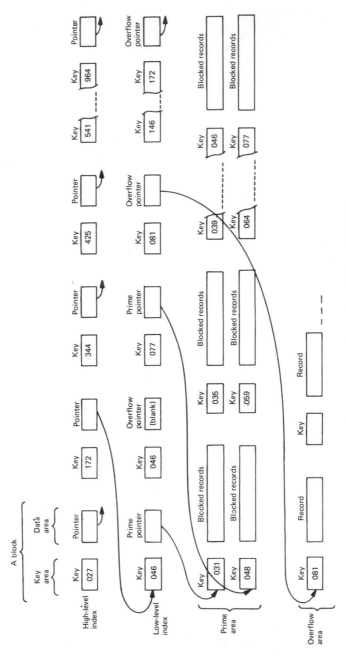

Fig. 12-13 An indexed-overflow design (OS/360).

238

1. When indexes do not share prime-area cylinders, the index and the prime area each resemble a sequentially organized file. This similarity can reduce the amount of added programming required to support the indexed organization.
2. The lowest-level index entries for any prime cylinder will usually occupy less than a full track. Therefore, either some space on the index track will be wasted as index entries and prime data must exist on the same track. Sharing a track complicates programming and increases the probability of accidental damage to both index and data records.
3. Many systems allow indexes to be stored on a device physically separate from the prime data. Storing all indexes on a high-performance device may yield better performance than distributing the lowest-level index.
4. Distributing the index causes an operational problem during the loading if index preformatting is performed. This problem is discussed a little later.

INDEXED-FILE PROCESSING

There are three major types of processing activities that affect indexed files: (1) file loading, (2) sequential retrieval, and (3) random processing. These three are discussed in the next three sections.

File Loading

The process of storing the initial collection of records in the prime area while creating indexes is called file loading. The preliminaries to loading indexed files are not unique; a control statement identifies the file as a new file, space is allocated, and the OPEN macro is issued. Following that, the user's program presents records in key sequence using an interface described in Chap. 4. As the records are accepted by the access method, the sequence of keys should be checked. If records are stored out of sequence, subsequent file processing will produce baffling results.

Sparse Loading.   For some files, a high rate of record additions and deletions is anticipated. Such files are called *volatile files,* and one technique useful in dealing with volatile files is called *sparse loading.* Sparse loading is simply the practice of leaving a portion of each prime-area space unit unfilled during loading. For example, if track capacity is 10 records, each prime track might be loaded with 8 records, leaving room for 2 records to be added before the track overflows. Sparse loading is effective only if each prime-area unit is large enough for several records. If a track could contain only 2 records, sparse loading would cost 50 percent of prime-area space, and even then the addition of only 2 records to a track would cause overflow. Sparse loading is not a highly effective technique for the following reasons:

1. It invariably wastes a significant amount of the prime area.
2. It increases the size of the index. In some cases, this increase will force

an extra level of index, thereby significantly affecting record storage and retrieval time.

3. Unless record additions are spread evenly throughout the file, the number of records overflowing will not be markedly reduced by sparse loading.

Sparse loading can be offered as a feature of the access methods. To use the feature, the user could furnish the desired loading factor in a table. As an alternative, the users might be instructed to accomplish their own sparse loading by interspersing dummy records marked as deleted records during the loading process. If this technique is to work, the I/O system must be designed such that it does not reject these dummy records.

Volume Initializing. Creating an indexed file includes development of indexes, an activity that requires periodic execution of reasonably intricate programs. To reduce the requirement for main storage space during loading, most contemporary systems preformat the tracks that will later contain indexes. Preformatting can occur during execution of OPEN. This practice is ill-advised and should be avoided in any new designs. The primary disadvantages are:

1. All volumes that will contain indexes must be made available during OPEN. If indexes are distributed across all volumes, this implies that all volumes must be mounted during OPEN and remain mounted until each is loaded or they must be demounted and later remounted. File loading is a serial process; only one volume at a time should be required.
2. Performing special activities during OPEN makes the loading process somewhat inflexible. For example, the programming to resume loading or to make massive insertions of new records is made more complex by the special actions to be performed only the very first time any file is opened.

Random Loading. You may have wondered whether it is really necessary to present records in order of their keys during loading. The answer is that key sequence is practically essential. If records are presented in a random order, there is no way to predict where in the prime area each one should be stored. Further, the loading time for random loading would exceed sequential loading by a significant factor, probably 10 times or more. The most efficient way to deal with records that are not in sequence is to sort them and then load them sequentially.

There are some situations where sequential loading is almost impossible. If records are continuously created or modified by a large number of keyboard-terminal operators, there may be no practical possibility of a preliminary sort. Such situations might be handled in the following general way:

1. During an initial period, possibly one working day, simply collect records in the order received.
2. During the first night, sort the collected records and load the indexed file. This initial set of records establishes the indexes and the expected distribution of keys.

3. Beginning the second day, new records are added to the file randomly. The number of new records will be very significant, and overflow chains may become very long.
4. Reorganize the file frequently, probably daily, until file size and key distribution become fairly constant. Reorganization is discussed later in this chapter.

This approach is not genuinely random loading, but it fulfills an important requirement, and it is used widely.

Mass Insertion of Records.   Not infrequently, there is a requirement to add a number of records to a localized area of an indexed file. For example, parts in an assembled product might have part numbers of the form AAAPP, where AAA identifies the assembly and PP distinguishes the part within the assembly. When record parts for this assembly are added to an indexed inventory file, using the customary random processing facilities, all of these records will be stored in a localized area of the file and all or most will be on a single overflow chain. This condition is very damaging for the following reasons:

1. Insertion time can be very long. This is particularly true if each new record is added to the end of a growing overflow chain.
2. The overflow area may become exhausted. If this happens, special action will be required to extend the overflow space or reorganize the file before the record insertion can be completed.
3. Record retrieval time for records on the long chain will be quite slow. This can be particularly important for files that experience the highest activity rate for the newest records.

The most desirable resolution of this problem would be to furnish special programs in the I/O system for mass insertion. These programs could create one or more new prime-data cylinders that could be treated somewhat as if they had been part of the originally loaded prime-data cylinders. Such programs might be quite complex, but their availability would avoid all of the problems listed above.

Resumption of Loading.   Closely related to the mass insertion programs suggested above would be programs than can add records in sequence to the end of an existing file. A few existing systems offer this capability. The principal challenge is the reestablishing of conditions that existed at the conclusion of the previous loading session.

Sequential Retrieval

A user may want to retrieve records from an indexed file sequentially to create a report, summarize information, search for records with certain attributes, or to accomplish reorganization of the file. The access method can furnish buffering because the order of retrieval is established by a combination of indexes, pointers, and physical proximity of records. For most file designs, the index is used infrequently during sequential retrieval. Several records can be retrieved with a single reference to an index entry.

Setting a Limit for Sequential Retrieval.   The user may be interested in retrieving only a portion of the file. To accommodate this need, I/O systems provide the ability to establish a starting point other than the beginning of the file. The EXEC-8 user establishes a starting point by ensuring that a particular table contains the key of the record that logically precedes the first record wanted. One way to do this is to retrieve the first record wanted using an individual record retrieval request. Following that, requests for sequential records will produce the desired records. OS/360 has a special macro, SETL, meaning set limit, that establishes a beginning point for sequential operations. One advantage of SETL is that the key of the first record to be retrieved need not be known precisely. For example, in an indexed parts file, all parts for a certain assembly might have part numbers of the form ABCxx where xx can be any value. To prepare for retrieval of all parts for the assembly, the user can issue SETL ABC00. The next record that will be delivered to the user will be the first record in the file whose key begins with ABC.

Sequential Update.   Sequential retrieval may include an update capability allowing records to be modified. Capability is limited to simple modification of existing records. New records cannot be added, nor can the length of an existing record be changed. These restrictions make it possible to replace the modified block of information without disturbing any other part of the file. Some systems provide the ability to add, delete, or change the length of a record by allowing the interleaving of random and sequential operations. This flexibility is not as easily achieved as one might think, particularly if the file structure acommodates new records by rippling existing records.

File Reorganization.   If a file is quite volatile, some overflow chains may become quite long with resultant reduced performance. To remedy this condition, occasional reorganization of the file may be required. Reorganization is accomplished by a combination of sequential retrieval of all records and a file loading operation that actually creates a new file. File reorganization is usually accomplished by a general utility program, but it can be accomplished by any user's program. A utility program might accomplish its task in two stages: (1) The entire file is copied to magnetic tape. To do this, records are retrieved sequentially and a magnetic-tape file with sequential organization is created. (2) A new indexed file is created and loaded using the tape file as a source of record.

This two-stage process has the advantages that the magnetic tape file can be preserved for back-up purposes and the direct access devices initially containing the file can be used to receive the reorganized file.

Some of the problems surrounding indexed file reorganization are these:

1. It is difficult for the user to know when reorganization is required. Even if some indicative statistics were accumulated by the I/O system, there would be a logistics problem in getting them to the person who would instigate reorganization.
2. The process of reorganization is time consuming, and it is not truly productive. For I/O devices that have large capacity but relatively low sequential data rates, reorganization can require several hours.

3. Reorganization can be required at an inopportune time. Indexed files are frequently used in communications based systems. An unexpectedly high rate of record additions to one area of the file early in the morning might cause marginal performance of the file. This would leave someone the choice between continuing service at a marginal level or halting service completely so the file could be reorganized.

Partial Reorganization. The ability to reorganize a part of a file would reduce the problems just listed. Such a capability is not generally available. One can readily see that the programming for partial reorganization would be similar to the massive insertion programs. Further, the availability of either of these two capabilities would reduce the requirement for the other capability. One problem in using a partial-reorganization program would be determining what area of the file requires reorganization. Possibly the program itself could identify the most overflow-ridden areas.

Random Processing

The principal value of an indexed organization is its ability to perform individual record transactions in any order. These random processing capabilities are described in the next several paragraphs. Random processes cannot be buffered by the system because there is no way to predict the order of requests. However, the user might accomplish the effect of buffering by requesting several random actions without waiting for the first action to be completed.

Retrieve an Existing Record. The simplest random process is individual record retrieval. For some uses, random retrieval is the only random process that is required, all other activities such as insertion of new records being performed sequentially during the reorganization. Because of its fundamental importance, many indexed organizations are designed to sacrifice performance in other functional capabilities as necessary to provide excellent performance for random record retrieval.

Typically, a random request involves searching indexes in a natural way beginning from the highest level. One alternative sometimes considered is for the I/O programs to prefix that search by a search of any conveniently nearby piece of the lowest-level index. The reason this possibility is considered is that, in many situations, the records required by random retrieval requests are not really randomly distributed over the file. For example, a handful of time cards contains data for people who are organizationally related, or a set of water meter readings may come from a small geographic area. Such naturally occurring relationships increase the probability that a required record may be found physically close to a record recently processed. A preliminary nearby search requires very little time, particularly if index blocks are already in main storage.

Delete a Record. To delete a record, the I/O system must retrieve the record using methods described above and then eliminate that record from the file. The most natural way of eliminating a record would seem to be simple erasure, setting all bytes to binary zeros or to blank characters. Erasure is not used because the simple practice of marking the unwanted record has several advantages. In several operating systems, a record is marked for deletion by setting all of the bits of the first byte of the record to ones. The advantages and disadvantages of marking rather than erasing are as follows:

ADVANTAGES

Erasing requires more time because all bytes of the record are affected.

The erased space must be accounted for somehow, so erasing must be supplemented by other conventions.

Marking has a potential advantage for recovery of accidentally deleted records, but has some obvious limitations in its use.

DISADVANTAGES

Any record containing data that accidentally conform to the deletion mark will be treated by the I/O system as if it were deleted.

The continued existence of deleted records exposes their contents to possible breaches of privacy conventions. This danger is significant, particularly if the deletion mark obliterates part of the key of the record, making later identification difficult.

Insert a New Record. When a new record is presented for insertion into a file, the I/O system must determine whether the key of the record coincides with the key of any other record in the file. This test is properly an I/O system responsibility even though a duplicate key would be presented only if the user has made an error.

Actual insertion is accomplished by inspecting the appropriate prime area, moving existing records as necessary, and utilizing any space that is either unused or is occupied by a record marked for deletion. Frequently, the prime area will overflow, and overflow chains are affected. Two special concerns are worth mentioning.

First, the ability of an I/O system to store and retrieve indexed records rapidly is affected significantly by the lengths of overflow chains and the order in which records are inserted into chains. In most existing organizations, the time required to store and retrieve records on overflow chains improved if records that are logically consecutive are presented to the system in order of descending value of keys.

Secondly, if appropriate space is not available, the new record must be rejected. Unless special care is taken in designing the record insertion programs, an I/O system might store the new record and then find that no space is available for a record that has been moved to accommodate the new record. It is not appropriate to reject such a displaced record; the user would be baffled by such an act.

Update a Record. When the users intend to update a record by changing the contents of one or more fields, they are required to notify the system of that intent. Notification can take the form of a random retrieval request with an exclusive option parameter. Having received such notification, the I/O system must protect against erroneous processing due to conflicting processes. The mechanisms used to establish exclusive use of records, indexes, or entire files are discussed in Chap. 19.

SUMMARY

Indexed sequential organizations and their related access methods called BISAM and QISAM furnish the abilities to process individual records or sequences of records from a file stored on a direct access storage device.

An indexed organization includes a prime-data area that contains most of the records of a file, an index area that makes it possible to find individual records without extensive searching through unwanted records, and an overflow area that accommodates records added to the file subsequent to the original file loading.

The order among records of an indexed file is established by relative values of record keys. In establishing a file, a user's program furnishes records sorted to ascending-key order. Records are blocked for recording in the prime area, and index entries consisting of keys and pointers are established during loading. Later, when new records are added to the file, the new records themselves or old records displaced by the new records are stored in the overflow area. Chains of pointers, supplemented in some system by entries in the lowest-level indexes, make possible the retrieval of prime-area and overflow-area records with equal facility.

The OS/360 and EXEC-8 systems are significantly different designs that furnish nearly identical functions. In the former system the lowest-level index includes absolute pointers to prime tracks or single-record overflow blocks. In the latter system the lowest-level index includes relative pointers to prime-area blocks which, in turn, include relative pointers to multirecord overflow blocks.

During file loading, record sequence is checked. For volatile files, sparse loading can be either specified by the user or actually accomplished by the user. Sparse loading is a partially effective technique for providing room for record additions within the prime-data area. As a prelude to actual loading, some systems require that the index areas be preformatted. Preformatting is operationally inconvenient and should be avoided if possible. File loading requires that records be presented in key sequence, but some of the effects of random loading can be achieved by partial sorting and frequent file reorganization.

Not infrequently, large numbers of records whose keys are nearly consecutive are added to a file. A mass-insertion feature, which would treat such additions as if they were continuations of the original loading process, would help avoid long chains of overflow records. A simpler, related feature extends the range of keys by resuming the loading process.

Sequences of records might be retrieved to create reports, summarize information or other purposes. Techniques are available for beginning a sequence of retrievals with any particular record or at any particular key value. During sequential retrieval, records can be inserted or old record lengths can be changed during sequential processing by interspersing random processing requests with sequential requests.

When overflow chains become excessively long, causing reduced performance, the file can be reorganized by combining sequential retrieval of the old file with loading of a new file. The cost and inconvenience of reorganizing are disadvantages of an indexed organization. An ability to reorganize a part of a file would offset some of those disadvantages.

Random processes include the ability to retrieve an individual record. Normally indexes are searched from the highest level downward when a record is requested. Prefixing that search with a search of the area immediately surrounding the area of most recent activity can improve retrieval time for many situations. Individual records are usually deleted by marking rather than erasing. When new records are inserted, either the space occupied by marked records or overflow space is used. When records are updated, the I/O system must protect against erroneous, conflicting processing.

Exercises

1.(e) Is the key value in a lowest-level index entry a highest key or is it a lowest key for a collection of records?
2.(e) Is an overflow always indicated in an index?
3.(e) What reasons are given for only limited effectiveness of sparse loading?
4.(e) What mechanism establishes the sequence among records that have overflowed from a single unit of the prime area?
5.(e) Are the terms *range index* and *dense index* synonymous?
6.(e) What unique advantage is ascribed to SETL for initializing a sequential retrieval?
7.(e) Is overflow space used at all during initial loading?
8.(m) Why might a sequential organization be more effective than an indexed organization when requirements are limited to sequential storage and retrieval?
9.(m) Does this chapter suggest that a record like Kiley's in Fig. 12-3 might be removed from the overflow area if space becomes available on a prime area track? Describe in a few words the merits of such a capability.
10.(m) Some files must be indexed by two different indexes. For example, an insurance policy file might be indexed by policy number and by policy holder's name. Describe why the indexes for such an organization cannot both be range indexes.
11.(m) List three processing features described in this chapter that are not essential but whose use might reduce the frequency of file reorganization.
12.(m) For some files, the most recently added records experience the most processing activity. What aspects of an indexed organization are detrimental for such files?

13 The Direct Organization of Data

The direct organization of data is an alternative to the indexed and list organizations for nonsequential storage and retrieval of records. The fundamental idea of the direct organization is this: Any record of a data set should be stored at a location such that the record key and the storage location of that record have some fixed arithmetic or logical relationship.

Think about that idea for a moment: The key and the location should have some fixed relationship. As an example, the key itself might be used as the storage location. In that case, the record would be stored at an address equal to its key and, if one knows the key, one also knows the address. Or, if the key contains too many characters, a truncated key might serve as the address, or the remainder after dividing the key by a certain integer might be used.

One of the problems in using the direct organization is choosing the key-location relationship. None of the operating systems in use today make that choice; it is the user's responsibility. To ease that responsibility, the storage space for the data set is considered to consist of numbered segments of uniform length called buckets,[1] and record keys are related to bucket numbers rather than to addresses. Bucket numbers are easier to use than storage addresses, because they begin with 1 and they are consecutive. In a separate operation, bucket numbers can be converted to physical addresses through use of a table relating bucket numbers to physical addresses. Figure 13-1 illustrates the relationship of records to buckets. The process of relating (transforming) keys to bucket numbers may result in several different records being related to the same bucket. For example, if a bucket number is derived by simply dropping the leftmost character of the key, keys 10123 and 20123 are both transformed to bucket 0123. To accommodate such cases, buckets may be defined to be large enough for several records. But regardless of bucket size, if records are added to the set continuously, bucket overflow will occur. Overflow records can be accommodated by several techniques; one of the most popular is to assign overflow from one bucket to the nearest unfilled bucket.

Several ideas have been suggested: Keys must be transformed; bucket size must be determined; and overflow records must be accommodated. These considerations are discussed in detail in the next several sections of this chapter.

---

[1] The term *bucket* has an unprofessional aura, but it is descriptive and it is in common industry usage.

Following that, initial loading of records into the space, random record processing, sequential record processing, and function subsets for small systems are discussed.

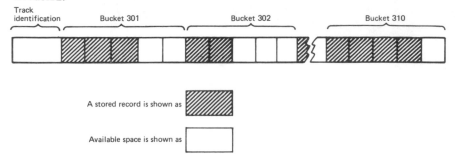

Fig. 13-1   A direct access device track illustrating the relationship of records to buckets.

KEY TRANSFORMATION

To retrieve a specific record from a data set, either one must know where the record is stored or one must search for the record. Both approaches have limitations; searching is too time-consuming for many situations, and knowing where a record is stored is a significant challenge. Some techniques that can reduce search time have been developed. Information can be extracted from records to form an index. An index can be examined more rapidly than a data set because it is smaller. As a refinement, the index can be sorted so that specialized searching methods can be applied. Another step results in multilevel indexes. These are good ideas; they are widely exploited; and they are discussed fully in Chap. 12. Indexes are mentioned here because in exploring the "know where the record is stored" alternative, one may consider maintaining a table, list, or catalog where record keys are related to locations. There is nothing wrong with that approach, but it is not the subject of this chapter.

What is needed is a process, algebraic or logical, for transforming a key into a bucket number. If there is to be a reasonable hope of finding such a process, we must be willing to make one major concession: We must allow the transformation to determine where the record should be stored as well as to determine where it can be found. Notice that this is different from an indexed organization where a record can be stored arbitrarily provided only that the index reflects the chosen location. Without this concession, finding a transformation might be hopelessly difficult. Making the concession implies that the order of records in storage is controlled by the transformation rather than by any consideration of the expected order of use of records.

The question now is, "What constitutes a good transformation?" For any particular collection of records, a good transformation has the following characteristics:

1. It wastes little storage space.
2. It overfills very few segments.
3. It meets the first two conditions continuously as records are added or deleted.
4. It is reasonably compact and simple to perform.

A good transformation is a simple process that transforms an evolving set of keys into bucket numbers so that all buckets are filled uniformly to near capacity.

Note that items 1 and 2 above are in opposition to each other. When a transformation is assigning records to a tightly constrained space, some buckets probably will overflow. Increasing the bucket size would relieve the overflow condition, but because all buckets have identical size, an increase would waste space. Bucket overflow is allowable, but it is undesirable because processing time for overflow records is much larger than for nonoverflow records.

The item 3 listed above requires that a good transformation should not deteriorate as records are added to or deleted from the data set. This requirement can be very important or not very important depending on the expected frequency of additions and deletions. In either event, the requirement is difficult to meet because it implies a knowledge of the future. However, some types of transformations can tolerate unpredictable additions and deletions better than others as we shall see in a few moments. For situations where changes to the record key set are unpredictable, such a transformation has a definite advantage.

The requirement that a good transformation be compact and simple to perform speaks for itself. A good transformation can be visualized as a subroutine of probably fewer than 100 instructions that accepts a record key as its input and produces a bucket number as its output.

In a few cases, it is possible to derive a good transformation by inspection. Example 13-1 illustrates a special case in which keys are very nearly equivalent to bucket numbers. This case can frequently be effected by good application planning. For example, a customer invoice consisting of a prepunched card can carry a prepunched bucket number that will be available for use as the record key when receipts are being processed. In some cases, the prepunched card resides in a file drawer and is furnished to the computer by a clerk.

Example 13-1

A company owns a fleet of 100 automobiles which are assigned identification numbers F001A, F002A, and so forth, up to F100A. Devise a key transformation that will use 50 buckets.
Solution
Step 1   Select the middle 3 characters.
Step 2   Add 1.
Step 3   Divide by 2 and discard the remainder.

The quotient is the bucket number.

Example 13-2 is another simple case resolved by inspection. The key set in Example 13-2 illustrates a common phenomenon: It includes strings of keys where the keys within a string are consecutive.

Example 13-2

A set of 365 records contains weather information for New York City for each day of 1969. The key for any record is of the form *mmdd* where *mm* is the month (ranging from 01 to 12) and *dd* is the day (ranging from 1 to 31). Devise a key transformation that will use approximately 400 buckets.
Solution
Observe that the *dd* portions of the keys are short strings of consecutive numbers. One good solution would result from letting January use the first 31 buckets, February the next 31, and so forth. This will waste a few buckets for short months, but it has a uniformity that allows a simple transformation.

Step 1   Subtract 1 from *mm*.
Step 2   Multiply result of step 1 by 31.
Step 3   Add *dd*.

The result will be as follows:

Month	Key	Bucket
Jan.	0101	01
	0102	02
	.	.
	.	.
	.	.
	0131	31
Feb.	0201	32
	.	.
	.	.
	.	.
	0228	59
Mar.	0301	63
	.	.
	.	.
	.	.
Nov.	1130	340
Dec.	1201	342
	.	.
	.	.
	.	.
	1231	372

Most application situations are much more difficult than these examples. Consider the following key sets:

item numbers from a mail-order catalog
names of students enrolled in a school
invoice numbers in an accounts receivable file

If a key set does not have definite patterns or if existing patterns can be expected to change over an operating period, a general purpose transformation may be the best choice. Most cases such as these require experimentation to determine whether a possible transformation is acceptable. Two good general purpose transformations are discussed in the following sections.

Division by a Prime Number

The best-known general purpose key-transformation technique involves division by a prime number.

Why divide? In all practical situations, the number of buckets is much smaller than the number of possible key values. For example, consider a set of approximately 100,000 records with 6-character alphabetic keys to be transformed into 20,000 bucket numbers. The keys can assume 26^6 (more than 300,000,000) possible values. Clearly, the transformation must reduce the range of keys so that each key within the range is associated with one of 20,000 bucket numbers. One way to reduce the range of keys is to divide. Dividing by 20,000, discarding the quotient, and saving the remainder would reduce any range of keys to 20,000 possible values.

Why use a prime number? Sets of keys frequently include patterns exhibiting a degree of uniformity which can be beneficial or detrimental to the transformation process. Two cases are especially important.

The first case is if the key set includes a long string of values where each differs from its predecessor by a fixed amount d, this string will be distributed evenly to buckets only if d and the divisor D have no common factors. This is illustrated by Example 13-3. The solution to Exercise 9 at the end of the chapter explains the phenomenon.

EXAMPLE 13-3

When D and d have a common factor, the remainders repeat in a short pattern.

Key set with $d = 3$	Remainder when $D = 6^*$	Remainder when $D = 5^†$
13	1	3
16	4	1
19	1	4
22	4	2
25	1	0
28	4	3
31	1	1

* Common factor $= 3$.
† No common factor.

Notice that the remainder sequence repeats in a short pattern when d and D have a common factor 3. When D has no factor in common with d, the pattern is much longer. In fact, it can be shown that when d and D have no common factor, the pattern will repeat only after every possible remainder value has occurred once.

The easiest way to ensure that d and D have no common factor is to choose D prime and larger than d; if D has no factors other than 1 and itself, it certainly has no factors (other than 1) in common with d.

Do strings exhibiting a common interval occur frequently? They occur whenever keys include any form of suffix. Example 13-4 illustrates this point.

EXAMPLE 13-4

The program modules of an I/O system are identified by 6-character keys where the last two characters are version number. These keys tend to differ by a common interval equal to 100.

Keys	Interval	
201501		
	100	
201601		
	100	
201701		
	100	
201801		←—— This is the end of
201502		the first string.
	100	
201602		
	100	
201701		
	200	←—— There is a record
		missing here.
201902		
	100	
202002		
	1000	
202003		

The second case is if there are two strings of key values such that the values in one string differ from the values in the other by a constant amount C which is a multiple of D, then the two strings will be transformed to identical bucket numbers, as illustrated in Example 13-5.

Strings related in this way occur whenever record keys include fixed prefixes. This point is illustrated in Example 13-6. Fortunately, the value of C is the product of an integer c and the number-base radix r raised to some power. That is, $C = c \cdot r^n$. If D is prime, it will not contain r as a factor and therefore C will not be a multiple of D unless $c = D$.

EXAMPLE 13-5

When C is a multiple of D, remainders are identical. The following keys and remainders have $C = 100$ and $D = 20$.

Key	Remainder	Key	Remainder
17	17	117	17
18	18	118	18
19	19	119	19
20	0	120	0
21	1	121	1

Neither the prefix nor the suffix case requires that D be prime; they require only that common factors be avoided. The easiest way to ensure against common factors is to use a prime number for D.

Which prime number? Because all remainders are less than the divisor, the divisor must be chosen slightly smaller than the number of buckets desired. There is always a prime number close to the desired value; prime numbers are surprisingly dense.

What if the key is not numeric? The answer to this question will depend on the specific hardware system to be used. In some machines, the binary representation of the key can simply be treated as if it were a binary number. In others, it may be necessary to manipulate the key one character at a time to provide a representation that is related to the original representation and that can be processed arithmetically

EXAMPLE 13-6

Parking-lot spaces are assigned identifying numbers of the form *LXXX*, where *L* is the lot number and *XXX* is the parking-space number. Strings of identifying numbers of this form differ by a constant amount.

Lot 1	Lot 2	Lot 7
1001	2001	7001
1002	2002	7002
1003	2003	7003
1004	2004	
	2005	
$C = 1000$	$C = 5000$	

Notice that C has the form $c \cdot 10^3$.

When the numeric representation of the key is too large for the registers of the machine, it can be shortened either by discarding some portion known to contain little key-differentiating information or by breaking it into two or more pieces and adding them together. In any of these preliminary manipulations, care should be taken to preserve as much as possible the variability that distinguishes one key from another.

Division by a prime number has one special property which has not been mentioned: It tends to preserve the consecutive order of a string of consecutive keys. This is an important property; strings of consecutive keys are very common.

Randomizing Transformations

If a transformation is to be truly general purpose, it should *not* preserve any relationship among keys. Rather, it should produce bucket numbers in a random sequence from any set of keys. The reasoning behind these statements is as follows:

1. To be truly general purpose, a transformation should be applicable to key sets having unpredictable repetitive patterns.
2. If patterns among keys are preserved, the resulting bucket numbers will exhibit unpredictable patterns.
3. An unpredictable repetitive pattern of bucket numbers may be desirable or it may be undesirable. For example, the pattern 2, 5, 10, 2, 5, 10, 2, . . . would be undesirable.
4. A random sequence of bucket numbers statistically guarantees a reasonably even distribution of records to buckets, provided only that the number of records involved is large.

A transformation designed to produce bucket numbers in a random sequence from any set of keys is called a randomizing transformation.

One randomizing transformation uses a radix-conversion process. The key is treated as if it were expressed in a radix foreign to the computing system; it is converted to the system's normal radix; and then the high-order digits are deleted. This process is illustrated in Example 13-7.

EXAMPLE 13-7
Assume that keys are decimal. Treat them *as if* they were expressed in base 11 and convert them to decimal. For example, the key 30102 will transform to $3 \times 11^4 + 1 \times 11^2 + 2$. Following transformation, truncate to three digits.

Original Key	Transformed Key	Truncated Key
30102	44046	046
30103	44047	047
30112	44057	057
30212	44178	178
40212	58819	819

Notice that a difference between the high-order characters of the last two keys is not lost during truncation.

Another randomizing transformation uses repeated division by a prime number, preserving the quotient in all but the last division. We shall not attempt to demonstrate that these methods produce a random set of bucket numbers. Experimental results are reported in trade journals dated after 1960.

Most of the existing I/O systems require that the users perform their own key transformation so that the bucket number along with the original key are submitted to the I/O system whenever a record storage or retrieval operation is to be performed. This mechanism provides the users complete freedom of choice, but it results in redundant code in each of the several application programs that use a single data set. It also exposes the users to coordination problems of two kinds whenever a transformation definition is changed:

First, when a transformation definition is changed, all affected programs must be modified and tested successfully within a limited period of time. At the actual time of the change, the data set must be reorganized to work properly with the new transformation. Following that reorganization, it is very difficult to turn back.

Second, after the programs are converted to use the new transformation, they can no longer process old copies of the data set. Old copies of the programs can be preserved but only with the hazard of clerical confusion. An improvement could be effected by storing the appropriate transformation with each data set for automatic use by the I/O system.

Developing and testing key transformations is an interesting avocation. Exercise 11 at the end of this chapter describes a utility program that is almost essential to the experimenter. You should be aware that no perfect general purpose transformation can exist. That fact is demonstrated in the solution to Exercise 15. On the other hand, some transformations are very much better than others, and it is essential that a good one be chosen. An inappropriate choice can result in inefficient use of storage or excessive processing time or both.

BUCKET DEFINITION

The storage bucket serves three major purposes:

1. It accommodates key transformations that produce nonunique results from unique record keys.
2. It allows the storage space to be expanded without redefinition of the transformation.
3. It isolates the key transformation from the addressing structure of the storage device.

Unless the record key set is completely predictable, the key-transformation algorithm will occasionally produce nonunique results, called synonyms, from unique keys. Synonyms can be accommodated by overflow mechanisms, as discussed in the next section of this chapter, or by buckets large enough to contain several records each.

Figure 13-2 shows that the effect of a change in bucket size is much more dramatic than one might expect. Assuming that record keys are transformed to randomly distributed bucket numbers, 37.6 percent of the records will overflow at 0.5 load factor when bucket size is 4. That is, when records have been stored in buckets until the average bucket is half full (0.5 load factor), 3.76 percent of the records will have required special handling due to lack of space in their assigned buckets. If bucket size is doubled to 8, the load factor can go almost to 0.7 before the same overflow rate occurs. This means that if 4 percent overflow is the maximum tolerable level, a bucket size of 4 would allow approximately 50 percent effective storage utilization, while a bucket size of 8 would allow almost 70 percent utilization.

Bucket Size	Load Factor											
	0.1	0.2	0.3	0.4	0.5	0.6	0.7	0.8	0.9	1.0	1.1	1.2
1	4.84	9.37	13.61	17.58	21.31	24.80	28.08	31.17	34.06	36.79	39.35	41.77
2	0.60	2.19	4.49	7.27	10.36	13.65	17.03	20.43	23.79	27.07	30.24	33.30
3	0.09	0.63	1.80	3.61	5.90	8.82	11.99	15.37	18.87	22.40	25.91	29.33
4	0.02	0.20	0.79	1.96	3.70	6.15	9.05	12.32	15.86	19.54	23.25	26.93
5	0.00	0.07	0.37	1.12	2.48	4.49	7.11	10.26	13.78	17.55	21.42	25.30
6	0.00	0.02	0.18	0.67	1.69	3.38	5.75	8.75	12.24	16.06	20.06	24.11
7	0.00	0.01	0.09	0.41	1.18	2.60	4.74	7.60	11.04	14.90	19.00	23.19
8	0.00	0.00	0.05	0.25	0.84	2.03	3.97	6.68	10.07	13.96	18.15	22.46
9	0.00	0.00	0.02	0.16	0.61	1.61	3.36	5.94	9.27	13.18	17.44	21.86
10	0.00	0.00	0.01	0.10	0.44	1.29	2.88	5.32	8.59	12.51	16.85	21.36
11	0.00	0.00	0.01	0.07	0.33	1.04	2.48	4.80	8.01	11.94	16.34	20.94
12	0.00	0.00	0.00	0.04	0.24	0.85	2.15	4.36	7.51	11.44	15.89	20.58
14	0.00	0.00	0.00	0.02	0.14	0.57	1.65	3.64	6.67	10.60	15.15	19.99
16	0.00	0.00	0.00	0.01	0.08	0.39	1.28	3.09	6.00	9.92	14.56	19.53
18	0.00	0.00	0.00	0.00	0.05	0.28	1.01	2.65	5.45	9.36	14.07	19.16
20	0.00	0.00	0.00	0.00	0.03	0.20	0.81	2.30	4.99	8.88	13.66	18.86
25	0.00	0.00	0.00	0.00	0.01	0.09	0.48	1.65	4.10	7.95	12.87	18.31
30	0.00	0.00	0.00	0.00	0.00	0.04	0.29	1.23	3.47	7.26	12.31	17.93
35	0.00	0.00	0.00	0.00	0.00	0.02	0.18	0.94	2.98	6.73	11.87	17.66
40	0.00	0.00	0.00	0.00	0.00	0.01	0.12	0.73	2.60	6.29	11.53	17.47
50	0.00	0.00	0.00	0.00	0.00	0.00	0.05	0.45	2.04	5.63	11.03	17.20
60	0.00	0.00	0.00	0.00	0.00	0.00	0.02	0.30	1.65	5.14	10.68	17.03
70	0.00	0.00	0.00	0.00	0.00	0.00	0.01	0.20	1.37	4.76	10.41	16.93
80	0.00	0.00	0.00	0.00	0.00	0.00	0.01	0.13	1.14	4.46	10.21	16.86
90	0.00	0.00	0.00	0.00	0.00	0.00	0.00	0.09	0.97	4.20	10.05	16.80
100	0.00	0.00	0.00	0.00	0.00	0.00	0.00	0.06	0.83	3.99	9.92	16.77

Example of use: When 500 buckets can hold 4 records each (bucket size=4) and 1000 records have been stored (load factor=.5), then 37.6 records (3.76% of 1000) can be expected to overflow.

Fig. 13-2 Percentage of records that overflow for randomly distributed bucket numbers.

There is a simple statistical explanation for this. Assume that the bucket size is 1, and records have been distributed randomly so that half of the buckets are completely filled and the others are partially filled. If another record is added to a bucket chosen at random, the probability is 0.5 that the bucket selected is already full. Now consider bucket size to be increased to 2 by coupling each of the original odd-numbered record locations with the succeeding even-numbered location without moving any of the records already in the buckets. When a record is added at random, the probability is 0.5 that the odd half of the selected bucket is already full, 0.5 that the even half is already full, and 0.25 that both halves of the bucket are already full. If locations had been joined in threes, the probability would be reduced to 0.125 (0.5^3).

Another insight can be gained from the limiting cases. If a small space is divided into 10 buckets each capable of containing one record, there is a significant probability that the second record to be stored will be assigned to the already-filled bucket. However, if all of the assigned storage space is considered one bucket, overflow will not occur until the entire space is filled.

On the other hand, increased bucket size has its disadvantages. Because a record assigned to a bucket may be stored anywhere within the bucket (for, if not, the bucket is entirely ineffective in reducing overflow), record retrieval requires that the bucket be searched. In the limiting case where the entire space is one bucket, one could expect to search halfway through the space to find a particular record. However, as illustrated in Example 13-8, modest increases in bucket size will not necessarily increase record retrieval time.

EXAMPLE 13-8

Effect of bucket size on record retrieval time. (Assume the device to be used is a magnetic drum and assume 100 characters per record, 1 record per data block, and 64 blocks per track.)

	Case A	Case B	Case C
Records/bucket	1	32	64
Rotations required to find the bucket (average)	1/2	1/2	0
Rotations required to find the record within the bucket (average)	0	1/4	1/2
Rotations required to read record	1/64	1/64	1/64
Total rotations	33/64	49/64	33/64

Notice that case A has the advantage that it requires no time to find the record within the bucket. Case C has the advantage that it requires no time to find the bucket. Case B has neither of these advantages.

In Example 13-8, the increase in bucket size from case A to case B did increase record retrieval time. But increasing bucket size again from case B to case C actually reduced retrieval time. The reason that case C is better than case B is that case C uses a natural subdivision of the physical space on the device. Some storage devices read and write data in sectors; for these devices, it is natural to choose bucket size equal to sector size.

For fixed total storage space, we have the following important conclusions:

1. Increasing bucket size will reduce bucket overflow or will improve storage utilization without increasing overflow.
2. Increasing bucket size *tends* to increase record retrieval time.
3. Some storage devices have natural space subdivisions that are attractive choices for bucket size.

The second major purpose of the bucket idea is to allow expansion of the storage space without redefinition of the key transformation. If a data set has grown to the point where the total storage space assigned to it is inadequate, the space must be increased. To use the added space, either the number of buckets must be increased or the size of each bucket must be increased. In either case, the records must be reloaded into the new space. An increase in the number of buckets would require a redefinition of the key transformation; the old transformation was specifically constrained to produce only the initial set of bucket numbers. If the old transformation is still a good transformation when measured against the requirements discussed earlier, it should probably not be discarded. Rather, the size of each bucket should be increased.

The flexibility to change bucket size is not widely exploited; no major operating system in use today provides for user control of bucket size. Several systems either require or allow bucket size equal to track length. In these systems, the user might achieve a change in bucket size by moving a data set from its present device to a device with a different track length.

The third purpose of buckets is to isolate the key transformation from the addressing structure of the storage device. There are several problems that would result from requiring that the key transformation produce storage addresses directly:

1. A transformation that would produce valid addresses only would be difficult to find because storage addresses are generally not consecutive.
2. A transformation that produces valid addresses for one type of storage device would be unusable on any device that has different addressing rules.
3. A transformation that produces one set of valid addresses for a particular device would be unusable if the data set were moved to a new area of the same device.
4. The use of storage space with discontiguous extents would complicate all of the above problems.

Buckets isolate the key transformation from these problems; bucket numbers are independent of address form, address changes, and address discontinuities.

But simply removing all of the addressing problems from the key transformation does not solve those problems. Bucket numbers must be converted to actual storage addresses. Example 13-9 illustrates a method that can be generalized readily. In an actual I/O system, the number of buckets per track probably would be derived by dividing track length by bucket length. Notice that the remainder in step 2, ranging from 0 to $n-1$, is the relative position of the particular bucket b on its track. Steps 3 and 4 are specific to devices with decimal addressing and 20 tracks per cylinder. In a system, steps 3 and 4 probably would be performed by a routine applicable to many types of storage devices.

EXAMPLE 13-9
Describe the process that will derive the physical address for any particular bucket b from the table below.
Assumptions
1. There are 2 buckets per track.
2. Addresses consist of *cctt* where *cc* is cylinder and *tt* is track.
3. Addressing is decimal with 20 tracks per cylinder.
4. The first track in each cylinder is track 00.

Extent	Beginning Bucket Numbers	Beginning Address
1	1	0103
2	170	2201
3	628	4000
4	988	8609

Solution
Step 1 Determine which extent contains b. Call the beginning bucket number of that extent B and call the related beginning address A.
Step 2 Calculate $(b - B)/2$. Discard the remainder.
Step 3 Add the quotient from step 2 to the tt part of A and divide the result by 20. The remainder is the required track number.
Step 4 Add the quotient of step 3 to the cc part of A to get the required cylinder number.

OVERFLOW RECORD HANDLING

The imperfections of any key transformation probably will result in overfill of some buckets. Several alternative designs for accommodating the overflow records can result from the following questions: Shall overflow records be stored inside or outside the space assigned to buckets? What storage and retrieval methods should be used?

One widely used technique is to store a record that overflows from a particular bucket in the closest unfilled bucket. This technique has the advantages of using space that is nearby and that would otherwise be wasted. But it causes several problems:

1. A record that should fit into a particular bucket may overflow because that bucket contains one or more overflow records from some other bucket.
2. If overflow records are restricted to a limited range of buckets, such as buckets within the same cylinder as the overflowing bucket, overcrowding in one area of the data set may force premature data set reorganization.
3. If no range restriction is made, any search to determine whether a particular record is present in the data set may involve the entire data set.

When overflow records are stored in the closest unfilled bucket, the definition of the bucket loses some of its significance. Some of the systems that use this overflow technique refer to the bucket as the beginning location for a record search. In a sense, overlapping buckets have been established with each bucket beginning one record location beyond its predecessor. In such cases, bucket size is effectively equal to the overflow search range.

When separate overflow areas are maintained, performance may be improved by having portions of the overflow area physically close to the buckets they serve. If this is done, provision should be made for a general overflow area so that overflow of one of the local overflow areas does not force premature restructuring of the entire data set. The time required to search for a particular overflow record can be reduced by "chaining" the records that overflow from any particular bucket together. Chaining can be accomplished by storing the address of any member of a chain with the preceding member of the same chain. The address of the first number of an overflow chain can be stored in the overflowing bucket. Chaining techniques are described in detail in Chap. 14, "Linked-List Organization."

Figure 13-3 can be helpful in determining how much space to allow for overflow records. Because the table entries apply to randomly distributed bucket numbers, an actual case may differ significantly. In case of doubt, it is usually advisable to err on the high side when estimating overflow space requirements.

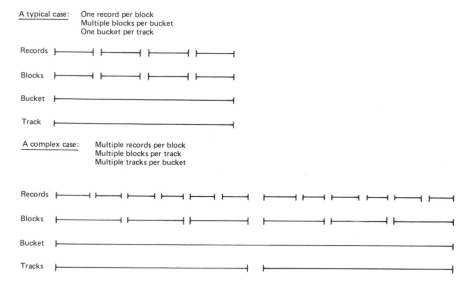

Fig. 13-3 Direct Organization Storage Format of the Minneapolis-Honeywell Series 200/Operating System.

Storage Formats

Figure 13-3 illustrates the relationships between records, blocks, and buckets in the Minneapolis-Honeywell Series 200/Operating System. In that system, a bucket can contain one or more blocks, and a block can contain one or more records (items, in Minneapolis-Honeywell terminology). A bucket can be larger than a track, but any bucket must be contained within a single cylinder.

A block is, of course, the unit of information stored or retrieved by a single channel program. When a data set intended for single record transactions has more than one record per block, the processing system incurs a significant data-moving burden. For example, to store a single record, an entire multirecord block must be retrieved; the single record must be inserted; and then the entire block must be stored. Alternatively, allowing only one record per block would be quite wasteful of storage space when records are small.[2] Most operating systems, including the Minneapolis-Honeywell system, allow the users of the system to decide whether a block will contain more than one record.

Device Loading

The records that are part of the initial data set can be loaded onto the direct access device randomly or sequentially. Random loading can be accomplished by treating every record as if it were an addition to an existing data set. It is conceptually the simpler method, but there are at least two reasons why it may be the less desirable method:

1. Random loading is time-consuming. For example, if 100,000 records are to be loaded and each record requires 0.5 s, 14 h, will be required. Sequential loading is faster by a factor of 2 or more, depending on device characteristics.
2. The storage space must be cleared before random loading so that residual information is not processed as if it were valid data either during and after the loading process. Sequential loading can avoid the separate clearing operation by clearing unused space as it is encountered.

Sequential loading involves three steps: (1) Transform all keys to bucket numbers. (2) Sort the records into bucket-number order. (3) Store the records in buckets beginning with bucket 1 and proceeding through the entire set. Bucket overflows that occur during sequential loading can be a serious nuisance. One method for handling the initially overflowing records is to load them randomly as a separate operation.

Whether loading is random or sequential, subsequent processing efficiency will be improved if records that will be used most frequently are placed in nonoverflow locations. Example 13-10 illustrates how significant this point is. The "80/20 rule" used in that example applies in many data processing situations. In cases where the assumptions in Example 13-10 apply, performance will be improved by approximately 20 percent by storing active records in nonoverflow locations.

EXAMPLE 13-10
The time required to satisfy 100 record retrieval requests from a particular data set is significantly reduced by storing active records in nonoverflow locations.
Assumptions
1. A total of 80 percent of the retrieval requests can be satisfied by only 20 percent of the records ("80/20 rule").
2. A total of 10 percent of the records are in overflow locations.

---

[2] Refer to Chap. 8 for more information.

3. The time required to retrieve a nonoverflow record is 50 ms.
4. The time required to retrieve an overflow record is 200 ms.

Solution

Of the 100 requests, 80 will be satisfied by high-activity records and 20 by low-activity records. Case 1 assumes that records have been stored without considering activity level; case 2 assumes that all active records are in nonoverflow locations.

Retrieval Time, ms	Case 1	Case 2
High-activity record	$0.9(50) + 0.1(200)$	50
80 high-activity records	5,200	4,000
Low-activity record	$0.9(50) + 0.1(200)$	$0.875(50) + 0.125(200)$
20 low-activity records	1,300	1,375
Total time, ms	6,500	5,375

During initial random loading, active records will tend to be stored in nonoverflow locations if they are loaded first. The same result can be achieved during sequential loading by including a record activity level, appropriately defined, as a low-order extension to the bucket number when sorting the records into bucket-number order. In either case, an activity-level indicator must be available. *Maintaining* the active records in nonoverflow locations during normal processing is a more difficult problem. It might be possible to accomplish this in part by forcing all records added to the data set into their proper buckets, displacing old records when necessary.

Random-Transaction Processing

The direct organization can support the following random-transaction processes:

Store a New Record   The process includes searching for available space, storing the record, and updating any control information.

Retrieve a Record   The process includes locating the appropriate bucket and comparing keys until the appropriate record is found. Special provision must be made for retrieving overflow records.

Store an Old Record   If the physical address is not available, this process will resemble record retrieval except that the record is recorded rather than retrieved. If the physical address is furnished by an application program, good design requires that the record at the given address be checked to ensure that it is the proper record.

Delete a Record   A record can be deleted by erasing it or by marking it with some distinguishing flag that can be detected by record retrieval programs. In all other respects, deleting a record resembles storing an old record.

Record retrieval may include an "exclusive" option so that the contents of a record cannot be modified by one application program while the record is being held exclusively by another application program. A record being held exclusively should be released by any of the other listed actions affecting that record. There are some problems involved with the exclusive feature, but they are not unique to direct organizations.

Sequential Processing

There are several situations that may require sequential processing. One of these, loading, has been discussed. Others include moving, copying, reorganizing, and generating reports. Some of these situations require a physically sequential process that simply stores or retrieves blocks of data as they are physically encountered without concern for records, buckets, overflow, and so forth. Several existing systems provide this through compatibility of the physical format of the direct organization and the sequential organization; this seems an ideal solution. Some applications, such as report writing, require that records be retrieved in order of ascending value of the key field. A form of this logically sequential processing can be provided through use of an auxiliary set of data consisting simply of the keys for all records to be included in a particular report. This set of data, called a *tickler file,* can be used by an application program as a source of keys for the conventional random retrieval operation.

Small-Systems Subsets

The direct organization allows significant restricting of function without losing its usefulness. As a limiting case, an I/O system can provide the ability to store or retrieve a record given the actual address in storage of that record. It is instructive to review the functions that have been described on the preceding pages of this chapter that would *not* be furnished in the limiting case.

> *Key Transformation* Key transformation is the user's responsibility in all major existing I/O systems. The small-system users can simplify their application programs by performing the key transformation completely outside the computer system. One method for accomplishing this is to maintain a printed list that relates record keys to storage addresses. Such a list can be produced and maintained by the computer system, and it can be used in about the same way that a telephone directory is used.
>
> *Buckets* In the limiting case, the record key is related directly to the storage address so buckets do not exist. With buckets eliminated, the key transformation is not isolated from the actual storage addresses. To make this restriction palatable, the I/O system must ensure that data sets are not moved indiscriminately within storage.
>
> *Overflow* In the limiting case, the I/O system cannot recognize an overflow situation. When the user requests the record from a particular location, that record is retrieved regardless of its key. When the user requests that a record be stored at a particular address, the record is stored at that address, destroying any record that may have been stored there previously. Such a restriction can be acceptable to system users provided it is clearly understood.

Furnishing the severely restricted function is a very simple matter. Every I/O system has the ability to store and retrieve records using storage addresses. The primary efforts required to furnish the limited functions are establishing, documenting, and supporting a usable interface to the already existing record storage and retrieval capability. Furnished in this way, the direct organization is in reality a direct processing feature for a sequential organization.

Strengths and Weaknesses

The primary advantages of a direct organization result from the simplicity of its fundamental concept. These advantages include:

Programming Simplicity   The programming required to store and retrieve records from a direct organization is significantly simpler than the programming required by other organizations. This simplicity is reflected in modest size, excellent performance, and low implementation cost. Because reliability and maintainability are related to complexity, these are also favorable.

Storage System Performance   The direct organization allows most records to be stored or retrieved in one reasonably simple operation. Other organizations may require several preliminary actions to examine or modify auxiliary records. The simple direct action can require significantly less channel and device time than other alternatives.

Weaknesses, centering around difficulty to use, include:

Choice of Key Transformation   Choosing an acceptable key transformation requires time, ingenuity, and experience. In many cases, computer analysis of potentially acceptable transformations is required.

Reorganization   When the data set grows to near capacity for the storage space assigned, or the key set has changed so that the transformation does not function effectively, the number of overflowing records will increase. When this happens, the processing time for transactions will increase, sometimes quite dramatically. To reduce processing time, the data set must be reorganized. Reorganizing a data set is time-consuming, and it usually requires selection of a new transformation.

Space Utilization   Some unused space must be provided to accommodate record additions, overflows, and nonuniform filling of buckets. Where record additions are frequent, the unused space may be 50 percent or more of the total space.

Logically Sequential Output   If logically sequential output is required frequently, the basic inability of a direct organization to furnish that output can be a serious inconvenience.

Extendability   There is no simple way to extend the direct organization to provide access to a record using an alternative key. For example, if an insurance policy record is stored using the policy owner's name as the record key, the direct organization can provide no direct way to retrieve that record using the policy number as the key.

The direct organization is an enigma. It is fundamentally appealing. It has been used by many people with good results. But one cannot avoid the feeling that its promise may always remain latent, that its full value may never be realized. The indexed and list organizations currently are enjoying popularity that significantly overshadows that of the direct organization.

SUMMARY

The fundamental idea of the direct organization is that a record should be stored in a location that is determined by a simple arithmetic or logical transformation of the record key. The fundamental idea is embellished by the use of buckets, and by automatic handling of overflow records.

Transforming a record key into a bucket number is the user's responsibility in current systems. A good transformation uses storage efficiently and is reasonably simple to perform. There are many methods for transforming keys, including division by a prime number and radix transformation. In some cases, a transformation can be chosen by inspection of the key set. In other cases, intuition, experience, and experimentation are required.

Buckets serve several useful purposes:

1. They accommodate key transformations that produce synonyms.
2. They improve storage space utilization.
3. They provide a convenient way to increase total storage space without requiring a new key transformation.
4. They isolate the key transformation from the storage device addressing structure.

Records that overflow from a bucket can be stored in nearby buckets or in separate overflow areas. Chaining overflow records together can reduce searching time in some cases.

The initial set of records can be loaded into storage randomly or sequentially. In either case, performance is improved by storing high activity records in nonoverflow locations. The random processing functions available for use during or after loading include storing a new record, retrieving a record, storing an old record, and deleting a record. A direct organization allows limited sequential processing of records. Use of a tickler file provides a form of logically sequential processing capability.

The direct organization facilities can be severely restricted for small-system use. In the limiting case, the ability to store or retrieve a record at a particular storage address can be furnished as an extension to the sequential organization functions.

The direct organization strengths result from its simplicity; its weaknesses are centered around difficulty of use. The direct organization is an enigma; its full capabilities are difficult to exploit.

Exercises

1.(e) What is the fundamental idea of the direct organization of data?
2.(e) List four attributes of a good key transformation.
3.(e) What is the prime number nearest to 24?
4.(e) List the three major purposes served by the storage bucket.

5.(e) Does increasing bucket size tend to increase or decrease record retrieval time?

6.(e) Using the table and assumptions in Example 13-9, calculate the address of bucket 623.

7.(e) How can one ensure that high-activity records are stored in nonoverflow locations during random loading?

8.(e) What function is described in this chapter as the minimal function that can be provided for the direct-organization data set?

9.(m) The key-transformation method that uses the remainder after division performs best when the divisor D is prime. Demonstrate mathematically that a string of keys separated by equal increments d will produce a shorter string of unique remainders when d is a factor of D than when D is prime.

10.(m) Assuming a random distribution of bucket numbers and a maximum allowable overflow rate of 5 percent which of the following will accommodate the greatest number of records?
   a. 5,000 buckets of size 4
   b. 2,000 buckets of size 10
   c. 1,000 buckets of size 20

11.(m) Flowchart a utility process that counts the overflow records that would result from use of a particular key transformation. Assume the transformation is available in subroutine form and that record size, bucket size, number of buckets, and the actual data records are available as input to the process.

12.(m) Assume overflow records are stored in the nearest available bucket without chaining. Explain why the search for a particular record should not be terminated when the first unfilled bucket is encountered.

13.(m) Flowchart a sequential loading process that places the most active records in nonoverflow locations. Assume that each record contains an activity count for the most recent operating period. Overflow records should be stored in the nearest available bucket. Use special care so that overflow from one bucket does not preempt space required by a high-activity record.

14.(m) Explain how two application programs processing records from a single data set in a multiprogrammed system, without exclusive option, could yield erroneous results.

15.(d) Prove that no perfect general purpose transformation can exist. (A perfect transformation would cause no bucket overfills provided the records in storage at any time do not exceed the total assigned storage capacity.) Suggestion: Assume m possible key values, space available for n records, and m greater than n. Observe that a perfect transformation must handle any collection of n or less records perfectly.

16.(d) As an extension of the above exercise, prove that if m is greater than n^2, then for any particular transformation, regardless of how it is chosen, there is at least one selection of records that is large enough to fill all of the available space whose keys all transform to a single bucket number.

17.(d) Describe the major functions of a load routine (or collection of routines) that features automatic transformation selection and ease of use. List the minimum set of parameters that must be furnished by the user of the load routine.

14 Linked-List Organization

In some cases, we are more concerned with file fabrication and alteration than reference or posting. When file alteration predominates, linked lists are generally most suitable. . . . Ivan Flores

A linked-list organization identifies relationships and establishes order among records through chains of pointers embedded within the records. A simple chain is illustrated in Fig. 14-1. The programs that process a linked-list file follow chains to retrieve or inspect records, and they insert and delete records from chains. Networks of chains have very interesting properties, and it is our task in this chapter to understand how and why such networks are constructed and how they are processed.

The principal philosophy behind a linked-list organization is that a group of files, which would be maintained separately if other organizations were used, can be combined into a single linked-list file serving a spectrum of requirements. As the files are combined, redundant information would be eliminated resulting in reduced storage space requirements, reduced file maintenance, fewer errors, and a generally more desirable capability. Just how integration is accomplished, what advantages accrue, and at what costs will become clear as we go along.

Of the four organizations described in this book, the linked-list organization is available in the fewest systems, but it is of great interest to innovators throughout the industry. The general purpose system serving as a source of information for this chapter is the Integrated Data Store (IDS), a product of the General Electric Company. The terms used in this chapter are those suggested in the October 1969 report to the CODASYL Programming Language Committee of the Association for Computing Machinery written by the Data Base Task Group (DBTG).

LISTS, CHAINS, AND INDEXES

There is a great and growing academic interest in lists and list processing. Chains and indexes are two forms of lists. The two forms are logically equivalent:

1. To convert a chain to an index, extract the pointers and organize them consecutively.
2. To convert an index to a chain, simply embed the index entries into the indexed records.

Chains and indexes differ significantly in their areas of utility. Chains are the more easily modified because consecutive members need not occupy consecutive storage space. Indexes can be searched more rapidly both because they are the more compact and because their structures allow binary searching. Sometimes a chain is called a linked list, the term used in the title of this chapter.

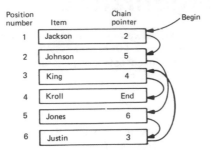

Fig. 14-1   A simple chain.

FUNDAMENTALS OF CHAINS

In the next few pages, we shall skim quickly through some fundamentals.

Pointers

A *simple chain* is a collection of records whose order is established by pointers as shown in Fig. 14-2. The record at the head of the chain can be considered the owner of the chain, and the other records are members. Simple chains are sometimes used in storing overflow records in the indexed and direct organizations described in previous chapters.

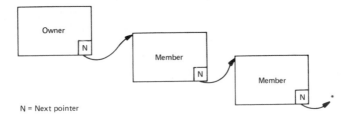

Fig. 14-2   Owner and members of a chain.

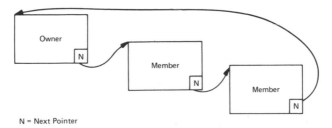

Fig. 14-3   A simple ring.

The last member of the simple chain contains a special form of next pointer indicating that no records follow it. One cannot help observing that the terminating pointer really should point somewhere. An inspiration results in the endless chain or ring shown in Fig. 14-3. The ring allows one to begin anywhere in a chain of records and traverse the entire chain passing through the owner enroute. Both the simple chain with the terminating pointer and the ring are useful. The term *chain* is ordinarily used to identify both forms, and the term *ring* is used only when one is particularly concerned with a chain that is endless.

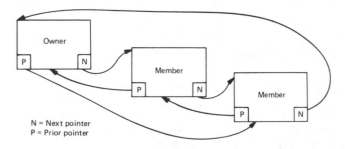

Fig. 14-4   A next and prior chain.

In some chains, prior pointers allow one to follow the chain in the backward direction. *Prior pointers* connect each member of a chain with its predecessor. Following prior pointers, one arrives finally at the owner of the chain. The *owner* might contain a special prior pointer that terminates the backward sequence, or it can contain a prior pointer to the last member in the chain as shown in Fig. 14-4. The chain as shown includes two rings of pointers. Notice that only one chain with two sets of pointers is shown, not two chains. The distinction is fundamentally important.

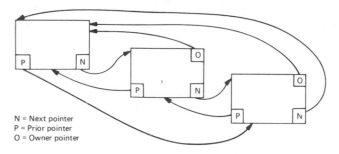

Fig. 14-5   A chain with owner pointers.

As the name implies, the owner record has special relationships to members of the chain. If, for example, each member contains information about a person assigned to department 803, the owner record might contain such information as the department name, the mailing address, and so forth for department 803. To make owner information more readily available, each member record might include an owner pointer as in Fig. 14-5. It is easy to see that owner pointers are not really required. One could simply follow the next pointers to arrive at the owner record, though for lengthy chains that might be a costly alternative.

Recapping quickly, we have looked at the following fundamental aspects of chains:

- next pointers connecting an owner and members in a forward direction
- prior pointers connecting an owner and members in reverse direction
- rings that are endless sequences of pointers
- owner pointers that connect each member directly with its owner

To be considered a chain, a collection of records must have next pointers. The other pointers listed above might be used in any combination with forward pointers to constitute chains having particular attributes.

Networks of Chains

A linked-list typically contains many chains, and the chains may be interdependent. Some of the possible interdependencies are illustrated in Fig. 14-6, where A is the owner of two chains, B is a member of one and the owner of another, and C is a member of two chains.

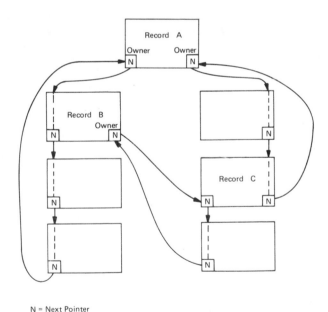

N = Next Pointer

Fig. 14-6   A network of chains.

UNDERSTANDING THE LIST ORGANIZATION

At this point, you should have a host of questions that fall into two classes: (1) Questions about *how* a list organization is designed. For example,

"How are chains represented?" or "What determines where a record should be stored?" (2) Questions about *why* one would want a list organization. For example, "What relationships can be represented by networks of chains?" or "Why would one use the various pointer alternatives?"

The *how* questions will be deferred for a while. As an aid to understanding list-organization motivations, a file containing information that is related to the personnel of a certain large company will be described. The file will contain several types of records as we shall see. The first type of record to be considered is called the employee record. There is one such record for each current employee. The record contains an employee name, social security number, date of hire, department number, telephone number, and so forth.

A Simple Next-Pointer Chain

From time to time, reports listing all personnel in alphabetic order are required. Editing the information for each employee in several different ways provides reports such as the company telephone book, a security clearance report, a credit union loan balance report, and a salary status report. To provide a basis for retrieval of records in alphabetic order, each employee record will contain a pointer linking it with its alphabetic successor. Figure 14-7 shows some of the records in this chain. The pointers are shown as L(Johnson), meaning "location of Johnson," L(Justin), meaning "location of Justin," and so forth.

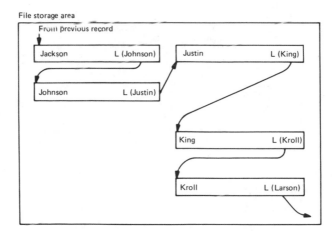

Fig. 14-7   A chain of employee records.

Following a Chain.   Following a chain is a simple matter: The record indicated by the next pointer is retrieved. The indicated record may or may not be available in main storage. Then the record is inspected to determine if the search is complete. If not, the old next pointer is replaced by the current next pointer, and the process is repeated.

It is worth noting that the steps of the process cannot be done in parallel. That is, chain following is a serial process frequently alternating I/O activity and computation at each step.

The Owner of a Chain

Adding a New Record to a Chain.   One of the principal advantages of a chain is that new records can be added at any point without affecting the location of other members of the chain. To insert a personnel record for a new employee, Jones, the following steps are performed (see Fig. 14-8):

1. Beginning with the owner, follow the chain until a record whose key exceeds Jones is found. In this case, it is Justin. Notice that Johnson precedes Justin.
2. Place L(Justin) in Jones' record and store Jones's record.
3. Replace the pointer in Johnson's record with L(Jones).

Notice that the actions required the availability of the predecessor of Justin's record. Because the predecessor of a record in a simple chain is not easily found, the program following the chain should retain the location of any record in the chain until the succeeding record has been inspected.

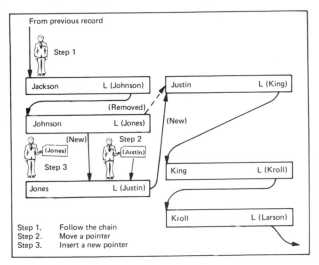

Fig. 14-8   Inserting Jones in the chain.

Though the members of a chain are frequently in order of increasing value of some key, they need not be in that order. Some alternatives for the ordering of records on a chain are as follows:

Sorted   Records on a chain can be in increasing or decreasing order of a key value within each record.

Chronological A new record can be added as the last member on a chain or as the first member on a chain.

Unordered A new record can be added just before or just after some other record identified by a user's program.

The rule used in establishing order on a chain is a part of the definition of that chain. That is, the rule is established at the time the chain is being defined.

The Owner of a Chain. It is easy to retrieve the member of a chain in succession; one simply follows the pointers. But where is the first member? The answer used in the linked-list organization is to identify some record in the file as the owner of the chain. The owner not only contains the first pointer, but it frequently includes other information that applies to the members of the chain. The owner should be a record that is easily located either because it is a member of another chain, because it is indexed, or because its key is related to its location. The latter technique you will recognize immediately as the basis of the direct organization. A record whose location can be calculated from its key is called a calc record.

Deleting a Record. Deleting a record for an employee, King, who has left the company, is even simpler than inserting a new record. One must simply move the existing pointer from King's record to King's predecessor. There is one very serious problem: If we found King's record directly without following the chain, how can we determine King's predecessor? One solution is to carry a prior pointer in each record. Figure 14-9 indicates how a prior pointer can be used during record deletions.

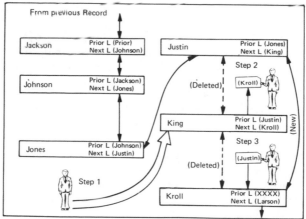

Step 1. Find King's record
Step 2. Move King's next pointer to King's predecessor
Step 3. Move King's prior pointer to King's successor

Fig. 14-9 Deleting a record from a chain.

There are two other alternatives that can be used to delete a record without knowing the record's predecessor. The first alternative is simply to mark the record as logically deleted, leaving it physically in the file. Marking for logical deletion could involve setting of a single bit in a field attached to the record reserved for I/O system use. Marking for deletion has two apparent disadvantages: (1) Overall file processing time is increased if chains include records that are essentially dead. (2) The space occupied by marked records is not available for reuse.

On the positive side, marking for deletion is a simple operation, and, further, retaining deleted records in the file may have some advantages in record recovery.

An example of the second alternative method for deleting a record without knowing its predecessor is as follows: One could delete King by simply moving its successor, Kroll, into the storage location currently occupied by King. This alternative is so simple and effective that it might properly be termed elegant. However, it must be used with caution, if at all, because other relationships already established may require that the location of Kroll remain fixed.

A special situation arises when a user's program requests deletion of a record that is the owner of a chain. Should all of the records of the chain be deleted? In IDS (Integrated Data Store), when a user requests deletion of an owner, all members of the chain are deleted. Further, if any of those members are owners of other chains, those chains are deleted as well. That action is necessary to force a file to conform to a fundamental IDS rule that each chain has exactly one owner. Automatic deletion of members has the danger that the users might inadvertently delete more records than they intend. That danger could be overcome, at least in part, by requiring that the users have authority to delete all of the types of records that are deleted and by requiring the users to indicate that they expect more than one record to be deleted.

Multilists

Returning to our employee records example, there is a frequent requirement to relate the employee records of a single department with one another. Some of the uses of this relationship are

- to provide efficient generation of periodic reports for each department
- to allow statistics for any department to be generated quickly when necessary
- to avoid unnecessary duplication of information common to members of the department

Some examples of this last point will be presented in just a moment, but first let us see what the file looks like with department chains (see Fig. 14-10).

It was stated above that establishing department chains would assist in generating periodic reports by department. Now that those chains exist, we can see that still another chain is required. We need a chain relating all of the department owners as in Fig. 14-11. This last chain will allow us to methodically step from one department to the next producing reports for each department.

With very little effort, we have found a need for a rather intricate multilist. Notice how any record in the file can be both owner and member:

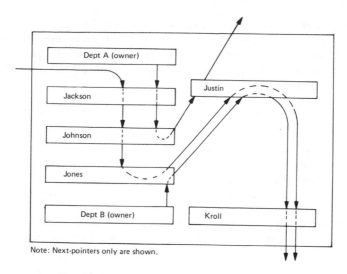

Fig. 14-10   Multilists in employee records.

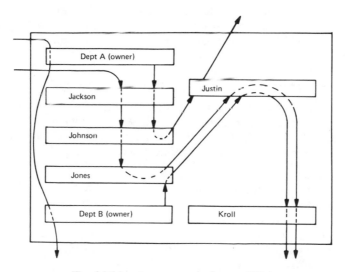

Fig. 14-11   A more complex multilist.

- One record is owner of two chains.
- Certain records are owners of one chain and members of another.
- Certain records are members of two different chains.

Owner Pointers.   Another requirement placed on our hypothetical file is that, in case of accident to any employee, an inquiry to the file will produce the name of the employee's manager. We shall assume that the department-chain owner contains the department manager's name or a pointer to the department manager's employee record. To find the name of Jones's department manager, one can either follow the department chain forward until the owner is encountered (this method assumes a ring structure) or arrange for each employee record to include an owner pointer designating the department owner directly. Owner pointers are particularly useful when the members of a chain are either calc records or are members of other chains.

Rings.   Connecting the end of a chain back to the owner to form a ring has several possible values:

1. It allows one to find the predecessor to any record when prior pointers do not exist. To accomplish this, one follows the chain until the entire ring has been traversed.
2. It allows one to find the owner for any chain when owner pointers do not exist.
3. It provides a basis for systematic searching of a multilist. Systematic searching is part of the data structures topic discussed next.

DATA STRUCTURES AND THEIR PROCESSING

In the preceding pages, we developed an example containing a network of chains where records played dual roles of owner and member. In this section, we shall explore classifications of data structures and systematic ways of tracing all paths through them.

Sequential Structures

A sequential structure of records is a relationship that can be represented by a single chain. As was discussed earlier, the chain might include next pointers only or both next and prior pointers. Further, the chain may be circular; that is, it may be a ring. Some examples of sequential structures are:

    a college class
        owner—an instructor record
        members—student records
        order—alphabetic by student name
    a COBOL source program
        owner—a program identification record
        members—COBOL records
        order—chronology established by programmer
    parts in inventory
        owner—an inventory summary record
        members—parts records
        order—alphabetic by part identification code

Notice that the records in these examples could have had more complex relationships described. A student may belong to several organizations; branching statements in a program refer to other statements; parts records are related to engineering drawings. If such relationships are indicated formally as relationships between records, the structure does not qualify as a sequential structure. A file might contain many sequential structures that are independent of each other. Figure 14-12, illustrating a sequential structure, is presented for comparison with the illustrations of trees and networks that follow.

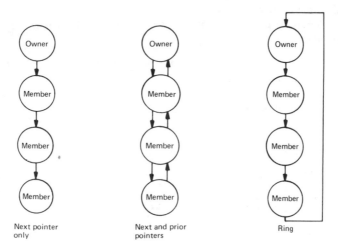

Fig. 14-12   Sequential structures.

Tree Structure

A tree structure is hierarchical. It is characterized by the fact that every record of the tree is a member of only one chain and may also be the owner of one other chain. The single exception is that the owner of the tree is not a member of any chain. A deceptive aspect of a hierarchical structure is that the pointers of the chains do not coincide with the lines traditionally used to indicate dependency in the hierarchy. Figure 14-13 illustrates this point by demonstrating how a hierarchical organization chart of a business enterprise is represented by a tree of chains. The three people reporting to manager B do not constitute three separate chains owned by B, but rather, they are three members of a single chain owned by B. Some tree-structure relationships are:

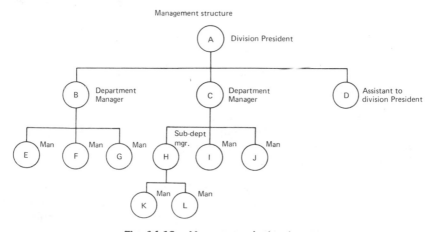

Fig. 14-13   Management structure.

- a management reporting structure
- the subassemblies and parts, including parts of subassemblies, that make up an assembled product
- subsections of a book including sections, chapters, pages, paragraphs, lines, and words

Systematic Coverage of a Tree Using Rings. There are probably many ways that one might systematically retrieve all of the records of a tree. Two methods are described here using the chains in Fig. 14-14 to illustrate. The first exploits the pointer connecting the last member of a ring to the owner.

Tree Structure

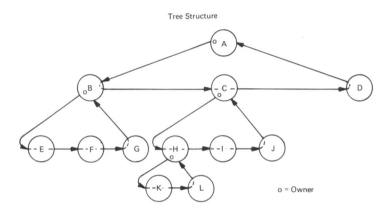

o = Owner

Fig. 14-14 A management tree.

Step 1   Retrieve the owner of the tree. The owner can be found because it is a calc record, because its location is in a table or index, or because its location is furnished by the user's program.

Step 2   Retrieve members of the tree-owner's chain until a member that is also an owner is encountered.

Step 3   Switch attention to the new chain, following it until another owner is encountered. Then switch chains again.

Step 4   Continue following chains, switching whenever an owner is encountered. The process is complete when the owner of the tree is encountered.

Notice that the chain-switching activity is simple because any record is involved in two chains at most.

Using the steps described, one would retrieve records from the tree in Fig. 14-14 in the following order: A, B, E, F, G, B, C, H, K, L, H, I, J, C, D, A. Notice that this kind of coverage results in retrieving every owner twice and always chooses to begin with the owner.

Systematic Coverage of a Tree Using Push-Down Stack. An alternative to the preceding coverage method uses a push-down stack. Such a stack is a programmed mechanism for queuing objects such that they can be dequeued in a last in, first out (LIFO) order. The mechanism got its name from the familiar spring-loaded stack of trays at the cafeteria; the stack that disappears into the counter so that the only tray that can be removed is the one added to the stack most recently.

The push-down stack is maintained as a table of variable size in main storage. The programs that process the stack respond to two service requests: (1) PUSH, which adds a new item to the stack effectively depressing all items currently in the stack, and (2) POP, which transfers the top item from the stack to the requesting program. The push-down stack and the two operations PUSH and POP are mentioned frequently in list-processing literature.

One algorithm that will accomplish systematic retrieval of a tree structure using a push-down stack is as follows:

1. PUSH a special item that, when it is POP'ed, will indicate that the entire process is complete.
2. Retrieve the owner of the tree and begin following the first chain.
3. Whenever an owner is encountered, PUSH the next pointer of the chain being followed, and begin following the new chain. The PUSH is omitted if the old chain is exhausted.
4. Whenever the end of a chain is encountered, POP a pointer and begin following that chain.

The combination of the stack and the processing steps may be a little mystifying. Figure 14-15 is a step-by-step example using the chains in Fig. 14-14 with ring pointers deleted. The process yields records in the same order as the

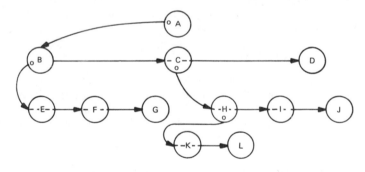

1	PUSH * as a special end indicator	*
2	Retrieve record A	*
3	Follow chain, retrieve 3	*
4	Because B is an owner, PUSH the pointer to C	C*
5	Retrieve E, F, G in order	C*
6	Because G is the end of a chain, POP	*
7	Retrieve C	*
8	Because C is an owner, PUSH the pointer to D	D*
9	Retrieve H	D*
10	Because H is an owner, PUSH pointer to I	ID*
11	Retrieve K and L	ID*
12	Because L is the end of a chain, POP	D*
13	Retrieve I and J	D*
14	Because J is the end of a chain, POP	D*
15	Retrieve D	*
I6	Because D is the end of a chain, POP	(empty)

Fig. 14-15   Using a push-down stack.

ring process described earlier except that owners are not retrieved twice. Variations in the algorithm would yield records in a different order. An exercise at the end of this chapter concerns a different algorithm.

Network Structure

A network is the most general structure of records. In a network, a record may have any number of owners, and it may own any number of chains. Every structure can be considered a network, though certain special cases of networks are considered trees or sequential structures. Hereafter, the term *network* will be used to include only those structures that are neither of the two simpler special cases.

It is surprisingly easy to establish relationships that constitute a network. The employee record file described as an example earlier in this chapter was a network; every employee record had two owners. One could expand any tree structure, such as the examples given earlier, to make it a network by adding another chain that contains some or all of the existing member records. Such a chain might establish an ordering by age, cost, date of hire, weight, or by any other attribute. A new chain might include precisely the same records as one of the existing chains but with a different ordering rule.

Systematic Retrieval of a Network.   There is no known general retrieval method for networks that does not either retrieve each record as many times as the number of chains that include it, or incur a heavy burden in avoiding multiple retrieval of records. Possibly, the best method for retrieving all of the records in a network would be to describe a collection of chain types that together constitute a tree covering the entire network. If no one tree covers the network, possibly two or more trees might be used.

Rules for Chain Structures

Listed below is a consistent set of rules concerning chain structures. The rules are identically those of IDS except that terminology has been changed slightly to conform to DBTG usage. These rules could be used as a starting point for a chained-list design. One might not use them identically, but one should probably deviate from them carefully.

1. A chain type is named with a symbolic name. There will be as many chains of the chain type as there are owner records for that chain type.
2. Each chain has only one owner record. The record type of the owner record is the same for all chains of the same type.
3. A chain is created whenever its owner record is stored. The chain is destroyed when the owner record is deleted.
4. A chain may contain more than one type of member record. Any number of member records may be in a chain.
5. Member records cannot be stored unless an owner record exists which qualifies as the particular owner according to the specified owner-selection rule for that chain.[1]

---

[1] Owner selection rules are discussed later.

6. Whenever an owner record is deleted, all of its member records are automatically deleted (and their member records too).
7. All records in a chain are associated in a ring, with the last detail linked back to the owner.
8. The owner record of the chain contains a pointer to the first member in the chain.
9. A record (owner or member) may be defined to be in as many chains as are required. It may be defined as owner in one chain and member in another.
10. A record cannot be defined as a member of a chain of which it is the owner, directly or indirectly.
11. As records are stored in the system, they are automatically linked into their defined chains.
12. When a record is deleted, the chains in which it is a member record are automatically modified to relink around the deleted record, which will eventually be physically deleted.

AN EXAMPLE: IDS

The Integrated Data Store (IDS) is a combination of conventions and programs that establish a particular list organization. The description that follows presents briefly those features that are the essence of the IDS design.

Pages, Lines, and Pointers

All storage space for a file is considered to consist of pages of uniform size. A page can contain up to 63 records of differing lengths. Each record on a page is given a line number between 1 and 63. Figure 14-16 illustrates an IDS page. The page header record contains information such as

    page number
    amount of space available for adding records
    line numbers available for use in adding records

Page header Record	Personnel Record; Line 1	Parts Record; Line 2
Vendor Record; Line 3	(Record Marked for deletion, was Line 4)	
Personnel Record; Line 5	Parts Record; Line 4	Parts Record; Line 6
(Prod. Record Cont.)		
	Available Space	

Fig. 14-16   An IDS page.

Notice that line numbers are not necessarily in sequence due to deletion and addition of records. A pointer to any record consists of the page and line number of that record. To retrieve a record, an entire page is moved to main storage, where it is searched for the line number wanted.

The page and line number for any record constitute a reference code for that record. Once assigned, a reference code is never changed regardless of change of location of a file or even change of the type of storage device. It is a relative address that is independent of physical parameters of the storage device used. I/O system programs map the reference code into the actual address of the page.

The user who creates an IDS file specifies page size. A page should be related to cylinder size of the device to be used so that a cylinder can contain one or more complete pages. Because complete pages will be moved to and from main storage, splitting a page across a cylinder boundary would increase processing time significantly.

Records and Chains

A file may contain many types of records. All the records of any one type are uniform length and have identical formats. Figure 14-17 illustrates that a record

Identification   Data fields   Pointers

Fig. 14-17   An IDS page.

has three parts: (1) an identification part containing line number, record-type code, and a record-length field, (2) data fields containing data available for processing by users' programs, and (3) pointers connecting the record with other records in chains.

Stored with the file is a description for each type of record and each type of chain. When a record is added to the file, this descriptive information is used to determine where the record should be stored and what chains are affected. A calc record is stored on a page whose number is derived by randomizing the key. Randomizing processes are described in the preceding chapter. A record that is a member of a chain identified as a prime chain is stored on or near the page that contains the owner of that chain.

Processing

While a file is being processed, an area of main storage is used to contain pages from the file. Figure 14-18 shows how records are retrieved for a user's program. In response to a STORE, RETRIEVE, MODIFY, or DELETE request, the I/O system programs determine whether the required page is in a buffer. If not, the required page is retrieved replacing a page that is already in a buffer. The buffer chosen for the new page is that buffer whose current page has had a longer period of inactivity than all other buffered pages. If the chosen buffer contains a page that has been modified while in its buffer, that modified page is stored in its proper position on the I/O device before the new page is retrieved.

Referring again to Fig. 14-18, the data fields of the record to be processed by the user's program are moved to working storage location. This action not only avoids confusing the user with pointers and control information, but it also allows protection of the page and its records from improper processing or unauthorized inspection.

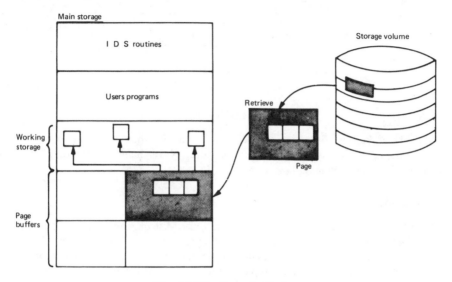

Fig. 14-18   Page buffering.

As a chain-following tool, a chain table like that shown in Fig. 14-19 is maintained for each type of chain. Receiving a RETRIEVE NEXT RECORD request might alter the table contents as shown in Fig. 14-20. Notice that the owner for any chain type is included in the table. The owner of a chain type may change frequently during processing. If that statement surprises you, you should reflect for a moment that there may be many occurrences of each type of chain in a single file. When a record is being inserted, the system must know which occurrence of each chain type is affected. The user's program may furnish information that, explicitly or implicitly, changes the owner entry in a particular chain table. In so doing, the user establishes a context for all subsequent actions that involve the chain table.

Chain type: ABC	
Owner	101
Prior	000
Current	101
Next	105

Page and line numbers

Fig. 14-19   A chain table.

Chain type: ABC	
Owner	101
Prior	101
Current	105
Next	208

Fig. 14-20   An updated chain table.

EVALUATION

The linked-list organization has been used less than the other organizations, and its design is somewhat less mature. Nevertheless, some qualitative evaluations can be made.

Redundancy

Possibly the most fundamental value of the linked-list organization is the ability of a simple file to serve a wide variety of user's program requirements. Using other organizations, several files including a great amount of redundant information might be required. For example, a purchasing information system for an enterprise might include three data files with record formats shown in Fig. 14-21. Redundant information is indicated by arrows. Using a single linked-list organization, most or all redundant information can be eliminated.

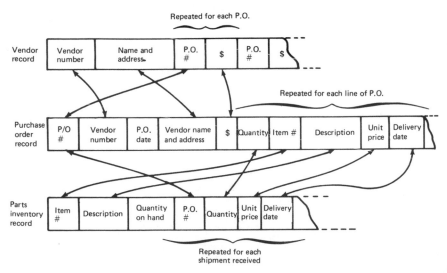

P.O. = Purchase order

Fig. 14-21   Redundancy in conventional files.

There are at least four advantages in eliminating redundant data:

1. Data maintenance effort is reduced. Since an item such as a vendor address would appear only once in a linked-list file, the cost of changing such an address is reduced.
2. Consistency is improved. When separate files are maintained, the purchase-order file might show parts delivered that are not reflected in the parts inventory record.
3. The possibility of errors in data is reduced. Correcting an error in one of several redundant files is less effective than correcting an error in a combined file.
4. Eliminating redundant information tends to save storage space. Eliminating redundant data could reduce space requirements by as much as 25 percent or more. The pointers that replace redundant information offset the savings somewhat.

Eliminating redundant data from files is so important that the DBTG Report states as its first objective: "allow data to be structured in a manner most suitable to each application . . . without requiring data redundancy."

Performance

The primary emphasis in the design of the data organizations described in the preceding chapters was how the data would be used. The primary emphasis in the linked-list organization is the data itself and how it will be maintained. As a result, one can expect the following general performance statements to apply:

1. A linked-list organization should yield excellent performance and cost for maintenance of general purpose data files.
2. A linked-list organization should yield relatively poor performance and costs for tasks that require retrieval of large quantities of information from files.

The statement by Ivan Flores quoted on the first page of this chapter is quite appropriate.

Overall Observations

The following observations are reasonably objective:

1. Eliminating data redundancy is an important or even essential consideration in many situations.
2. Chains are frequently cumbersome. Scanning an index is very much faster than following a chain.
3. Intermingling data with large quantities of control information and pointers is philosophically undesirable for the following reasons:

   • There is no apparent way to use a high-performance storage device to advantage as one can do readily with an indexed organization.
   • The intermixing implies transfer of large quantities of auxiliary data that are not useful in any specific situation.
   • Intermingling is detrimental to security, privacy, and recoverability of data.

4. To achieve reasonably good performance, pages of data must be transferred. Transferring pages tends to overload channels with data that will not be used. Further, these transfers expose the unused data to accidental damage unnecessarily.

SUMMARY

A linked-list organization utilizes networks of chains to establish relationships among records. This philosophy allows several files to be combined eliminating redundant data. Chains and indexes are alternative forms of lists; either can be derived readily from the other. Chains are the more easily modified, while indexes can be more rapidly searched.

Chains consist of sequences of pointers. A next pointer connects the chain owner to the first member which, in turn, is connected to the second member, and so forth. A special form of chain called a ring includes a pointer from the last member to the owner. A chain can have prior pointers connecting each member with its predecessor, and it can have owner pointers connecting each member with its owner. Further, any record can participate in many chains as owner or member in any combination.

Following a chain is a serial process that alternatively retrieves and inspects records. To retrieve all the records of a chain, one can begin with the owner and follow the pointers. The owner can be found either because it is a member of another chain, it is indexed, or its location may be calculated from its key.

A new record can be added to a chain by following the chain to reach the appropriate point and then adjusting a few pointers. The records on a chain might be chronological, sorted by key value, or unordered. There are several ways of deleting a record from a chain:

1. The next pointer in the record's predecessor can be modified. A prior pointer can be used to identify the predecessor.
2. The record can be marked deleted but be left in the chain.
3. The record's successor can be moved into the storage location of the record being deleted.

Deleting a record that is an owner probably implies that all members should be deleted.

Complex multilist structures can result from establishing chains for such purposes as producing reports or statistics for a class of records and removing redundant information from records to the owner of a chain of those records. Owner pointers and rings allow one to find the owner of any record. Rings are also an aid in finding the predecessor of a record as in systematically searching a data structure.

Three classes of record structures are: (1) the sequential structure where relationships are represented by a single chain, (2) the tree structure where any record is a member of one chain and may also be the owner of another chain, and (3) the network where any record may be a member of several chains and an owner of other chains. Tree structures can be searched systematically using rings or using a push-down stack. Systematic searching of a network is more difficult; there may be no simple and efficient general method. The design of a linked-list organization will include chain-structure rules similar to the following:

1. A chain type has a symbolic name.
2. A chain is created or destroyed when its owner is created or destroyed.
3. A chain may contain any number and variety of members.
4. Members cannot be stored unless the appropriate owner has been stored.
5. An owner points to the first member, and the last member points back to the owner.
6. A record may be a member of several chains and owner of several others. Storing or deleting a record implies automatic modification of chains.

IDS considers storage to consist of pages. Pointers in IDS consist of page numbers and line numbers within pages. Pages and line numbers are not affected by actual storage addresses; an IDS file can be moved from one device to another without affecting pointers. The IDS program maps page numbers to actual storage address. A file may contain many types of records. Each record contains identification, data fields, and pointers. Record descriptions and chain descriptions are used in storing new records. A record described as a calc record has its page number calculated from its key; a record in a prime chain is stored near its owner.

During processing, entire IDS pages are moved to and from main storage buffers, and individual records are moved from buffers to and from a work area by IDS programs. Chain tables reflect a current processing position for each type of chain.

The linked-list organization features the elimination of redundant information from files, thereby reducing the number of errors and saving storage space. Performance for maintenance operations is excellent, but performance for other processing of data is poor. Performance improvements might result from a carefully designed organization combining indexes with linked lists.

Exercises

1.(e) According to chain-structure rules, may a record have more than one owner? Might such a record have more than one owner pointer?
2.(e) If the records of a chain are to be retrieved frequently in a first in, first out (FIFO) order, what rule for ordering the records would be most appropriate?
3.(e) If a record deletion is accomplished by marking the deleted record, why is the space occupied not available for reuse?
4.(e) Why is the location of a calc record computed on a page number rather than an actual physical address?
5.(e) Why might the term *line* used in IDS be considered a misnomer?
6.(e) Are linked lists more suitable in cases where file alteration predominates or where reference and posting predominate?

7. (m) List a set of steps that would adjust pointers properly when a new member is inserted into a chain having next and prior pointers.

8. (m) In the discussion related to deleting a record, a problem arose when King's record was found without following the chain. Suggest at least two ways in which that might occur.

9. (m) The third step of the tree-searching algorithm using a push-down stack can be modified to say: Whenever an owner is encountered, PUSH the pointer to the first member of the new chain. List the records from the tree in Fig. 14-14 in the order of retrieval by this modified algorithm.

10. (m) Suggest why the following chain-structure rule is imposed: A record cannot be defined as a member of a chain of which it is the owner.

11. (m) Eliminating redundant data has several apparent advantages. Give at least three reasons why a user might want to keep files separate.

12. (d) Describe the major aspects of an organization combining indexing with linked lists.

15 ⫶ Labels

Label: A block at the beginning or end of a volume or a file,
which serves to identify or delimit, or both identify and delimit,
that volume or file. . . . American National Standards Institute,
Document X3.27-1969

This chapter concerns machine readable labels used to identify storage volumes and collections of data. Such a label is a block of information that can be retrieved and modified by the operating system just as can any other data. Labels are separated into classes depending on their use:

1. A volume label identifies a volume.
2. A file label identifies a file or a section of a file.
3. A user label contains information related to a file or a section of a file.

A label is a single block of data. Frequently several labels are used as a group. It is appropriate to say "the volume label group" or "the file label group." The form and content of some types of label blocks are rigidly prescribed by an operating system. Other label blocks may be designed by the users to fill their own needs.

The most apparent purpose of labels is to identify, but equally important are the purposes of describing and delimiting data and of providing the basis for an operating system to control access to data.

Label Whereabouts

Labels are recorded on the volumes to which they apply. The reasons for this are almost obvious:

1. The volume label must be on the volume to serve its function of positive identification of the volume.
2. Having labels on the volume eliminates an operational problem; the volume and its labels cannot be separated accidentally.

Label Standards

If there were a single standard description of each kind of label and if that standard were universally applied, label processing would be simplified significantly. However, there are several label standards in use. Any computer installation can enforce use of a particular standard only at the expense of being unable to process data with labels that do not comply.

In many computer installations, a mandatory label standard is applied to direct access storage. The operating system used in such an installation may reject any direct access volume that does not comply. A more tolerant rule is often applied to magnetic tape. In many installations, magnetic tape labels can comply with any of several standards; they can have labels that comply with no recognized standards; or they can have no labels at all. Magnetic tape is allowed these special freedoms in recognition of the vast libraries of reels that conform to obsolete standards and the use of magnetic tape for interchange of information between installations that employ different standards.

The vendors of any operating system are at liberty to define and support any standards they prefer. Consequently, many detailed specifications such as block size, field size, alignment of values within fields, and definitions of special codes differ from one label standard to another. But because all systems of labels have the same purposes, most differences are minor, and the overall content of most labels is the same.

ANSI Standards

The American National Standards Institute, Incorporated (ANSI) fosters the definition of industry-wide standards. ANSI standards are developed cooperatively by representatives of several computer vendors and computer users. Where ANSI standards exist, they represent a good cross section of many professional opinions.

One ANSI standard, the American National Standard Magnetic Tape Label for Information Exchange, is recognized by several operating systems. For example, Burroughs MCP recognizes both the ANSI standard and the B5500 standard for magnetic tape input, and it creates only unlabeled or ANSI Standard labeled output tapes. The B5500 standard is a Burroughs standard. OS/360 honors several tape-label standards including ANSI. Information about ANSI standards is available from American National Standards Institute, Incorporated, 1430 Broadway, New York, N.Y. 10018.

VOLUME LABELS

A volume label serves much the same purposes as a label on a carton or on the cover of a book: It identifies the volume, and it may identify the owner of the volume and restrictions in use of the volume.

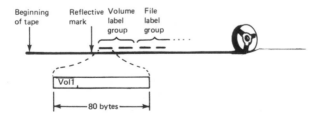

Fig. 15-1 The volume label group.

Figure 15-1 illustrates the physical position of the volume label group on magnetic tape. The conventions shown are consistent with the ANSI standard and are similar to the conventions of several other standards. An exception is the GCOS-III standard. GCOS does not use volume labels; rather, it incorporates the volume label information into the file labels. The first, and frequently the only, label in the volume group is identified by VOL1 in the first 4 bytes.

The volume labels of direct access storage volumes are placed at predetermined addresses so that they can be found routinely. On OS/360 storage volumes, for example, the first label block is always recorded on cylinder 0, head 0, block 3, as shown in Fig. 15-2.

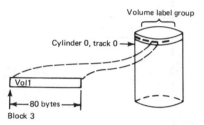

Fig. 15-2   The volume label group (OS/360).

Volume labels are usually 80 bytes long. This convention undoubtedly stems from the 80-column card.

Volume Label Contents

The first volume label (VOL1 label) includes the following information:

> *Label Identifier*   The label identifier indicates to the operating system that this data block is a label. The ANSI and other standards use the identifier VOL followed by a 1 as the first 4 bytes of the first or only volume label on a volume.
>
> *Volume Serial Number*   The volume serial number identifies the volume. Frequently, the serial number is also recorded on a visible label attached to the volume.
>
> *Owner Identification*
>
> *Space Reserved for Future Use*

Additionally, the following information is included in some VOL1 labels:

> *VTOC Address*   Included in direct access volumes only, the volume table of contents (VTOC) is a file, stored on a direct access volume, that lists and locates all of the files on the volume. The address of the VTOC must be stored in the volume label. Having found the VTOC, one can find all other files, but one must have help to find the VTOC.
>
> *Accessibility Code*   An accessibility code can be used to indicate to the operating system that access to data on this volume is restricted.

Figure 15-3 shows a typical VOL1 label format.

As the label identifier VOL1 suggests, the volume label group might contain other labels. Additional volume labels could contain any information desired by the enterprise processing the volumes. Care should be taken to avoid violation of standards in designing such labels. For example, the ANSI standard prohibits the use of identifiers VOL2, VOL3, and so forth, for additional volume labels.

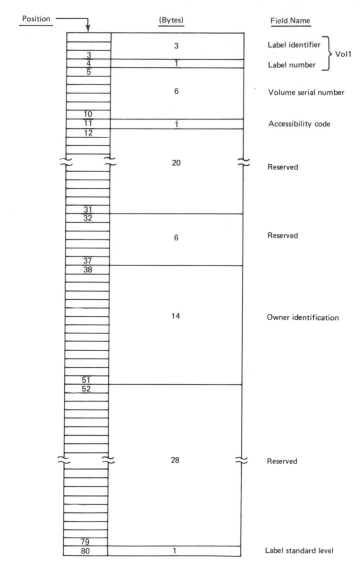

Fig. 15-3   ANSI Standard, volume label.

Volume Label Processing

There are four possible ways to process labels: inspection, creation, modification, and deletion.

Inspection.   Whenever a volume is mounted on a magnetic tape or direct access device, an I/O system program must retrieve the volume label or labels and store appropriate information in tables. For example, in OS/360 the volume serial number is placed in the unit control block (UCB). The I/O system should assume that a volume has been mounted whenever the interruption system indicates that a unit has become ready for processing or the operator indicates that he or she has complied with a volume mounting request message from the system.

Creation, Modification, and Deletion. Philosophically, the volume labels should have been written on a volume before the operating system encounters that volume, and those labels should never be deleted. Practically, there are problems in that philosophy.

First of all, someone must place volume labels on a volume. If those labels are to exist before the operating system encounters that volume, they cannot be recorded by the operating system. This implies that some computer or device not under operating system control creates volume labels. Such a practice is a nuisance, and it can result in destruction of valid data due to operator error.

Secondly, if magnetic tape is used heavily, the first few feet of it wears out and must be cut off. In the process, the volume labels are destroyed.

Thirdly, if an operating system can process labels conforming to any of several different standards, there will be occasions when volume labels conforming to one standard must be destroyed and labels conforming to another standard must be created.

The best solution seems to be for an operating system to provide a special volume labeling service. This service can work cooperatively with the operator, using special precautions such as issuing warning messages, checking for existing volume labels, and confirming expiration dates while creating new volume labels or modifying old labels. No other system service and no user's program should be able to destroy or create standard volume labels. For many I/O devices, the I/O supervisor can protect against illicit label processing by intercepting attempts to process beyond the tape marks or extent boundaries of a file.

FILE LABELS

File labels serve to identify, delimit, and describe files or parts of files. Though the purposes of file labels for magnetic tape and direct access storage volumes are the same, the fundamental differences in these two classes of storage media cause significant distinctions in file labeling conventions.

Magnetic Tape File Labels

Figure 15-4 shows file labels on a magnetic tape. Notice that the file labels for any file are divided into header and trailer groups. These are two reasons for the split:

1. Some of the file label information must be available to a user's program before file processing can begin. That information should be in header labels.

2. Some information about the file was not known at the time file recording began. An example is the number of blocks that would ultimately
be recorded. Because magnetic tape blocks cannot be updated in place
and because it would be inconvenient to reposition the tape to the
header-label area, information developed during file recording is placed
in trailer labels.

A file label on magnetic tape is typically 80 bytes long.

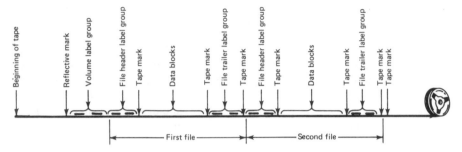

Fig. 15-4   File label groups on magnetic tape.

Magnetic Tape File Label Contents.   The magnetic tape file header label group
usually consists of two labels. In the ANSI and some other standards, file labels
1 and 2 are identified by HDR1 and HDR2, respectively, as their first 4 bytes.
HDR1 contains identifying information, such as file name, the sequential position of the file on the tape, the date when the file can be scratched, and an
accessibility code restricting use of the file. HDR2 contains descriptive information such as block length, record length, record type (fixed length, variable
length, etc.).

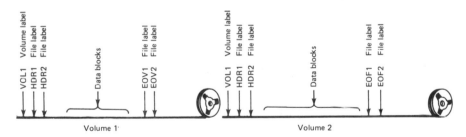

Fig. 15-5   A two-volume magnetic tape file.

The file trailer label group also consists of two labels. If the labels signify
the end of a section of a file, they are identified as EOV1 and EOV2, where
EOV stands for end of volume. If they signify the actual end of the file, the
identification codes are EOF1 and EOF2.

Interestingly, EOV1 and EOV2 are almost identical to HDR1, while
EOV2 and EOF2 are almost identical to HDR2. The only differences are in the
identifiers themselves and in the values recorded in the fields that are identically

named. For example, HDR1 contains a field named block count, but the field always contains 0. The same field in EOV1 and EOF1 shows the actual block count for the blocks of the file on that volume. The most important reason for repetition of HDR information in the trailer labels is to allow files to be processed backward on a unit capable of reading backward.

Figure 15-5 shows the labeling conventions for a two-volume file. The volume label group shown consists of the typical single VOL1 label on each volume. Figures 15-6 and 15-7 show file label contents for ANSI standard labels.

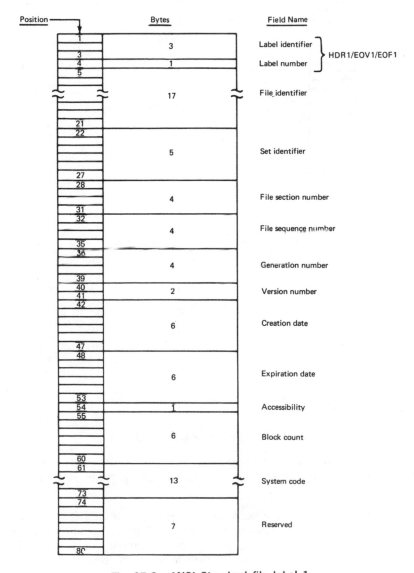

Fig. 15-6 ANSI Standard file label 1.

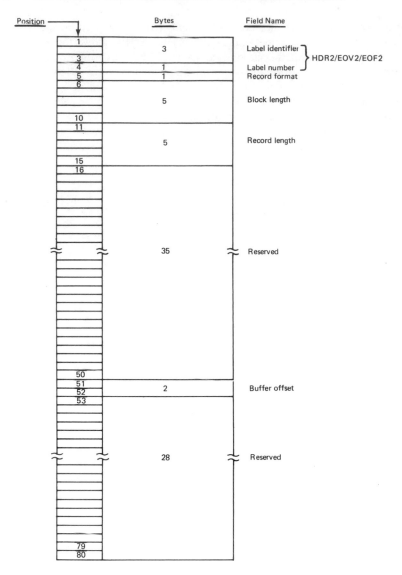

Fig. 15-7   ANSI Standard file label 2.

File Labels on Direct Access Storage Volumes. Placing file labels at the beginning and end of files on direct access volumes would not be desirable because of the following reasons:

1. An operating system needs to know where each file begins so that the data from other files can be bypassed. That is, an operating system needs a table identifying files and their locations just as a book has a table identifying chapters and their locations. Storing the file labels for all of the files on a volume together allows those labels to serve as a table of contents (VTOC) to the volume.

2. Placing a variable number of blocks from the label groups at the beginning of the first track assigned to each file might upset the symmetry of the file, thereby complicating address calculation. For example, if the data block size of a certain file is such that 10 blocks can be recorded on a track, each track of the file would have 10 blocks except the first, which might have from 8, 9, or 10 blocks.

3. There is no need to separate header and trailer information on direct access volumes.

If we are agreed that labels should be stored together, we face two related questions:

First, how much space will the labels require? The answer depends on how many files the volume will contain. One could set an arbitrary maximum, but to do so would jeopardize the standard: The maximum will be too high for some users, causing label space to be wasted, and it will be too low for others, causing file storage space to be unusable.

Second, where on the volume should the collection of labels be placed? We cannot answer this question completely unless we know how much space is required.

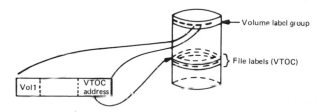

Fig. 15-8   File labels on a direct access storage volume.

One good answer to these questions is to consider the collection of label blocks to be a file and to store that file on the volume just as one would store any other file. The label file is called the *volume table of contents* (VTOC).

Finally, then, the label-storage conventions for direct access storage volumes are these:

1. The volume label is placed at a location arbitrarily fixed for all volumes.
2. File labels are stored together as a file on the volume.
3. The volume label contains the address of the label file.

Figure 15-8 illustrates these conventions. Direct access device file labels are usually larger than 80 bytes to accommodate file location information that is not required for magnetic tape.

Direct Access Storage Volume File Label Contents.   File labels for direct access storage volumes differ from magnetic tape file labels in several ways:

1. They are not typically 80 bytes long. This reflects both a more distant relationship to cards and the unnecessary rotational delay that might result from two blocks rather than one larger block. A more typical

label length for direct access volumes is the 140 bytes used by RCA and IBM.

2. There is no separation of headers and trailers. Elimination of the redundant labels simply reflects the more flexible processing ability of direct access devices.

3. The direct access volume labels contain some additional information such as:

Data Set Organization Code Data in a direct access file can be organized in any of the several ways described previously in this book.

Extent Boundaries The space allocated to a file may be in several discontinuous pieces called extents. The extent boundaries define the location of the file.

Key Description If the organization of the file is such that retrieval of the records can be based on their key values, the position of the key within each record may be part of the label information.

Some of the important fields in a file label for a direct access storage volume are:

file name
volume sequence number (for multivolume files)
creation and expiration dates and security codes
file-organization code
record and block description
extent boundaries

File Label Processing

Creation. The I/O system must create file labels whenever a new file is created or an old file is extended to a new volume. Additionally, because writing on a tape effectively deletes all data beyond the point of writing, file trailer labels must be recreated whenever a magnetic tape file is modified. The information to be recorded in the labels comes from a control statement or a table in the user's program area.

Modification. Some fields in file labels must be changed whenever the file is modified. The most important example is block count.

Deletion. File labels on direct access storage volumes are deleted whenever the file is deleted. On magnetic tape, it is customary to delete labels as a by-product of reuse of the tape. The expiration date in the file labels is used by the operating system to challenge premature deletion. In using a magnetic tape reel, it is impractical to check the expiration date for any file other than the one about to be deleted. Thus, files and their labels on a multifile volume have limited system protection against premature deletion.

USER LABELS

Some standards provide for the file label groups already discussed to be augmented by 80-byte blocks called user labels. In ANSI terms, the user labels are:

UHL1 through UHL9   These labels extend the file header label group.
UTL1 through UTL9   These labels extend the file trailer label group.

In each case, the user labels are 80 bytes long. The existence of each label and the contents of each label are completely under control of a user's program except that the label identifier and number must be coded as the first 4 bytes shown. The single file volume case shown in Fig. 15-9 includes user label groups.

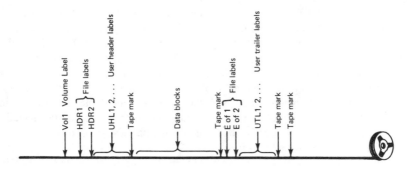

Fig. 15-9   User labels.

User Label Processing

User labels should be read and recorded by the operating system, but the information content must be furnished by the user's program. The whole reason for user labels is to provide a place for the users to store information about their files.

Creation.   After creating file labels, either header or trailer, the operating system can utilize a system exit allowing a user's program routine to furnish data for a user label. The exit can be exercised repeatedly until some form of coded response indicates that no more user labels are to be recorded. If the user's program has provided no system exit for user label creation, the file being created will not have user labels.

Inspection and Modification.   Exits similar to the user label creation exit can be used to furnish user label contents to the user's program for reference and modification.

Deletion.   User labels should be deleted whenever file labels are deleted.

NONSTANDARD LABELS

The enterprise using an operating system may find it necessary to process volumes conforming to standards not honored by the operating system. To satisfy this need, an operating system can provide a carefully described way to add nonstandard-label processing routines. Any such routines become part of the operating system for the computer installation.

SUMMARY

Machine readable labels are used to identify, describe, and delimit collections of data. Frequently, several complementary labels are used as a label group. Labels are recorded on the volumes to which they apply. There are many magnetic tape label standards in the data processing industry. The American National Standards Institute, Incorporated has published a magnetic tape label standard used by several operating systems.

The volume label group usually consists of a single 80-byte label identified as VOL1. On magnetic tape, VOL1 is the first data block. On a direct access storage volume, it is placed at fixed location such as cylinder 0, track 0, block 3. VOL1 contains information such as the VOL1 identifier, the volume serial number, and owner identification. On direct access storage volumes, VOL1 also includes the address of the volume table of contents (VTOC). Volume labels should be inspected whenever a volume is made available for processing. Philosophically, standard volume labels should never be created or destroyed by an operating system. Practically, both creation and destruction are necessary, and they must be controlled carefully.

File labels identify, delimit, and describe files or parts of files. File labels are created whenever a new file is created or an old file is extended, and they are deleted when the file is deleted.

On magnetic tape, file labels are split into header labels and trailer labels. Header labels are identified as HDR1 and HDR2, and trailers labels are identified as either EOV1 and EOV2 or EOF1 and EOF2, depending on whether they delimit a segment of a file or the complete file. The header labels and trailer labels have fields that are nominally the same. The values in the header label fields represent conditions before file creation, and the values in the trailers contain final conditions. In general, the first label of each file label group identifies the file, and the second label describes the file.

File labels on direct access storage volumes are part of the volume table of contents (VTOC). The VTOC is a file of data not conceptually different from other files. The labels in the VTOC contain information similar to magnetic tape labels, and they can also include data organization, extent boundaries, and record-key descriptions.

User labels can be identified by UHL1, UHL2, and so forth, when they augment the file header label group, and UTL1, UTL2, etc., when they augment the trailer group. The information in user labels is furnished by the user's program. User labels can be processed using a system exit.

A computer-using enterprise may find it necessary to process volumes whose labels are not honored by an operating system. A carefully described way of adding routines to process these nonstandard labels should be provided.

Exercises

1.(e) List the customary 4-byte identifying codes for the following labels:
   a. first volume label on magnetic tape
   b. first trailer label on the last volume of a magnetic tape file
   c. second header label on a magnetic tape file
   d. third user-trailer label on a magnetic tape file

e. first volume label on a direct access storage volume

f. second trailer label on the last volume of a magnetic tape file

2.(e) What do the letters ANSI stand for?

3.(e) Give two reasons why the block count of a magnetic tape file is not placed in a file header label.

4.(e) What reasons were given in this chapter for providing a volume label creation capability in an operating system?

5.(m) Do you think the expiration date in a file label for the second file on a magnetic tape is an effective indicator for preventing premature destruction of that file? Why?

6.(m) The magnetic tape command "forward-space file" moves a tape forward so that it comes to rest beyond the first tape mark encountered. How can an I/O supervisor allow this useful command and still ensure that a user's program does not process beyond the tape mark?

7.(m) What purpose is served by the adjacent tape marks after the labels of the last or only file on a reel of magnetic tape?

8.(d) Magnetic tape devices that use reflective marks to indicate physical bounds of a tape could recognize a short preliminary section of tape for use as a VTOC and the second section of tape for storage of files. Describe how such a convention might work and compare its merits with those of the ANSI conventions.

16 Catalogs and Space Allocation

Catalog: A complete enumeration of items arranged systematically with descriptive details.
Allocate: To apportion for a specific purpose. . . . Webster's Seventh New Collegiate Dictionary

Keeping track of files and the storage space available for files is a formidable task. Not only is the number of files recorded on auxiliary storage media large, but new files may be created and old files deleted at a rate of several files per minute. To complicate the task even further, the set of volumes containing a file may change during processing.

Just keeping track of files and available space is a big job. Add to that the responsibility of responding to dozens of inquiries per minute and you have an activity that is barely manageable by clerks but that is a very natural activity for a computer.

The vehicles that an operating system uses to control and identify files and space are the catalog and the volume table of contents (VTOC).

Catalogs and VTOCs are stored on direct access storage volumes. The catalog itself and each VOTC may be thought of as a file. In some systems, they are formally treated as files because they have the following characteristics:

1. They consist of records and blocks.
2. They have file labels including file names, expiration dates, and passwords.
3. Space is allocated to them as it is to any other file.
4. They can be processed by standard utility programs that process files.

The interesting aspects of catalogs and VTOCs include not only what they contain and how those contents are organized, but also the special facilities provided for their processing.

CATALOGS

Requiring each user of a file to identify the volumes containing that file has two disadvantages: The clerical effort to keep volume identification current for all programs that use any particular file is significant. The opportunity for error in these clerical operations is substantial. The use of a system-maintained file catalog alleviates these problems. A catalog allows a user to name a file at the time it is created and to simply refer to it by that name whenever it is to be used.

Several of the principal features of catalogs are apparent:

1. The word "catalog" as used in an operating system context has the same meaning as it has in other usage. A *catalog* is an enumeration of items with descriptive details.

2. The items enumerated in a catalog are files. A catalog must be organized for storage and retrieval of information about any file. Insertion of new information and modification or deletion of old information must be accommodated.

3. The information about any file will include at least the volume identification codes of each volume that contains any part of that file.

In most general purpose systems, the user decides whether any particular file should be cataloged. A method for indicating that a file is to be cataloged was discussed in Chap. 5. Figure 16-1, illustrating a control statement request for cataloging, will refresh your memory. That control statement would cause cataloging of the file named PERS.JONES.TEMP. In that example, TEMP is the simple or unqualified file name; PERS is the first qualifier; and JONES is the second qualifier. PERS.JONES.TEMP is the fully qualified name. Several operating systems allow as many as 10 or more qualifiers. The object in qualifying a simple name is to distinguish between identical simple names, and this might be accomplished by an enterprise through use of a set of rules similar to the following:

1. The user who creates a file can give it any simple name he or she chooses subject only to the restriction that the user gives no two files identical simple names.

2. The first qualifier of any file name must identify the creator's department.

3. The second qualifier must be the file creator's name.

```
//FILE1    DD   DSNAME=PERS.JONES.TEMP, . . . ,DISP=(NEW,CATALOG) , . . .
```

Fig. 16-1 A control statement for file cataloging (OS/360).

Some systems, particularly time sharing systems, automatically catalog all files. Alternatively, systems for small computers may not offer a cataloging capability. In the situation illustrated in Fig. 16-1, the user would not necessarily know, nor does the user need to know, what volumes will contain the file. At any time, the catalog can supply the appropriate volume identification codes.

Catalog Structure

The requirements to retrieve, update, insert, and delete catalog entries for files in an unpredictable order suggest that a catalog should be indexed in some way. Further, the use of qualifiers for file names suggests the general form of indexing that is used. As you may have guessed, the file naming conventions were established with the indexing problems in mind.

Trees and Subcatalogs.   Nearly all general purpose I/O systems have multilevel catalogs of file names. Figure 16-2 illustrates how a catalog identifies the storage volumes that contain any particular file. Each subcatalog has a name of its own and contains the names of the subcatalogs related to it. A structure like that shown is called a *tree structure;* the subcatalogs fan out like branches of a tree. In some operating systems, subcatalogs are called *indexes*.

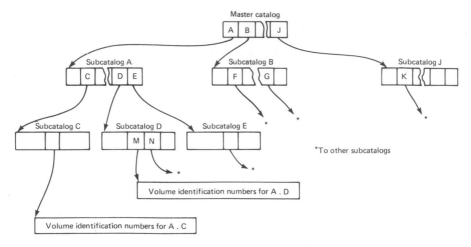

Fig. 16-2   A catalog illustrating the tree structure.

Physical Organization of the Catalog.   The catalog is stored on one or more direct access storage volumes. The highest level or levels of the catalog are stored on a permanently mounted volume called the system residence volume, or, simply, "sys res." Other levels can be stored on the system residence volume or on other volumes. Other volumes might be chosen for either or both of the following reasons: (1) to improve system performance by distributing the burden of catalog activity over several devices, and (2) to improve file portability by allowing pieces of the catalog to be removed from one computer system and used temporarily on another computer. A storage volume that contains a part of the catalog is called a *control volume*. Figure 16-3 illustrates the control volume conventions used in OS/360. In OS/360, the catalog levels are called indexes, and the highest level index on any volume is called the volume index. Notice that the portion of the catalog that resides on any volume is identified by a file label in the VTOC of that volume.

Uses of the Catalog

The three principal uses of the catalog are (1) to identify the volumes containing a file in the typical, uncomplicated situation, (2) to identify the volumes containing files used by the operating system itself, and (3) to identify the volumes containing generations of files that result from periodic processing. The first of these three has been discussed in this and in preceding chapters. The other two uses are discussed in the next two sections.

System Files.   The operating system uses several files that are usually identified and cataloged just as users' files are. Examples of such files are:

    program libraries
        • libraries of control program modules in executable form
        • libraries of compilers and utility programs

• subroutine libraries that contain modules of generalized code that compilers can include in compiled programs

• libraries of control statements available to users for requesting standard types of services

• libraries of messages to be issued to the operator or the user to communicate information or requests for operator action
statistics files

• files of accumulated operating statistics to be used for allocating costs to system users

• files of error statistics to be used for diagnosing and improving performance of components of the computer

• journals of services performed for use in reinstating files in the event of system malfunction

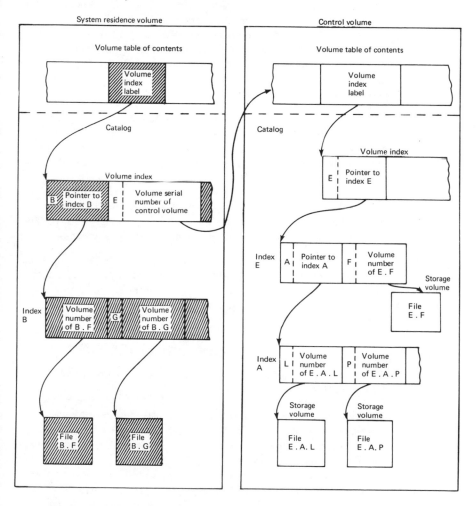

Fig. 16-3 A control volume connected to the system residence volume.

These files may be cataloged so that the components of the system can gain access to them using system mechanisms that must exist for other purposes. Additionally, cataloging these files makes processing of them with standard utility programs convenient.

Generations of Files.   Frequently, the processing of a file results in an updated copy of the file. With respect to the newest copy, the older copies are called the father, grandfather, great-grandfather, and so forth. For some files, one older generation might be preserved to be used in the event of accidental destruction of the newer copy. For other files, a larger number of generations might be required to support quarterly or annual reports.

To avoid ambiguity in identifying files, each generation of a file is given a unique name. However, requiring that the users change their control statements to include the name of the newest generation each time they process a file would be a nuisance and a source of clerical errors.

A catalog facility that provides unique file names without the requirement to change control statements is called a *generation data group facility*. If a group of files has been declared a generation data group and the group has been given the name A.B, then each individual file within the group can be identified by either of two names as follows:

1. An absolute name of the form A.B. G*xxx*, where *xxx* is the generation number. The correct absolute name is given to each new generation automatically. That is, if the most recent generation has the name A.B.G015, then the operating system will automatically name the next generation created as A.B.G016.

2. A relative name of the form A.B(*y*), where *y* is an integer. The father of the most recent generation of the group has the name A.B(−1), the grandfather has the name A.B(−2), and so forth. The most recent generation has the simple form A.B with no *y* value.

The absolute name can be used whenever a particular generation must be singled out for processing not related to the systematic development of generations. To make such usage practical, the user can be informed of the system-devised absolute name for each new generation as it is created.

```
//FILE1    DD    DSNAME=A.B, . . . DISP=(OLD). . .

//FILE2    DD    DSNAME=A.B(+1), . . . DISP=(NEW,CATALOG) , . . .
```

Fig. 16-4   Control statements using relative names in a generation data group (OS/360).

Figure 16-4 illustrates the use of relative names in the control statements that create a new generation of the group. The relative name A.B(+) refers to the generation to be created; it will be one generation newer than the existing newest generation. The whole point in relative names is that they are relative. If the relative name A.B refers to the file named A.B.G015, then after one newer generation has been created, the name A.B will refer to the file named A.B.G016 and A.B(−1) will refer to the file named A.B.G015. Because the relative names constantly refer to files relative to the most recent generation, control statements using relative names can be used repeatedly without change to process new generations.

Catalog Processing Facilities

The routines that inspect or modify the catalog, either its contents or its structure, are part of the control program. In OS/360, routines are available to perform the following actions:

1. Catalog, uncatalog, or modify the cataloged information describing a file.
2. Locate a file. This routine searches the catalog and yields the identification of the volumes containing any cataloged file.
3. Build or delete a subcatalog. This routine is used to modify the structure of the catalog.
4. Connect or disconnect a control volume. This routine is used to modify the catalog by introducing or removing the collection of subcatalogs on a control volume.

The routines are activated by execution of a particular system call. Any user's program or control program routine in OS/360 can cause catalog processing at any time.

Processing the Contents of the Catalog.   There are two reasons why it is not usually convenient for the system user to instigate processing of catalog contents by executing a system call.

The first reason is that the catalog and its contents are usually of concern to the user only by implication:

● Locating a file is an activity implied by the user when he or she specifies the name of an existing file.
● Uncataloging a file is an activity implied by a user's request to discard a file.
● Modifying the information describing a file is an activity implied by the actual change of that information.

Secondly, catalog-content processing activities are frequently auxiliary to a user's program and consequently must be specified by control statements. Control statements offer a user no ability to execute a system call directly.

Changing the Catalog Structure.   There are two fundamentally different approaches to processing structural changes to the catalog:

1. Structural changes can be accomplished by the control program as requested by control statements submitted by a system user. This approach is used in GCOS-III. Underlying this approach is the idea that parts of the catalog belong to individual users, and the parts that belong to a user should be subject to the same kinds of capabilities and controls as are available to the user for creating, modifying, and destroying the contents of the catalog.
2. Structural changes can be accomplished by a utility program executed as any other user's program is executed. This approach is used in

OS/360. Underlying this approach is the idea that the catalog is a file. Changes in its structure should be accomplished by scheduling and executing a user's program just as other file processing is accomplished.

Contents of the Catalog

Figure 16-5 illustrates the very comprehensive catalog system of GCOS-III. The first qualifier of the name of a cataloged file in GCOS-III is a user's master-catalog name; the next qualifier is the name of a subcatalog emanating from the user's master catalog, and so forth. At each step of the way, the name given must be unique within the subcatalog being used at that step. The system master catalog includes the following information:

SYSTEM USER	USER'S MASTER CATALOG AND SUBCATALOG
User identification code	Its own name
A password that the user is expected to present to prove his or her identity	Addresses of all subcatalogs emanating directly from it
Some accounting information such as amount of file space in use and the amount reserved for each user	Device type and volume identification codes for all files emanating directly from it
Identification of the user's master catalog	Passwords and permissions used to control access to subcatalogs and files. (Passwords and permissions were described in Chap. 5.)

THE VOLUME TABLE OF CONTENTS

In several operating systems, a special file called the volume table of contents (VTOC) is maintained on each direct access storage volume. The VTOC serves to identify and describe all files and pieces of files stored on the volume and to inventory all unused storage space.

The VTOC and the Catalog

The catalog identifies the storage volumes that contain any particular file. For a magnetic tape file, the catalog indicates not only what volume is involved but also the relative position of the file on the volume. For example, the file named PERS.JONES.TEMP might be identified as the third file on volume VOL23. For files stored on direct access storage volumes, the situation is more complicated because a single file may occupy discontinuous addresses on the volume. In some systems, the lowest-level subcatalog for a file stored on direct access storage volumes includes the addresses of the file extents. Such systems typically use catalogs in the following ways:

1. Files that are created and destroyed during execution of a single service request are not cataloged.

2. All other files are cataloged.
3. The catalog is invariably used to locate existing files.
4. VTOCs are not created, recognized, or used.

The alternative catalog design philosophy, used by an approximately equal number of systems, does not include extent addresses in the catalog. In these systems, the VTOCs of the direct access storage volumes serve as extensions to the catalog.

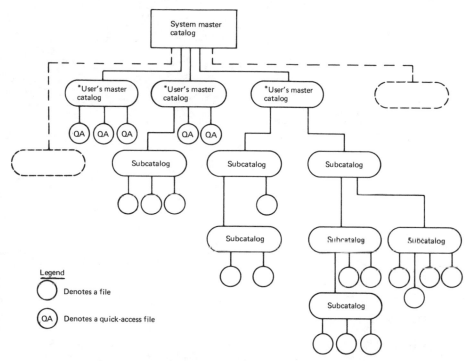

Fig. 16-5   Honeywell Series 60/Level 66 GCOS-III file system.

The following conventions, illustrated in Fig. 16-6, are typical for systems that use VTOCs:

1. The user indicates whether any particular file should be cataloged.
2. The user of a file is allowed to identify a file by name and volume, in which case the catalog is not used.
3. The user of a file is allowed to identify a file by name only, in which case the catalog is used.

The principal value of the VTOC is that its use makes each direct access volume self-describing. This can be particularly important if volumes are moved from one system to another during processing. The principal disadvantage of the use of VTOCs is the effect on system performance. When extent information is included in the catalog, the system can retrieve that information with very little effort beyond that required to retrieve volume identification.

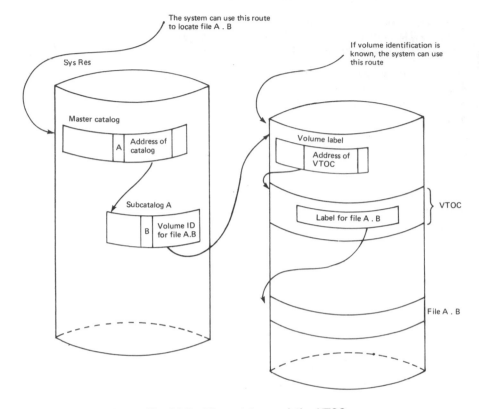

Fig. 16-6   The catalog and the VTOC.

VTOC Contents

A VTOC contains blocks of information about files and about available space. Though the kinds of blocks and their descriptions differ from one system to another, the following types of blocks might be included:

- A file label for each file recorded on the volume. File labels were described in Chap. 15.
- Extensions to file labels. Depending on data organization and on the number of discontinuous extents, a file label may require extension to an additional block.
- Blocks that describe unused space.
- A block that describes the VTOC itself.

In OS/360, the block that describes the VTOC is always the first block in the VTOC. In addition to describing the space occupied by the VTOC, it includes the address of a block that describes unused space. Unused space is described simply by the addresses of the first and last tracks of each available area. If there are too many unused areas to be described in one block, an additional block is identified by the first block.

The blocks within a VTOC could be ordered in some way to improve the time required to find a particular file label block. However, this is not usually done. Rather, new file label blocks are simply stored in the first available space. If a user can arrange to store frequently used files on a volume before other files are stored, this unordered label method will yield particularly good performance. The performance difference probably would not justify asking the user to store frequently used files first. However, the fact that the first files stored will each get continuous space may be important enough. If frequently used files are stored first, performance will be benefitted on both bases.

STORAGE SPACE ALLOCATION

Most operating systems assume responsibility for allocating storage space. To do this, they maintain inventories of available space; they fill requirements for space; and they accept space that is no longer required returning it to the available inventory.

Classifications of Space

Some systems, such as OS/360, consider all direct access storage space to be available for general purpose use. For example, VTOCs and libraries of system programs are considered to be files, and the space they occupy is accounted for using the general purpose mechanism. Several other operating systems recognize special space requirements. For example, EXEC-8 considers storage space to be divided into three classifications:

> *System Residence Space*   This space is assigned during system genera-tion, and it is not changed during processing. System programs and tables are stored in this area. Typically, system residence space is assigned from the highest-performance device in the system.
> *Scratch Space for Temporary Files*   This space is also assigned during system generation. It is available for use by users' programs during their execution. Scratch space is automatically returned to the scratch space pool when execution of the user's program ends. Files stored in scratch space are never cataloged.
> *All Other Space*   This space is available for allocation to permanent files. As pieces of it are allocated to files, the inventory of available space is reduced. When files are scratched, the space is returned to inventory.

The differences between designs illustrated by OS/360 and EXEC-8 are more than academic. Using the former design, system residence space is one or more files in every sense. The system residence files can be processed by any user's program provided the proper file name and password are used and the expiration date is not violated. Also, temporary files are distinguished from permanent files only by the fact that the latter are not scratched. The principal advantage of the general approach is that it is general. The design illustrated by EXEC-8 has the following advantages:

1. Files that should not be processed by users' programs are specially protected because they are outside the areas controlled by allocation programs.
2. The time required to make scratch space available to users' programs is reduced significantly by the use of programs designed especially for that purpose.

The Inventory of Space

If a system uses VTOCs, the inventory of space available on each volume is maintained there. Systems that do not use VTOCs must maintain the space inventory by other means. The Burroughs' MCP maintains an *available disk table* consisting of available extents in ascending order of disk addresses.

Whether available space is indicated in a VTOC or in an available disk table, special provisions must be made to ensure that the inventory is adjusted properly despite incidents due to system malfunction. For example, if a CPU malfunction were to cause abnormal termination of processing after the inventory of available space on a volume has been reduced but before the new file label has been recorded, the VTOC for that volume would be out of balance. Depending on the order of processing in a particular system, disruptive incidents could result in permanent loss of space or in destructive use of space for two purposes at the same time. Good design principles suggest that the order of operations should be such that the jeopardy is loss of space rather than loss of data. MCP ensures inventory balance by recreating the available disk table whenever the system is restarted. The reconstruction routines assume that available space consists of all of the space on the volume reduced by the amount allocated to files. Reconstruction requires a scan of the catalog. OS/360 accomplishes the same result by using a "set-must-complete" feature of the system. Whenever a sequence of events that will temporarily cause a VTOC to be out of balance is begun, a "set-must-complete" indicator is set. If an incident of any sort interrupts the system before the indicator is reset, the operator will be notified so that special procedures to reconcile the affected VTOC can be undertaken.

Control Statements	Meaning
@ASG, CR FILEX, F/5	Allocate 5 tracks to the file named FILEX.
@ASG, T FILEX, F/2/POS/5	Allocate 2 positions to FILEX. Extend space as required during processing. Do not exceed 5 positions total size.

Fig. 16-7   Control statements illustrating granularity (EXEC-8).

Granularity

The term *granule* as used by EXEC-8 can be defined as the unit of space to be allocated to a file or returned to available inventory. The user can specify granularity for a particular file to be either 1 track or 1 position (i.e., 64 tracks) of magnetic drum space. Figure 16-7 illustrates some of the alternatives available. The default case provides granularity of 1 track. As described in Chap. 5, other systems may recognize data blocks, sectors, tracks, or cylinders as units of granularity.

Allocation Routines

An operating system capable of allocating space will include routines that perform the following functions:

1. Allocate space to a file.
2. Extend the space already allocated to a file.
3. Release to the available space inventory any space that is not being used by a file.
4. Scratch a file and return the space to available inventory.

Some of the important activities of allocation routines are described in the following sections. A particular system, OS/360, is used throughout to allow consistent and specific descriptions. Most systems do not include all of the variations described, nor are all OS/360 features described.

Allocate.   This routine is used whenever a new file is about to be created on a direct access storage device. Parameters specified in the call for this routine identify the volume to be used, the amount of space required, and any special requirements. If the requirements can be met, the inventory of available space in the VTOC is adjusted appropriately, and the new file label is recorded. If the requirements cannot be met, a special return to the caller indicates that allocation was not accomplished. Some of the special requirements that can be specified are:

Maximum Extent   The space allocated should be the largest available extent on the volume provided that extent is at least as large as the requested amount.

Continuous Extent   The allocated space must consist of continuous addresses. If this requirement is not specified, the request may be satisfied by a combination of small extents.

Suballocate   The space allocated should be taken from a specifically named file rather than from available space. Suballocating related files from a single large file can ensure that the related files are physically close to each other.

Extend.   The extend routine is used to increase the space available to an already existing file. Although extend might be considered a special case of allocate, there are several significant differences:

1. The amount of space and any special requirements for extend are specified in an existing file label.
2. Extend usually does not create a file label, but rather it modifies an existing label.
3. Extend should attempt to find available space that is continuous with the space already being used by the file.
4. If available space on the volume is not adequate to fill the requirements, extend must attempt to fill the requirements using another

volume. This case can be quite complex because it involves volume mounting and file-label creation.

Release.   The release routine fills a very important need that arises in the following way:

1. The user who creates a file usually does not know precisely how large the file will be.
2. If the user specifies too little space for an initial allocation, the resulting file may become unnecessarily fragmented.
3. More important, if extend is unable to find space to augment existing space, the user's program may be unable to continue.
4. If the user specifies too much space for the file, the excess should not be wasted.

Release is used to return unused space to the available inventory. In accomplishing this, release must modify the file label properly, and it must ensure that the released space is represented properly in the available space inventory. Specifically, if the released space is continuous with an existing available space extent, the two should be merged to form a single extent. In EXEC-8, the release function is performed automatically at the time a file is being closed. Most systems require the user to specify by control statement whether release should be accomplished.

Scratch.   Scratch includes several of the activities required in release. Some of the additional activities of scratch are as follows:

1. Scratch must deal with all volumes of a file, requesting volume mounting as necessary.
2. If the expiration date in a file label has not passed, scratch may be required to take special action. One possible action might be simply to notify the operator that the file has not been scratched.
3. If a file is protected by a password, scratch may be required to clear the entire space. Alternative actions that might be employed to avoid clearing are discussed in Chap. 18.

Executing the Space Allocation Routines

The space allocation routines are initiated by system calls. However, the user's program does not usually issue the call. Rather, the following comments apply:

First of all, *allocate* is usually called by the scheduler. This convention allows known requirements for space to be filled before a user's program begins execution. It is important that allocate be executed before the user's program is started whenever possible for two reasons:

1. Space allocation can be quite time-consuming. In EXEC-8, files that are not in use may be staged to magnetic tape to make space available. In other systems, volumes may be unmounted and other volumes mounted to provide space. If these activities are performed during execution of a user's program, significant resources of the system may be tied up unnecessarily.

2. Space allocation may be unsuccessful. If the required space is not available, that fact should be discovered before the user's program begins execution. An unsuccessful start of a user's program not only wastes execution time, but may necessitate time-consuming recovery procedures before a second attempt can be made.

Allocate also may be called by OPEN in a system that allows new files to be identified during user program execution or that allows deferred mounting of volumes that will store new files.

Second, *extend* is usually called by the access methods. However, it may be called by any program.

Third, *release* is usually called by CLOSE.

Fourth, *scratch* is usually called by the scheduler in accordance with the file-disposition specification in a control statement. Action is delayed until the user's program has ended so that the file can be reopened if required and so that special file disposition can be applied in the event of abnormal termination of the user's program. The user's program might occasionally call scratch.

SUMMARY

Keeping track of files and storage space usage would be a formidable task for clerks, but is a natural activity for a computer. The catalog and a volume table of contents (VTOC) for each volume, themselves stored on direct access storage volumes, serve as vehicles.

The principal function of the catalog is to maintain continuous records of the volumes used to store individual files. The catalog is usually organized as a tree structure allowing easy addition and deletion of information. Each level of the structure represents a qualifier of a file name. The highest level of the catalog is stored on the system residence volume, but other levels may be stored on other volumes. A volume containing part of the catalog is called a control volume. Use of control volumes spreads the burden of catalog processing to several devices and allows sections of the catalog to be moved to other computer systems when necessary.

One special use of the catalog is to identify the files of programs and statistics used by the operating system itself. Another special use is for the special handling of generations of files.

Catalog processing is accomplished by routines that catalog, uncatalog, or modify cataloged information, locate a file using the catalog, build or delete a subcatalog, and connect or disconnect a control volume.

The routines that modify the contents of the catalog are used by the system itself in satisfying users' requirements. In some systems, the routines that modify catalog structure are activated by control statements. In others, catalog structure modifications are requested by a utility program.

A VTOC is used as an extension of the catalog to identify actual extents used by a file. In some systems, VTOCs are not used, and extent information is carried in the catalog. A VTOC contains file labels and label extensions, blocks and space-inventory blocks. Typically the blocks are maintained in any particular order.

In some systems, space is dedicated to special purposes during system generation. When this is done, dedicated space is permanently unavailable for allocation. In other systems, all space is allocated. Whether records of available space are maintained in VTOCs or in available disk tables, special steps must be taken to ensure that available space records approximately complement the space being used by files.

Space is allocated in units called granules. The collection of routines that apportion granules to files typically include:

- An allocate routine that fills the initial space requirement for a file. Allocate is usually called by the scheduler.
- An extend routine that augments the space required by a file. Extend is usually called by the access methods.
- A release routine that returns any space unused by a file to available inventory. Release is usually called by CLOSE.
- A scratch routine that returns all space used by a file to available inventory. Scratch is usually called by the scheduler.

Exercises

1.(e) Would inclusion of passwords and permissions be appropriate in a catalog such as that illustrated in Fig. 16-6? Explain your answer.
2.(e) Why is a tree structure a convenient structure for a catalog?
3.(e) What is the principal advantage of recording extents in a VTOC as compared to the alternative described in this chapter?
4.(e) What convenience is afforded by the relative names of files provided by a generation-data-group facility?
5.(e) What reasons are given for activating the scratch routine after the user's program has terminated rather than at the time a file is being closed?
6.(m) Why is it preferable to allocate too much space and then release part of it rather than to allocate a small amount and extend it as necessary during file creation?
7.(m) Give two reasons why a user might request that the space allocated to a particular file be continuous.
8.(m) Why does it require more time to determine the extents of a file when extents are recorded in a VTOC rather than in the catalog?
9.(d) Suggest a mechanism that will reduce or eliminate searching the VTOC for the file label when the catalog is used together with a VTOC to locate a file.

17 Program Libraries

Library: A place in which books, manuscripts, musical scores, or other literary and artistic materials are kept for use but not for sale. . . . Webster's Seventh New Collegiate Dictionary

The organizations described in Chaps. 11 to 14 are for storage of data. In a Von Neuman computer, programs are data. Therefore, one might conclude that programs require no special consideration. That conclusion is not correct. All general purpose systems provide special organizations or special tools for manipulating programs. Several systems use a special data organization called a partitioned organization that was designed specifically for program storage. One very special tool is the program loader that moves a program to main storage and makes final adjustments for execution.

It is so natural to feel that special provisions should not be required that the SHARE organization of computer users resolved in 1966 that users of OS/360 should not utilize the special provisions made for programs. Even further, they recommended revision of the system itself to eliminate those provisions. Special provisions are justified by the importance to system performance of efficiency in handling programs and by the differences between the way a user deals with the data that are a program under development and the way he uses that program to process other data. In the earlier days of computing preceding, say, 1965, computer systems did not store the users' programs for them. Rather, the compiled program was punched on cards or paper tape by the system and returned to the users to store in their desks. A major change in a program required a recompilation just as it does today, but the users themselves made minor modifications by changing the compiled programs directly. Though it seems almost unbelievable today, programmers routinely modified cards containing machine instructions in binary form by manually pressing chads gleaned from a card punch into the several improper holes in a card and then punching a few holes using a simple electromechanical punch. The pressed-in chads were held in place by friction, and particularly rough treatment could dislodge a chad yielding a faulty program. That early mode of handling programs was quite undesirable for at least two reasons:

1. The source language versions of most programs were not maintained as true reflections of the machine language programs. Indeed, there was no practical way such maintenance could be accomplished. Continued development of such programs was frequently impossible. Programs simply got out of control.
2. Program decks were frequently lost, misidentified, or accidentally damaged. Critical processing was occasionally accomplished by the wrong program or by an old version of the right program. Not infrequently the processing was not accomplished at all because a manual

change was improperly made or a card was dropped from or misplaced within a program deck.

The current practice is, of course, to leave programs within the computing system. Programs are modified under computer control by revising the source language program and recompiling. While this practice is expensive and sometimes frustrating, no one who has used the older process would seriously suggest returning to it. The current practice poses some challenges to the I/O system that are discussed in the three major parts of this chapter:

capabilities required of libraries
organization of information in a library
tools provided for manipulation of libraries

LIBRARY REQUIREMENTS

Libraries are used to store collections of data in a way that makes use of any collection convenient and efficient. A collection of data in a library can be called a member of the library. Typically, a member is more than a record and less than a file. The principal use of libraries is the storage of programs, so libraries and the tools for manipulating libraries are designed to accommodate program storage and retrieval.

As the reader is probably aware, most operating systems recognize three forms of any program:

• The source language form consists of program statements in symbolic form conforming to the syntactic rules of a language such as FORTRAN, COBOL, or PL/I.
• The object form is produced from the source language form by a language processor. This form is an intermediate stage, not executable by the computer or easily interpreted by a programmer. Its value is that it can be processed alone or in combination with other object programs to form a single executable program.
• The executable form consists of operation codes and operands that can be interpreted by the electronic circuits of a central processing unit.

Figure 17-1 illustrates these forms.

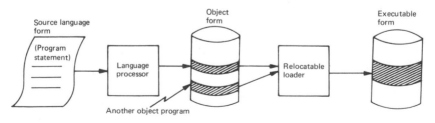

Fig. 17-1 The three forms of a program.

Use of Libraries in Program Development

Suppose a programmer wishes to modify an existing program. Some of the requirements and activities affecting libraries are these:

1. The old source program must be modified to yield a new version. The older version is usually preserved at least until the newer one has proved to be correct. Sometimes several versions must be maintained for extended periods.
2. During compilation, a complex source language statement might be replaced by a standard collection of simpler statements called an open subroutine. A library of such subroutines in source language form is modified rarely. Primary emphasis is on ability to deliver frequently used members quickly.
3. The language processor will produce a new object program. The older object program might be preserved for an extended period for use in other program development work. The new object program simply becomes a new member of a library.
4. The new version of the object program is processed to yield a new executable program. The executable program will be moved from auxiliary storage to main storage for execution by a system program called a loader. As before, the older executable form of the program might be preserved so that ongoing work using it will not be affected.
5. The entire process of creating new members of libraries, compiling, and testing requires other libraries that are mentioned here simply to indicate the variety used.

Notice that the members of libraries need not be programs. Collections of control statements for standard procedures such as compiling and testing a revised program can be stored as members of a library. Messages that the system presents to the users or to the operators to notify them of conditions requiring attention can be members of a library. I/O system programs are stored in libraries from which they are loaded by the loader. The supervisor and scheduler may be stored in one or more libraries. Language processors may constitute one or more libraries.

LIBRARY ORGANIZATION

Objectives

The uses to be served by libraries impose organization objectives as follows:

1. The organization must allow rapid location of any member.
2. The organization should assume that an entire member will be retrieved or stored during a short period of time.
3. The organization must recognize that members may vary in size.
4. The organization should allow an individual member to be treated as if it were a sequentially organized file.

The first three objectives are readily apparent. The fourth allows general purpose utility programs, compilers, sort programs, report writers, and so forth, to process a member of a library as if it were a file. While this capability is not essential, the economy and convenience that accrue make it an important objective.

The Partitioned Organization

Several operating systems utilize a modified sequential organization called a partitioned organization for libraries. Modifications include addition of an index and partitioning of the main data space into parts called members. Modifications are accomplished in such a way that most of the sequential access method conventions apply. The partitioned organization is usually restricted to direct access storage devices, but at least one system provides a partitioned organization on magnetic tape.

Figure 17-2 illustrates a partitioned organization. The index, or directory, is usually a simple list of member names and their locations in order by member name. One system uses a multilevel index, thereby providing rapid search for a large library. The simpler list form presupposes a larger number of smaller libraries. Each partition is delimited by file marks, providing a convenient means for terminating transmission of a member.

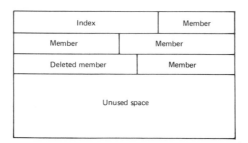

Fig. 17-2   The partitioned organization.

Reuse of Space.   The ability to reuse space occupied by deleted members is a serious design question. Figure 17-2 shows a deleted member embedded among active members. There are several ways such space could be reused, but each has its own problems:

1. A new, smaller member could be stored in the space.
    Problem: There is no convenient way to determine in advance whether the new member will fit.
2. A new member could be stored partially in the space overflowing to other unused space as necessary.
    Problem: Fragmenting a member complicates both storing and retrieving, and, most important, it increases member-retrieval time.
3. When a member is deleted, the members following could be moved up to fill the space.
    Problem: This method might result in moving large quantities of data frequently. To avoid erroneous processing, other use of the library would be severely restricted during the move.

4. A library could be reorganized to consolidate the unused space. *Problem:* It is difficult to know when reorganization is required.

The best design choice will depend on many factors. However, one factor is particularly important: The library conventions must allow excellent retrieval time for those executable programs that are frequently used parts of the control program. The best design might be the second alternative using a chaining technique to link parts of a fragmented member. Critical executable programs could be those stored first in a new library, thereby avoiding fragmentation and also ensuring the preferred placement near the index.

One serious shortcoming of the partitioned organization is that there is no simple way to expand the index space in the event of its overcrowding. One could consider moving the first member to allow the index to expand. There is probably no system that provides such a capability and, indeed, that design would have its shortcomings.

LIBRARY PROCESSING TOOLS

The tools needed for library processing include (1) library access method tools, (2) system facilities that fill special requirements of library use, and (3) general utility programs that affect entire libraries or library members. These tools are described under the headings that follow.

Library Access Methods

If the library organization conforms sufficiently to the rules of the sequential organization, the storing and retrieving of members can be accomplished a record or block at a time using sequential access method system calls. The appropriate macros from a sequential access method augmented by some indexing macros can be termed a library access method.

Indexing Macros. To locate a member of a library and prepare for its retrieval, one issues a system call as illustrated in Fig. 17-3. The macro program responding to the call can search the index serially using a channel program, or it can perform a binary search on a main storage copy of the index. The choice will depend on the characteristics of the storage device and on the form of the index. The result in either case is that tables are modified so that a sequential access method macro such as MSGET (OS/200) or READ will begin retrieval of the desired member. The table modifications are similar to those resulting from the POINT macro described in Chap. 8.

System	Operation	Operands	Meaning
OS/200	SETM	FILE1,L(MBRX) ,IN	Prepare to retrieve
OS/360	FIND	FILE1,L(MBRX) ,D	MBRX from FILE1

Note: L(MBRX) means the main-storage location containing the name MBRX

Fig. 17-3 Finding a library member.

Figure 17-4 illustrates how an index entry is made for a new member. The call ENDM or STOW causes the last data blocks and a file mark to be recorded. The two systems illustrated use slightly differing logic. OS/200 identifies the new member before the member itself is stored. OS/360 stores the member and then identifies it. In either case, the programs that make the index entry should be executed after the member is stored. This design avoids situations where the index might identify a member that was not successfully stored.

System	Operation	Operands	Meaning
OS/200	SETM	FILE1,L(MBRY),OUT	Prepare to store MBRY in FILE 1
	(instructions that store blocks of data)		
	ENDM	FILE1	Stop processing the current member
OS/360	(instructions that store blocks of data)		
	STOW	FILE1,L(MBRY)	Stop processing the current member and index it with the name MBRY
Note:	L(MBRY) means the main-storage location containing the name MBRY		

Fig. 17-4   Storing a new member in a library.

Calls similar to those shown can cause updating of an existing member, replacing of an old member by a new member, renaming of an old member, or adding an alternative name for a member.

Alias.   An alternative name for a member, aptly called an alias, can be used as suggested by the following example. A library contains two versions of the POINT macro. One, named NPOINT, is the standard macro. The other, XPOINT, performs the usual actions and also causes statistics about its use to be recorded for later analysis. The operator can select either version for use by assigning the alias POINT to that version. This technique allows each version to retain its original name, thereby avoiding errors in identifying programs during modification or replacement. It also allows all programs that use POINT to use the proper version automatically.

Member Names.   Most systems attach little significance to member names. They simply establish a few simple rules controlling the number and variety of characters. EXEC-8 offers a semiautomatic naming capability where names have meanings that are related to the steps of a program development process. That naming system is described in the next several paragraphs. The EXEC-8 terms have been changed to conform to the use established in this chapter.

An index entry includes the following information:

Member Name   A 1-to-12 character name is specified by the user.
Version   A 1-to-12 character adjunct to the member name. Version is also specified by the user.

Cycle   Whenever a source member is updated, the system increases the cycle number by 1.

Type   A member is either source, object, or executable.

Two examples will indicate how the name and its qualifiers are used.

1. The user specifies JOE/OLD(4) as input to a language processor. This name identifies cycle 4 of the OLD version of member JOE. The system infers that the type should be source because the language processor requires source language input.
2. The user specifies JOE as a program to be executed. This simple name implies the most recent cycle of member JOE. Absence of a version name implies that there is only one version of JOE. The system will infer that the executable type of program is required.

The use of version, type, and cycle as name qualifiers allows a library to include a great many variations of a single program, all with a single member name.

The mechanisms used to provide several cycles of a source program at modest cost in storage are quite interesting. A user updates a cycle by requesting insertion of new statements and deletion of old statements. The new statements are inserted in the existing member, each new statement carrying the cycle member of the cycle being created. Statements being deleted are similarly marked. Now, if a user requests cycle 4 of JOE, the system creates that cycle dynamically while the composite member is being retrieved by ignoring all insertions and deletions with cycle number greater than 4 and 5, respectively.

System Facilities

Creating a Library.   There are several actions that must be performed to convert storage space into a library. Depending on design details, such actions might include:

Initializing the Index   This can be done by storing blank index-entry blocks followed by a file mark.

Identifying the Start of Unused Space   This might be done by storing a special index entry identifying all unused space as a pseudo-member.

Preformatting the Space for Members   Some systems preformat member space by storing blocks of uniform size. This process is time-consuming, and, by implication, it restricts the block size of members to a fixed size. Preformatting is avoided in most systems.

Initializing Pointers and Counts   This is done in order to reflect the starting condition.

There are at least four alternatives for accomplishing the initializing actions:

1. The space allocation programs could accomplish these preliminary actions whenever space is being allocated to a file designated as a library. This alternative has the disadvantage that system facilities including CPU time, channel time, and main storage space are preempted at a time that may not be consistent with other priorities.

2. The OPEN macro could be expanded to include library initialization. This alternative adds complexity to an already overly complex program.
3. A library initializing macro could be included in the system. The macro would be issued by a user's program after the new library file had been opened.
4. A library initializing utility program could be furnished with the system.

The last two alternatives are the simplest, and one of them should probably be favored, though they are less convenient for the user.

Opening a Member.   A valuable feature offered in several systems is the ability for a user's program to treat a member as if it were a sequential file. This can be accomplished by any one of the following three mechanisms: (1) The file name on a control statement can indicate both file name and member name. An acceptable syntax is illustrated in Fig. 17-5. (2) When OPEN detects an input situation with a member name on the control statement, it accomplishes a normal OPEN followed by an indexing operation like the SETM shown in Fig. 17-3. (3) When CLOSE detects an output situation with a member name on the control statement, it accomplishes an indexing operation like the ENDM shown in Fig. 17-4 followed by a normal CLOSE.

```
//INPUT   DD     DSNAME=FILE1(MBRX) , DISP=(NEW,KEEP)
```

Meaning: FILE1 is the name of the file.

MBRX is the name of a member.

Fig. 17-5   A control statement syntax for a file name with member name.

Using this feature, one can design language processors and other general purpose programs to process a file without losing the ability to process a member of a library.

```
//TEST     JOB
//JOBLIB   DD     DSNAME=LIBA,  DISP=(OLD)
          EXEC   PGM=INVNTRY
```

Meaning: The library named LIBA is to be concatenated with the library containing user's executable program.

Fig. 17-6   Concatenating libraries.

Concatenation of Libraries.   A user may want to augment or override a system library temporarily. For example, a user might be developing a replacement for a phase CB17 of the INVNTRY program. If the user replaces the existing CB17 with his or her experimental member, all users of INVNTRY will be unwilling participants in the experiment. Use of an alias would not correct that problem. A library concatenation feature providing the desired flexibility can be used as follows:

1. The user can place his or her experimental CB17 in a library. We shall call the library LIBA.
2. The user can furnish a control statement identifying LIBA for concatenation with the system library. An acceptable syntax is shown in Fig. 17-6.
3. The user's intent is detected by the indexing macro such as the FIND described in Fig. 17-3. Whenever a phase of the compiler must be retrieved for execution, FIND searches the index to LIBA automatically before it searches the index to the system library.
4. Whenever LIBA contains a member with the desired name, that member will be retrieved for execution. In particular, CB17 will be retrieved from LIBA.

Note that the concatenated library applies only to the user who specified its use.

The Program Loader.   As stated earlier, a member can be retrieved using sequential access-method-like macros. However, an access method is not an acceptable tool for loading programs for execution. The reason is simple: Program loading is a very specific task where speed is essential. Few realize that even a medium-size, general purpose system may require loading an average of one or two programs every second. Assuming that programs are loaded from a rotating storage device such as a magnetic drum, allowing one or two extra rotations while loading a program would affect system performance significantly.

The program used to retrieve programs and prepare them for execution is called a loader, program loader, relocatable loader, or program fetch. Most of the details of the loader are not appropriate material for this book; they concern program relocation, symbol resolution, and program dispatching. The actual I/O part of the loader is programmed specifically to retrieve executable programs from libraries. The loader is part of the control program nucleus, and it can avail itself of such privileges as may be reserved to supervisory programs.

The principal challenge in designing an effective loader stems from the fact that a certain amount of interpretation of the executable program is required during loading to direct the loading process properly. The interpretation and reaction must occur within the time limits imposed by a continuously rotating device. The challenge is particularly great if the loader will be used on any one of several different CPU models to retrieve programs from any of several different types of storage devices.

General Utility Programs.   A system might include several utility programs that deal with libraries. The list below includes some of the utility programs typically available:

- a copy program that reorganizes a library as it makes a copy
- a library status program that reports statistics such as space remaining, number of members, member names, and activity rates (if available)
- a program that moves members from one library to another
- a program that deletes, renames, or creates aliases for members
- a program that modifies a source-program member by adding or deleting statements

The designs of most of these programs are sufficiently simple and natural that no comment is required here. However, the program that modifies source-program members is worth discussing. Typical input to that program is illustrated in Fig. 17-7. There is a long-standing design question that has never been resolved too well: If a member is updated twice, are the statements in the member renumbered between the updates? If statement numbers are revised each time the member is updated, the user must either get a revised listing of the member or renumber the statements on the obsolete listing manually. If statements are renumbered infrequently, a special technique must be invented to allow modification of statements inserted since the renumbering. Renumbering at the user's request is a reasonably good solution.

Operation	Operands	Meaning
ALTER	2,4	Delete statements 2 through 4
ALTER	6,6	Delete statement 6 and insert
(Source statement 6.3)		6.3 and 6.5
(Source statement 6.5)		
ALTER	7	Insert statement 7.5 after 7
(Source statement 7.5)		

Original statements: 1, 2, 3, 4, 5, 6, 7, 8

Resulting statements: 1, 5, 6.3, 6.5, 7, 7.5, 8

Fig. 17-7   Input to a library utility program.

SUMMARY

Program libraries are afforded special processing tools and, frequently, a special organization called a partitioned organization. Before 1965, users stored programs at their desks, and they modified the executable form manually. Current practice retains the source language, object, and executable forms within the system.

Some of the uses of libraries are:

- to store the user's source, object, and executable programs
- to store open subroutines for insertion into users' programs during compilation
- to store collections of control statements
- to store operators' messages
- to store the I/O system programs

To serve the user adequately, libraries must be organized for rapid location and retrieval of members of varying size. Some economies accrue if a member of a library can be processed as if it were a sequential file.

The partitioned organization contains an index followed by members that are separated by file marks. The requirement for excellent retrieval time makes reuse of library space difficult. The partitioned organization includes no simple way to accommodate index overcrowding.

An I/O system will include calls such as SETM and ENDM, or FIND and STOW to perform index searching or index modifications. Variations of the calls allow inserting, deleting, renaming, or providing an alias for the existing name of a member. Most systems attach little significance to member names. However, EXEC-8 recognizes an entire library structure based on version, cycle, and type of each program. Cycles, formed by updating source programs, are stored in a composite form allowing dynamic formation of any particular cycle.

Library initialization can include index initializing, member-space preformatting, and initializing of pointers and counters. Initializing could be done when space is being allocated, when the file is being opened, or it could be done at the user's request either by macro or by a utility program. The macro or utility alternatives are the simplest.

Processing a member as if it were a sequential file gives added usefulness to language processors and general utility programs. A workable mechanism for accomplishing this extends OPEN and CLOSE to perform indexing whenever a control statement specifies a particular member of a file. Another control statement specification can concatenate one library with another, thereby overriding or augmenting the index of the second library.

The program loader is designed specifically to retrieve executable programs in the shortest possible time. The challenge includes limited interpretation of the program during loading. A loader might be required to work efficiently for any of several CPU and storage device combinations.

A system will usually include utility programs for reorganizing libraries, reporting library statistics, moving members between libraries, and for modifying, deleting, or renaming members.

Exercises

1.(e) Name at least two kinds of information other than programs that might be kept in a computer library.

2.(e) Is member space preformatted in most systems?

3.(e) When a member is given an alternative name without deleting the original name, what is the alternative name called?

4.(e) In the EXEC-8 system, does updating a source member create a new version or does it create a new cycle?

5.(e) What indication can a user furnish that a member should be treated as if it were a sequential file?

6.(e) What are some other names for a program loader?

7.(e) Why might one use concatenation of libraries while testing a new phase of a widely used program?

8.(m) What fundamental problem makes it impossible to maintain a source program matching an executable program when the latter is modified manually?

9.(m) Punch the binary equivalent of $(4173AC)_{16}$ in card columns 1 and 2 of a card. Use the standard column-binary form where the binary digits begin in the 12th row of column 1, proceed down the column, and then down column 2. Modify the third character from a 7 to an 8 by punching the required new hole and manually filling old holes with chads.

10. (m) After reading this chapter, what do you consider the most important objective in the design of a library organization?

11. (m) Suggest how a system might accumulate member-usage statistics for use during reorganization of a library.

12. (d) Describe briefly an organization and a set of operating conventions that provide rapid access to frequently used programs and that recover space freed by deletions. You may want to try an unordered index and possibly a test that instigates space recovery whenever embedded, unused space becomes excessive.

18 Operating Characteristics

A glance at the topic headings of this chapter reveals that the chapter is devoted to abilities (reliability, availability, serviccability, accountability, operability, recoverability, and practical ability). Each ability is an important attribute of an I/O system. In general, they are by-products of good design rather than adjuncts attached as after-thoughts. Just as a Boy Scout is trustworthy, courteous, and kind without the addition of new parts, so are the abilities described in this chapter woven throughout the fabric of an I/O system.

There is a great deal that must be said about I/O system design. An I/O system shares many design challenges with other kinds of systems programs. These common challenges are discussed briefly in this chapter, but concerns unique to I/O systems are given emphasis just as they have been throughout the book. Chapter 19 deals with security and privacy, burning issues that concern the present and future of the entire computer industry. Chapter 20, "Flexibility," is devoted to independences, notably device, data, and organization independences.

RELIABILITY

Electromechanical equipment can be described as reliable or unreliable. A reliability specification can be stated, and a representative sample of a production run can be tested against the specification. Before the advent of operating systems, reliability was not thought to be descriptive of a computer program. A program was either correct or incorrect. If it was correct, it worked; if incorrect, it did not. As computer programs become more complex, they begin to exhibit reliability characteristics not unlike electromechanical devices.

Surprisingly, an operating system may run while its programs include dozens of errors. Over long periods of time, the existence of these errors will be evidenced in unreliable operation. For some reason, apparently unexplainable, a major system will fail in a way that may be as innocuous as a strangely truncated message displayed on the operator's console or may be as dramatic as abrupt termination of all activity. Such failures may stem from unreliability in the computer itself, from improper operator action, from improper user program activity, or from an error in an operating system program.

High reliability in an operating system results from two qualities easily stated but not easily achieved. *A reliable system must be tolerant.* Unsolicited action by an operator, improper execution of an instruction by the CPU, incorrect forms of a control statement, and an endless instruction loop in a user's program must all be anticipated in the design of a general purpose system. *A reliable system must be relatively free of programming errors.* Some parts of the system must be absolutely free from errors, and other parts must be reasonably free. If we accept the realistic view that the number of errors committed by a programmer increases with the complexity of a program, then we must conclude that simplicity is essential to reliability.

The two qualities above are somewhat at odds with each other. The first requires that a system be comprehensive and the second that it be Spartan.

All of the rules of programming that promote reliability in other system programs apply equally to I/O systems. Some reliability rules that apply only to generalized programs that accomplish input or output are as follows:

1. Where possible, programs should not depend on the relative speeds of devices and the CPU for correct operation. If such a dependence is unavoidable, the program must be afforded special privileges so that no interference will occur during its execution. Further, the program should be marked so the timing constraints are not inadvertently strained by modifications to the program.
2. Programs should not depend on the accuracy of unchecked data. For example, an absolute address recorded in the first few bytes of a magnetic tape block should not be used to modify the channel command that reads the remainder of the block. Rather, the entire block should be read into a prearranged area, and then, when the transmission has been verified, the data can be moved.
3. A program should not assume that it has exclusive use of any resource unless exclusive use has been guaranteed.
4. Any program that deals with I/O devices must be tolerant of device idiosyncracies. A reliable system must continue to operate correctly despite any combination of exceptional conditions created by I/O devices.
5. Some provision should be made for identifying storage volumes of unsatisfactory condition. Continued use of a few marginal volumes can give a system the appearance of unreliable operation. Unreliable devices have the same effect, but that problem is more easily detected by routine maintenance of equipment.

AVAILABILITY

A quality called availability is important in systems where the user, human or otherwise, interacts directly with the system. An acceptable level of availability for a particular system might be:

Hours of Service   24 h per day, 7 days per week, including holidays.
Gross Availability   System must be capable of furnishing service at least 98 percent of every 24-h period.
Hours of Unavailability   No period of continuous unavailability shall exceed 10 min.

An availability specification can become very detailed including definitions of recovery time for damaged files, separate requirements for full service and for several levels of limited service, and so on. Clearly, an availability specification will affect the computer system itself. To meet a stringent requirement, a system might include two or more CPUs, channel switching for all I/O devices, and extra I/O devices.

Some of the special I/O system capabilities that might be required in a highly available system are these:

- ability to allow I/O devices to be repaired and tested during system operation
- ability to diagnose failures and identify a failing component
- ability to operate correctly despite temporary loss of any I/O device or reasonable combination of devices
- ability to continue to run despite consistent failure of a portion of main storage or an I/O channel
- ability to continue to run responsibly despite computational errors indicating intermittent failures in the ALU
- ability to continue to run responsibly despite incorrect or inappropriate operator action
- ability to create logs and journals adequate to reconstruct critical files and the ability to undertake file reconstruction automatically when necessary

Availability and reliability are closely related, but there are several important differences. Reliability is closely related to accuracy and dependability, while availability concerns the continuity of service. In an extreme case, a system might be highly available but very unreliable. A trivial example might be a system that is functioning normally except that the floating-point ADD instruction is giving wrong results intermittently. Frequently, the availability requirements are such that it is more important that service be continuous than it is that service be comprehensive. The colloquial term, graceful degradation, is used to describe the ability of a system to restrict the type of service given rather than to fall hopelessly behind in an attempt to furnish full service when portions of the system are not operating properly. A limiting case of graceful degradation might be the continued ability of a system to respond to all requests for service with the message that the system is incapable of executing the request. Such a response from a system can be of much more value both psychologically and practically than no response at all.

SERVICEABILITY

A system is highly serviceable if reasonably well-trained technicians can diagnose and correct its problems quickly. Some items that contribute to serviceability are:

Symbolic Listings of System Programs   These carefully commented, up-to-date symbolic listings of the system programs should appear on nearly all lines describing intent of the code and warning of interdependencies.

Supporting Documents   These documents should be comprehensive and should explain table formats, who references and who modifies individual table entries, and should illustrate overall logic in flowchart form.

Collections of Test Cases   These test cases can be used to detect malfunctions and, equally important, to confirm that a modification made to eliminate one error has not introduced other errors.

General Conformance to Standards   The problems of service personnel are simplified if they can safely expect that CPU registers are assigned according to a standard pattern, that code is reenterable, that code is not timing dependent, and that instructions are used in a straightforward manner free of programming tricks.

Activity Logs   Logs and journals of activities such as system calls, overflows of counters, recovery from intermittent failures, operator actions, I/O activities, and so on, can be useful in discovering clues or patterns contributing to malfunctions.

ACCOUNTABILITY

A major difficulty in any multiprogramming, multiprocessing, or time sharing system is accounting for the use of system resources as a basis for billing users. The problem is particularly vexing because it is at once vitally important, significantly taxing of system resources, and not directly productive. A good accounting capability must be consistent and auditable, and it must allow billing that is closely related to costs. The next paragraphs explore these requirements, and then some alternative solutions are described.

Clearly, the users would expect that if they requested identical services on two separate occasions, the system would assess them consistently for the two services. The implication of this requirement is that users' assessment should be unaffected by concurrent unrelated activities in the system. This goal is difficult to achieve for several reasons:

1. The I/O devices used on any occasion depend on the sequence of activities preceding a particular service. Not only might different devices be used on separate occasions, but devices of different types might be used, and the selection of channels and control units may yield different interactions.

2. When storage devices, control units, or channels are shared with other service requests, the activities of those other requests can affect performance. For example, simple competition for use of a channel could affect magnetic tape writing time by 50 percent or more.

3. Depending on relative priorities, a service request might have resources allocated to it for 5 min or 5 h.

4. Intermittent failures can affect performance. For example, intermittent failures in reading a file either because of a faulty recording medium or marginal condition of an I/O unit could affect reading time by a factor of 2 or 3.

Computer systems are quite expensive, and it is realistic to expect that users will occasionally challenge a billing. To support a contested billing, the operating system should provide a detailed analysis for each service request indicating date, time of day, and resources used. If the accounting system is consistent, it should be possible to rerun individual service requests to demonstrate that the accounting was not in error. The possibility of demonstrating consistency should avoid its necessity, particularly if the user is billed for costs incurred in proving that an existing bill is correct.

The relative prices charged for system resources are important in determining how a system will be used. For example, the prices charged for magnetic tape units and magnetic drum units might determine whether a particular major use of the system is accomplished using a sequential approach with magnetic tape or a random approach using drums. If the billing price for the use of magnetic drums is accidentally set too low, heavy demand for drums might result causing excessive competition for use of drums. The addition of more drums would alleviate the competition. However, with drums priced too low, total billings may not cover system costs properly.

There is no simple solution to all of these concerns. The following brief description of one very comprehensive accounting capability may serve as a source of ideas.

A *significant events journal* is created as a by-product of system operation. This journal indicates the time of day for such events as

- receipt of a user's request
- devices allocated indicating number
- main storage space allocated
- amount of ALU time utilized
- amount of time spent waiting for an I/O activity to complete
- amount of direct access storage space used

All significant events for all service requests are intermixed in a single journal as they occur. At some later time, the journal is processed to sort out the events related to each request. Then, using the accumulated statistics and some approximation formulas, a normalized time for each class of system resource is calculated. The approximations furnish a realistic estimate of the resource usage that would have occurred for each service request if that request had been executed without competition or interference by other requests. By using those estimates and a set of billing rates carefully devised to encourage balanced use of all resources, billing amounts can be calculated.

The significant-events-journal approach has a disadvantage that is important for certain uses: The customer billing is not available immediately after the request has been run. The principal advantages of the approach are these:

1. Creating the journal is a relatively minor burden. Accumulating comprehensive billing data as events occur is a much larger burden that reduces the effective peak-load capacity of the system.

2. Processing the journal at non-peak-load times allows significant analysis and elaborate approximations using resources that would otherwise be idle.

3. The journal serves as a chronology that may be useful in analyzing system activities or customer requirements with an eye toward improving the service offered.

OPERABILITY

A computing system in operation is a bewildering phenomenon. If one visualizes a column of numbers with a million entries being summed in a second, one is impressed. But a system that is making thousands of decisions a second affecting hundreds of individual matters is really beyond human comprehension. Yet, operators must deal with operating systems. The ease or difficulty an operator experiences in dealing effectively with a system is a measure of the operability of the system.

In about 1960, Dr. Fred Brooks described an important philosophy of the relationship between an operator and an operating system. That philosophy holds that an operator should serve as the hands of a computer, furnishing only those services that require dexterity and mobility not easily incorporated in a computer. The trend in the industry is in that direction. For the present, operators are required to do more; they serve as hands and also as the decision makers for all decisions not programmed into the system.

System operators as a group are frequently disparaged for the quality of the decisions they make. Operators as a group are surprisingly capable, and the fault, if one exists, should be laid at the feet of the operating-system designer. It is inefficient, unjust, and hazardous to require operators to make decisions for which they have inadequate information.

In a comprehensive operating system, there should be no reason for the user to communicate with the operator directly. Rather, the user should make his requirements known to the system, and the system should communicate with the operator as required. Less comprehensive systems may require that the user's program instruct the operator using a system call or, even more basic, that the user himself instruct the operator through written or spoken instructions. It is philosophically undesirable for the user to communicate with the operator since such communication can be ambiguous and the operator responses to such instructions may be imperfectly checked resulting in processing errors which are very difficult to trace.

The principal means of communication with an operator is through messages and replies to messages using the console display. Some factors affecting the quality of this communication are as follows:

1. Instructions must be complete and unambiguous. If the system requires that a labeled scratch tape be mounted, the message MOUNT SCRATCH TAPE is ambiguous.
2. Messages should be brief and pertinent. Messages that are unnecessarily wordy or lack any real purpose tend to obscure important information. A plethora of messages causes confusion and may even restrict system performance while critical instructions wait their turn for use of the console printer.
3. If the operator is expected to act as overall supervisor, as is often the case, status information must be given. For example, the operator needs to know how much work is backlogged, whether high-priority work is being accomplished satisfactorily, whether intermittent failures are occurring excessively, and so forth.

An important observation made by Dr. Nathaniel Rochester and borne out by experience is that operability is best achieved by trial and error. It is very difficult to anticipate and evaluate all of the factors that will affect the operator/system relationship. Some of the factors are psychological; others concern level of intelligence and training; and still others, such as visibility of messages and economy of physical motion of the operator, are the mechanics of operating a system. Dr. Rochester's sound advice is this: One should expect to revise and improve operability based on actual experience.

Dr. Robert Fano has made an interesting observation concerning the psychology of operability. He observed that people react to computers in much the same way as they react to other people. If an operating system directs an operator in ways the latter considers curt, unreasonable, or ambiguous, the operator may lose his or her temper. Operators have been observed kicking machines, hammering on keyboards, and muttering disparaging comments. An operator motivated by resentment or a desire to retaliate can hardly be expected to be cooperative.

A basic technique that accommodates most of the special problems related to operator messages is this: All operator messages should be stored in one centralized location within the system libraries. Some of the advantages that accrue are these:

1. It is easier to control or improve the wording of messages that are centralized.
2. Centralization makes it easier to substitute abbreviated message forms for experienced operators, a technique that improves operator and system efficiency.
3. Centralization makes it easier for the system to furnish clarification of messages in a systematic way if an operator requires such clarification.
4. Centralized messages tend to serve as their own documentation.
5. Centralized messages can readily be replaced with non-English equivalents to accommodate operators in foreign countries.

A good method that can be used to cause printing of a centralized message is for the program that requires the message to furnish a message code identifying the message and any variable parameters for handling by a centralized routine.

RECOVERABILITY

When an unusual event occurs during running of a rudimentary operating system, the system might stop abruptly, loop continuously, or cause erratic activity of I/O devices. When any of these conditions occur, the operator's experience and intuition are used to resolve the problem. Usually, the last step in resolving the problem is to reexecute the user's request that was in process. As systems have become more complex, the cost of that simple solution has grown. In a complex system, several users' requests might require reexecution and, further, many users who are communicating directly with the system through terminals would find service temporarily suspended and rework wasteful of their time. For these and other reasons, systems that feature automatic recovery with a minimum of lost time and a minimum of rework are being developed.

Many control programs in existence today consist almost entirely of subprograms that do not modify themselves during execution. Using an industry colloquialism, these control programs are reentrant. Creating a reentrant program may require extra programming effort. The primary value is that reentrant programs can perform two or more services concurrently. Somewhat surprisingly, reentrability has significant recoverability value as well. The reason is this: In the event of actual or suspected malfunction of a section of main storage or actual or suspected damage to a program, a reentrant program can simply be replaced by a new copy of that program. Programs that are not reentrant usually cannot be refreshed in this manner.

Another principle important to recoverability is that control programs should be designed for nonstop operation. Each subprogram of a control program should make a reasonable effort to complete its intended service. Failing in that effort, a subprogram should furnish information indicating what happened and relinquish control to some other appropriate program. A subprogram should not halt, loop, or otherwise force an abnormal termination of system control. Nonstop design is quite difficult, but it is important. Recovery is very difficult following disorderly termination of system control.

Reenterability and nonstop design are important features of all parts of a highly recoverable control program. Two design features are important to I/O system recoverability:

First, channel programs must be restartable. One acceptable design requires the program requesting channel program execution to furnish a code indicating which of several standard restart procedures can be used with that program. Some possible restart procedures are:

1. Simply restart the channel program from the first command.
2. Issue a backspace command to the device and then restart the original channel program from the first command.
3. Restart the channel program from beginning with some specific command other than the first command.

Second, device error routines should be comprehensive. The state of the art in I/O devices is such that solid failures will occur infrequently, but intermittent, correctable errors are common. Several important principles that should be observed in designing device error routines are:

1. Corrective actions should be designed in accordance with engineering facts and actual failure statistics for the particular type of device.
2. If error routines try too hard to record on a medium of marginal quality, subsequent attempts to retrieve that data will probably fail.
3. The collecting statistics that can identify devices and storage media that are operating marginally is extremely important. Without such statistics, good device error routines can be detrimental; they tend to defer the action necessary to remedy basic problems.

Transaction journals must be provided for files that are persistently updated by random transactions. The cost of creating a journal is significant, but there is no apparent alternative. Careful design might allow a single journal to support several files. Journals supplemented by periodic copies of a file can provide recoverability adequate for most needs. An adequate journal might contain one of the following classes of information:

- transactions that can be reprocessed to recreate changes to a file
- the changes themselves
- copies of the information obliterated by each change to a file

This last type of information can be used in reverse chronological order to return a current file to its condition at any earlier time. Such action can correct for erroneous processing, but it is not effective for recovering an illegible file.

PRACTICAL ABILITY

There are several other abilities that, while they are extremely important, they are less specific to I/O systems than those already discussed. These abilities are listed below, each with limited comment. A major contributor to all of them is simplicity or, alternatively, a major deterrant to all of them is complexity. Like Charles Babbage, any good designer can imagine systems that are impractical. The entire computing industry sometimes suffers from the enthusiasm to build whatever can be imagined. The authors are aware of only one design that was scrapped before the product was built due to complexity, but the history of the industry is strewn with programs and systems whose complexity doomed them.

Testability   A program whose complexity makes testing impossible is an impractical program. A good design allows exhaustive testing with only modest effort. Bear in mind that a system program might be retested hundreds or even thousands of times.

Maintainability   The design of a practical program must be simple enough that most errors can be fixed by changing only a few instructions. Complex programs frequently require extensive rework to fix a minor problem. Extensive rework is not only expensive, but it tends to introduce new errors. New errors are particularly frustrating to users because they can unexpectedly affect scheduled production processing. Old errors are less serious because they are usually encountered by a user testing his or her program rather than during scheduled production.

Extendability   A simple program is easily extended to include new capabilities. Operating systems are simultaneously being maintained and extended. If either or both of these activities require extensive rework of a program, coordination becomes difficult. For example, if an extension to a program will require one year of development time and it requires an extensive rewrite of the program, errors being fixed during that year may reoccur in the extended program. From the user's view, such a program has regressed.

System Capability   In today's environment, the design of a system is a committee effort. A committee cannot design a simple product because committee action requires compromise, and compromise consists of incorporating everyone's ideas into the product. In our largest and most general systems, this committee effect has resulted in excessive embellishment. Providing several ways for a user to fill each of his or her needs is confusing to the user, and it adds cost and complexity to the system.

Performance   Any reasonably knowledgeable designer can design a system that is big and slow.

Predictability   No would-be user of a system can be expected to invest heavily in development of a use for the system unless the result is predictable. Some examples of factors that should be predictable are cost of use, cost of development of the process, responsiveness of the system, total running time, cost of maintenance, and life expectancy of the system.

Approachability   A good system should be easy to teach and easy to learn and easy to use. Documentation should be thorough and explicit, but it should be brief; a system should not require a lifetime of study. An approachable system is one that is as simple as possible and that is described in the most effective way.

SUMMARY

Reliability, availability, serviceability (sometimes referred to as RAS), accountability, operability, recoverability, and practical ability are vital qualities of an effective I/O system or, for that matter, any operating system. High reliability results from two qualities. One is tolerance of "goofs" whether by humans or program or machine, and the other is a relatively high degree of error-free programming. The following rules will help promote system reliability:

1. Programs should not depend on the relative speeds of devices and the CPU for correct operation.
2. Programs should not depend on the accuracy of unchecked data.
3. A program should not assume it has exclusive use of any resource unless exclusive use has been guaranteed.
4. Any program that deals with I/O devices must be tolerant of device idiosyncracies.
5. Provision should be made for identifying storage volumes of unsatisfactory condition.

Availability is closely related to reliability. It is a particularly important quality where the user interacts directly with the system. For example, an airline reservation system servicing many ticket agents by remote terminals must maintain an extremely high availability factor.

A good accountability capability is necessary in most systems. It must be consistent and auditable and allow billing which is closely related to costs. It is especially difficult to achieve in multiprogramming, multiprocessing, or time sharing systems.

There is a continuing trend to try to make the operations of a computing system as easy and foolproof as possible. However, as new computing systems evolve, they become more complex, thus making ease of use even more difficult to achieve. Computer operators must not only serve as the hands of the computer, but as the decision makers for decisions not programmed into the system.

Recoverability, availability, and serviceability are all interrelated. Program reenterability and nonstop design are important features of a highly recoverable control program. In I/O systems, channel programs must be restartable, and device error routines should be comprehensive.

Exercises

1.(e) Give some examples of computing-system applications which require a high level of reliability and availability.
2.(e) To what class of computer professional is serviceability important?
3.(m) Describe ways in which reliability and availability can be designed and implemented in today's systems.
4.(m) Why is an accounting capability more difficult to achieve in multiprogramming, multiprocessing, time sharing systems?
5.(m) How would you rank the "abilities" described in this chapter from most important to least important?
6.(m) What are some desirable operational characteristics of a computer system?

19 ⫶ Privacy and Security

> To its profound distress, the American public has recently learned of a revolution in the technique by which public and private authorities can conduct scientific surveillance over the individual. . . . Dr. Alan Westin

In his landmark book, *Privacy and Freedom,* Dr. Alan Westin defines privacy as "the claim of individuals, groups, or institutions to determine for themselves when, how, and to what extent information about themselves is communicated to others." There is no way to provide that kind of privacy in a computer system for one fundamental reason: In a computer system, data do not belong to the person they describe, but rather they belong to the person who collected them! A more appropriate definition of privacy of data within a computer system is this: the claim of the owner of data to determine to whom the owner's data shall be disclosed. Security is closely related. It is the freedom from unauthorized modification, destruction, or disclosure of data.

This chapter concerns privacy and security. Another closely related subject, integrity, is discussed in Chap. 20. Integrity can be defined as the safeguarding of data from untoward interaction of programs. The safeguards that provide integrity are of a different kind than the privacy and security safeguards. Integrity problems are system failures or system shortcomings, but they do not involve an intruder. Privacy and security violations do involve an intruder, though in cases the intrusion may be accidental.

EXPOSURES AND THREATS

When data are placed in a computer system, they could potentially be exposed to compromise by a wide variety of threats.

Exposures

The privacy and security features of a system are safeguards against

$$\left. \begin{matrix} \text{accidental or} \\ \text{intentional} \end{matrix} \right\} \quad \left\{ \begin{matrix} \text{disclosure or} \\ \text{modification or} \\ \text{destruction} \end{matrix} \right\} \quad \text{of data}$$

The following examples indicate that all six candidates are realistic exposures:

Accidental Disclosure Personal information about employees left in main storage by one program might be included in a main storage dump triggered by a subsequent program.
Accidental Modification An operator might accidentally modify an inventory file by processing the same transactions twice.

Accidental Destruction   A failure in the recording circuits of a storage device might cause a file to be destroyed during an update-in-place process.

Intentional Disclosure   Identifying himself as an authorized user, a person might list criminal records of political leaders to be used to discredit them.

Intentional Modification   A programmer with a detailed understanding of the security features of the system might circumvent those features to add friends to a company payroll.

Intentional Destruction   A disgruntled employee might plant a bomb in the computer center intending to destroy a company by destroying its vital records.

Threats

You may have noticed that the examples of exposures included a wide variety of threats such as incomplete system design, operator error, device failure, masquerading by a user, insider's knowledge, and lack of physical security of computer facility. Figure 19-1 lists these and other common threats to data.

Accidents	Physical Security
Control program error	Fire, flood, earthquake
User's program error	Theft
Operator error	Magnetic destruction of files
Communications system error	Bombings

Surveillance   (Deliberate passive intrusion)

Wiretapping

Electromagnetic pickup

Inspection of trash (carbon paper, listings)

Programmed Infiltration   (Deliberate active intrusion)

Browsing through unprotected files

Masquerading as an authorized user

Bypassing protection using detailed knowledge of the system

Bypassing protection using special features inserted by an accomplice

Fig. 19-1   Threats to the security or privacy of data.

A complicating factor in protecting data is that threats may occur on many fronts. Protection is not a simple matter of posting a guard at the door, though that is a significant fundamental step. Figure 19-2 indicates where opportunities to violate protective measures may occur in a system. The communication lines and terminals present a significant challenge because they are outside the physical boundaries of the computer center.

Costs of Protecting Data

An idea broadly accepted today is that security and privacy cost money and that the more comprehensive the protection, the greater the cost. An important

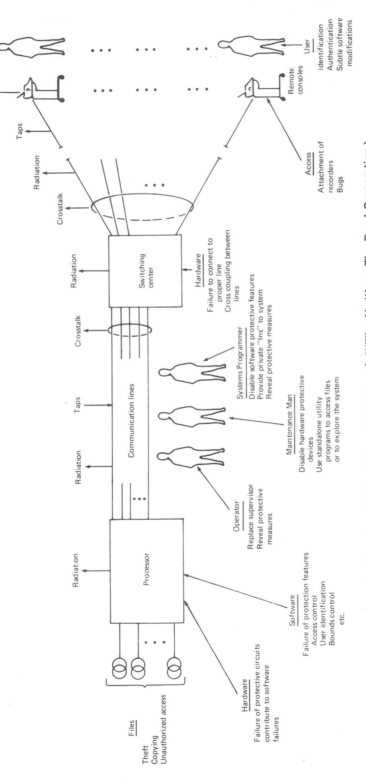

Fig. 19-2 Opportunities to violate data. (Courtesy of Willis H. Ware, The Rand Corporation.)

corollary is that an enterprise should establish values for its data so that it does not foolishly pay more to protect data than the data are worth. Furthermore, it is at least theoretically unnecessary to protect data more than enough to deter an intruder. Figure 19-3 relates the class of the intruder to the cost of preventing his intrusion. Intruders range from the curious kook, who simply wants to find out what happens if certain things are done, to a malevolent government at whose whim data can be neither private nor secure.

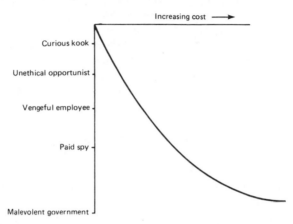

Fig. 19-3   Cost of deterring an intruder. (Based on a talk by Paul Baran.)

Another important aspect of protecting data is that it is foolish to protect against exotic threats while ignoring the mundane. For example, protecting against wiretapping or electromagnetic surveillance is hardly worthwhile if operators and programmers are not screened to ensure their loyalty. An intruder would rather pay a disgruntled employee $250 for a perfect copy of a reel of tape than pay $25,000 for surveillance equipment to collect 100 reels of jumbled characters from which the useful data must be extracted.

Governmental Controls

The military establishment and certain government agencies such as the Federal Bureau of Investigation and the Atomic Energy Commission have very rigid rules for classifying data and for protecting classified data. However, there are very few laws or governmental controls relating to commercial data.

In 1965, when the idea of a national data bank was the subject of great public attention, the federal government held lengthy hearings on the rights of privacy and the effects of computers on those rights. At present, several state governments have passed or are considering privacy laws that may establish legal responsibility for protecting data.

The absence of laws and legal precedents has a double-edged debilitating effect on attempts to protect data:

1. The computer owner or vendor has very little established legal responsibility under which accuracy or privacy must be guaranteed.

2. The would-be intruder has little threat of legal penalty from committing a dishonest and unethical act.

GENERAL COUNTERMEASURES

The countermeasures that can be included in an I/O system are described later in this chapter. At this point, we shall discuss general countermeasures, measures which, though they are not part of the I/O system, are essential to the protection of data and without which, protection of data is flatly impossible. The general countermeasures discussed include responsibilities of the computer manufacturer and the computer-center administration. Throughout the remainder of this chapter, we shall assume a general purpose multiprogrammed system with terminals connected by common carrier lines such as telephone lines.

Computer Countermeasures

There are certain features of a computer itself that are particularly essential to data protection. Some of these features apply to the CPU, channels, and storage devices, while others apply to terminals and the communications lines attaching the terminals. Fail-safe design should be used throughout so that failure of a single component results in more rather than less restraint in the processing of data.

CPU, Files, and Storage Devices.   Certain CPU instructions must be reserved for the exclusive use of the control program. Any attempt on the part of a user's program to execute such instructions must be restrained so that a control program can either honor or disallow the action. Among the restricted instructions are any that initiate I/O activity, and any that establish processing constraints must also be restricted.

Communication Lines and Terminals.   There should be a provision for each terminal device to identify itself so that the system can test for improper action of a switching network or for intrusion of an uninvited terminal. Additionally, a terminal can include an operator identification feature such as:

● an ignition switch that either enables the terminal to operate or supplies an identifiable code that can be inspected at the CPU
● an identification card reader, possibly including a magnetic-stripe feature allowing periodic changes to eliminate use of obsolete cards
● other more exotic but currently less practical features to identify the operator's voice, thumb print, lip print, or even the shape of the operator's head (!)

Cryptographic devices can afford some protection of data being transmitted. A cryptographic scheme might be supported by features in a terminal and programs in the CPU.

Computer Center Administration

As things currently stand, computer manufacturers are providing reasonably good data protection features, and operating systems are using those features reasonably well. That leaves computer center administration as the principal variable in data protection. No amount of expense or effort within an operating system will substitute for the basic measures necessary to make the computer center physically secure.

Personnel.   The most important single requirement is that the people who are in direct contact with the computer, the stored data, and the control program must be loyal, competent, and emotionally stable. This requirement suggests that computer operators, repair people, and system programmers must be screened to ensure their qualities and that all other people be kept physically away from the computer system or that their presence be carefully monitored. If, as is so often the case, the computer facility is open to all employees of an enterprise or even to the general public, precious data may be compromised in every inexpensive way. Magnetic disk volumes may be lost or stolen; entire tape libraries may be destroyed magnetically; or the computer system itself may be destroyed by bombing. Less dramatically, errors in processing, misappropriation of computer time, and casual invasions of privacy will occur without management's knowledge.

Some simple examples of the way disloyal employees can compromise data are these:

1. Operators can copy storage volumes or substitute a modified control program for a highly protective control program.
2. Computer repair people might possibly disable protective circuits or they can intentionally or accidentally modify or destroy files.
3. System programmers can modify protective features of a control program so that their confederates can penetrate its defenses or they can describe existing weaknesses in a defense thereby aiding an intruder.

The Security Officer.   A person, or possibly a small group of people, should be given responsibility for devising and monitoring administrative security measures. Some of the concerns of the security officer should be:

- Whether the personnel policies described above are being observed properly.
- What files should be duplicated for backup and where the copies should be stored.
- Whether backup procedures are being tested periodically to ensure their effectiveness.
- Whether certain operating conveniences offered by the computer center expose data in excess of their value.
- If electronic surveillance is anticipated, whether radiation shielding, private lines, and/or exclusion of nonessential people for the entire building and grounds may be justified.
- Whether a production schedule that makes erroneous processing unlikely is being used.
- Whether logs of all significant activities are maintained and inspected frequently. Significant events include suspension of control program operation and shipment of duplicate files to storage.

- Whether precautions against natural disasters such as fire and flood have been taken.

One cost of adequate protection of data is continual awareness. A high-ranking officer of the enterprise should require periodic full reports from the security officer, and the officer should personally check whether the precautions and procedures described are actually in effect. Most enterprises find it difficult to maintain tight security against an unidentifiable enemy.

I/O SYSTEM COUNTERMEASURES

The principal matters of interest in this chapter are I/O system countermeasures. Of the features to be discussed, data access control and processing restraints are included in current general-purpose systems. The other topics, monitor design, threat monitoring, auditing, and cryptography, include ideas that are within present capabilities but are at best only partially included in current systems.

Monitor Design

A control program imposes its authority by prudent use and jealous control of those features of the computer designed for its exclusive use. Throughout the remainder of this chapter, the term *monitor* is used to describe those parts of the control program that respond to, modify, or activate these protective features of the computer. The monitor is a very small part of the I/O system, probably not more than 5 percent. In existing systems, the monitor has not been identified and segregated from other parts of the system. A very important early step in developing effective countermeasures is the careful identification of the monitor.

A monitor can protect against threats both accidental and intentional only if it works the way it is designed to work. In short, the monitor must be free of errors. Not only might a monitor containing errors fail to protect data, but it may itself constitute a threat to data. Close adherence to the following two rules should provide the necessary quality in a monitor:

1. The monitor should contain a minimum of programming. Relegating unessential programming to other parts of the system reduces the opportunity for error in the monitor and improves the chances that the monitor can remain unchanged over long periods of time.
2. The monitor should be designed, written, and modified only by experts who are thoroughly familiar with their assignments. A small number of people should be involved so that close communication can be established.

Data Access Control

Some files are sufficiently valuable that restrictions on their use are enforced by the monitor. This activity has two facets: (1) an authorization system allowing the file owner to declare in advance who should be granted access and (2) positive identification of a user who requests access to restricted files.

Identification.   The users might identify themselves by inserting a magnetically coded card into a slot on a terminal or by using another of the terminal features suggested earlier. However, the most widely used identification mechanism is a password. The mechanics of using passwords were discussed in Chap. 7. The effectiveness of passwords has three basic limitations:

1. Normal use of a password exposes it. A user typically presents a password for inspection using the keyboard of a computer terminal. An intruder can acquire the password rather easily by personally observing its use, by inspection of a carbon ribbon, or by electronic surveillance.
2. A password can be duplicated at no cost, and a copy cannot be detected until it is used. An observer can effectively steal a password simply by observing it in print, and the observer can transport the stolen copy past a guard with no fear of detection.
3. Users forget passwords. Experience has shown that a significant proportion of the users of a system cannot remember necessary passwords. This results in telephone calls which are a nuisance and, in themselves, detrimental to security. Further, passwords can predictably be found secreted in obvious places around a user's office.

But on the positive side, passwords are acceptable by a variety of terminal types, and they require no special devices for their use. Furthermore, passwords can be changed easily and quickly to confound intruders.

Some interesting techniques for changing passwords have been invented. One way is to replace the single password with a set of passwords to be used in endless rotation. For example, if passwords A, B, and C are defined as a set, a user would present A on the first occasion, B on the second, C on the third, A on the fourth, and so on. This scheme requires that an intruder have more information than a single password.

Another password-changing technique has the I/O system respond to a proper password by presenting the user a new password to be used next time. This scheme requires an intruder to use a stolen password quickly to avoid its obsolescence.

Both of the above schemes have the advantage that successful use of a password by an intruder causes a stepping action that provides the authentic user clear evidence that an intrusion has occurred. Both suffer from two drawbacks: (1) After an intruder successfully uses a password, the monitor will treat the intruder as legitimate and treat the legitimate user as an intruder. (2) Remembering continuously changing passwords is more difficult than remembering single passwords.

Authorization.   It was mentioned earlier that the person who collects a file of data is considered the rightful owner of the data. That idea is worth examining for a moment. One's initial reaction is that it would be ethically better if data belonged to the person they describe. That reaction is not realistic for several reasons:

1. Data may not describe a person but may describe inanimate objects such as the parts of an assembly. Such data would have no apparent owner.

2. Data may describe more than one person. For example, something pur-
chased by A is something sold by B. Such data would have two owners.
3. Much data about persons are ethically the property of other persons.
For example, a sales representative has a right to know his or her
customer's address.

It is clearly more practical, and hopefully just as ethical, to assume that the
collector of data owns them.

A responsibility of the owner of data is to authorize or restrict their use.
There are two schools of thought represented in current systems, and both rely
principally on passwords. In one school, a password is associated with a file
and anyone knowing the password is presumed authorized to process that file.
In the other school, a password is used to prove a user's identity, and authority
to process is given to certain users. Both schools yield workable systems.

The second school has some important advantages that make it the better
alternative:

1. A system may require proof of a user's identity for billing and logging
purposes. Using the same proof to control access to data is sensible
from the user's viewpoint.
2. Requiring a different password for use of each file requires the user to
remember too many passwords and causes an unnecessary delay in
processing as passwords are being verified.
3. The second school is readily adaptable to magnetically coded identification cards or other proof of identity; the first school is not.
4. The distribution of any password to many users limits its effectiveness.
The first school requires relatively wide distribution.

In either case, it is undesirable to use automatic authorization where, for
example, authority to process a particular file implies authority to process all
other files of a certain class. The reason is simply this: Effective protection of
data in any security system requires authorization to be on a "need-to-know"
basis only.

In many current systems, authorization to process applies to a complete
file of data, and separate authorizations frequently apply for retrieving records
from a file and for updating records or otherwise modifying the same file. In the
future, authorizations may limit a particular user to inspection or modification
of certain fields within records. Providing these limited authorizations is an
essential step in integrating separate files into a data base.

Other Processing Restraints

A monitor must restrain a user's program in many ways to ensure that it does
not exceed the limits of the authorizations described above or other limits of
orderly processing. Most of these restraints have been mentioned in earlier
chapters so their reiteration here will be brief:

Expiration Date   Most file labels include an expiration date used to protect the file against premature scratching. If a user's program requests
scratching earlier than the expiration date indicates, the monitor can re-

quest confirmation from the operator that scratching should be performed. This procedure protects against accidental scratching of a file.

Write Inhibit   When a file is being opened, the user is required to specify whether he or she intends to retrieve only. A monitor can note this intent and force a user's program to comply. This restraint prevents accidental modification of a file that might result from a user's program error, and it also enforces conformance to the restricted authorizations described earlier.

Extent Restrictions   A monitor can restrain the channel programs issued on behalf of any user's program to affect only the appropriate direct access storage space or the appropriate magnetic tape file. These restraints ensure that a user's program does not accidentally or intentionally modify or inspect files other than those identified during file opening.

Extent Clearing   A few systems are optionally providing automatic obliteration of any file that is being scratched if that file contains confidential information. Unfortunately, obliteration requires the writing of blanks or other useless information over the entire file space, a time-consuming process which not infrequently requires remounting of volumes that were removed during processing.

Main Storage Protection   Each user's program should be restrained by the control program supervisor to execute instructions and inspect or modify data only within the main storage space allotted to that program. Any requirement that exceeds those restraints should be handled by system call or other special provisions ensuring that no program accidentally or intentionally modifies or inspects another's data.

Activity Logging.   An operating system should record all activities that affect or might affect protected data. Such a log can be useful not only for reconstructing events when data are compromised but also for determining the legitimate uses of that sensitive data. Some of the activities that should be logged are these:

1. Successful opening of a password-protected file should be logged. This information serves the same purpose as logging the use of a classified document in a manual system. As an example, the logged information can furnish a list of users who have had access to certain private data that have become public knowledge.

2. Unsuccessful attempts to open a password-protected file should be logged. The data protection features of an operating system offer a special kind of challenge to a would-be intruder. The intruder can work anonymously in broad daylight, using the outstanding capabilities of the system to systematically probe for weaknesses in the system. A log of unsuccessful attempts to open a protected file can reveal that systematic probing has occurred.

3. The copying of a protected file should be logged. It is not always possible to detect that a file is being copied. However, instances when system-furnished utility routines are used to copy a file can be logged by the utility program. Just as with classified documents, copying should be restrained, but there is no completely effective way to

eliminate it. Clearly, if a file is copied and the copy is not protected, the data in the file are subject to compromise.

4. Termination of control program operation should be logged. To be effective, a monitor must be in control of the system. A dishonest operator can terminate that control. The best protection against this threat is careful screening of personnel combined with close supervision of operators. In addition, the control program should log its own termination. Additionally, the command to terminate will be printed on the operator's console. Good practice requires that the printed record from the operator's console be preserved and that any discontinuities in that record be explained. For example, the console record should be on continuous forms, and any break in the physical continuity of those forms should be approved and initialed by an operation's supervisor.

In addition to logging events affecting protected data, a monitor could undertake audits both periodically and on certain special occasions. One type of audit consists of comparing parts of the monitor that are in main storage with the master copies in the system libraries. For this audit to be of any value, the master copies must be carefully protected. If possible, these master copies should reside on a read-only storage device, that is, on a device that has no recording capability. Such an audit can be performed periodically to protect against accidental or intentional disabling of the monitor's protective features. Another type of audit that can be performed by the monitor is a systematic test of the protective features of the computer itself. Such a test can ensure that those features essential to effective monitoring have not been disabled either accidentally or intentionally by computer servicing personnel.

While the auditing activities in the preceding paragraph seem practical, the authors know of no general purpose system that employs them. The reader is cautioned to use the ideas carefully, exploring all ramifications to ensure that auditing accomplishes its purpose without interferring with efficient and convenient operation of the entire system.

Cryptography

No discussion of data protection can be complete without a mention of cryptography. Cryptography is particularly appealing in a computer system because imaginative encoding and decoding schemes can be performed efficiently by a computer. However, cryptography is rarely used in nonmilitary systems today. A would-be intruder can accomplish his aims by theft, bribery, or bold action more easily and at less expense than by line tapping or electronic surveillance. Stated another way, cryptography is not appropriate until other more basic steps are taken to establish security. Such steps are presently being taken in many computer installations, so cryptography will become more important.

Because there has been little general purpose use of cryptography, there is little that one can report about the state of the art in current general purpose systems. Therefore, the discussion here will be limited to a simple academic review of the three major classes of cryptographic encoding.

Substitution.   The simplest form of cryptographic encoding simply substitutes one character for another. The encoding process is easily reversed for decoding. For example, a typewriter with a replaceable printing element can be adapted to perform automatic decoding simply by substituting the appropriate printing element. Anyone reasonably adept in cryptographic analysis can break a substitution code very quickly by analyzing a message for repetitive patterns of characters and for frequency of occurrence of each character. Even though the code is easily broken, encoding by substitution is of significant value; an intruder cannot tell by glancing at encoded data whether the data are of interest to him or her.

Transposition.   Another basic form of cryptographic encoding uses transposition of characters according to some fixed or varying pattern. Transposition is not an attractive method in a computing system because transposing requires that several characters be manipulated as a group. This obstructs the smooth flow of data, complicates error correction, and increases the cost of terminal devices.

Addition.   Using an addition method, a message is encoded by adding it character by character to a predefined base message. To decode, the base message is simply subtracted. Ideally, the base message should be as long as the message to be encoded. In practice, a shorter base message is simply repeated as many times as necessary. The use of short base messages makes the code easier to break, but longer base messages cause a hardship in automatic decoding using a terminal device with limited storage capability

One technique that seems particularly adaptable to computer systems uses a base message consisting of pseudo-random characters. Some advantages of this technique are as follows:

1. Base messages need not be stored, but rather they can be generated as needed.
2. Generation schemes that can be accomplished economically in a terminal device are possible.
3. Base messages that are very long can be generated.

Information for Users

Experts generally agree that an operating system cannot furnish a perfectly safe environment for data. That is, an intruder who is sufficiently rich, clever, and dedicated can overcome most any protective system. Further, because protective measures reduce operating efficiency, most systems will be run with less than the most comprehensive safeguards.

The manuals that describe a system should declare major aspects of the protective system including its limitations. This information will allow a concerned user to either supplement the safeguards or to search out a more appropriate system. Some safeguards the users can furnish for themselves are storage clearing, cryptographic encoding of a file, and physically locking a storage volume in a vault. Any description of the limitations of the system protective measures must be carefully worded so that it does not assist a would-be intruder. A detailed description of the programmed safeguards would be of significant help to anyone trying to bypass or disable these safeguards.

SUMMARY

Data placed in a computer system are potentially exposed to accidental disclosure, modification, and destruction or to intentional disclosure, modification, and destruction. In most computing installations, some level of safeguards are implemented to substantially reduce or eliminate these exposures.

Safeguards may take the form of appropriate personnel and building security procedures, certain computer hardware checks like privileged CPU instructions, or the use of passwords to gain access to data files or to the use of terminals.

Some countermeasures can be taken through proper I/O system design. Features such as data access control and processing restraints are included in current general purpose systems. A properly designed and implemented monitor can help protect against both accidental and intentional threats. The monitor is typically no more than about 5 percent of an I/O system.

Other security measures may include activity logging and some form of a cryptographic capability. Data logging is useful for both reconstructing events when data have been compromised as well as determining legitimate uses of sensitive data.

Exercises

1.(e) What are some measures that can be taken at a computer installation to reduce exposures to privacy and security?
2.(m) Security and privacy cost money. How would you view the ratio of costs for protection versus the total DP costs for a computer installation?
3.(m) What are some of the hardware features found in computers today that aid in providing data or program protection?
4.(m) Discuss the pros and cons of the use of passwords.
5.(m) What are some of the advantages of activity logging with respect to security and privacy?

20 Preserving the User's Environment

Operating systems exist for one fundamental reason: to furnish a desirable environment for users' programs. If you have observed an enterprise as it develops a major new use of a computing system, you may have noticed that progress is remarkable after the groundwork is laid until the new programs become operational. After that period, progress begins to slow, and it is only by continued, conscious effort of management that improvements and extensions to the original programs can be accomplished. One reason major efforts tend to bog down is that maintaining the already completed programs absorbs much or all of the resources of the department. Figure 20-1 illustrates this point. The budget for the programming department starts low, gains rapidly, and, typically, levels off when the first set of programs becomes operational. Beginning on that date, maintenance costs rise rapidly. Maintenance costs would drop dramatically after a few months except that follow-on programs add to the maintenance costs in three ways.

1. The follow-on programs must be maintained.
2. The follow-on programs expose errors in the original programs that were previously of no consequence.
3. As the cumulative number of corrections made by maintenance personnel increases, the design of the programs gradually degenerates, making maintenance more difficult.

There are three apparent ways that the resources required for significant continued design and development could be made available:

1. The total budget could be increased. Whether this alternative is realistic depends on factors outside the scope of our discussion. However, it is noteworthy that an increase would furnish only temporary relief.
2. Eliminate rework of programs by improving the quality of the corrections to errors. There are important reasons why this solution is usually not practical: Maintenance fixes usually must be made quickly to satisfy operational needs. Corrections should be constrained to affect as little of the existing code as possible. If this principle is not rigidly enforced, not only is comprehensive retesting required after each error is fixed, but new errors may be introduced at a rate exceeding the elimination of old errors.
3. Reduce or eliminate the cost of adapting old programs to a new environment. This could be accomplished by rejecting environmental changes regardless of their apparent value, or somehow allowing the environment to change without affecting existing programs.

353

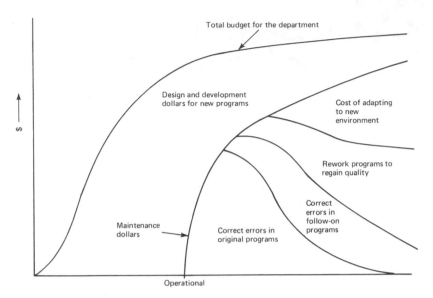

Fig. 20-1

The remainder of this chapter is devoted to those features that an operating system can offer to insulate users' programs from the adverse effects of changes to its environment. Three major topics are discussed:

Device Independence This is the quality that allows a program to perform correctly without change despite changes in the I/O devices serving that program.

Data Independence This is the quality that allows a program to perform correctly without change despite change to the form or content of the records processed by that program.

Integrity This is the quality that allows a program to perform correctly despite the simultaneous use of data by other unrelated programs.

DEVICE INDEPENDENCE

An executable user's program is said to be device-dependent if it contains commands, instructions, or constants that make the program applicable only to a specific type of I/O device. A program that contains no such dependencies is called device-independent. The principal value of device independence is that it tends to allow the I/O requirements of a program to be satisfied by any of several types of devices.

It is important to recognize at the outset that device independence does not imply that the choice of I/O devices is arbitrary. There are at least three factors that may affect the choice of I/O device for a device-independent program:

1. There may be no conceivable way for a particular device to fill the specific need. For example, a card reader simply cannot receive and record a file of data.

2. The user may have designed his or her program to require capabilities not present in all I/O devices. For example, a user might have used update-in-place logic, thereby eliminating conventional magnetic tape drives from consideration.
3. Use of certain devices might be impractical. For example, a typewriter terminal would be impractical if 1,000 pages of output are to be printed.

These three factors should not be considered limitations in the degree of device independence but rather as limitations on the usefulness of particular I/O devices. Notice that none of the three factors limiting the choice of I/O device contradicts the definition of device independence stated in the previous paragraph.

The Value of Device Independence

Most people acquainted with computers would agree that device independence is valuable but might be hard-pressed to say why. Some of the most important values are as follows.

Device independence allows scheduling flexibility. A device-independent program might be executed at a time when a device-dependent program would be forced to wait. In an extreme case, the device-dependent program might be delayed for hours while a particular device is being repaired. Further, during that waiting period, equipment that a device-dependent program could have used may be idle.

Device independence allows easy upgrading of a computer system as new I/O devices become available or as higher-performance devices become justified.

Device independence allows broadened use of general-purpose programs. For example, a single device-independent utility program might copy a file to and from any of several types of devices.

The mechanisms that provide device independence tend to provide flexibility in I/O system design. This value is simple recognition of the fact that wide latitude in choice of I/O devices tends to imply wide latitude in other parameters as well. For example, between one day's processing to the next, an existing rudimentary I/O system might be replaced with one that does automatic staging of input data or that provides automatic recovery ability for files being modified. To the system designer, this flexibility may be the most important value of all.

Designing for Device Independence

From a conceptual viewpoint, device independence is easy to provide: One must simply provide a device-dependent interface for users' programs. Using such an interface, an I/O system accepts device-independent service requests and interprets them into the appropriate device-dependent actions. Thus, the problem in designing for device independence reduces to the problem of designing a device-independent set of calls, tables, and exits that is comprehensive and effective. If the set is not comprehensive, most users will be compelled to use device-dependent services to accomplish their work. If the set is not effective, users will resort to device-dependent services to gain acceptable efficiency. In either case, device independence will have been sacrificed.

DATA INDEPENDENCE

Definition

Most executable programs in existence today have a degree of immunity to changes in their environment. For example:

- A program might be insensitive to I/O device characteristics as discussed in the preceding section.
- A program might be unaffected by changes in the storage addresses used to store the data to be processed.
- A program might be tolerant of changes in the blocking factor used in its files.

However, few executable programs have the ability to cope with any significant changes in the definition of the records they process. A simple illustration of this inflexibility might be that a change in the employee-identification-number field from 4 bytes to 5 bytes would require modification, recompilation, and retest of every program that uses the personnel file. Data independence, providing the ability for programs to be unaffected by changes in the form or content of the records they process, is considered essential for the data base systems of the future. Though data independence has been a feature of special purpose systems as early as 1954, contemporary systems do not include this quality. The discussion here is limited to defining the concept, justifying its use, and discussing the deterrents to its general availability. Methods for accomplishing data independence can be suggested but not demonstrated; data independence is not within the current state of the art.

Data independence need not be an all-or-nothing capability. A combination of I/O system features and user's program disciplines might provide data independence in the user's program to any of the following increasingly difficult levels:

Level 1   Tolerate only those changes affecting fields that are not processed by the user's program. Most of today's programs have this level of data independence.

Level 2   Tolerate extensions to a record.

Level 3   Tolerate changes in the positions of fields within a record.

Level 4   Tolerate changes in the sizes of fields within a record.

Level 5   Tolerate division of a record into two or more records (not record segments but, rather, separate records).

Level 6   Tolerate elimination of a field from a record, provided the value of that field can be computed from other data that are available in the system. Data that are not stored but, rather, are computed by the I/O system are called virtual data.

One's intuitive grasp of these levels might be aided by visualizing an I/O system that furnishes data independence through a GET/PUT-level interface. To do this, the buffering and blocking programs within an access method could be augmented by programs that restructure records to reconcile the definition of the stored record that exists in a file and the definition of the logical record assumed by the user's program. Level 3 could be achieved by simple rearrangement of fields. Level 5 might require that the access method programs store two or more records for each PUT or that they retrieve several records to fabricate a single record satisfying a GET. Level 6 might require the I/O system to summarize data from several records or to calculate total price from the fields representing unit price and quantity.

Justification

The urgent need for data independence is a relatively recent event. Historically, an enterprise recognized a few separate areas of their business where computers would pay. Typically, these areas might have been payroll, accounts receivable, and parts inventory. Each was considered independent of the others, and each area established its own record formats. As equipment and know-how improved, other application areas such as personnel statistics, customer billing, and forecasting of parts use were developed. It was quite evident that the files for these areas contained redundant information and that a great deal of cost, confusion, and frustration were resulting from requirements to maintain all files separately. Frequently, the payroll file would show Tom Brown in department A, while the personnel file showed him in department B. Customer invoices were reflected into accounts receivable but only after cards were manually punched from a copy of the invoice. And not infrequently, the use of part P was forecasted ridiculously high because part P was being ordered frequently, but the inventory file showed an excessive quantity on hand. The term *integrated data processing* was coined to describe the consolidation of many files into a few larger files that could be processed by dozens of separate programs to accomplish interrelated tasks. The advent of large storage devices with random access capability and the widespread use of manned terminals dealing directly with a computing system have both added urgency to integration of files and programs. That trend is expected to continue. The result is variously described as on-line systems, transaction-oriented systems, or data base systems.

If a data base system is to be successful, the files of the data base must be readily adaptable to new or modified uses. But, because many programs use records from the data base, any change in record content might affect dozens of programs. Even further, the use of manned terminals makes it imperative that such changes are made with very little interruption to the normal reliable operation. Realistically, the only way dozens of programs can be simultaneously adapted to a new record format is for the adaptation to be automatic. Therefore, experts in the field agree that data independence is essential.

Problems

There are, in the authors' opinion, three major obstacles that must be overcome to make practical data independence available:

Performance   The most apparent obstacle is performance. The continued reformatting of records during processing is costly both in dollars and in responsiveness of the system. In some ways, such reformatting during execution is like emulation of obsolete processing systems; one can justify it only as a temporary measure.

Definition   The entire data processing industry is involved in defining the properties of data base systems. Getting agreement on direction is a problem of international scope.

Discipline   It is clear that the higher levels of data independence described earlier are difficult to provide. Level 4 is a problem; level 5 may be unreasonably difficult; and level 6 raises credibility questions about the entire matter. Carrying the fundamentally simple idea of data independence to such extremes is a factor delaying the advent of a realistic, practical capability.

INTEGRITY

The October 1969 report of the Data Base Task Group of CODASYL defines integrity as the safeguarding from untoward interaction of programs. That report is interested in one particular aspect of integrity, the errors that can be introduced into a file by allowing two or more programs to simultaneously update a single record in a way that the resulting record is in error. For our purposes here, integrity is expanded to include three topics:

Deadlock   This is the detrimental condition wherein two or more programs become interlocked so that neither can continue processing.

Simultaneous Update   This is the condition mentioned above that results in errors due to undetected interaction.

Must Complete   This is a condition that exists whenever a partially completed process causes critical tables to be temporarily out of balance.

Deadlock

In a multiprogramming or multiprocessing system, programs must compete with each other for system resources such as I/O devices and files. The control program is involved in all such competition, and it has the responsibility to adjudicate the conflict in accordance with preestablished rules. The resolution gives an advantage to one of the combatants but, under most circumstances, does not penalize the other combatant. Under certain conditions, a deadlock can arise. The resolving of a deadlock always penalizes the loser, causing an undetermined amount of rework. Deadlock can and should be avoided.

Conditions Causing Deadlock.   In the simplest case, deadlock between programs A and B can arise by the following sequence of events:

1. Program A acquires the exclusive right to use resource 1.
2. Program B acquires the exclusive right to use resource 2.
3. Program A requires resource 2 in order to complete its work.
4. Program B requires resource 1 in order to complete its work.

Neither program A nor B can proceed until the other has completed its work, or has at least proceeded to a point where its already acquired resource can be relinquished. An impasse exists. The two are deadlocked. To resolve the impasse, one program must relinquish a resource, possibly at considerable cost in rework at a later time.

Dependencies can exist among many programs, each requiring exclusive use of a resource already held by another. Such dependencies are undesirable because they affect system performance detrimentally. However, unless the chain of dependencies is actually a ring of dependencies, the required resources will be freed one at a time, and no impasse will result. If the chain closes on itself to form a ring, a deadlock exists.

The resources that could be involved in deadlock are those that must be devoted to the exclusive use of one program for an extended period. Such resources can be termed serially reusable; they can be reused, but use cannot be shared or interleaved. Some examples of resource classification are shown in the following table:

Resource	Classification
Magnetic tape reel being used to record a new file	Serially reusable
Card reader	Serially reusable
Arithmetic unit	Sharable
File of reference data on a magnetic drum	Sharable
Main storage in a multiprogrammed system	Serially reusable
Main storage in a time-sharing system	Sharable
Direct access storage device with a volume of private data mounted	Serially reusable
Direct access storage device with a public (scratch) volume mounted	Sharable
Record being held exclusively by a program during updating	Serially reusable

You may feel that deadlock is highly unlikely and that the best strategy is to let it happen, if happen it will, and resolve it in an arbitrary manner when it does happen. There are some important arguments that oppose such a strategy:

1. Deadlock is not unlikely. It is an unfamiliar occurrence because operating systems include restrictions or procedures that avoid its otherwise natural occurrence.
2. Deadlock is not readily evident. It is a very common event for one program to be waiting for another to free a resource. To detect deadlock, every such dependency would require analysis to ensure that a ring of dependencies did not exist.
3. The cost of rework might be. very high. In some applications requiring high availability, rework might be completely unacceptable because of the processing delays it entails.

Avoiding Deadlock.   There are several strategies that can be used to avoid deadlock. The four listed below have been suggested by James Havender of IBM.

1. Establish an order among all serially reusable resources and allow no program to request such resources in any other order. To understand why this strategy works, assume that program A requests resource number 27 that is already held by B. B might be the beginning of a chain of dependencies, but if it is, that chain can never close into a loop. To do so, one or more of the programs in that chain would have to be holding a resource numbered 27 or more while it requests a resource numbered 26 or less—a violation.
2. Require a program to request all its serially reusable resources at one time. By using this strategy, a program may be delayed, but a program that is delayed holds no critical resources and consequently it cannot participate in a deadlock.
3. Require a program to free all the serially reusable resources it holds before requesting additional resources. The request can include the original resource if necessary.
4. When a program requests a serially reusable resource while holding other resources, interpret that request as a desire rather than a demand. This strategy ensures that no program holding resources can be delayed for lack of resources. That is, no program can be involved in a resource-dependency chain.

Probably the most generally used strategy is the second one presented above. Using that strategy, no program begins execution until all of the resources it will require have been reserved. A principal reason for having control statements is to inform the control program of these requirements.

Staging of data eliminates most of the opportunity for deadlock. In a system that is heavily oriented toward staging, users' programs deal almost completely with sharable resources, while most of the serially reusable resources are permanently assigned to the control program.

Simultaneous Update

The inadvertent interaction of two programs can cause processing errors in the following way: Program A retrieves a particular record. Program B retrieves the same record, updates one or more fields, and stores the record in its original location. Program A updates one or more fields of its now-obsolete copy of the record and stores the revised record in the original location obliterating program B's action.

As you can readily observe, simultaneous update is closely related to deadlock. It arises in the same way and for the same reason: A record being updated is a serially reusable resource.

Avoiding Simultaneous Update.   There are at least three strategies that can be used to avoid simultaneous update:

1. The entire file that contains one or more records to be updated can be considered a reusable resource subject to the same disciplines as other reusable resources. This strategy is frequently used. Its primary drawback is that it tends to be overly restrictive, particularly when it applies

to large files that are actively processed by large numbers of manned terminals.

2. The control program can furnish an exclusive-use mechanism by which a user's program can be assured that no other program will interact unfavorably. An exclusive-use mechanism is described below.

3. The control program can furnish a mechanism that informs a user's program when simultaneous update has occurred. This strategy makes corrective action a user's program responsibility. A method for detecting that simultaneous update has occurred is described later in this chapter.

Exclusive Use.   Some systems provide a mechanism that can be used to protect against simultaneous update. In OS/360, the mechanism is called the enqueue mechanism, and the system calls that activate the mechanism are ENQ and DEQ, standing for enqueue and dequeue, respectively. The mechanism is explained by the following example. Assume program A has executed an ENQ R1, where R1 is any symbolic name. Now, if program B executes ENQ R1, the control program will force execution of program B to be suspended until program A issues DEQ R1 or until program A terminates. If program C executes ENQ R2 where R2 differs from R1, the control program will allow program C to execute.

You can see that the mechanism is quite simple. The control program maintains a list of symbolic names that can be searched to determine whether a program should be delayed. To be effective, the mechanism must be augmented by two agreements among users. (1) All users must recognize a common naming convention for all reusable resources. (2) Every user of the system must agree that, before using a serially reusable resource, the user will issue an ENQ naming that resource. The control program is not really controlling resources. Rather, it is enforcing the serial use of names.

The control program has no way to force use of ENQ. If any program fails to use it, that program can cause a simultaneous-updating error. At first, the voluntary nature of ENQ seems unorthodox. Won't programs intentionally avoid its use? The answer is that there is no more incentive for a program to cause a simultaneous-update error than there is for it to cause any other kind of error.

The ENQ mechanism must be used carefully to avoid deadlock. Two or more programs using ENQ could easily deadlock in just the way described earlier in this chapter unless they observe careful discipline. This exposure to error is again no different from other exposures that programmers face.

System Detection of Simultaneous Update.   While the mechanism just described is effective, it is not altogether good. Not the least of its drawbacks is that it takes main storage space and it takes CPU time at a moment that can affect system responsiveness significantly. That cost would be more readily accepted were it not for the fact that simultaneous update of records is, in most circumstances, highly unlikely.

Recognizing the high cost and the marginal value, the Data Base Task Group report to CODASYL in October 1969 recommends an alternative approach. This alternative allows the activities leading to simultaneous update to occur, but the control program is responsible to warn programs of impending simultaneous update errors. The following sequence of events illustrates the DBTG alternative: Program A retrieves record R. Program B retrieves, updates, and stores record R. Program A updates R and requests that R be stored. The control program uses a system exit to inform the user's program of the impending error. Program A re-retrieves record R, updates, and stores it.

Assuming, for the moment, that the control program can detect the impending error easily, this alternative has the advantage that extra effort is expended only in cases where it is needed. The most apparent disadvantage is the fact that every program that updates records would be required to have a workable, tested exit program.

The DBTG report does not suggest a mechanism that can be used to detect the impending error. One possible method follows:

1. Each record in a file could include a 1-, 2-, or 3-byte field used to indicate record-version number.
2. Whenever a record is updated, its version number is increased by 1.
3. Whenever a program retrieves a record for the purpose of updating that record, the control program can note the current version number in a convenient table.
4. Whenever a program requests that an updated record be stored, the control program can determine whether an intervening update has occurred by inspecting the version number in the table with the one in the currently filed record.

Whether this detection method or some other detection method would really provide an advantage is a debatable point. In the authors' opinion, a specialized enqueuing mechanism designed specially for simultaneous update would be a superior alternative.

SUMMARY

There are three major things an operating system can provide to insulate users' programs from adverse effects of changes to their environment:

The first is device independence—the quality that allows a program to perform correctly without change despite changes in the I/O devices serving that program. The principal value of device independence is that it tends to allow the I/O requirements of a program to be satisfied by any of several types of devices.

The second is data independence—the quality that allows a program to perform correctly without change despite change to the form or content of the records processed by that program. However, few executable programs have the ability to cope with any significant changes in the definition of the records they process.

The third is integrity—the quality that allows a program to perform correctly despite the simultaneous use of files by other unrelated programs. Integrity includes the following three topics:

Deadlock   This is the detrimental condition wherein two or more programs become interlocked such that neither can continue processing.

Simultaneous Update   This is the condition mentioned above that results in errors due to undetected interaction.

Must Complete   This is a condition that exists whenever a partially completed process causes critical tables to be temporarily out of balance.

Exercises

1.(e) Explain why it is desirable, if not necessary, to have various capabilities in an operating system to help insulate users' programs from changes to their environment.

2.(e) Explain device independence and indicate why it is valuable.

3.(m) What are the six levels of data independence discussed in this chapter? Give an example of each.

4.(m) What are some of the problems associated with trying to achieve data independence?

5.(m) Discuss what is meant by deadlock including conditions causing it.

6.(m) What is a simultaneous update of a record and how can it be avoided?

Index

Index